Is This Yoga?

This book provides a rigorously researched, critically comparative introduction to yoga. *Is This Yoga? Concepts, Histories, and the Complexities of Contemporary Practice* recognizes the importance of contemporary understandings of yoga and, at the same time, provides historical context and complexity to modern and pre-modern definitions of yogic ideas and practices. Approaching yoga as a vast web of concepts, traditions, social interests, and embodied practices, it raises questions of knowledge, identity, and power across time and space, including the dynamics of "East" and "West." The text is divided into three main sections: thematic concepts; histories; and topics in modern practice.

This accessible guide is essential reading for undergraduate students approaching the topic for the first time, as well as yoga teachers, teacher training programs, casual and devoted practitioners, and interested non-practitioners.

Anya Foxen is Assistant Professor of Religious Studies and Women's and Gender Studies at California Polytechnic State University, San Luis Obispo, USA. She is a yoga teacher and long-time practitioner.

Christa Kuberry is a yoga teacher, yoga student, and yoga scholar. She is the Vice President of Standards at Yoga Alliance.

"Foxen and Kuberry meticulously trace the historical paths of yoga and delineate its key concepts, posing important questions, for example, about gender. They manage to balance recovery and critique, complicating any straightforward narrative of an authentic yoga tradition undergoing change and eventually morphing into its modern practice. There is no competing study, but much demand, for a textbook like this one."

Andrea R. Jain, Indiana University School of Liberal Arts, USA.
Author of *Peace Love Yoga: The Politics of Global Spirituality*

Is This Yoga?

Concepts, Histories, and the Complexities of Modern Practice

Anya Foxen and Christa Kuberry

Routledge
Taylor & Francis Group
LONDON AND NEW YORK

First published 2021
by Routledge
2 Park Square, Milton Park, Abingdon, Oxon OX14 4RN

and by Routledge
52 Vanderbilt Avenue, New York, NY 10017

Routledge is an imprint of the Taylor & Francis Group, an informa business

British Library Cataloguing-in-Publication Data
A catalogue record for this book is available from the British Library

Library of Congress Cataloging-in-Publication Data
Names: Foxen, Anya P., 1986– author. | Kuberry, Christa, author.
Title: Is this yoga? : concepts, histories, and the complexities of modern practice / Anya Foxen and Christa Kuberry.
Description: Abingdon, Oxon ; New York : Routledge, [2021] | Includes bibliographical references and index.
Identifiers: LCCN 2020050580 | ISBN 9781138390058 (hardback) | ISBN 9781138390072 (paperback) | ISBN 9780429422973 (ebook)
Subjects: LCSH: Yoga.
Classification: LCC B132.Y6 F69 2021 | DDC 181/.45—dc23
LC record available at https://lccn.loc.gov/2020050580

ISBN: 978-1-138-39005-8 (hbk)
ISBN: 978-1-138-39007-2 (pbk)
ISBN: 978-0-429-42297-3 (ebk)

Typeset in Times New Roman
by Apex CoVantage, LLC

Contents

Figures

Preface

This book is meant to be a bit teleological—that is, it has a goal in mind. Specifically, it assumes that the reader wishes to understand the history and theory behind yoga because they are already somewhat familiar with one version of it, and that this version is some form of modern global yoga.

No book can speak to the whole world, and no author can speak *for* the whole world. We, the coauthors of the book in front of you now, are two middle-class women of European descent, living, practicing, and teaching in the United States. Our scholarly background is in the Western academy, and our background as practitioners of modern postural yoga stems from a mixture of global lineages as well as more generic and deeply syncretized forms of modern yoga as spiritualized physical culture. It's inevitable that our lenses, both scholarly and personal, have been shaped by this positionality. As scholars, our goal has been to present the South Asian roots of yoga as faithfully as possible while simultaneously keeping an eye on the larger global frameworks, second-order concepts, and cultural homologies that can help up to better understand yoga's complex evolution and its vast diversity, both past and present. The modern material, especially, is sourced from and enlivened by our experience as practitioners embedded in their own lineages and communities, whose histories we have come to know and live both as insiders and as scholars.

It should go without saying that this book is not intended to be a final or universal word on "Yoga." In fact, as the title suggests, it's meant to highlight the inherently ambiguous and multivalent nature of "yoga" as a label. And, in the end, while this book explicitly strives to center the idea of diversity, conversation, and change when it comes to the story of yoga, even this is one perspective from one set of voices. We encourage the reader to place this text alongside others.

The book is divided into three sections: "Concepts," "Histories," and "Modern Practice." The last section will be most useful to readers whose primary goal is to understand the social and political dimensions of contemporary global yoga practice, including how it intersects with other aspects of our modern world, including identity, economics, medicine, and so on. While we will occasionally gesture towards pre-modern yoga traditions in this section, the focus will remain firmly on global yoga as we know it today. Despite past tendencies by scholars to dismiss or trivialize the importance of modern global yoga practices, a growing field of scholarship has turned to making sense of these manifestations of yoga as authentic and serious in their own right. We hope our efforts here strengthen these efforts.

If it's yoga's historical evolution and variability that you're after, these will be most apparent in the middle section. However, that diachronic (meaning, tracking change through time) portion of the book is meant to complement the more synchronic (meaning, focused on a single historical moment, in this case the one representing the system's most standard and robust form) of the first section. There, you'll find some of yoga's core concepts, including how they might vary not just across time, but across different religious, philosophical, and cultural contexts. We placed these conceptual chapters at the front of the book because it seemed to us that it helps to get comfortable with the general nature and shape of a complex thing before trying to understand how it has evolved and changed. In this initial section, we'll still keep an eye on variability but, to the extent that we may sometimes treat concepts in an ahistorical manner, this should not be used to conclude that this kind of standard and timeless version actually exists. The same goes for cross-cultural parallels and analogies.

When it comes to our academic university audience, we hope that this book might serve as a useful introduction to the relevant topics, and create a baseline of knowledge from which the instructor might guide students to go deeper.

For practitioners, we hope that this will offer a glimpse of yoga's rich history and range of potential meanings, as well as offer new opportunities for questions and self-reflection.

Acknowledgements

This book would not have been possible without the support of our family, dear friends, and generous colleagues. Among the latter, Christopher Miller, Aaron Ullrey, Carryn Mills, and Patrick McCartney read parts of the manuscript and provided vital feedback. Several others, including Amanda Lucia, Christopher Miller, Andrea Jain, Jerome Armstrong, and Stuart Sarbacker provided advance copies of their work to help us be as thorough as possible. We would also like to specifically thank our friends and colleagues in the yoga industry and community, many of whom did not wish to have their names mentioned for the sake of privacy, but who served as invaluable sources of experience.

Guide to Sanskrit pronunciation

Sanskrit pronunciation is actually very simple in that it's entirely phonetic. Meaning, each letter always corresponds to a single specific sound. The only issue is that the Devanāgarī alphabet, in which Sanskrit is written, has 47 primary characters, whereas the Roman alphabet used to write English has only 26. This means that when we transliterate Sanskrit words, meaning we render Devanāgarī letters into Roman ones, we have to use additional symbols, called "diacritical marks" to indicate that the character represents a sound that's close to but not quite the same as the letter it's attached to. Below is a guide to the characters, including these marks, and the sounds they represent (note that we skipped a couple of the rarer characters that are difficult to approximate in English and do not appear in this book).

Vowels

a as in "come"
ā as in "father" (held twice as long as *a*)
i as in "fit"
ī as in "seen" (held twice as long as *i*)
u as in "full"
ū as in "root" (held twice as long as *u*)
ṛ as in "rim"
e as in "they"
ai as in "rice"
o as in "oracle"
au as in "cow"
ṃ is a nasal n or m, influenced by whatever sound follows it, as in "bingo" or "hunch"
ḥ is a final "h" sound that produced a slight echo of the preceding vowel, so *aḥ* as in "aha"

Consonants

k as in "kayak"
kh as in "stick-house"
g as in "god"

gh as in "big-house"
ṅ as in "ring"
c as in "churn"
ch as in "ranch-house"
j as in "jump"
jh as in "hedgehog"
ñ as in "canyon"
ṭ as in "fort" but with the tip of the tongue flexed back to touch the roof of the mouth
ṭh as in "smart-head" but with the tip of the tongue flexed back to touch the roof of the mouth
ḍ as in "bird" but with the tip of the tongue flexed back to touch the roof of the mouth
ḍh as in "hard-head" but with the tip of the tongue flexed back to touch the roof of the mouth
ṇ as in "ton" but with the tip of the tongue flexed back to touch the roof of the mouth
t as in "tuck" but with the tip of the tongue touching the teeth
th as in "light-house" but with the tip of the tongue touching the teeth
d as in "dove" but with the tip of the tongue touching the teeth
dh as in "red-house" but with the tip of the tongue touching the teeth
n as in "neck" but with the tip of the tongue touching the teeth
p as in "play"
ph as in "upheaval"
b as in "bog"
bh as in "lab-hand"
m as in "mother"
y as in "yellow"
r as in "run"
l as in "life"
v as in "vole"
ś as in "shape"
ṣ as in "shore" but with the tip of the tongue flexed back to touch the roof of the mouth
s as in "spirit"
h as in "hope"

Note on transliteration

Sanskrit and other non-English terms appear in italics and are transliterated following standard lexicographical usage, with the following qualifications: (1) terms that have entered the standard English lexicon, such as "yoga," appear without italicization or diacritical markers; (2) where common terms such as "mantra" or "karma" are italicized, it is with the intention of reminding the reader that they bear technical meanings different from English colloquial usage; (3) modern proper names are rendered without diacritical marks and follow the transliteration and spelling preferred by historical sources; (4) diacritical marks have been added to quotations for consistency and to avoid confusing the reader.

Part I

Concepts

1 What is yoga?

When we think about defining terms, our first impulse is often to consult a dictionary. Actually, this is a pretty helpful exercise where yoga is concerned, though not because it helps us arrive at anything like a simple or even useable definition. Here is the first half of the entry for "yoga" in the *Monier-Williams Sanskrit-English Dictionary*, which has served as an essential reference for scholars of South Asia in the English-speaking world since it was first published in 1850:

> Yoga:
> The act of yoking, joining, attaching, harnessing, putting to (of horses); a yoke, team, vehicle, conveyance; employment, use, application, performance; equipping or arraying (of an army); fixing (of an arrow on the bow-string); putting on (of armour); a remedy, cure; a means, expedient, device, way, manner, method; a supernatural means, charm, incantation, magical art; a trick, stratagem, fraud; undertaking, business; acquisition, gain, profit, wealth, property; occasion, opportunity; any junction, union, combination, contact; to agree, consent, acquiesce in anything; mixing of various materials, mixture; partaking of, possessing; connection, relation; in consequence of, on account of, by reason of, according to; putting together, arrangement, disposition, regular succession; fitting together, fitness, propriety, suitability; exertion, endeavour, zeal, diligence, industry, care, attention; application or concentration of the thought , abstract contemplation, meditation, (esp.) self-concentration, abstract meditation and mental abstraction practised as a system (as taught by Patañjali and called the Yoga philosophy); [...]

Monier-Williams does then go on to list several more "sectarian" meanings of the word, belonging to many of the groups we'll survey in the course of this book, like the "the union of the individual soul with the universal soul" (the Pāśupatas), "the union of soul with matter" (Sāṅkhya), and "contact or mixing with the outer world" (the Jains). The convention here, like in many dictionaries, is to list the most common usages for a word first, and then move towards the increasingly obscure.[1] So, as we can see, the most common meanings of "yoga" actually have very little to do with the kind of practices, be they physical or spiritual or both, that we'll be discussing in this book. Indeed, if there is a connection to such generic usages to be found here, that connection is first and foremost figurative and metaphorical.

The fact of the matter is that "yoga" is a very basic and generic kind of word. It derives from the Sanskrit root √*yuj*, which means something like "to connect," "to join," or, in a more applied sense, "to yoke." In fact, our English word "yoke" is a true cognate—meaning that it derives from the same common linguistic root. And so, if we want to understand why the meanings of yoga, even the more technical ones, have been historically so diverse, a helpful starting point is precisely to think about the basic and generic nature of the word itself and how this might lend itself to all sorts of imaginative applications. The simplest tools are often the ones that can be used for the greatest variety of purposes.

English speakers don't tend to use "yoke" as robustly but, as yoga scholar David Gordon White has suggested, perhaps we could instead think of a word like "rig."[2] Potentially functioning as either a noun or a verb, "rig" has a similar kind of range of meaning to "yoga." A rig can be a structure or a device, as in a "sailing rig" or an "oil rig." It can also be the act of assembling this structure, or really of assembling anything, as in "to rig the sailboat" or "to rig up a tent." You can even "rig an election," similar to the use of "yoga" to mean an illusion or trick.

So, imagine that, a few millennia ago, there emerged a spiritual practice called "rigging" based on, let's say, the metaphorical likening of the complex arrangement of ropes, cables, and chains necessary to hold together the components of a sailing vessel to the complex and systematic self-discipline needed to achieve a particular spiritual state. Fast-forward two and a half millennia or so and, on the other side of the world, now you have people heading into fitness studios to get themselves "rigged up." That, essentially, is the story of "yoga."

But of course this is still all very general. Even if we're talking specifically about spiritual practices, these still tend to be pretty diverse. Throughout human history, people have engaged in all sorts of spiritual disciplines to achieve all sorts of goals, depending on how it is that they imagine the universe to operate, what they imagine the highest purpose of this universe to be, and so on. If yoga is about "yoking," then we might start by looking at the vast variety of things that people might have historically wanted to yoke or bring together in the context of South Asian worldviews. There we find that "yoga" describes the union of the individual soul with the absolute, but also to the union of one person's consciousness and will with that of another, or else (perhaps most literally) to the union of warriors to the celestial chariots that were believed to carry them into the afterlife after a particularly glorious death on the field of battle. Add to this the fact that, as we'll discuss imminently, there are things that we might want to call "yoga" in hindsight—maybe because they shared some crucial commonality with later yoga practices or eventually evolved into things that are called "yoga"—but that were not called this at the time. In other words, pinning down the history of yoga is very messy.

In the end, there's a two-fold trick to wrapping your head around yoga (or anything else historical). The first step is to realize that people are people. Meaning, regardless of time and place, human society is complicated. It's colored by diversity and disagreements, social and political and above all economic interests, power grabs, noble intentions, and the vast distance between ideals and their lived realities. From this perspective, to imagine that there was a time in the golden past when everyone sat down in perfect isolation from the hustle-and-bustle of daily life, read a single text (say, the *Yoga Sūtras*), understood it perfectly, practiced it to the letter, and mutually agreed to call this "yoga"—well, it just isn't very realistic.

The second step, though, is to recognize that people can and do have radically different worldviews. Especially when separated by time and place. Think about it: a few hundred years ago, you could have lived your life thinking that the sun revolved around the earth. This would have been perfectly rational and supported by the day's most advanced science. So, from this perspective, to project our modern understanding of bodies, minds, and everything in between onto pre-modern yoga texts and their practitioners isn't very realistic either. If we're going to understand yoga practices, we have to think about them in the context of their culture and their time. This includes recognizing variability and change, as well as letting go of the notion that ancient practices are somehow more authentic or that modern practices are somehow more rational.

Given all of this, it should come as no surprise that not only has there never been a universally agreed upon definition of yoga, but yoga practices (the entire spectrum of them) have continuously changed and evolved in tandem with the culture around them. So, when we attempt to define yoga, we can take one of two fundamental approaches. We can really double down on the historically and contextually variable meanings of yoga and try to trace the intricate relationships between these. How do groups define the methods and goals of yoga differently based on their specific understanding of the world? How do they interact and respond to one another based on these different definitions and understandings? How do the usages and applications of yoga change through these interactions? Otherwise, we can look for common trends. What, in the end, seems to stay more or less constant across time and space and context? Is there some shared story or set of assumptions that tends to characterize "yoga" wherever it pops up? For our part, we'll be doing some of both.

Before we dive deeper into various ways or defining yoga, though, one caveat: we won't really be focusing on postural practice. That is, the idea of moving the body or putting it into different poses, with which the casual Western observer might be most familiar. After all, the idea of moving the body is not in and of itself very interesting. We do this all the time. What's interesting is *why* we move the body in specific ways, and in order to get at the "why" we have to (for instance) consider what's going on inside the body. What is putting the body in one pose or another, moving it this way or that supposed to be *doing*? And towards what purpose? In other words, if we want to understand the specifics of yoga practice, postural or otherwise, it's these framing questions that we have to answer first.

To this end, let's look at some of the traditional ways in which South Asian texts have talked about and defined yoga. From this, we'll move to examine a few modern scholarly definitions. And finally, at the end of the chapter, we'll propose a few helpful frameworks of our own.

Traditional definitions

Historically, Indian sources have tended to use the word "yoga" to designate the goal of a certain practice, rather than the practice itself. That is, traditionally, one doesn't "do yoga," one achieves yoga by doing some other designated thing or set of things. Sometimes, of course, these two ideas can overlap, insofar as the state of yoga is described as the successful accomplishment of some actionable goal.

One of the first places the term "yoga" becomes linked with a body of mental (meditation) and physical (asceticism) practices is in the early Upaniṣads, a set of mystical texts mostly composed between the 5th century BCE and the 1st century CE. The *Kaṭha Upaniṣad* (6.11), for instance, tells us: "They consider yoga to be firm restraint of the senses. Then one becomes undistracted, for yoga is the arising and the passing away."[3] The same text famously compares the human mind-body organism to a chariot, wherein the Self is the rider, driven by an intellect, which grasps the reigns of the mind yoked to the senses or horses. So, in this case, we can very clearly see the connection between "yoga" in its more generic sense as hitching up a chariot and its more figurative sense as restraining the senses. A well-yoked mind is a yoga.

Somewhat similarly, the *Yoga Sūtras* of Patañjali, a famous compilation of aphoristic verses probably dated to sometime between 325 and 425 CE, tells us that "Yoga is the suppression of the fluctuations of the mind" (*yogaś-citta-vṛtti-nirodhaḥ*, 1.2). The traditional commentary for the text's opening verse also equates yoga with the state of *samādhi* or completion, wherein the mind is single-pointed in such a way as to reveal reality in true nature, thereby cutting off psychological afflictions, loosening the bonds of *karma*, and creating the proper conditions for the full stilling of cognition.[4] This definition, like the previous, focuses on the mechanics of the mind, or its internal rigging, so to speak.

Other definitions treat yoga as a way of connecting some aspect of oneself to something else. For example, the *Pañcārtha Bhāṣya*, a 4th-century CE commentary on the earlier *Pāśupata Sūtra*, specifies that "in this system, yoga is the union of the self and the Lord" (1.1.43).[5] The Lord, in this case, is God and specifically Śiva. Yoga, then, is the state of being connected to Śiva. Notably, the Pāśupatas, to whose tradition this text belongs, did not believe that the human Self could merge with God so as to become one. What they mean by this is, rather, that one comes to share in Śiva's nature as being omnipotent and free. Somewhat similarly, the *Śiva Purāṇa Vāyavīya Saṃhitā* (29.6) says that "yoga is the state of a mind fixed on Śiva, its other states restrained."[6] In these cases, yoga is a rigging together of two otherwise separate things. This tends to be the case in dualistic worldviews where the highest levels of reality maintain a distinction between the Self and material nature, or the Self and God, and often both.

On the other hand, non-dualistic systems, where the highest form of reality is a single and undifferentiated thing, might seek to combine the idea of yoga as an internal rigging up of the mind with yoga as a connection to something external (because, in the end, the internal and the external are one and the same). So, for example, Kṣemarāja, an 11th-century philosopher in the non-dual Trika-Kaula school of Śaivism, says that "knowledge is experience of one of the various elements (*tattvas*) which are to be known; yoga is the attainment of union with that [element]."[7] Here, he's talking about the idea of mentally parsing the layers of reality, its constituent elements or *tattvas*, and eventually merging into them as one climbs the ladder of creation in a visionary journey all the way back to its source. In a similar vein, the *Yogabīja* (89–90), a 14th-century text on *haṭha* (forceful) yoga that might have Buddhist origins, tells us: "The union of outward breath and the inward breath, one's own menstrual blood and semen [that is, the female and male sexual fluids], the sun and moon, the individual soul and the supreme soul, and in the same way the union of all dualities, is called yoga"[8] In other words, yoga is joining and therefore collapsing all dualities until all that remains is oneness.

As we noted, these definitions tend to foreground the goal aspect of yoga. Even when they seem to point to a practice (like restraining the senses), they give us little in the way of information regarding how this should be done. Historically, just as there hasn't been a single definition of yoga, there also hasn't been a single method ascribed to it. In fact, even more-or-less the same goal might be attained via a variety of methods. Practical texts on yoga often present the term as part of a compound of words where the other member points to the type of yoga, or rather the means of attaining it, being discussed. So, for instance, *haṭha* yoga isn't just "forceful yoga," but more accurately "yoga by means of force," which would have entailed various mental and physical practices to control the body's vital energies, including manipulating the breath or placing the body into various poses. By the 2nd millennium CE, there are four types of yoga that are understood to be the most common, *haṭha* being one of them. The others are *mantra* yoga (yoga by means of reciting *mantras*, or incantations associated with deities), *laya* yoga (yoga by means of dissolving the mind via a variety of visionary and contemplative practices), and *rāja* yoga ("royal" or "the best" yoga, which meant one entered directly into the state of *samādhi*).[9] Texts also tend to talk about the limbs or auxiliaries (*aṅgas*) of yoga, by which they usually mean the specific practices that lead to yoga. The most famous of these is the *aṣṭāṅga* (*aṣṭa* [eight]-*aṅga* [limb]) method of Patañjali's *Yoga Sūtras*, although historically there has been a variety of other systems with varying numbers of limbs. The auxiliary practices can and do include everything from moral observances, to physical techniques and austerities, to philosophical reasoning, to the pursuit of meditative states.

Scholarly definitions

Scholars have generally avoided defining yoga in any conclusive fashion, largely because the task is considered more or less impossible. In the end, if you're going to confine the cultural and historical variability of yoga to a couple of sentences, you tend to wind up with something either so general that it doesn't really clarify things much, or so specific that it excludes a good portion of the aforementioned variability. So, in this section, we'll look at three modern scholarly definitions: one that tries (and generally succeeds) in treading the line between the general and the specific, and two others that usefully focus on specific historical manifestations of yoga (one ancient and one modern).

Attempts to define yoga in general terms tend to look something like statement given to us by Stuart Sarbacker, who proposes that

> yoga is a set or a system of techniques of mind-body discipline, rooted in Indian religion and philosophy, that aims to transform a practitioner into a

> more perfect being so as to 1) make them more powerful and/or to 2) facilitate liberation from worldly affliction.[10]

Notice that Sarbacker's definition doesn't tell us much about what yoga actually looks like in terms of methods or practices, and only talks about its goals in very broad terms. This leaves lots of room to fill in the details of individual traditions.

On the other hand, David Gordon White, whose primary interest is in pre-modern yoga and even more specifically in popular and practical (rather than philosophical) understandings of yoga, suggests that, historically,

> yoga involved yoking oneself to other beings from a distance—by means of one's enhanced power of vision—either in order to control them or in order to merge one's consciousness with theirs. When those other beings were divine, even the absolute itself, this sort of yoking was cast as a journey of the mind across space, to the highest reaches of transcendent being.[11]

If we combine White's definition with the more general picture painted by Sarbacker's, we can get some sense of the mechanics of yoga. How does one become more powerful or free of worldly affliction? By using one's mind and sense organs to establish connections—ones that make sense based on pre-modern South Asian understandings of metaphysics—with other beings, both mortal and divine. White's definition, by virtue of being more specific, does exclude certain things that would have historically been called yoga, and certainly it excludes most modern yoga practice, but it does give us a more substantive idea of what a lot of pre-modern yoga practice would have looked like.

Alternatively, Andrea Jain, a scholar of modern yoga, suggests that

> postural yoga refers to a collection of complex data made up of a congeries of figures, institutions, ideas, and practical paths involving mental or physical techniques—most commonly meditative, breathing, or postural exercises. It is believed to resolve the problem of suffering and to improve health, both defined in modern terms. Postural yoga often betrays a desire to repair what is perceived as an imbalance of "body–mind–soul." Finally, it is tied to mythologies about the historical transmission of yogic knowledge, accumulating around a transnational community that has engaged in and transmitted what participants call yoga—and sometimes refuse to call yoga—since the twentieth century.[12]

Jain's definition has some major issues if one wanted to apply it to yoga in South Asia in 500 CE, but of course this isn't her goal. Notice, though, that Jain's definition still has quite a bit in common with Sarbacker's more general one. However, Jain also manages to put her finger on a very important social dimension of yoga, one that has been important historically but has become even more crucial in our modern age of global interaction. In order to count as yoga, a practice must define itself with relation to that category, even if only in the negative, hence the inclusion of things that participants "refuse to call yoga." In other words, yoga is a function of language and group identity rather than practice. Jain's definition points to the possibility that we might call things yoga for social reasons—it is yoga if practitioners call it yoga (even if their application doesn't have a whole lot of historical precedent), but it might also be yoga if practitioners stridently insist that it's not despite all formal evidence to the contrary.

Rigging up our framework

Definition as conversation

Ultimately, as Jain's statement suggests, definitions and the ideas and practices they seek to represent exist in a complex system of cultural conversations. Nothing means anything in a vacuum. Nothing exists or happens in a vacuum, either. And so, if we want to understand what yoga is and has been throughout history, we have to understand the ways in which things called (and not called) yoga have interacted with and responded to one another. How they've been rigged together.

Even if we're being historically conscious by understanding that practices change and evolve over time, it might be tempting to think of yoga as something like a tree, with sprawling roots and branches, but a solid trunk at its center. But this is still too simple. Instead, if we want to stick with plants, we might choose something a little less centralized. Yoga, and really any "tradition," functions more like a rhizome, a continuously growing plant that spreads via a vast subterranean network of roots and stems. There are things like bamboo, ginger, asparagus, and (conveniently in the context of yoga) lotuses. In a rhizome, there's no center or core. Instead, each node can send off shoots in all sorts of new directions, take root in new types of soil, and on, and on. So there is no single definition of yoga, and there is no single yoga tradition, only a web of interconnected nodes.

We can extend this analogy even further to talk about how ideas and practices that ultimately arise from different cultures might intertwine and interact. For example, modern postural yoga[13]—meaning, the gymnastics-oriented styles found in most yoga studios and gyms—has roots belonging to more than one cultural species. If pre-modern South Asian yoga is a rhizomatic lotus, modern global yoga is not just that same lotus, transplanted all over the world. Instead, it's more like a hybrid. It's the product of some ingenious grafting and splicing with other ideas and practices that look similar but have different cultural roots. After all, it's pretty easy to look at a lotus and decide that it has something in common with a water lily. And so, if we want to understand modern yoga, we have to take into account not only the vast network of South Asian traditions where yoga has sprung up, but also other analogous traditions (for instance Western "harmonial" traditions of spiritual practices that likewise included contemplative, breathing, and movement practices) which influenced yoga through colonialism, and which served as host contexts when yogic ideas and practices made their way around the world. Incidentally, if we were looking for an actual cultural analogue (rather than just a semantically appropriate translation) for the concept of "yoga," then "harmony," from the Greek *harmonia*, "fitting together" or "union," might be the our best candidate.

Finally, another important area of messiness (and therefore conversation) to pay attention to is the somewhat artificial way that we tend to fence off certain cultural areas from one another. For instance, yoga pops up in contexts that we might call philosophy but also religion. And, of course, historically these two things have been fairly difficult to distinguish from one another, whether in Asia or in Europe. Which seems like it wouldn't be much of a problem until one is tasked not only with explaining the differences between Hindu, Jain, and Buddhist yoga practices, but with making sense out of Jewish yoga or Christian yoga. After all, our modern secular sensibilities tend to be fairly accepting of disagreements in philosophy, but tend to get very anxious when it comes to ideas of competing ideas in the area of religion and faith.

In this context, we also shouldn't forget that both religion and philosophy have been closely entangled with another field that aims to explain the world as well as to solve its practical problems. This field is science. If we're talking about bodily practices, then we might be specifically concerned with medical science. Why is this important? Because it helps us explain how it is that popular modern yoga came to be largely about exercise. In truth, the physical and the spiritual have never really been separate. Not in India, and not really in the West either—our mainstream culture's insistence that they are is a very recent phenomenon, and by no means universal. Throughout South Asia, there is a long history of yoga being used towards practical ends, whether for the cultivation of something that might be best translated as "superpowers" (*siddhi*) or even more mundane notions of health. On the other hand, bodily fitness has long been associated with spiritual virtue, both in South Asia and in the West. Again, even if the type of yoga we want to understand is purely "gymnastic," we might still ask ourselves why practitioners are doing what they're doing. What kinds of assumptions are they making about the mechanics of their practice? What are their goals?

Identifying yoga

Ultimately, we, the authors, don't think there's much to be gained by putting forth yet another general definition of yoga. Instead, what we'd like to do, working off the three scholarly definitions as well as the more traditional ones we've already cited, is to propose some avenues of approach that try to extrapolate from the historically and culturally specific into a more general framework.

First, let's say that if we really want to capture the full breadth of relevant material when it comes to yoga, we'll have to assemble something of a Venn diagram. Specifically, we might want to think about what yoga is from at least three perspectives: (1) terminological, i.e. things that have historically been called "yoga"; (2) morphological, i.e. things that look like yoga; and (3) functional, i.e. things that accomplish the goals that have been ascribed to yoga.

The first of these—the terminology—is of course to some extent foundational to the other two. Without some set of things objectively called "yoga," we can't determine either yoga's forms or its goals. But having determined these, we can then set out to find other things that seem to be related. Are there other ideas and practices out there that look similar to or accomplish the same goals as the things we call "yoga"? Specifically, since we're working cross-historically, we might look for ideas and practices that may have originally developed outside of the "yoga" context but have since been absorbed into it. This can even apply across cultures. For instance, using our earlier analogy, if we were to untangle the roots of modern yoga, we might find some lotuses that started out as water lilies in the mix. Meaning, if we can identify the Western ideas and practices that look and work most like yoga and identify the historical nodes where they tangled up and, in some cases, hybridized with their yogic counterparts, we can gain a much deeper understanding of modern yoga's character and its sprawling variability. Or, in a more culturally localized way, we might think about how the category of yoga came to overlap with other, technically independent practices like *tapas* (asceticism) or *dhyāna* (meditation). For example the *tapas* and *dhyāna* practices of ancient Jain and Buddhist movements are not called "yoga," but they sure do look and work a lot like things that would even eventually come to bear that label.

A very short story of yoga

In the end, yoga forces us to get comfortable with complexity and even with contradiction. There is no one story of yoga, what it is, or how it came to be. But what if someone asked you to summarize yoga in five minutes? What might that look like? After all, it can also be useful to have a relatively simple narrative, if only so that we can go back and complicate it later. So, here's one version of yoga's origin story.

We might say that if there's anything that yoga traditions have historically had in common, it's the idea that our current experience of the world is not as good as it gets. As soon as we try to get more specific than that, we're forced to answer two basic questions: what does the cosmos look like and how does it work?; and, what does the human body look like and how does it work? One specific characteristic that yoga systems have tended to share across time and space is their way of thinking about the answers to these two questions in related terms. In particular, they've tended to think in terms of a microcosm, or the "little world" of the human body as being not only analogous, but homologous and continuous with the macrocosm, or the "big world" of the universe. The human being is a small world, and the world is a large being.

This kind of logic allowed yoga and related systems to build on what are perhaps even older and more basic ideas about the cosmos: the notion that we can escape our ultimately unsatisfactory ordinary world and go to a better one, often by going upwards towards the heavens. This is the very literal "yoga" of dying warriors hitching themselves to their chariots to ascend into the heavenly realms of their forefathers. David Gordon White, incidentally, argues that this is more or less the original yoga—that is, it's the first kind of stuff that's called "yoga" that also shares anything in common with the later spiritual practices we usually label as such.[14] Not surprisingly, we find this kind of ascension practice in all sorts of places across the world, though only in the Vedic Indian context could it be accurately called "yoga." Specifically, we might follow White in calling this a kind of "yoga of going." A spiritual practice based in the idea of literally traveling to some higher level of reality.

However, over time, by relying on the logic of big and little worlds, the yoga of going turns into something else. Journeys to other realms become less literal and more visionary. Rather than happening in literal space, they are imagined to happen inside the mind and the human body. So, the yoga of going, which we usually understand today to be mythological, turns into a "yoga of knowing" that relies on a transformation of consciousness rather than a change in one's surroundings.[15] Because the human body (the microcosm) and the universe (the macrocosm) are understood as two homologous sides of the same Möbius strip, the idea is that everything that exists in the outside world has some corresponding principle in the human body. The grand Mount Meru might become the column of the spine, for instance, or the highest heavenly realms might be compared to the cranial vault. Consequently, something that used to be done externally—that is, by physically going somewhere—can be miniaturized, ritualized, and eventually internalized so that it can be done within the controlled environment of the human body. Rather than imagining an ascent into the heavens, you might perform meditative and visualization practices that involve an energy traveling up into the head, which is precisely what happens in some medieval yoga traditions. In the end, though, the yoga of knowing often depends on the idea of going somewhere, even if only metaphorically. In other words, both of these yogas are about the destination.

Alongside this, there has historically been another kind of yoga, and it's what we might call the "yoga of doing." Arguably, the yoga of doing is what has often provided the toolkit for transitioning from going to knowing. In particular, the yoga of doing is comprised of techniques of the body and mind that developed among ascetic renouncers. These ascetics were interested in controlling the body, usually with the end goal of stilling it altogether, so that they might in turn still the mind, so that they might escape the burdens of *karma* (literally "action") and with it *saṃsāra* or the cycle of rebirth. The yoga of doing can be external, such as holding the body in a specific position or surrounding oneself with five fires in the heat of high noon, usually for the purpose of creating an uncomfortable environment for the body in order to generate a kind of thermal energy from the resulting exertion (this is one meaning of *tapas*). The yoga of doing can also be internal, such as controlling or stilling the breath, or practicing techniques that stop, divert, or reverse the flow of semen (believed to be the physical essence of life). The idea was to control the body's vital energies and substances, either with the goal of ultimately shutting down the body to break down the causal chain of *karma*, or to harness their power. This yoga is very much about the method.

The evolving history of yoga in South Asia, as well as the ways in which yogic systems have blended with analogous ideas and practices from other cultures, has been an ongoing mixing and matching of these ideas of going, knowing, and doing. After all, as we mentioned at the outset of this chapter, yoga has historically referred both to the goal (where you're going, or the state of consciousness and/or being that you attain) and the practice to achieve that goal (the doing). We might also suggest that one way of thinking about modern yoga is to say that the practice has become the goal. In a modern quasi-secular cosmology, there is no place to go. And yet, even in our modern culture, we might still think about the ways that practitioners approach yoga as fitness with the goal of transforming their bodies and Selves. Even the most physical yoga might be a way of practicing with one's body (doing) in order to realize (know) some better version of oneself.

Conclusions

- Yoga is a fairly generic term, that refers to the idea of joining something together, perhaps analogous to our English word "rig." In addition to this more generic sense, it has also come to refer to a diverse body of South Asian spiritual concepts and practices that involve manipulating the internal mechanics and external connections of the human Self.
- Traditional texts define yoga in various ways, though they usually use the term to denote a goal more so than the practice itself. This goal can be, among others, a state of mental and physical self-control (getting one's internal rigging into good order), a state of union or connection with some external thing (God, but also another being, or even a layer of reality), or realizing a kind of absolute interconnectivity and oneness inherent in all reality.
- It is best to think of yoga not as a single unified tradition but as a rhizomatic network of concepts and practices. Modern yoga especially, though we could also make this argument for premodern traditions, is not only rhizomatic but also hybrid. In other words, it is the product of interactions between a number of different cultural clusters, both South Asian and those stemming from other geographic locations.
- Yoga has never been easily confined to a single "field," such as philosophy, religion, or medicine. Yogic practices have always included a variety of techniques, both mental and physical, and have been used to achieve a variety of goals, including spiritual liberation, but also worldly power, perfection (including health) of the body, and other practical ends.
- Historically, we might think about models like the yogas of "going" and "knowing," based on the idea of transporting oneself to some better, higher, transcendent state through either a literal or a visionary journey. Alongside these we have yogas of "doing" that ground themselves in mental and physical techniques of manipulating the human organism for a variety of goals. In practice, these yogas tend to overlap, mix, and match with one another.

Notes

1 David Gordon White, *The Yoga Sutra of Patanjali: A Biography* (Princeton, NJ: Princeton University Press, 2014), 3. White also makes this point about yoga's "dictionary" definition by quoting from Monier-Williams.
2 David Gordon White, *Sinister Yogis* (Chicago: University of Chicago Press, 2009), 63.
3 James Mallinson and Mark Singleton, *Roots of Yoga: A Sourcebook from the Indic Traditions* (London: Penguin Classics, 2017), 15.

4 Mallinson and Mark Singleton, *Roots of Yoga*, 18.
5 Mallinson and Mark Singleton, *Roots of Yoga*, 18.
6 Mallinson and Mark Singleton, *Roots of Yoga*, 19.
7 Mallinson and Mark Singleton, *Roots of Yoga*, 21.
8 Mallinson and Mark Singleton, *Roots of Yoga*, 23.
9 Jason Birch, "The Yogatārāvalī and the Hidden History of Yoga," *Nāmarūpa*, no. 20 (2015): 1–13.
10 Stuart Ray Sarbacker, *Tracing the Path of Yoga: The History and Philosophy of Indian Mind-Body Discipline* (Albany: State University of New York Press, 2021), 34.
11 White, *Sinister Yogis*, 44–5.
12 Andrea R. Jain, *Selling Yoga: From Counterculture to Pop Culture* (New York: Oxford University Press, 2014), 172.
13 Elizabeth De Michelis, *A History of Modern Yoga: Patañjali and Western Esoterism* (London: Continuum, 2004).
14 White, *Sinister Yogis*, 59–67.
15 White, *Sinister Yogis*, 83.

2 Cosmologies

Yogic theories of the big world

This chapter will likely strike you, the reader, as the one least directly related to yoga. After all, yoga is very much about practices, whereas this chapter is very much about concepts. But here it's important to remember that "yoga" can refer both to something one does, as well as to the state one attains by doing it. Throughout this book, we will emphasize the fact that yoga (in both of these senses) has always been multifaceted, diverse, and occasionally contradictory. What yoga is and isn't—and conversely, what is and isn't yoga—is all about context. So, context is the focal point of this particular chapter.

Cosmology (literally, from the Greek, "the study of the world") is that set of philosophical questions that tries to describe the universe in its totality: how it works, what it's made of, whether it has a meaning or purpose. And cosmology is important precisely insofar as it creates a context for practice. It gives us a schematic of how the world works, and therefore a roadmap for how to get to where we want to go.

So, we can then ask some important questions: what does yoga look like in each of these different contexts, with their attendant worldviews and assumptions? How might yoga look different from a Buddhist perspective as opposed to a Jain one? What about the various philosophical flavors of Hinduism? And since we're also looking at global modern yoga practice, might there be comparable concepts in Western philosophy that served as a host context for yoga once it arrived in Europe and North America? What are the kinds of non-South Asian concepts that have historically been most primed to blend with yoga?

Big-picture concepts

The one, the two, and the many

The first philosophical question that can help us distinguish one type of yoga from another is very simple: how many things are there? This is meant in the absolute sense. When you reduce the whole world to its most basic components, that is to say to the level of absolute reality, how many of these components are there? Sometimes the answer is one, sometimes it's two, and sometimes there is a possible third. From there, how you understand the one, or else the relationship between the two, determines how you explain the existence of the many things we actually perceive our world as containing.

The one thing, if there is just the one, is something that we can most generally call "absolute reality"—that is, the absolute truth of the cosmos. In varieties of Hinduism that stick close to Vedic roots (that is, those that accept the authority of the ancient Vedas, texts composed beginning around 1500 BCE), this generic ultimate thing is usually called *brahman* or the "expansion," the essence of which is pure consciousness. Typically, this one thing will in one way or another become, emit, or at least produce the appearance of the many. Depending on the specific system, the resulting creation might either be real or only an illusion, but it is in all cases reducible back to the one. The schools of thought that most vociferously assert that reality consists of one thing and one thing only will say that this thing is impersonal and beyond all quality or description. In this case, we might call it *nirguṇa* ("without qualities") *brahman*. Buddhism tends to be even less forthcoming when it comes to nailing down the one (or indeed the many) in any sort of permanent way, but the most standard answer to "how many things are there?" is *advaya*—"not two." Here, absolute reality is not precisely a thing at all, but rather the inherent emptiness (*śūnyatā*) of all things.

If there is a second thing, that thing is usually material nature as distinct from consciousness. Dualistic systems will say that both consciousness and matter are eternal and uncreated but fundamentally different from one another. In atheistic systems (like Sāṅkhya or Jainism), consciousness is often not singular but plural. Meaning, insofar as it represents something like a soul, there are as many souls as there are living beings. In the most basic kind of theistic system, then, God is simply another soul, albeit a very special one. Specifically, God is a soul that has never been subject to the constraints of matter. In theistic systems, the goal is often to become as much like God as the rules will allow. In some cases, this means absolute identity (the Pāśupatas, for instance maintained that the human soul can become exactly like Śiva, just not Śiva himself). In other cases, one can only go as high as becoming a member of God's divine entourage.

This brings us to the possible third thing we mentioned earlier. If the supreme deity is somehow different (higher) than the individual human souls, this of course means that there are, in effect, not two but three kinds of things that eternally exist—God, souls, and nature. It's unusual, within Hinduism, for a deity to "create" souls in the manner that we might expect God to do in one of the Abrahamic monotheisms (Judaism, Christianity, Islam). Nor does God precisely create nature. Often God might function as the efficient but not the material cause of the cosmos. That is, rather than creating the universe, God causes the universe to develop itself from its latent unmanifest state. God's complete freedom from the limitations of matter and his control over it is what ultimately distinguishes him from other souls.

Another option is to say that God ultimately contains and manifests everything else that exists (that is, the material world and individual souls) and yet also transcends it all as an unreducible oneness. In fact, the traditions that come closest to advancing the idea of a full-on creator God usually do this from a position that they call "qualified non-dualism" (*viśiṣṭādvaita*) or "difference in non-difference" (*bhedābheda*). Such positions will claim that, yes, everything is one (*brahman*) and yet there are distinctions within that one between a personal God, the individual soul, and the material world. They might explain this by pointing to the way in which waves on the ocean are the ultimately just the ocean and yet they are also distinct. Or else, the way the sun emanates its rays and yet the rays are not the sun itself. Sparks from a flame are also a popular metaphor. The point being, individual souls are part of God, but not wholly indistinguishable from him. As we'll see, this distinctness becomes especially important in devotional traditions, though tantric traditions can have some of the same concerns. In order to worship God, you need to be in some way distinct from him. Tantric traditions, however, will add the interesting qualifier that in order to worship God, you must first become a kind of god yourself.[1]

Little and big worlds

There is a saying in ancient Greek—"*anthropos mikros kosmos*," man is a small world. In Sanskrit, the analogy tends to flow the other way. *Ṛg Veda* 10.90 tells of the Puruṣa, a man with a thousand heads and a thousand feet, who pervades the whole earth and everything that is, was, and ever will be. This "Cosmic Man" is the first sacrifice, and from that sacrifice the whole world is born. His head becomes the sky, his navel the atmosphere, and his feet the earth. The moon is his mind and the wind is his breath. Even the four traditional social classes of Indian society—and with them, the order of human society—emerge from the Cosmic Man's body. In short, if for the ancient Greeks man was a little world, for the ancient Vedic folk the world was a big man. (Both cultures, it's worth noting, considered the male body to be the default human body. So, when we use masculine pronouns for yogis in this chapter, we're being quite intentional. While female practitioners certainly existed, we almost always have to read between the lines to imagine what their practice might have looked like.)

We'll return to the ancient Greek version of this equivalency towards the end of the chapter. Drawing correspondences between the microcosm and the macrocosm—the little world of the human body and the big world of the universe—is not a rare phenomenon. It's impossible to track it to a single time period or to a single culture. For our intents and purposes, it doesn't so much matter whether the Greek and Indian versions of this motif are actually related, but that people in the 19th century who became familiar with both sets of ideas thought they were. And, even more importantly, that they used this perceived relationship to mix Indian ideas with European ones, creating a whole new context in which yoga practice could take root.

Ultimately, the logic of the macro/microcosm is a logic of corresponding categories. The primary correspondence is between the human body and universe as a whole. That is, again, the universe is a kind of body and the human body is built like a universe. However, this also means that everything within the universe—seasons, minerals, plants, and animals—is classified according to the same common set of categories and therefore related through a set of metaphysical links. For example, the cosmic quality of *brahman* (in an early Vedic context best translated as something like "generative power"), corresponds to the mouth and head of the Cosmic Man, and therefore also to the mouth and head of the human body. Among gods, it is Agni, who rules the sacrificial fire. It's also spring among seasons, morning time, the goat among animals, and of course the Brahmin priest among social classes.[2]

In Western sources, this notion of correspondence is what the Stoics and the Neo-Platonists called sympathy (*sympatheia*), which literally means something like "common feeling" but comes to signify the way in which individual parts of the cosmos are able to function in harmony with one another. In Sanskrit, these connections were called *bandhus*. *Bandhus* hold the universe together and allow it to function as a coherent whole.

In Vedic times (1500–500 BCE), this model would have been used to explain how human action in the ritual of sacrifice could have cosmic import. The universe was created as a primordial act of sacrifice, after all, and so through sacrifice (now on the micro scale) it was to be maintained. In a somewhat later body of texts called the Upaniṣads (500 BCE onwards), ultimate reality is *brahman* or the "expansion," but *brahman* is also *paramātman* or the "supreme self." Insofar as the Upaniṣads claim to reveal the true secret meaning of the ancient sacrificial rituals, they too make use of the hidden correspondences that run through every fiber of reality. In fact, the earliest usage of the term *upaniṣad* is not so different from *bandhu*. It means precisely something like "connection" or "correspondence."[3] This logic of correspondence allows the Upaniṣads to move the older Vedic rituals from out there in the macrocosm (where is it a literal thing that happens in the physical world) into the microcosm of the human body, where is becomes a metaphor for the contemplative process.

So too in later tantric traditions (a new type of ritualism that emerges in South Asia beginning around 500 CE), Hindu, Buddhist, and Jain alike. The world and the human body share a common structure, both of which can be mapped onto the ritual diagram of a *maṇḍala* (circle, Figure 2.1). Even more importantly, both are

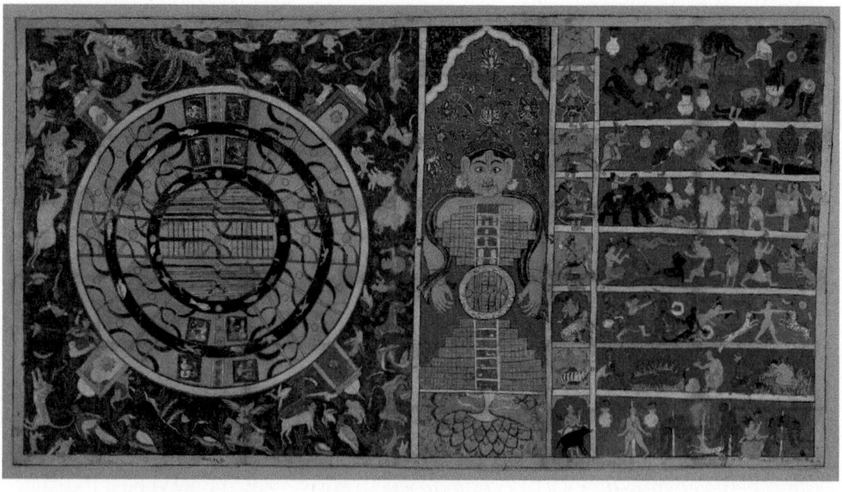

Figure 2.1 Jain cosmology depicting the universe as a human body, with the earthly world at the navel and seven layers of hellish and heavenly realms extending above and below. India, Gujrat, 1613.

Source: Courtesy of the Cleveland Museum of Art, from the Catherine and Ralph Benkaim Collection.

pervaded and inhabited by the same divine energies. This becomes all the more true in the medieval *haṭha* yoga tradition, which is based on the idea that external tantric ritual can be fully internalized and then acted out within the body. By understanding that the human body is not only continuous with, but ultimately identical to the divinely manifested cosmos, the *haṭha* yogi is able to transmute the elements of his mortal body into a perfected divine form that allows him not only liberation but mastery over the material universe.

Scholar of South Asian religions Wendy Doniger has described this idea as a "Möbius universe, in which the inside is the outside."[4] Like the Möbius strip, a surface whose two sides are really just one, the little world flows into the big world and back again in an infinite loop. Insofar as the practice of yoga has relied on this correspondence of microcosm to macrocosm (not all yoga has), it has operated at that impossible place where the curve seems to reverse its orientation. In this model, yoga is a way of revealing hidden connections that allow us to navigate our reality in new ways.

The core problem

As we suggested in Chapter 1, if there's anything that yoga traditions have historically had in common, it's the idea that our current experience of the world is not as good as it gets. And, as we'll see in Chapter 5, practices that we might loosely recognize as yoga (even if they're not called "yoga" quite yet), begin to emerge in response to a specific view of how the world works. This view is grounded in the concept of transmigration, or the cycle of birth, life, death, and rebirth. Though we normally associate such ideas with Asian religions, it was also the common perspective in ancient Greece, where it was known as *metempsychosis*. Abrahamic religions, though, have tended to conceive of time, both human and cosmic, in linear terms, and so the idea of a reincarnating soul generally faded in the West, appearing only occasionally in esoteric contexts. In South Asia, however, this concept eventually became central to of all the area's major religions, including Hinduism, Buddhism, and Jainism, and is called *saṃsāra*.

The general idea behind *saṃsāra* us that desire, and the actions born of desire, trap us in an endless cosmic chain of action and reaction, keeping us in our fragile material bodies navigating an often unpleasant material world. The Buddhists, who become the resident experts on analyzing this unpleasantness, summarize it quite pithily: *sarvam duḥkham*, "all is suffering." Why? Because *sarvam anityam*, "all is impermanent." That is, even the best human life is not that great, since nothing ultimately lasts. Things may be good now, but that could change at any moment. Even if nothing spontaneously terrible happens, one day you'll get old and die. And what's worse is, you know this. So no matter how good things are, you're still living with the low-key existential dread that one day this too shall pass.

So, the question becomes, what do we do about this?

The answer depends on how you understand the nature and mechanics of the world, and the human being's place in it. In order to escape the suffering that arises from the impermanent and corruptible nature of our world, you need to transcend that nature. In the South Asian context, "yoga" is often (though certainly not always) the word used for the methods of doing this. As we saw in Chapter 1, however, the meanings of "yoga" are multiple as, therefore, are the methods it describes. In its earliest forms, the idea of yoga might have entailed a literal kind of ascension, an upward "going" that allows one to leave behind the physical world of the earth and enter some immortal heavenly abode.

When it came to actual practice however, this "going," was usually abstracted into either "doing" or "knowing." Yogas of doing focused on physical techniques, usually ascetic ones, that either shut down the body in order to free the consciousness from its confines or else manipulated its vital forces and energies in ways that were supposed to transform it into something superpowered and immortal. Yogas of knowing, on the other hand, entailed realizing, sometimes spontaneously and sometimes through complex contemplative techniques, that one was never limited by the body to begin with.

In the earliest dualistic systems, true liberation tended to only be possible once one left one's physical body behind. Towards the end of the 1st millennium CE, however, non-dual Vedāntic and tantric traditions led to the advent of a new idea—embodied liberation, sometimes called *jīvanmukti*. In this state, the liberated yogi remained in an embodied state rather than merging into the absolute, either in order to help others along the path to liberation or simply to enjoy (*bhukti*) the splendid abilities of his new perfected body.

Before proceeding to more specific traditions, then, it's worth knowing that liberation was never the exclusive goal of yoga practice. From the very start, the very same techniques that were believed to lead to liberation, could also be used to endow one's body with *siddhis*, literally "accomplishments" but more clearly translated as something like "superpowers." In a sense, *siddhis* too presented a solution to the problem of suffering, but in a different way. The impermanence of the material world likely seemed less troublesome if you were immortal and could, for instance, use your mind to bend reality to your will or fly through the air.

Mapping concepts onto traditions

Ascending upward and inward in the Vedic tradition

The oldest stratum of texts we have access to in South Asia are the Vedic hymns, which present us with a relatively simple physical cosmology consisting of three worlds: the earth, the atmosphere, and the firmament. These three realms, which were most likely common to all Indo-European cultures, were inhabited by gods associated with various cosmic phenomena.[5] The idea of a transmigrating soul emerges only in the late Vedic period, and so we find it in the Upaniṣads, which, as we said, purport to reveal the true hidden meaning of the older Vedic texts. This idea is shared by early Buddhism and Jainism, which emerge around this same time.

The Upaniṣads tell us that, upon death, human souls go up to the moon as smoke or vapor, condense there, and come back down as rain. Rain begets plants, plants are consumed by male animals, and from the semen of males souls are then reborn into the wombs of females. This is the cycle. True immortality, and therefore freedom, lies beyond the disk of the sun. Those who manage to free themselves from the cycle of *saṃsāra* pass through the sun at death, never to return.[6]

In the Upaniṣads, for the first time, we find some of the contemplative techniques for effecting this ascent on a visionary rather than literal level being referred to as "yoga." As we'll see in Chapter 6, this idea may have an older history stemming from the battlefield ascensions of fallen warriors, who were said to rise upwards to pierce the sun on their chariots (called "yogas," on account of the word's association with "yoking"). But the Upaniṣads, doing as they do with many old Vedic tropes, take the idea of going up to the sun and reinterpret it as metaphysical and symbolic. *Brahman*, the ultimate Self of the macrocosm, is the *ātman*, the Self in the microcosm of the body. The whole world is the body of the cosmic Puruṣa, and the individual *puruṣa* dwells in the human body, as a man the size of a thumb in the cave of the heart. In the outside world, *brahman* is the luminous disk of the sun and, as the *Chāndogya Upaniṣad* (8.6) tells us,

> The channels (*nāḍīs*) of the heart are made of a fine essence that is tawny, white, blue, yellow and red. Verily, the sun on high is tawny, it is white, it is blue, it is yellow, it is red. Like a road between two villages goes from one to the other, so too the solar rays go to two worlds, this world below and the world above … One hundred and one are the channels of the heart. One of them runs through the crown of the head. Going up by it, he reaches the immortal. The others, in their ascent, spread out in all directions.[7]

Some portions of the Upaniṣads will say that simply knowing this secret correspondence is enough to liberate one from the cycle of rebirth. Other sections, however, suggest that this knowing requires a bit of effort. The *Kaṭha Upaniṣad* (3.1–13), for instance, identifying the cave of the heart with the highest world beyond, gives us a very famous metaphor that likens the human organism to a chariot. "Know the self as a rider in the chariot," it tells us, "and the body as simply the chariot. Know the intellect as the charioteer, and the mind as simply the reins. The senses, they say, are the horses, and the sense objects are the paths around them."[8] Poor understanding and leads to an uncontrolled mind, which leads the senses to act like disobedient horses. Truly liberating knowledge (*jñāna*) therefore requires a well-yoked system. Yoga is the method and the goal of this yoking.

From ayoga *to yoga in Jainism*

For the Jains, everything is a substance. They're also dualists, dividing reality into two fundamental kinds of substances—*jīva* or "animate," and *ajīva* or "inanimate." The *jīva* is the subject and *ajīva* is its object. However, unlike most of the systems we'll review in this chapter, the Jains also consider the *jīva* to be an agent. That is, it is actually the *jīva* that desires, and acts, and thereby accrues *karma*. A *jīva* is itself a kind of special substance, fundamentally different from the other five substances (matter, motion, rest, space, and time) that make up the category of *ajīva*, distinguished specifically by its primary essence of consciousness. *Jīvas*, which we can also loosely translate as "souls," are therefore actually plural. Meaning, there isn't just one single *jīva* for the whole world, but instead every being is the combination of a *jīva* and a body (which is *ajīva*).

The condition of *saṃsāra* is the entanglement of *jīva* and *ajīva*, which happens through the mechanics of *karma*, which is also a specific kind of very subtle material substance. When the *jīva* experiences passions and desires, it becomes increasingly "sticky" and therefore prone to picking up the fine particles of *karma*, which in turn attach it to a series of bodies. The first time the word "yoga" shows up in Jainism, it's actually being used to describe this situation. Yoga is the union of *jīva* and *ajīva*. The goal of Jain spiritual practice, therefore, is actually *ayoga*, or the separation of the two.

Jainism evolves in concert with other South Asian traditions and so shares many of their innovations and general trends. Eventually, the term "yoga" does gain some currency as a salvific method, even though the goal of Jain practice continues to be separating the *jīva* from its worldly and material attachments—that is, the goal technically remains *ayoga*. Jain ideas of the dualism between *jīva* and *ajīva*, the inescapable material nature of *karma*, and the ethical focus on non-violence have led to an emphasis on ascetic techniques. If *karma* binds *jīva* to *ajīva*, the simplest and most logical solution is to do everything in one's power to eliminate *karma*. Practically speaking, this would have involved putting an end to action and its seeds though various austerities, but also meditative practice or *dhyāna*. Nevertheless, despite this focus on asceticism, we can still find in Jainism the same techniques geared at developing superhuman powers as well as other staples of tantric practice, which we'll review in greater detail shortly.

A prime example of Jainism's participation in the constantly evolving body of yoga traditions can be found in the modern Preksha Dhyana tradition. Preksha Dhyana is a meditation-based technique that blends together traditional Jain ascetic practices, *haṭha* yogic subtle body techniques, and modern ideas rooted in biomedicine and psychology into a program through which the practitioner can transcend the physical body.[9]

Deconstructing the Self in Buddhism

Buddhism is an ancient and extremely diverse global body of traditions. For this reason, it's quite difficult to give a definitive summary of its worldview, even when we're limiting ourselves to something more specific, like yoga. As we'll see in Chapter 5, some of the core features of yoga, namely asceticism (*tapas*) and meditative practice (*dhyāna*) were likewise foundational features of early Buddhism. If there is one thing, however, that differentiates Buddhism from the other traditions we're covering in this chapter, it's the idea of *anitya*, the inherent impermanence of all phenomena, including consciousness.

In Buddhism, the basic building blocks of reality are called *dharmas*, here best translated as something like "principles." Beyond this, Buddhist schools have a number of ways of parsing reality. We might talk about the eighteen elements (*dhātu*), which sort the world into sense objects, sense organs, and sense consciousnesses, and which are similar to some of the Sāṅkhyan concepts we'll review shortly. Otherwise, we might look at the five "aggregates" of personhood: form or body (*rūpa*); sensation (*vedanā*); ideation (*saṃjñā*); conditioned factors (*saṃskāra*); and consciousness (*vijñāna*). The crucial thing about *dharmas*, though, is that they are momentary—that is, impermanent. Contrast this with the special and foundational nature of consciousness as conceived by the Jains or in the Upaniṣads.

The Upaniṣads, as we mentioned, describe the Self or *ātman*, whose eternal and abiding nature is consciousness, as the rider in a chariot. The Buddhists have a chariot metaphor too. In their metaphor a monk, Nāgasena, patiently explains (via a kind of Socratic dialogue) to Indo-Greek king Milinda (Menander) how the human self is like a chariot. Just as a chariot is not its wheels, axle, carriage, or reins, so too the person is not the hair, or the flesh, or the organs, or the sensations, or even the consciousness. Why? Because all of these are merely parts that make up the mere appearance of a coherent whole. And so, just as there is no chariot, since the chariot is merely an impermanent aggregation of impermanent parts, so too there is no Self.

Thus, the Buddhist worldview begins from the position of *anātman*, or "non-self." Everything in reality, including consciousness and the self, is impermanent (*anitya*) and inherently empty (*śūnya*). In other words, there is no *there* there. The world is an ever-flowing matrix of interdependent phenomena that appear and pass away. This caused some proponents of the newer Mahāyāna (the "Great Path") tradition of Buddhism, which began to emerge around the first couple of centuries of the Common Era, to declare that phenomenal reality was not real at all, but an illusion of the mind. This is the general position of the Yogācāra ("Yoga Practice") school, among others.[10]

If the assertion that nothing exists and liberation thus equals total annihilation sounds kind of bleak, it's with good cause. And sure enough, even in the face of these assertions of total emptiness, ideas about a kind of perfect, eternal, and blissful "something" creep right on back into Buddhist thought. This ultimate thing might be called the *dharmakaya*, the "collection of the Buddha's teachings" but also potentially the "body of the perfected principles." Or else the *tathāgatagarbha*, the "buddha embryo" that represents the latent buddhahood of all living beings.[11] Tantric Buddhism, especially, is invested in such ideas, embracing the inherent emptiness of all phenomena as a means towards deconstructing one's reality only so that it can be reconstructed as something luminous and perfect.

On the landscape of early "yoga" practice, Buddhism contributed the idea that it was not sufficient to simply stop the mind but that liberation actually required a kind of psychological transformation.[12] Note, however, that as in our discussion of Jainism above, the principal technique used to accomplish this is *dhyāna* (meditation) and not yoga—or, at least, the techniques in question are often not referred to as "yoga." Buddhist meditation techniques have their own history of evolution, especially outside of South Asia. For instance, as we'll see in the final section of this book, "mindfulness" practices in the modern world often align with but are not identical to yoga.

Enumerating reality in Sāṅkhya

Sāṅkhya is best translated as "enumeration." Specifically, it is the enumeration of the twenty-five *tattvas*—literally something like "that-nesses" but we can say "principles"—of reality (Figure 2.2). Sāṅkhya is a dualistic system, so ultimate reality consists of two eternal principles, *puruṣa* (the "person") and *prakṛti* ("nature"). Like Jainism's *jīvas*, *puruṣas* are plural. The essence of *puruṣa* is pure consciousness—it doesn't do anything, it simply is. *Prakṛti*, on the other hand, is defined by the balance of three essential *guṇas* or "qualities"—*sattva* ("existence"), *rajas* ("ardor"), and *tamas* ("darkness"). As long as the *guṇas* remain in perfect equilibrium, *prakṛti* remains in an unmanifest state. But, as you may have already guessed, this isn't what typically happens. As soon as one quality begins to dominate over the others, nature begins to manifest, to change states, and therefore to devolve into reality as we know it. We say, "devolve" rather than "evolve" because this process is not considered a good thing. *Prakṛti*'s ultimate and ideal state is the unmanifest equilibrium.

So, why the disruption? The relationship between *puruṣa* and *prakṛti* is an interesting one, and a bit of a paradox. They exist for the sake of one another. *Puruṣa* is the subject and *prakṛti* is the object. *Puruṣa* is consciousness and *prakṛti* is the thing it is conscious of. Technically, the ideal state of *puruṣa* is *kaivalya* or "isolation," but it's only through an understanding of *prakṛti*'s true nature (which is fundamentally different from its own) that it can realize this state.

And so, it is precisely the conjunction of *puruṣa* and *prakṛti* that causes the *guṇas* to fall out of balance. The first *guna* to dominate is *sattva*, which is closest in its character to consciousness itself. This results in the first transformation of undifferentiated *prakṛti* into *buddhi* or "intellect." And then something else happens, the intellect (colored by *puruṣa*'s luminous nature) mistakes *it*self for *the* Self (that is, for *puruṣa*) and so emerges the *ahaṃkāra*, literally the "I-maker." We can call this the "ego," which says, "Hey, I exist. This is *me*." And things go downhill from there, so to say. Driven by the frenetic energy of *rajas*, the *guṇas* are now shifting and percolating. At this stage, the predominance of *sattva* yields the mechanical mind (*manas*), whereas the predominance of *tamas* yields the five subtle elements (*tanmātras*) of the outward physical world.

And thus, things branch off, the five subtle elements (sound; touch; visible form; taste; and smell) in turn produce the gross materials (*mahābhūtas*) of the physical reality we actually experience (ether; air; fire; water; and earth). *Manas*, on the other hand, brings with it the components of a sentient individual. These are the sense capacities (*buddhīndriyas*) that allow us to perceive the material world (hearing; feeling; seeing; tasting; smelling) and the action capacities (*karmendriyas*) that allow us to interact with it (speaking; grasping; walking; excreting; generating).

The Sāṅkhya model of the world is like a big metaphysical nesting doll—at every level, reality is contained within and can be collapsed (or reabsorbed) into the preceding level. This is a literal objective process, but it's also a psychological subjective one. Recall that *prakṛti*'s objective manifestation happens for and

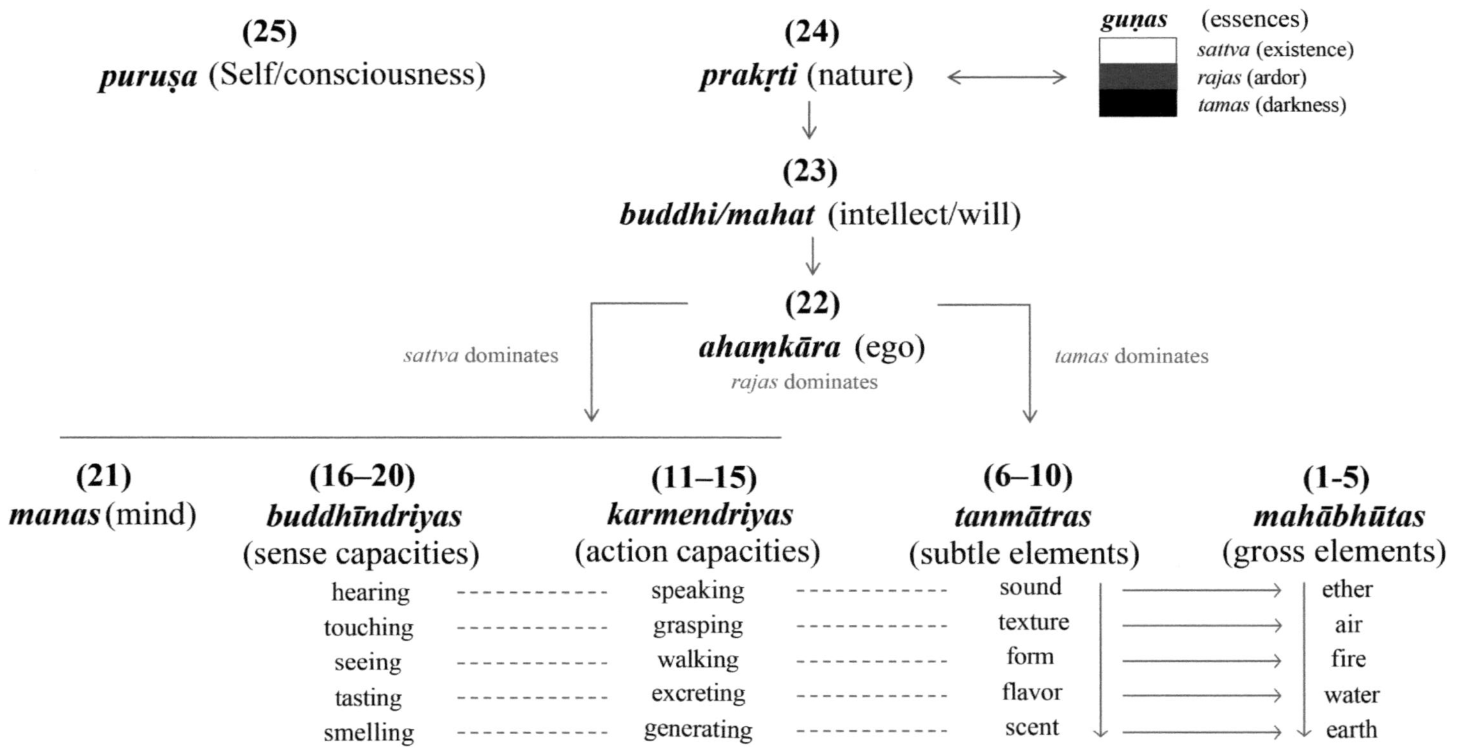

Figure 2.2 The *tattvas* (principles) of Sāṅkhya.

Note: This figure is based on a schematic of the *tattvas*, as originally presented by Gerald James Larson, *Classical Samkhya: An Interpretation of Its History and Meaning* (Delhi: Motilal Banarsidass Publishers, 2011), 236.

by virtue of *puruṣa*'s subjective consciousness. Through the process of *jñāna* (philosophical knowledge but also contemplative gnosis), the mind can be used to reverse the direction of *puruṣa*'s consciousness, pointing it away from external objects, away from the action of the senses, and all the way back to the root cause. If physical matter is the hardware, the mind is the software, but *puruṣa* is the ghost in the machine of *prakṛti*. The ultimate goal is to extract the ghost.

This reverse "hacking" of the software, however, is interesting in its own right insofar as it presents a fully consistent explanation for the other major goal of yoga—not liberation from, but mastery of the material world. Unlimited by the organism's lower constraints, the intellect becomes so expansive that it potentially pervades all of reality.[13] Getting all the way back to reality's source code allows you a back door into its basic functions. We previously used the word *siddhis* to describe the resulting accomplishments of such a state, but the *Yoga Sūtras* (which take Sāṅkhya as their model of the world) call them *vibhūti*, or something like "pervading" or "omni-presencing."[14] In other words, the yogi becomes potentially everywhere and everything.

Sāṅkhya is usually understood to be a sister school to the philosophical tradition stemming from the *Yoga Sūtras* of Patañjali. So, one reason it behooves us to understand Sāṅkhya is so that we might understand the *Yoga Sūtras*, which have historically been (and still remain) an important reference point for yoga. We'll turn to the *Yoga Sūtras* at other points throughout this book but, for now, it's enough to say that the text provides us with a systematic contemplative method for distinguishing between *puruṣa* and *prakṛti*. On the other hand, elements of Sāṅkhya and its analysis of reality are absorbed into later schools of thought that become important to yoga's evolution, namely tantra and Vedānta.

The divine matrix of tantra

Tantric traditions emerged over the second half of the 1st millennium CE and went on to influence nearly every aspect of South Asian culture, from religion to statecraft. Because of its sprawling diversity, tantra is famously difficult to define, but historian of religions David Gordon White has supplied the following encapsulation: "Tantra is that Asian body of beliefs and practices which, working from the principle that the universe we experience is nothing other than the concrete manifestation of the divine energy of the godhead that creates and maintains that universe, seeks to ritually appropriate and channel that energy, within the human microcosm, in creative and emancipatory ways."[15]

Tantric traditions share with Sāṅkhya the idea of an emanated cosmos. Unlike Sāṅkhya, however, Hindu tantric traditions are emphatically theistic. That is, they begin with an absolute deity, whether personal or impersonal. Even Buddhist and Jain tantras, despite the general atheism of the schools, incorporate a myriad of lesser deities and essentially god-like Bodhisattvas ("Awakened Beings") and Tīrthaṅkaras ("Ford-Makers"). Practically, this means that the cosmos gains more layers beyond the original *tattvas* of Sāṅkhya. Both Vaiṣṇava and Śaiva-Śākta tantras tend to imagine the uppermost levels of reality as "pure" (*śuddha*) creation in which the absolute godhead manifests in a succession of very subtle material forms. Below that is an intermediate or mixed level of creation, where individual souls fall into a succession of metaphysical constraints. Then comes "impure" creation, where souls are materially bound, and which tends to look basically like Sāṅkhya's *tattvas*.

And, like in Sāṅkhya, yoga practice allows the practitioner to potentially reverse engineer the *tattvas* and thereby to get back to their purer forms. One place we see this sort of process is in the standard preliminary practice of *bhūtaśuddhi*, the purification of the body's elements. In this ritual, the tantric practitioner visualizes his body as continuous with the *tattvas* of the material world and collapses them back upon one another until he reaches the desired level. How high up the chain this process goes depends on the specific system. Systems that place a high emphasis on the superiority of God will typically stop at the level of *prakṛti*. Other systems, though, will extend the process all the way up into pure creation and potentially up to absolute identity with the deity itself (usually God, but sometimes Goddess).

This is also the idea behind the process of *tattvajaya*, literally the "conquest of the realities," which is precisely what it sounds like. In this practice, the yogi contemplatively ascends up through the levels of reality, gaining full control and mastery of them along the way. The result, as you might imagine, is a dizzying array of superpowers, all the way up to total omnipotence.

The logic behind all this, again, is that of the big and little worlds. The microcosm of the yogi's body is identified with and, in doing so, extended out to pervade the macrocosm of the universe. Tantric cosmologies, however, are incredibly intricate and complex and, for this reason, the *maṇḍala* ("circle," Figure 2.3) or *yantra* ("instrument") is a crucial tool in tantric practice. The *maṇḍala*, usually represented as a circular array, is a fractal emanation. The primal and primary thing—the supreme deity, Buddha, or principle—is at the center. Everything around it is a series of reduplications. The many in the one, the diversity that forms the unity. Creation (or wisdom, in the Buddhist case) flows down from the center top. The yogic path reverses this process, starting at the lower periphery and moving in and up to the apex. In this sense, the *maṇḍala* is less of a flat circle and more of a three-dimensional cone. As we'll see in Chapter 3, the human body (the microcosm) is also a *maṇḍala* and so the emanation and reabsorption of the universe is mirrored in the elements of the tantric, and in this case yogic, body.

The primary conceptual linchpin of tantric cosmologies, however, is the idea of a masculine–feminine polarity. Consciousness tends to be gendered masculine whereas matter tends to be gendered feminine. In dualistic systems both of these principles are independently absolute and eternal. In monistic systems, they tend to be viewed as two sides of the same basic reality. Historian and philologist Alexis Sanderson has argued that most tantras are actually dualistic, asserting a distinction between consciousness (both God's and that belonging to individual souls) on the one hand and material creation on the other.[16] Perhaps the most important exception to this is found in the non-dual system of the Trika-Kaula Śaivas, as well as the goddess-centric Śākta and tantric Buddhist traditions with whom they often shared fluid boundaries.

Figure 2.3 The Cakrasaṃvara *maṇḍala*, featuring the deity (here an enlightened being called Heruka) with his feminine counterpart, Vajravārāhī. They are surrounded by six goddesses (Ḍākinīs) and the external borders are framed by cremation grounds populated with lesser deities and tantric practitioners. Nepal, ca. 1100.

Source: Courtesy of the Metropolitan Museum of Art.

Overall, Sanderson concludes that dualism is a more natural position for tantric traditions because of the high value they place on ritual. The logic here is that the soul isn't bound simply by ignorance but by the specific ways that matter entraps and tethers it in a different but equally *real* reality. And so material (that is, ritual) methods are necessary to undo the soul's material bonds. When it comes to yogic methods, such traditions may highlight yogas of doing. For instance, it is in dualistic Vaiṣṇava texts that we first find some of the core physical techniques of *haṭha* yoga being taught *as* yoga.[17] In nondual traditions, on the other hand, matter is consciousness. Or, in the case of the Buddhists, *saṃsāra* is *nirvāṇa*. In other words, you're already free (and always have been), you just don't know it. Here, then, we are more likely to find yogas of visionary knowing.[18]

Haṭha yoga, a complex and syncretic medieval tradition with which modern yoga is most directly continuous, draws on nearly every one of the traditions we've mentioned so far. Specifically, the classical texts belonging to this tradition combine ascetic and tantric methods. In this sense they inextricably combine knowing and doing. Often less obviously theistic (or at least less sectarian) than their tantric predecessors, *haṭha* frameworks absorb and naturalize tantric cosmologies into the physical body of the practitioner. Because of the overwhelmingly bodily focus of these systems, we will examine them in greater detail in Chapter 3.

Western parallels

Now that we've reviewed some of the major concepts central to yoga's development in South Asia, let's zoom back out and return to the broader frameworks with which we started this chapter. As we'll see in Chapter 7, when a cluster of ideas and practices (like yoga) spreads out across different cultural environments, it will tend to take root in places that most resemble its original habitat. In other words, it'll cluster with the ideas and practices that are most like itself. Eventually, it'll blend with these analogous ideas and practices, forming something new—a hybrid. Modern yoga is such a hybrid. So, what's the other half of the picture here?

The most fundamental parallel is between South Asian and Western understandings of little and big worlds. Here, we're using "Western" as a kind of shorthand. We really mean ideas that first developed in the ancient Greek world, which encompassed Southern Europe, but also northern Africa, and Western Asia. After the breaking up of the Roman Empire, these ideas (like most Greek philosophy) survived and continued to evolve in the Muslim world. It was actually through Muslim culture that they first found themselves in proximity to yogic frameworks, with which they blended in the writings of South Asian Sufis among others.

Scholars sometimes call this complex of stuff "Western esotericism," or otherwise "occultism." These terms, both of which are grounded in the notion of something "secret," point to two features of the traditions in question. These traditions claim to be about discovering the hidden order of the cosmos (how the world *really* works) and they were often passed down in ways that required the initiation into a secret or exclusive social group (religious, scholarly, or both). In this way, the idea here is not so different from the original meaning of "*upaniṣad*" as we discussed it above. *Upaniṣad* points to the "occulted" (that is hidden) web of correspondences that governs the laws of nature, but it also comes to refer to the intimate relationship between teacher and student—*upaniṣad* is sometimes translated as "to sit down next to"—through which such knowledge would have been passed. So here we have our first parallel, in both places we find systems of knowledge that claim to reveal the hidden links between human beings and the world at large.

Introducing harmonialism

For the purposes of this book, we're going to call this Western system "harmonialism." We'll do this partially because such a word has less baggage than something like "occultism," but also because it gets at the actual content of the associated ideas in the same way that the basic meaning of the word "yoga" tells us something about the content of yogic traditions. Harmonialism tends to be rooted in the ideas of Pythagoras, an ancient Greek philosopher-cum-mystic, but it also draws important elements from Plato (and especially the Neo-Platonists), Aristotle, and the Stoics. It tells us that the universe is arranged according to a framework of (often mathematically and musically) ordered proportions, which are interconnected on every level, all the way up from the cosmos at large down to the human body. Remember: *anthropos mikros kosmos*. Man is a small world. These systems can be dualistic, distinguishing the human soul and God from nature. However, in Europe, they came to lean more towards monism, at least in part because they represented a divergence from the mainstream dualism of institutional Christian doctrine. Ultimately, the point of harmonial traditions would have been to use this web of connections between the levels of reality to bring all three (human, cosmos, and the divine) into alignment or *harmony* for the benefit of body on the one hand and soul on the other.[19]

This use of the word "harmony" would have originally been quite literal. For the Pythagoreans, cosmogony was arithmogony, and reality was on a fundamental level numerical. The One (*to hen*, equated to the intellect or *nous*) generated all other numbers just as the creative fire that burned at the center of the cosmos generated all other celestial bodies—even the One itself was a *harmonia*, or a "fitting together" of the odd and the even, the limited and the unlimited. When the One would differentiate itself, however, it would do so in a way that maintained harmony among the parts of the whole. The universe was therefore arranged musically, precisely following the proportions of the diatonic octave. In Western musical theory, the diatonic musical scale is made up of five whole steps (whole tones) and two half steps (semitones), producing a total of seven "intervals." Further down the line, this kind of thinking resulted in Newton's conviction that the spectrum of light must have seven colors (even though, let's face it, indigo is basically blue). Relevant for our purposes, this is also the reason that everyone eventually settles on the idea that there are seven *cakras* (and that they're correlated with the colors of the rainbow, no less), even though such frameworks are not terribly common in pre-modern India.

But let's not get too far ahead of ourselves. Back in ancient Greece, Plato expanded on this idea of the universe's harmonic proportions, describing the cosmos as a set of nestled rings representing the orbits of the celestial bodies and set concentrically to form the whorl of the Spindle of Necessity (the "spindle whorl" is an ancient tool used for spinning fibers into thread), which was attended by the three Fates. Each whorl was mounted with a singing Siren, uttering a single pitch, such that their eight voices formed a perfect harmony to which the Fates sang the past, present, and future.[20] This was the structure of the World Soul (literally the "Soul of the All," *he tou pantos psyche*), which was the perfect pair to the human rational soul. By the Renaissance, it also became a standard model for understanding everything from astronomy, to medicine, to architecture, to dance. Because the whole world was arranged according to this standard set of musical proportions, all parts of nature inherently "resonated" with certain other parts. And so, one always sought to maintain harmony in the world, and to restore it via complementary methods if the balance should falter.

Reascending to the celestial spheres

So, as with the three realms of Vedic and Upaniṣadic thought, we're talking about features of the physical cosmos, but we're also talking about metaphysical realities. The ancient Greeks understood that the earth was spherical (rather than flat), but they also envisioned it as being at the center of the cosmos with the other celestial bodies revolving around it in the hierarchically arranged spheres that were their proper domains. Things on the Earth were made out of the four gross elements (fire, air, water, and earth). Beyond this, Greek philosophers often posited another special kind of element, which we'll generically call ether, and which was creative and not corruptible like the four terrestrial elements. It was out of this very subtle element that the stars and the heavenly bodies were made. Among the celestial bodies of the planets and stars, the sun held a place of special importance. It sat at the center of the other celestial spheres, and was the living heart of the universe (the big world). If the earth was the physical center of the cosmos (just as the navel is the "center of gravity" within the little world of the human body), then the sun was its metaphysical center, the origin of life.[21] Beyond all this (and through the disk of the sun) there was another world that was not material at all. Plato would have called this the divine world of the Forms, comprised entirely of eternal ideas. Renaissance Christians, who readily adopted the ancient Greek cosmology with certain modifications, would come to call this world the "Empyrean" realm, or the Kingdom of God.

Plato also gave us one final chariot metaphor that, like its Upaniṣadic and Buddhist counterparts, elucidates the inner workings of a person. In his *Phaedrus*, Plato likened the soul to a chariot, governed by a charioteer who wields the reins of two winged horses. One horse is white, well-bred, honorable and obedient. The other horse is a malformed lumbering animal, not only insolent and prideful but deaf. Zeus, in his winged chariot, leads the other gods in a circuit around the heavens. The gods' chariots glide around the heavenly spheres evenly and with ease. The human soul, though, unable to control the unruly horse is pulled downwards until it loses sight of the divine world of forms. On its downward fall, it sheds the wings that are a marker of its divinity and, having dropped to the earth, forgets the world of forms altogether. More conceptually, then, Plato identified three parts or capacities of the soul: reason (the charioteer), spirit (the white horse), and appetite (the dark horse). The first of these is rational and immortal, created by the same divine Demiurge that conceived the cosmos, while the latter two are irrational and mortal, and are created by the lower gods.

On earth, the soul becomes embroiled in its material existence and so it transmigrates, life after life, through a series of bodies. The soul's point of origin, its true nature, and therefore its rightful place is the divine abode that lies beyond the material world. And so, it must seek to return there—to regrow its wings and reascend.

In Plato's allegory of the chariot and the soul's fall to earth, we have a kind of parallel to the mythic yoga of going. Like those Upaniṣadic passages that point to liberation beyond the disk of the sun, so too the Platonists imagined the souls escape out of matter in quasi-spatial terms. And the goal was very much to escape. The Middle Platonists as well as the Neo-Pythagoreans, emerging just at the turn of the millennium into the first two centuries of the Common Era, came to regard matter as fundamentally evil. This opinion was shared by a slew of religious sects, whom scholars have collected under the general label of Gnosticism. "Gnosis," cognate with our verb "to know" (and, incidentally, also with the Sanskrit *jñāna*), referred to salvific knowledge received through revelation.

The general tendency towards Gnosticism can be located among Jewish, Christian, as well as "pagan" groups, all of whom generated complex mythological narratives to explain the prevailing philosophical idea of matter as evil. Though the particular actors of these myths varied with each sect, they all shared the following basic form: there is a transcendent God who created a perfect divine world, which is the original home of the human soul. But then something went wrong, and this led to the rise of an evil Demiurge (a lower Creator, often gendered feminine) who created the material world, into which the human soul fell, forgetting its divine origins. Certain sects, however, had a more optimistic perspective on the whole thing. The Hermetists, for instance, held to the fundamental unity of the universe, represented by the essential interrelatedness of God (the One), the cosmos, and man.[22] They tended to view the cosmos as a beautiful creation of the transcendent God, the first reflection of his image, and infused everywhere with his presence.[23] The World Soul was a sister to the human soul, both sharing divine parentage, and for this reason (rather than to completely escape the evil material world) it was the destiny of the human soul to reascend to this absolute cosmic status. In either case, to do this, one would need to pass through the ethereal realm of the planetary spheres, along the rays of the sun, which was the heart of the universe and the cosmic manifestation of the divine intellect of the One.[24]

Some philosophers, like Plotinus (c. 204–270 CE), insisted that the soul is inherently divine and therefore can never actually be trapped by matter. And so, it has only to realize its identity with the divine intellect that lies at the origin of the cosmos which it can do through philosophical contemplation—in order to achieve the desired state of *henosis*, or unity with the One. So here we have something like an analogue to the yoga of knowing. Other philosophers, like Iamblichus of

Chalsis (c. 245–325 CE), insisted that the transcendence of matter's limitations must happen through matter itself. In this context, knowing was not enough, and so emphasis was placed on the rituals of theurgy, *theourgia* or "god-work." Here we have something closer in kind to the yoga of doing, and even more so to the kind of frameworks we often tend to find in tantric traditions. Like tantra, theurgy is a complex, diverse, and historically fraught term, but historian of medieval Christianity Claire Fanger provides the following generalizations as a tentative definition. Theurgic practices: "(1) tend to involve rituals to effect the soul's purification; (2) tend to involve fellowship with intermediary beings (gods, angels, *daemones*); and (3) tend to be oriented toward revelation, or experiences in which something is transmitted by the divine powers."[25] And so, without saying that theurgy is the same as tantra (because it isn't), we could suggest that it has historically served as an analogous framework for spiritual practices that involved practices of spiritual going, knowing, and doing.

Mapping the cosmos of Allāh

These Neo-Platonic themes of purification and ascension took on new meanings in the Muslim world. Islamic culture, which flowered dramatically with the rise and expansion of the Islamic empire from the 7th century onwards, preserved and elaborated on much of Greek thought (in fact, it is through translations from the Arabic that many classical sources made it back to Europe during the Renaissance). But Muslim thinkers, drawing on a variety of sources, also developed a new and original set of cosmological models, images, and mystical practices.

Early Islamic philosophers reshaped Greek cosmology to talk about the universe as an emanation of God (Allāh), produced through a series of ten intelligences. The first intelligence corresponds to the highest heavenly realm that lies beyond the celestial spheres, which then produces the fixed stars, which in turn emanates the seven celestial bodies, all the way down to the tenth intelligence that produces the sublunar earthly realm.[26] These ideas turned out to be especially appealing to the Sufi mystical tradition, which used them as a kind of roadmap to chart a return to God.

Out of all this, Sufi thinkers systematized an idea of four hierarchically layered realms, which were as much spiritual states as they were "places." Human beings and our world are the sphere of *mulk* ("kingdom," that is, the realm over which God is king) or *nāsūt* (humanity), which stands in contrast to the angelic realms of *malakūt* (sovereignty) and *jabarūt* (omnipotence). Higher than all of these is the realm of *lāhūt* (divinity).[27] While God, and therefore the realm of *lāhūt*, is ultimately inscrutable, the other realms act as a progressive series of mirrors for God's attributes. So the idea, again, is one of correspondences. Everything that exists in the physical realm corresponds to some (metaphysically greater) entity in the spiritual realm.

The Islamic idea of an ascent through the heavenly realms goes all the way back to Muhammad himself (Figure 2.4). The history of Sufi mysticism is full of diverse elaborations on this theme, some more spatial, others more intellectual and emotive, and many a good deal of both. Stages of spiritual progress are often referred to

Figure 2.4 The *mi'raj* (ascent) of Muhammad. From the Khamsa of Nazimi. Iran, Tabriz, 1539–1543.

Source: Courtesy of the British Library.

as *maqāms* (places or stations), which incidentally is both the word used to signify a shrine that a might be visited by a pilgrim and also a melodic mode in traditional Arabic music. The number of *maqāms* that a spiritual aspirant must pass through on his path to God as well as their precise nature vary from tradition to tradition. Generally, though, the journey is conceived as being as much a matter of going from down to up as from out to in. It's worth mentioning that Sufi traditions in northern India and especially Bengal often combined such frameworks with yogic and tantric practices.

The Sufi systems are not always precisely harmonial, though they incorporate some of those elements, especially when it comes to cosmology. However, insofar as Islamic philosophy and proto-science drew heavily on their Greek predecessors, harmonialism continued to thrive in the broader framework of Muslim thought. For instance, al-Kindī, a 9th-century Muslim philosopher who lived in what is now Iraq, combined Aristotelian, Neo-Platonic, and Pythagorean ideas to suggest that every single thing in the world (elements, bodies, objects, planets, images, words, musical notes, souls) transmits rays, which are ultimately responsible for all correspondences and causal relationship.[28] And if one could understand the mechanics of these energetic rays—that is, if one managed to harmonize oneself with their forces—one could become a powerful mage, capable of bending the natural world to one's will. [29] Notably, we see very similar ideas emerging in Europe during the Renaissance.

So, why spend all this time on non-Indian ideas in a chapter on yoga cosmologies? Mainly, because these similarities have not escaped the notice of practitioners, modern and pre-modern alike. Any claims of influence or transmission between Indian and Western systems prior to the 2nd millennium CE tend to be tenuous at best. This is not to say that influence or transmission did not occur—it almost certainly did—but only that we do not have the concrete evidence to trace precisely when, how, and in which direction it happened. However, we can see (originally Greek) harmonial models drawing on practices like theurgy already being synthesized with Indian yogic systems in Islamic sources from the 13th century onwards.[30] For Western practitioners of modern yoga, who often swim in the water of Western spirituality, these parallels continue to resonate today.

In other words, if we really want to make sense of all of the ideas that underpin modern yoga, we need to understand all of their diverse cultural sources, Indian and otherwise. And we also need to understand that our current moment is not the first time that these histories have met, overlapped, and blended.

Pulling it all together: the metaphysics of early modern yoga

Early international yogis who taught in America and Europe were well-versed in the metaphysical assumptions of their audiences and especially in how those assumptions might overlap with their own Indian systems. What's more, they capitalized on this understanding, eagerly building bridges between the two worldviews.

Swami Vivekananda, a pioneering popularizer of yoga in the West who made his debut at Chicago's 1893 World Parliament of Religions, set the tone for all those who would follow him. In his lectures, collectively published along with a translation and commentary on Patañjali's *Yoga Sūtras* under the title *Rāja Yoga* in 1896, Vivekananda doubled down on the scientific nature of yoga. For Vivekananda, the universe boiled down to two principles, *prāṇa* and *ākāśa*, which he translated as "energy" and "matter," respectively. Notably, his notion of *ākāśa* was closer to what Western metaphysicians had long called "ether" than it was to the Indian element bearing that name. *Ākāśa* was the raw subtle matter of the cosmos, while *prāṇa* was the energetic current that flowed through it. What's more, towards the end of his time in the United States, Vivekananda reportedly met with the visionary engineer Nikola Tesla, who shared his ambition to demonstrate that force and matter were, in the end reducible to the same basic cosmic principle.[31]

Vivekananda was of course well versed in the Indian systems of Sāṅkhya as well as non-dual Vedānta. However, he also spoke the languages of contemporary physics and Western metaphysics. When he described the mechanics of yoga, he brought all of these frameworks into play. It's worth noting that Vivekananda wasn't being terribly unorthodox when he invested modern physics with spiritual meaning. Western physicists beginning with Isaac Newton and ranging well into the 19th century speculated on the spiritual nature of electromagnetism, which inherited many of the qualities traditionally associated with the celestial element of ether.

So what happens during yoga practice? According to Vivekananda,

> from rhythmical breathing comes a tendency of all the molecules in the body to move in the same direction. When mind changes into will, the nerve currents change into a motion similar to electricity, because the nerves have been proved to show polarity under the action of electric currents. This shows that when the will is transformed into the nerve currents, it is changed into something like electricity. When all the motions of the body have become perfectly rhythmical, the body has, as it were, become a gigantic battery of will. This tremendous will is exactly what the Yogi wants.

Having transformed himself into an energetic battery, the yogi is able to exert his will like a beam of electromagnetic radiation, over objects and bodies, near and far.

Vivekananda was a monist (generally an Advaita Vedāntin, so for him the one reality was the expansive *brahman*), but he was a modern and a comparative monist. To some extent, his idea of the yogi as an all-powerful figure who, as Vivekananda himself claimed, could "control everything in the universe, from the atoms to the biggest suns" was also not a little bit tantric. And beneath Vivekananda's scientific language, there lay a further set of harmonial assumptions on which his audiences would have surely picked up. But when Vivekananda advised his readers to use the breath to "harmonize the system" of their bodies, he almost certainly meant something different than contemporary American writers drawing on a history of European astrological medicine.[32]

Another great example is Paramahansa Yogananda, author of the modern spiritual classic, *Autobiography of a Yogi* (1946), where he described (among other things) how his guru, Sri Yukteswar, was resurrected on the "astral planet" of Hiranyaloka after his death. The idea of an astral realm—or, as we'll see in Chapter 3, an astral body—are Western concepts stemming once again from ancient Greek cosmologies. Hiranyaloka, on the other hand, derives from the Indian notion of Siddha realms, inhabited by semi-divine sages and perfected yogis.[33] On the surface, they are not dissimilar concepts, if only because both are ultimately grounded in the logic of big and little worlds. Certainly, the translation would have been compelling to Yogananda's audiences, who would have understood the notion of an astral planet but not a *siddhaloka* (perfected world). The same could be said for Vivekananda's translation of *ākāśa* into ether or *prāṇa* into electricity. But it's also worth with noting that these are ultimately different concepts with different histories.

Which is not to say that such translations are misguided or somehow inauthentic. As we've seen in this chapter, even if we confined ourselves to South Asian traditions we would find them to be full of diverse, historically variable, and often conflicting frameworks and concepts that have nevertheless continuously interacted, combined, and recombined. Our task, going forward, will be to pay attention to this complex interplay of similarity and difference.

Conclusions

- Dualistic cosmologies, like those of Sāṅkhya, Jainism, or certain tantric traditions, tend to focus on the idea of extracting and isolating the Self from matter. This can be a contemplative psychological process but, more often, it also involves external physical actions like ritual and/or austerities that worked to neutralize the binding effects of matter and/or the material body.
- Monistic (non-dual) cosmologies, like those of the Buddhist and Kaula Śaiva and Śākta tantras, as well as Advaita Vedānta, tend to focus on expanding and erasing the boundaries of the Self such that it becomes coextensive with the greater material cosmos. These traditions often focus on contemplative and visionary methods.
- Both of these systems have at times relied on the idea of a correspondence between the big world (macrocosm) of the universe and the little world (microcosm) of the human body, as well as themes of ascent. This ascent through the layers of reality can be either an extraction mechanism, or it can be a way of realizing reality's ultimate continuity by drilling down (or up, as the case may be) to its most fundamental essence.
- Analogous systems in the Western world, including ancient Greek, Islamic, and early modern European models, have interacted and blended with these Indian frameworks to produce blended and hybrid cosmologies for today's global yoga systems.

Notes

1 Gavin D. Flood, *The Tantric Body: The Secret Tradition of Hindu Religion* (London and New York: I.B. Tauris, 2006), 11.
2 Brian K. Smith, *Classifying the Universe: The Ancient Indian Varṇa System and the Origins of Caste* (New York: Oxford University Press, 1994), 70.
3 Patrick Olivelle, *The Early Upaniṣads: Annotated Text and Translation* (Oxford and New York: Oxford University Press, 1998), 24.
4 Wendy Doniger O'Flaherty, *Dreams, Illusion, and Other Realities* (Chicago and London: University of Chicago Press, 1984), 242.
5 Olivelle, *The Early Upaniṣads*, 19–20.
6 Olivelle, *The Early Upaniṣads*, 21.
7 Translation adapted from Patrick Olivelle, *The Early Upaniṣads: Annotated Text and Translation* (Oxford and New York: Oxford University Press, 1998), 279. See also David Gordon White, *Sinister Yogis* (Chicago: University of Chicago Press, 2009), 86.
8 Translation adapted from Olivelle, *The Early Upaniṣads*, 389.
9 Andrea R. Jain, "Jain Modern Yoga: The Case of Prekṣā Dhyāna," in *Yoga in Jainism*, ed. Christopher Key Chapple (New York: Routledge, 2015), 229–42.
10 Johannes Bronkhorst, *Buddhist Teaching in India* (Boston: Wisdom Publications, 2009), 115–35.

11 Bronkhorst, *Buddhist Teaching in India*, 154–5.
12 Johannes Bronkhorst, *Greater Magadha: Studies in the Culture of Early India* (Leiden and Boston: Brill, 2007), 52.
13 Edwin F. Bryant, *The Yoga Sutras of Patañjali: A New Edition, Translation, and Commentary: With Insights from the Traditional Commentators* (New York: North Point Press, 2009), 713–14.
14 David Gordon White, *Sinister Yogis* (Chicago: University of Chicago Press, 2009), 39.
15 David Gordon White, ed., *Tantra in Practice* (Princeton, NJ: Princeton University Press, 2000), 9.
16 Alexis Sanderson, "Meaning in Tantric Ritual," in *In Essais Sur Le Rituel III*, ed. Anne-Marie Blondeau and Kristofer Schipper, vol. CII, Bibliothèque de l'École Des Hautes Études, Sciences Religieuses (Louvain-Paris: Peeters, 1995), 15–95.
17 James Mallinson, "Yoga and Yogis," *Nāmarūpa*, 3, no. 15 (2012): 1–27.
18 White, *Tantra in Practice*, 12.
19 Anya P. Foxen, *Inhaling Spirit: Harmonialism, Orientalism, and the Western Roots of Modern Yoga* (New York: Oxford University Press, 2020), 23–4.
20 Franceso Pelosi, "Eight Singing Sirens: Heavenly Harmonies in Plato and the Neoplatonists," in *Sing Aloud Harmonious Spheres: Renaissance Conceptions of Cosmic Harmony*, ed. Jacomien Prins and Maude Vanhaelen (New York: Routledge, 2017), 16–20.
21 Lucas Siorvanes, *Proclus: Neo-Platonic Philosophy and Science* (Edinburgh: Edinburgh University Press, 1996), 307.
22 Roelof Van den Broek, "Hermetism," in *Dictionary of Gnosis and Western Esotericism*, ed. Wouter J. Hanegraaff et al. (Leiden and Boston: Brill, 2006), 559.
23 Roelof Van den Broek, "Gnosticism and Hermetism in Antiquity: Two Roads to Salvation," in *Gnosis and Hermeticism from Antiquity to Modern Times*, ed. Roelof Van den Broek and Wouter J. Hanegraaff (Albany: State University of New York Press, 1998), 10.
24 Ruth Majercik, ed., *The Chaldean Oracles. Text, Translation, and Commentary*, trans. Ruth Majercik (Leiden and New York: Brill, 1989), 38–9.
25 Claire Fanger, "Introduction," in *Invoking Angels: Theurgic Ideas and Practices, Thirteenth to Sixteenth Centuries*, ed. Claire Fanger (University Park: Pennsylvania State University Press, 2015), 16.
26 Jamal J. Elias, *The Throne Carrier of God: The Life and Thought of Ala Ad-Dawlah as-Simnani* (Albany: State University of New York Press, 1995), 152.
27 Elias, *The Throne Carrier of God*, 155.
28 Pinella Travaglia, "Al-Kindī," in *Dictionary of Gnosis amd Western Esotericism*, ed. Wouter J. Hanegraaff et al. (Leiden and Boston: Brill, 2006), 59.
29 Liana Saif, *The Arabic Influences on Early Modern Occult Philosophy* (New York: Palgrave Macmillan, 2015), 30–36.
30 Carl W. Ernst, "The Islamization of Yoga in the 'Amrtakunda' Translations," *Journal of the Royal Asiatic Society*, series 3, 13, no. 2 (2003): 199–226; Shaman Hatley, "Mapping the Esoteric Body in the Islamic Yoga of Bengal," *History of Religions*, 46, no. 4 (2007): 351–68.
31 Anya P. Foxen, *Biography of a Yogi: Paramahansa Yogananda and the Origins of Modern Yoga* (New York: Oxford University Press, 2017), 78.
32 Foxen, *Inhaling Spirit*, 226–38.
33 Foxen, *Biography of a Yogi*, 209n46.

3 Bodies

Yogic theories of the little world

This chapter will deal with yogic approaches to the body in the broadest possible terms. Although techniques grounded specifically in the mechanics of the physical body—putting the body into certain poses, manipulating its inhalation and exhalation of air, and so forth—have certainly been part of yoga practice, meditative practices have been equally if not more important. This might mean attempting to still the mind to decouple it from external reality, or it might mean visionary practices that use the mind to literally reshape reality or even to create it anew. Either way, such practices are still very much relevant in a chapter on bodies, even if that might seem counterintuitive at first. To understand why and how, we must get away from the notion of meditation as something that happens only in the mind. Or else, we must get away from the mind as being somehow separate from the body—either separate from the rest of the body by virtue of being in the head (indeed, many pre-modern thinkers, including quite a few Indian ones, actually located the mind in the heart) or, more importantly still, as being something other than the body entirely.

Consequently, we'll be treating the body less as a discrete physical object, and more as a continuum. The body's internal mechanics (how it works on the inside) flow directly into understandings of mind and Self. The body also has a relationship to the outside world and, if we bring in the logic of macro- and microcosms, our big and little worlds, we find that all of these things are intimately interconnected.

As an aside: it's worth mentioning that for the vast majority of this chapter, and unless otherwise specified, we'll be talking about male bodies by default. This isn't because female practitioners of yoga did not exist, though we have few records of them or of what their practice might have looked like as distinct from that of men. But, as far as the texts are concerned (and texts are largely what we have to go by when it comes to pre-modern traditions), if there's a default human body that reflects the proper order of nature, that body is represented as male.

Another important premise is that, just as there's no one single understanding of the cosmos (cosmology) or doctrinal context in which yoga happens, so too there is no one universal understanding of the yogic body. This is especially true when we factor in modern traditions, which tend to be more about therapy (yoga as a fitness or relaxation technique) rather than spiritual salvation or enlightenment. But it's also worth noting that using yoga for therapeutic goals is not precisely a new thing. Looking at the role of the body in yogic traditions makes this abundantly clear. There are certainly those traditions that regard the body as nothing but an obstacle to be overcome. Even then, however, overcoming the obstacle often means subjecting the body to certain internal processes that neutralize its potential to act as a prison, by drying up its impure and leaky insides and burning up its karmic fetters, for instance. Such practices might not be considered therapeutic in the medical sense, but they are certainly a form of biophysical intervention that aims to "treat" the body.

Maybe the simplest way to approach the matter is to admit this most basic and fundamental axiom: any practice undertaken by humans has to begin in the human body. It's where we go from there, how we understand the body and what we do with it, that tends to separate one kind of practice from another. So, if we wanted to make some generalizations about yogic positions on the body, we might do so along the following lines: is the body an obstacle or an asset? It is something to be escaped, or is it the ground on which liberation occurs? Should it be destroyed or transformed?

Big-picture concepts

The subtle body

There is the gross physical body (in Sanskrit, the *sthūla śarīra*) and then there is the subtle body. In Sanskrit, this other body is often referred to as the *sūkṣma śarīra* or the *liṅga śarīra*, but these terms and their historical specificity don't necessarily capture the full extent of what we might conceptually mean by "subtle body" when we look at South Asian traditions. Likewise, many of the terms we use to translate these Sanskrit words into English (or other European languages) have their own histories that we'll briefly explore at the end of this chapter. Western subtle bodies tend to be referred to as "etheric" (from the ancient Greek, *aitherodes*) or, better yet, astral (*astroeides*)—that is, made of the same stuff as the stars, which are in the end just "heavenly bodies." When we call this body the "spiritual body," we do it because our word "spirit" ultimately comes from the Latin *spiritus*, which is used to translate the ancient Greek *pneuma*. All of these words refer to a kind of subtle life-force but they also refer, more mundanely, to breath and air. Not unlike, of course, the Sanskrit word *prāṇa*, and likewise *ātman*. In other words, people the world over have tended to think of the human body in ways that transcended the purely tangible. And they did it in ways that were similar, but also different.

In India, some of the most in depth pre-modern discussions of the subtle body occur not in the context of yoga practice, but with regards to much more practical matters like psychology and embryology. The subtle body is way of talking about mind and life-force, and in this sense helps to explain the inner mechanics of a sentient being. It is also the repository of *karma*, governing the process of life, death, and rebirth. But, in some sense, the way pre-modern cultures understood "subtle" bodies, that is features of the body that are not literally tangible and immediately apparent, is not so different from the way we understand the body's inner mechanics today. We might talk about enzymes, and hormones, and neurotransmitters. Premodern people talked about spirits, and humors, and winds, and vital energies.

But, in another sense, the subtle body is also much more than this.

Little and big worlds, revisited

Historian of religions David Gordon White has proposed that, in addition to a micro- (the "little world" of the human body) and a macrocosm (the "big world" of the universe), we can also think of a mesocosm.[1] That is, a kind of middle world that literally *inter-mediates* or goes between the human body and the larger world around it. On the other hand, Barbara Holdrege has suggested the idea of the "processual body" or a way of thinking of the inner nuts and bolts of the body as a process that gets us to a specific goal.[2] Focusing on concepts like these lets us think a bit more generically about what this intermediary "subtle" body might look like, and why it might look different from context to context. It's all about the frame of reference. What is the larger world in which the human body stands and, even more importantly, what do we want to accomplish within it? What's the goal?

When we talked about cosmologies in Chapter 2, we inadvertently ended up saying quite a bit about the basic ingredients of the human being. Remember all those chariot metaphors? In addition to the physical body, which was part and parcel of the material world in general, and the Self/soul, which shared the nature of ultimate reality, there was a lot of "connective tissue" and most of it was fairly psychological in nature. Most yogic paths involve some process, whether ritual or contemplative or both, of working through these layers of one's being. This could mean peeling them back, or destroying them, or perhaps transforming them.

So, ultimately, the major function of the subtle body is to triangulate between the human being (body and conscious Self), the greater cosmos, and ultimate reality. It is to create a kind of middle ground on which the processes that connect these things take place.

In South Asia, we find models of the universe contained within the human body as early as the *Ṛg Veda* (c. 1500 BCE). In formal Vedic ritual, the body of the sacrificer becomes the measure of the sacrifice—this is quite literal: the dimensions of the sacrificer's body are used to scale the geometry of the ritual ground. This mirrors the "Cosmic Man" of *Ṛg Veda* 10.90, whose body becomes the world in an act of primordial sacrifice. His eye becomes the sun, his breath becomes the wind, and his two feet become the earth. We see this same kind of continuity of substance between the human and natural worlds in the foundational texts of classical Indian medicine, or Āyurveda (literally, "the knowledge of longevity"). For example, the *Caraka Saṃhitā*, an Āyurvedic text gradually compiled sometime between the 3rd century BCE and the 5th century CE, tells us: "Earth is that which is solid in man, water is that which is moist, fire is that which heats up, air is breath, ether the empty spaces, *brahman* is the inner self (*ātman*)" and that "indeed, this world is the measure (*sammita*) of the man. However much diversity of corporeal forms and substances there is in the world, that much [diversity] there is in man; however much there is in man, that much there is in the world."[3]

Āyurvedic models of the body are based on the idea of three *doṣas*: *vāta* (wind); *pitta* (choler); and *kapha* (phlegm). We tend to translate *doṣa* as "humor," in analogy to the four humors of pre-modern Western and originally Greek medical theory. The Greeks correlated their humors with the four gross elements: blood with air, yellow bile with fire, black bile with earth, and phlegm with water. The word "humor" is a translation of the Greek *chymos*, literally something like "juice" or "sap" but more figuratively "flavor" (we'll talk more about the Greek model towards the end of this chapter). *Doṣa*, on the other hand, actually means something like "fault" or "deficiency" or, in more medical terms, "disease." We should not make too much of this literal meaning, because the *doṣas* do ultimately come to represent the neutral state of their associated substances within the body. However, the etymology may point to the importance of proper order and equilibrium in the body. The body's substances become a problem when they become imbalanced, displaced, or, in other words, deranged.[4]

Here we could perhaps find a parallel to the philosophical system of Sāṅkhya, which shares major overlap with yogic traditions. As we saw in Chapter 2, Sāṅkhya's idea of primordial nature (*prakṛti*) depends on an equilibrium of its three qualities or *guṇas*. It is only when the *guṇas* fall out of their state of perfect equilibrium that the psycho-physical organism develops out of raw unmanifest matter and bondage in the cycle of *saṃsāra*. Now, it would be incorrect to say that the Āyurvedic *doṣas* are identical to the *guṇas* of Sāṅkhya. There are many technical reasons on both sides that don't allow for a direct equivalence. But, perhaps a better statement would be that they are analogous to one another in the same way that the little world is analogous to the big one.

Body basics in pre-modern South Asia

Not surprisingly, the Āyurvedic literature offers by far the most rigorous discussion of the body in pre-modern India. However, technical Āyurvedic terminology is not found in yoga texts until fairly late. In this section, we'll limit ourselves to basic understandings of the body that are elaborated in Āyurveda, but that are more or less culturally pervasive in their simplified forms.

Generally, the gross material body was understood as made up of seven constituents, or *dhātus*. The *dhātus* are supposed to derive from one another through a process of gradual refinement. In order, they are: lymph (*rasa*); blood (*rakta*); muscle (*māṃsa*); fat (*medha*); bone (*asthi*); marrow (*majja*); and semen (*śukra*). The vital material of all of these is *ojas*, which can be found in its most concentrated form in semen. The body's vital energy, or *tejas*, is embodied in the digestive fire. Finally, there are the *vāyus* (winds) that govern the internal movement of the body's vital substances. These are multiple in number and subdivided by direction and function. Over time, five emerged as the most important, and these are *prāṇa* (inward), *apāna* (downward and outward), *vyāna* (pervasive), *samāna* (homogenizing), and *udāna* (upward). Note that *prāṇa* is the name of a specific wind, but is also often used as a generic term for all of these forces as they flow in, out, and within the body.

The heart was viewed not only as the seat of all vital functions, but also of mind. In other words, in pre-modern South Asia, you didn't think with your head—you thought with your heart. This isn't such an unusual position in the ancient world. Western philosophers and physicians continued to disagree well into the Renaissance about whether the body's ultimate control center, the rational soul and the seat of intelligence, was to be found in the heart or the brain. Aristotle famously favored the heart, though consensus eventually swung the other way. In India, the mainstream view remained focused on the heart until fairly close to the modern period.

From the time of the Upaniṣads (500 BCE) onwards, we find an image of the heart as an inverted lotus bud, with its stem running upwards to the head. It is in that enclosed space that the ultimate essence of existence—the Self—is often believed to be housed. This Self might be described as a person (*puruṣa*) the size of a thumb, a minute thing akin to a grain of rice or a mustard-seed, or else simply space and effulgent light. And it is in the heart that the macrocosm and the microcosm, the big world and the little one, converge. The *Chāndogya Upaniṣad* (8.6) tells us:

> Now, these channels of the heart consist of the finest essence of orange, white, blue, yellow, and red. The sun up there, likewise, is orange, white, blue, yellow, and red. Just as a great road traverses both this village here and that one there, so also these rays of the sun traverse both worlds, the one down here and the one up above. Extending out from the sun up there, they slip into these channels here, and extending out from these channels here, they slip into the sun up there. . . . One hundred and one are the channels of the heart. One of them runs through the crown of the head. Going up by it, he reaches the immortal. The others, in their ascent, spread out in all directions.[5]

Unsurprisingly, this model becomes important for a number of yogic practices. As we'll see, however, the details of *how* the model shows up depend on the type of yoga one is aiming to engage in. And this largely depends on how one understands the relationship between the absolute Self and the world, and especially the body.

The ascetic body

An ascetic approach to the world tends to take a negative view of the body. For example, one medieval text has the following to say:

> Let him abandon this impermanent dwelling place of the elements. It has beams of bones tied with tendons. It is plastered with flesh and blood and thatched with skin. It is foul-smelling, filled with feces and urine, and infested with old-age and grief. Covered with dust and harassed by pain, it is the abode of disease. If a man finds joy in the body—a heap of flesh, blood, pus, feces, urine, tendons, marrow, and bones—that fool will find joy even in hell.[6]

This kind of approach is especially at home in dualistic cosmologies, where the body (gross and subtle, alike) is viewed as fundamentally different from consciousness or absolute reality.

In renouncing the social order that keeps the wheel of *saṃsāra* turning, the ascetic also renounces any attachment to the body that inhabits it. On the surface, then, the activities of the ascetic body are meant to flout and therefore drop out of the social order that is synonymous with *saṃsāra*. To exit the realm of *karma*, one must stop perpetuating its cycle. On a most basic level, this means one must stop acting. This, for instance, is the basic approach of Jainism.

Once you dig below the surface, though, things get more complicated. It's actually pretty difficult to stop acting entirely. Some ascetic practices (some *āsanas* or postures, for instance) aim to completely still the body on the outside, but this does little for the body's inner workings. One can stop eating (another typical ascetic method), but in the end one must also put an end to more involuntary internal processes like breathing and thinking. Here we get into the realm of things like breath control (*prāṇāyāma*) and meditation (*dhyāna*). And it's here that we discover that the ascetic body can also be a bit of a paradox. By renouncing the ordinary body—mortifying it and, essentially, destroying it—the ascetic potentially gains access to a special kind of bodily power.

The word we most often translate as "asceticism" is *tapas*, which most literally means "heat." We'll come back to the many meanings of *tapas* as we examine yoga's history in other chapters. For now, though, it's enough to point out that heat is, above all, energy or power. Heat can create as well as destroy. So, on the one hand, the *tapas* energy generated by the effort of ascetic techniques burns up and destroys the binding seeds of *karma*. As much as an ascetic might strive towards inaction, stopping all vital processes is clearly impossible for a living body. Some traditions resolve this issue by positing death as the natural end of ascetic practice, such as for instance the great Jain vow of *sallekhanā*, in which the practitioner fasts until death. A different approach, however, might be to assert that once the ascetic has harnessed the energy of *tapas*, he can use its purifying power undertake action without reaping any negative consequences. And so, on the other hand, *tapas* can also result in some very creative worldly outcomes. There are many stories that feature ascetics undertaking austerities not in the interest of liberation, but of worldly power.

But, since this chapter is about bodies, let's spend some time discussing the ascetic understanding of how the body works. In addition to the external body, ascetics have focused on the manipulation of the body's internal vital forces, which often come down to a basic triad: mind, breath, and semen. Mind and breath might, by now, seem obvious. Semen perhaps requires a bit more explanation. There is an old belief among ascetics, which persists to this day, that these three elements of life are inherently linked. Controlling one facilitates control of the others.[7] Celibacy is, of course, a staple of ascetic practice across cultures. On a social level, it implies one's opting out of the cornerstone institution of marriage and with it the legacy ensured by children. On an individual level, it reflects a detachment from sexual desire. But, for us, what's most important is the way celibacy affects what's going on inside the body.

In the outside world (the macrocosm), the year is balanced between the cool and wet seasons, during which the moon gathers and pours out its cooling moisture in the form of rain, and the hot and dry seasons, during which the sun dries it out again.[8] In this manner, as the Upaniṣads tell us, upon death, human souls go up to the moon as smoke or vapor, condense there, and come back down as rain. Rain begets plants, plants are consumed by male animals, and from the semen of males, souls are then reborn into the wombs of females. This is the cycle. In the older Upaniṣadic model, true immortality, and therefore freedom, lies beyond the disk of the sun. Those who manage to free themselves from the cycle of *saṃsāra* pass through the sun at death, never to return.[9] And so too, in the microcosm of the human body, food is distilled into increasingly more refined *dhātus*, all the way up to semen, which is the purest concentrate of vital *ojas*. Later *haṭha* yogic texts get even more specific in saying that this vital fluid, which they often refer to as *bindu* (the seminal drop) drips down from its proper reservoir in the head into the abdominal pit housing the digestive fire, where it feeds the lifecycle that inevitably ends in death and rebirth. Worse yet, this vital substance might be ejaculated and either wasted entirely or implicated in furthering the ultimate example of *saṃsāra*: procreation.

Again, in its most fundamental form, ascetic practice might seek to simply arrest this cycle, which requires arresting the internal mechanics of the body. But in order to stop something, you have to be able to control it. This also makes sense in other, more worldly forms of asceticism—control is power. Philologist and yoga historian Sir James Mallinson has argued that many of the core physical techniques that we associate with later medieval *haṭha* yoga traditions actually have their origins in the ancient practices of ascetics, focused on building up the internal heat of *tapas* and on preserving their *bindu*. Among these were various *mudrās* and *bandhas*, or seals and locks, meant to close off the passageways of the body to prevent the fall of *bindu*. Otherwise the body could be physically inverted either by hanging upside down or, later, through postures like the headstand. Such ascetics were said to be *ūrdhvaretas*, that is those whose seed is turned upwards.[10]

What about poses? To the extent that something like postural practice was a part of early ascetic traditions, it would have had the same goals as the techniques we just described. *Āsana*, which literally means "seat," would have almost always referred to seated and generally unelaborate postures meant to keep the body perfectly still. This is probably what the *Yoga Sūtras* of Patañjali (2.46, c. 325–425 CE) mean when they declare "*sthira-sukham-āsanam*"—"the posture should be steady and comfortable." However, there are also those other techniques, the primary purpose of which would have been to forcefully arrest the flow of the body's vital substances, or to otherwise mortify the body in order to produce the energy of *tapas*. The object of these, as one might suspect, would have been very much the opposite of making the body comfortable. These are the types of poses—standing on one leg, or standing on your head, for instance—that we would today identify as *āsanas*, but which would not have originally carried this label.

So, once again, in its strongest form, the ascetic model focuses on disciplining and ultimately destroying—literally burning up or "baking"—the body through the fiery power of *tapas*. In this framework, *bindu* is kept in the head and the body's other substances (those gross leaky *dhātus* the ascetic texts love to hate) are dried up by additional heat-building ascetic practices. This reflects a traditional, body-negative ascetic approach in which the physical body is ultimately an obstacle to be overcome if one seeks to achieve ultimate freedom.[11]

The tantric body

It's the tantric model of the yogic body that a modern practitioner, even a casual one, would probably find the most familiar. This is where we encounter the idea of *cakras* and the active flow of breath as energy. For this reason, it's especially important not to impose our modern understanding of these features onto the pre-modern framework where they are first found. Remember: it's all about context. For example, the earliest understanding of *cakras*, what we today call energy centers, did not locate them physically in the anatomy of the body, gross or subtle. As we'll learn in Chapter 6, *cakras* were originally features of the outside world, specifically circles of deities, that were visualized and meditatively imposed onto the human body in order to reinforce the links between micro- and macrocosm and, ultimately, to transform the human body into a divine one.

The other trouble with tantric models is that there are so many of them. Because tantras (the texts to which this term generally refers) are theistic—meaning, there's a God at the center of it all—they are also sectarian, meaning their contents, including their models of the body, vary depending on the deity (and, really, deities) in question. This is because the tantric body is ultimately a visionary one. It is not the physical body as such, but a perfected form that the practitioner meticulously constructs out of the divine energies that pervade the cosmos. However, since what this divine order looks like ultimately varies from system to system, so does the way that it maps onto the human body. And so there is no standard and universal blueprint for charting the body's relevant features when it comes to tantric ritual and visualization techniques. As the philologist Alexis Sanderson has pointed out, when one reads the tantras one variably finds "six 'seasons,' five 'knots,' five voids (*vyomas*), nine wheels, eleven wheels, twelve knots, at least three sets of sixteen loci, sixteen knots, twenty-eight vital points (*marmans*), etc."[12] This, again, is because all of the aforementioned are visionary rather than strictly anatomical realities.

All in all, though, tantric traditions, even dualistic ones, tend to take a favorable view of the material world and, with it, of the material body. As we discussed in Chapter 2, the tantric cosmos is a complex series of emanations from the supreme godhead that resides at its center. Tantric traditions are vast and complex, and most of them actually foreground ritual over yogic visualization and meditation. One place where such practices do crop up, however, is during the construction of the practitioner's perfected body. Just as the concentric circles of the *maṇḍala* are a map of this external world, so too the *cakras* represent this same order on the level of the human form. David Gordon White suggests that *cakras*, just like the *maṇḍala*, should be considered from the top down as a series of conical concentric rings[13] (Figure 3.1). Following the logic of little and big worlds, creation (or wisdom, in the Buddhist case) flows down from the center top. The yogic path reverses this process, moving from the lower periphery back up to the apex.

Figure 3.1 The six *cakras* in Buddhism. Central Tibet, ca. 19th century.

Source: Courtesy of Los Angeles County Museum of Art.

This is what we mean when we say that the *cakras* were originally tools for visualization rather than literal anatomical features. The yogi's gross physical body does not *actually* contain a miniature universe inside it. At the start, the analogy between microcosm and macrocosm is only that—an analogy. However, by visualizing and ritually installing the circles (*cakras*) of deities into his body, the yogi transforms and expands his ordinary mortal body into a subtle divine body that is in fact metaphysically continuous with if not identical to the divine energy that makes up the outside world. In other words, in this earlier model, no one has *cakras* in their body by default. One is not naturally born with them, rather one must create them through ritual and meditative practice. Notably, too, not all tantric systems even use the language of *cakras*—there are many other ways to talk about how divine bodies relate to mortal ones.

We'll outline tantric ritual and visualization practices in Chapter 6 but, for our purposes here, the most relevant aspect of this larger process is something called *bhūtaśuddhi*, or the purification of the elements. During this step, the practitioner ritually dissolves his mortal body through a complex series of visualizations and potentially other (more physical) techniques. Progressively collapsing the elements of his body, which are also the elements of creation at large, into one another, the practitioner works his way up the cosmic ladder. Just as the evolutes of reality are reabsorbed into the primordial matter from which they originally emanated, so too the practitioner's Self ascends from its living seat in the heart, up the central channel and towards the divine to which it's connected through the crown of the head.[14]

Sometimes this process is accompanied by images of the body being burned up or scorched, until all that remains is a heap of ash to be washed away by the milky ocean of cosmic dissolution.[15] In this sense, it might not seem so different from the ascetic understanding of baking the body until its impurities dry up and the seeds of its *karma* shrivel. However, in tantric traditions this is only a part of the journey and not the endgame. Once the body (or microcosm) is symbolically destroyed, then creation happens again, and the practitioner's now-perfected form is recreated in the image of the macrocosm. He does this by meticulously reconstructing his body out of pure *mantra* energies—the *mantras* belonging to deities specific to his particular tradition—such that he becomes a true embodiment of a "cosmic" being.

In some texts, we find discussion of obstacles, or "knots" (*granthis*, Figure 3.2), within the body that must be broken or pierced so that the Self can ascend to its unconstrained divine state. This can be done by using the breath to push through the blockages in the body's subtle channels (*nāḍīs*), such that the subsequent process of dissolving the body's fundamental elements can flow unimpeded.[16] Still other texts may talk of piercing not knots, but *cakras* of deities, as one traces this path of ascension. Likely, there are many moving pieces here, many of which may have originally been independent but have over time come to blend and intertwine. Such recombination, and especially the close association of tantric visionary practices with physical techniques that rely on anatomical understandings of the body, becomes a hallmark of classical *haṭha* yoga practice, to which we will now briefly turn.

Figure 3.2 The three knots of the subtle body represented by their associated deities, Brahmā in the navel, Viṣṇu in the heart, Śiva in the cranial vault. India, Nurpur, ca. 1690–1700.

Source: Courtesy of the Cleveland Museum of Art.

The *haṭha* yogic body

Classical *haṭha* yoga, which begins to emerge in earnest from the 13th century onwards, is in many ways a synthesis of the ascetic and tantric models we just reviewed. It uses both physical and visionary techniques. As we already mentioned, Mallinson has argued that the techniques most emblematic of *haṭha* yoga, the physical locks and seals that manipulate the body's internal functions, have their start in ascetic traditions. However, during the later medieval period, the forces those techniques are supposed to manipulate became increasingly imagined in tantric terms.

In addition to *cakras* and *granthis*, which we find in tantric texts, *haṭha* yogic texts likewise often feature a discussion of *kuṇḍalinī*, a coiled energy associated with the power of the divine feminine (*śakti*), which the practitioner must raise from its resting place within the body up towards the divine masculine principle located in or just beyond the crown of the head. In Buddhist traditions, she is known as *caṇḍalī* (the "Fiery One"). This suggestive name might point to the concept's complex origins. *Kuṇḍalinī* is said to reside at the opening of the body's central channel, the *suṣumnā*, which later texts (including most modern understandings) tend to locate at the base of the spine. Along with the central *suṣumnā*, two other channels eventually become part of the standard model. The *iḍā* (on the left and associated with the moon) and *piṅgalā* (on the right and associated with the sun) travel alongside the *suṣumnā*, sometimes described as forming a bowed circuit on either side of it, sometimes weaving around it, intersecting and alternating between right and left. They begin at the base of the torso and terminate at the nostrils. However, some earlier texts importantly talk about the central channel as stemming from the heart, perhaps in the same vein as the image given to us by the *Chāndogya Upaniṣad*, echoing back to the heart as the correlate of the sun and the residence of the Self. Other texts place the channel's opening in the space just below the heart, in the navel, or lower still, possibly incorporating that notion of the destructive force of the digestive fire.

It is perhaps in light of these references that we should understand an often-quoted definition of *haṭha* yoga as the union of sun and moon. In the tantric world, these come to represent the masculine and feminine poles. However, they also have older associations upon which the tantric models are almost certainly building. And so, the *kuṇḍalinī*, at once the destructive heat of the sun and of time, the divine feminine, the human Self, goes up by the central channel to join the cooling moon that holds the elixir of immortality, the divine masculine, and God. This visionary ascent through the human body, as the practitioner meditatively collapses and dissolves the constituents of his organism into their increasingly subtler forms essentially reverses the process of cosmic creation.

Once the *kuṇḍalinī* reaches her goal, there are essentially two options, which again reveal the varying goals of *haṭha* yoga's source traditions. On the one hand, this is a process that brings about final liberation, as the *kuṇḍalinī* dissolves into the eternal oneness of God (this is usually the model of Śaiva tantric *laya* yoga). On the other hand, this is the path to embodied immortality, as the *kuṇḍalinī* breaks open the store or immortal nectar in the crown of the head and floods the body with it upon her return,[17] essentially re-enacting cosmic creation within the body in the image of fully realized divinity.

And so, *haṭha* yogic texts, though more standard than the tantric ones, are still not entirely consistent when it comes to their goals or the means of getting there. Their synthesis of ascetic and tantric models leaves them with a pretty serious paradox, which you may have already begun to intuit from our description of *kuṇḍalinī*'s function. Some of her fiery, scorching character is very consistent with ascetic goals of using the practices of *tapas* to dry up, and thus "perfect" through a kind of baking, the body's gross substances. We might argue that the idea of dissolving the body's constituents through the tantric practice of *bhūtaśuddhi*, uses visionary methods to accomplish something very much in the same spirit. In this sense, when *haṭha* yogic texts advocate using the breath along with other physical techniques that would have once been used to raise *bindu* to instead raise the *kuṇḍalinī*, the mashup seems like a natural fit, despite the fact that the two represent very different concepts and "substances."

However, once we get into models where *kuṇḍalinī* is allowed to make a return to render the body immortal, then we run into a real conceptual problem. The *amṛta*, or immortal nectar, that tantric and *haṭha* yogic traditions place in the reservoir at the crown of the head is closely analogous, if not identical, to earlier understandings of *bindu*. So, on the one hand, we have ascetic ideas of the body that tell us to keep the *bindu* on the head at all costs, lest in drip down into the body's lower fire, where its destruction leads to sickness and death. On the other hand, we have *haṭha* yogic traditions that tell us to drive that lower fire up to the head so as to release the nectar stored there, allowing it to flood down, which is supposed to make the body impervious to all sickness and death.[18] These are, of course, opposite and contradictory goals. Both make sense, however, in the context of their respective understanding of the body, and especially the body's subtle functions.

Importantly, though, even when the *haṭha* yoga texts aren't entirely consistent, many of them do try to be universal. For instance, the most famous among them go to great pains to strip out sectarian markers of the type that give tantras their fascinating and occasionally frustrating specificity.[19] In the *haṭha* texts, terms that would have once been associated with the deities of a specific tantric system, like the *kuṇḍalinī*, which is often identified with the Crooked Goddess Kubjikā of the *Kubjikāmatatantra*, or the *cakras*, that would have been inhabited by any number of sect-specific divinities, are slowly transformed into natural features of the physical body.[20] As part of this process, they are woven into existing cultural models of the body, both gross and subtle. The result is something that claims to be increasingly generic and universal, even as it remains very much culturally specific.

It's also in this context, and likely as a result of the transition to a more natural view of the body's subtle features, that postural practices begin to become more prominent, We see ascetic techniques (like inverting the body to reverse the flow of *bindu*) being reinterpreted and converted into *āsanas*, and we see seated meditative *āsanas* becoming more elaborate in ways that might apply pressure to or otherwise stimulate certain parts of the torso in order to manipulate the energies there. Finally, we see complex *āsanas* that may well have had their origins in other traditions, such as the martial arts, being absorbed into *haṭha* practice for the purpose of cultivating strength and fitness within the body[21]—a more quotidian road to perfection.

Perfected bodies, and what they're for

All yogic systems, in one way or another, must deal with the body. And ultimately, though ascetic traditions take a more body-negative approach, even they leave room for ideas about perfecting the body. As we mentioned earlier, asceticism is not exclusively a path to renouncing the world in favor of liberation from it. Insofar as ascetic practices can build up the transformative energy of *tapas*, they are also a means to great worldly power. For some ascetics, this may even be the ultimate goal. Nevertheless, their efforts and therefore their powers are ultimately grounded in a specific model of how power is generated within and works through the human organism. An ascetic yogi's powers are different from those of a tantric yogi in part because they stem from a different kind of body.

The typical practitioner of the tantric traditions was not usually referred to as simply a yogi but as a *sādhaka*, an "aspirant," engaged in a *sādhana* or a "means for accomplishment." What is the accomplishment? *Siddhi*, which we've been translating in this book as superpower, but which translates more literally as precisely something like "accomplishment" or "attainment." When he has attained his goal, the *sādhaka* thus becomes a *siddha*, or an "accomplished" or "perfected" one. As you may have guessed, it's not a coincidence that these words all look similar—they all share the same verbal root. The Siddhas are quasi-mythological and semi-divine beings who may have potentially served as models for yogis seeking ascension. Appropriately, then, some tantric texts use *sādhaka* and yogi more or less interchangeably to refer to their practitioners. Others, however, insist that the tantric *sādhaka* is actually superior to the generic yogi, who might simply be a *tapasvin*, one who performs *tapas* or austerities.[22]

So why might one want to be a tantric *sādhaka* rather than a *tapasvin*? Both, as we've seen can be used as means towards liberation (though what liberation looks like in each case might actually be different). Both can also lead to worldly power. It's actually in this latter goal that we find the most important difference. *Tapas*, which is imagined as a kind of building up of mystical heat, works like a battery. It supercharges the practitioner's body, burning up his binding *karma*, but also giving him the power to perform superhuman feats. However, like the charge in a battery, it's depleted by use. If the *tapasvin* wishes to retain his power, he must perform more *tapas*. A *sādhana*, on the other hand, is a fundamentally transformative practice. The *sādhaka* doesn't gain power, he *becomes* power. His human body is transmuted into a perfected body made entirely out of the sonic energy of *mantras* and so his power is permanent—it cannot be lost or depleted because it's intrinsically part of him.[23]

To some extent, this latter model for the body is a more comfortable fit for tantric traditions because of their more positive view on matter in general. Even in dualistic tantras, the material world is understood to be laced through with divine energy. As a result, the idea that a human body can come to partake in that divinity requires less of a leap of logic than it would in a ascetic system where matter is something to be conquered so that, in the end, it can be overcome. Of course, none of this really represents hard and fast distinctions. As the *haṭha* yoga synthesis shows us, ascetic and tantric ideas are not mutually exclusive, though their combination does require some accommodation and reinterpretation from both sides.

So, we could say that an ascetic perfected body is a body that has gained complete control over matter, including the matter of which it itself is composed. It has reached an optimum state of being save for one thing: it remains material. If the ultimate goal of yoga is liberation, then a perfected ascetic body does not quite represent this goal. In the end, the body must still be abandoned. Ascetic liberation tends to be disembodied liberation. This is not necessarily the case for a tantric perfected body. Generally, disembodied liberation does remain a possibility in both dual and non-dual forms of tantra, but it is not the only possibility. Tantric traditions often allow for embodied liberation (or *jīvanmukti*) and, in some cases, this entails a true state of divine immortality. Meaning, a tantric perfected body is a divine body—the pinnacle of existence.

And, just to illustrate the diversity of goals towards which yogic practices might lead us, we could also consider the devotional perfected body, as found in some *bhakti* traditions. The devotional body is sort of like the tantric body, insofar as it is a perfected body intentionally constructed for the sake of transcendent experience. However, unlike the tantric body, the goal of which is to *be* the deity (or at least a deity), the devotional body is optimized to experience the deity. But, in practice, the lines are blurry. For instance, Gauḍīya Vaiṣṇava practice (a form of Kṛṣṇa *bhakti* that today has global reach as the International Society for Krishna Consciousness) follows a fairly standard tantric *sādhana* with some key modifications. The body is purified, deconstructed, and reconstructed through the practices of *bhūtaśuddhi* and *nyāsa* as per usual, with the qualification that the practitioner should not establish the deity in the parts of the body below the navel. However, when it comes to the next steps, authors explicitly emphasize that the visualization and worship of Kṛṣṇa should take place in his *dhāman*, or eternal abode, as is appropriate for *bhaktas*, and *not* in the lotus of the heart, as is done by yogis. This is important because to do otherwise would lead to the practitioner to identify with and worship himself as identical to the deity.[24] In *bhakti* systems, this distinctness from the deity can be a sign of God's ultimate uniqueness and supremacy, but it can also be important for the same reasons that this kind of (perfected) embodiment is important. It allows for an optimally blissful experience. As the famous mystic Ramakrishna (guru to Swami Vivekananda) once said: "I want to taste sugar, not become sugar."[25]

The Vedāntic body

There is one final model of the subtle body that we need to mention, even though it has not been particularly relevant to yoga for the majority of its history. This is the model of the five sheaths, or *kośas*, the first instances of which can be found in the *Taittirīya Upaniṣad* (2.1–5). There, we learn that the *ātman*, or Self, is encased in a series of bodies, beginning with the gross physical body made of food (*anna*), and growing ever more subtle. In the writings of later Vedāntic philosophers, who set out to analyze the Upaniṣads, the food body comes to be called the *sthūla śarīra* or gross body. The next three layers are the vital breath (*prāṇa*) sheath, the mind (*manas*) sheath, and the discernment (*vijñāna*) sheath, and together these are called the *sūkṣma śarīra* or the *liṅga śarīra*, which translated as the subtle body. Finally, there is the bliss (*ananda*) sheath, which constitutes the causal body or *karaṇa śarīra*.

This model of the body becomes most prominent in Vedānta and is not generally referenced as "yogic" (that is, it doesn't help us accomplish anything with regards to yoga) until the two traditions begin to blend in the late medieval and early modern periods. Though early Vedānta philosophers did not set much store by yogic methods, this began to change after the 13th century. Even still, the earliest references to the *kośas* as being connected to *haṭha* yoga appear in the "Yoga Upaniṣads," but not until the 17th century and even then only tangentially.[26] The prominence of this model today likely reflects the Vedāntic leanings of late 19th- and early 20th-century modernizers and popularizers of yoga.

One of the most famous pioneers of global yoga, Swami Vivekananda (1863–1902), was quite fond of Vedānta. So much so that the international branches of his organization, the Ramakrishna Mission, are referred to as the Vedanta Societies. An even better example might be Paramahansa Yogananda (1893–1952), who, in his famous *Autobiography of a Yogi* (1946), essentially adapted this Vedāntic model, in part by also combining it with Western Neo-Platonic ideas, to talk about a kind of embodied liberation.

In his book, Yogananda describes three kinds of body: (1) the idea or causal body; (2) the subtle astral body; and (3) the gross physical body. Astral bodies, he tells us, are composed of *prāṇa* or, as Yogananda translates it, "lifetrons." Beings with astral bodies normally inhabit the astral universe, which is made up of many astral planets and is in fact hundreds of times larger than the physical universe. Yogananda compares the two to a hot air balloon, where the physical universe is the solid basket beneath the much larger, lighter, and more vibrant balloon of the astral universe. The causal universe, in turn, is not a manifest entity but the ideas of the other two universes, just as the causal body is composed of the 35 ideas that are reified into the elements of the astral and physical bodies. Causal-bodied beings, Yogananda tells us, exist beyond the "finer-than-atomic energies" of lifetrons in "the minutest particles of God-thought."[27] The yogi must progress through these stages of embodiment on his way to absolute freedom.

Western parallels

By referring to Yogananda's use of Neo-Platonism, we have already indicated that talking only about Indian ideas of the subtle body is not sufficient if we want to understand how this concept functions in modern yoga. We should not pretend that Indian models of subtle bodies, yogic or otherwise, developed in complete isolation from other cultural systems. There are some interactions that we can definitively substantiate, such as the syntheses of Bengali Sufis that we'll discuss shortly. Others are a little trickier, especially if we're concerned with the ancient world. What we do know, however, is that ideas about the subtle body are not unique to South Asia. In fact, as we mentioned at the beginning of this chapter, they're a pretty common feature of how pre-modern people talked about the body's inner mechanics and its relationship to the outside world.

It should be no surprise, then, that we also find many examples of such bodies across Western and Near Eastern cultures, both ancient and early modern. The Christian apostle Paul, for instance, drew on what is likely a combination of contemporary ideas in the ancient Mediterranean to speak of the *soma pneumatikon* (the "spiritual body") of the faithful resurrected in 1 Corinthians 15:44. The 3rd-century Church Father Origen borrowed directly from Neo-Platonic formulations to describe how the soul, initially pure mind, upon its fall away from God acquires first a fine ethereal body and eventually a coarse physical form. Muslim philosophers, and especially Sufi thinkers, developed a system of *laṭīfas*, or subtle substances, that are at once bodily sheaths, organs, and realms of being to describe the soul's return to God. In Europe, such ethereal, pneumatic, or spiritual bodies were ubiquitous in Renaissance sources and persisted well into the modern period. Gottfried Wilhelm Leibniz (1646–1716), for example, asserted that having a body is necessary for the soul's individual existence and distinctness from God, whereas Thomas Hobbes (1588–1679) went so far as to declare the having of a body as a necessary condition for existence itself and therefore concludes that God himself must have a body composed of very fine ethereal matter.[28]

Pneumatic chariots

In Chapter 2, we discussed Plato's chariot metaphor for the Self, which represented a kind of three-part soul composed of reason, spirit, and appetite. Plato's student, Aristotle, also proposed a tripartite soul but gave more thought to how the soul interacts with the body and, indeed, what kinds of bodies the soul's different capacities yield. For Aristotle, there was the nutritive (later also called "vegetative") soul, which is responsible for generation and growth and is found in all living organisms including plants; the sensitive soul, responsible for movement and perception and found only in animals; and finally the rational soul, responsible for intellect and exclusive to humans. In order to explain how these different capacities (which were, in the end, abstract and immaterial) manifested in the material body, Aristotle proposed a concept that Stoic philosophers had long been using to talk about the interactions between different parts of our reality: *pneuma*.

While it might be tempting to think of the soul (or the spirit, which derives from *spiritus*, the Latin translation of *pneuma*) as something immaterial, pre-modern people believed them to exist on a continuum. So matters of the soul weren't simply a religious concern, they were also a medical one. As we mentioned earlier, *pneuma* essentially means breath, though Aristotle also tells us that *pneuma* is the human body's counterpart of the element of which the stars and heavenly bodies are made—ether.[29] But Aristotle was less of a mystic than Plato. He didn't generally consider the soul to be something separate from the body, instead it was the body's "form," the organizing principle that allowed a body to become a being. As such, there was no question of the soul escaping the body or ascending to some other realm. Instead, Aristotle's ideas, along with those of the Stoics, became central to the development of Greek medicine and especially the Galenic school, which took its name from the physician Galen of Pergamon (129–210 CE).

For Aristotle, physiologically speaking, *pneuma* was generative animal heat or "soul-heat," akin to the heat of the sun. Distinct from external air, it did not derive from respiration but rather was innate to the living organism, passed through reproduction and generated within the living body.[30] The nutritive soul was the first instance of this heat within the body but, in order for the body to grow and thrive, Aristotle suggested that nutritive fluid from the stomach is "boiled" by the heart to produce blood, and some even further to produce additional *pneuma*, which would then circulate with the blood into the body's various organs. Notably, this also meant that for Aristotle, as for the Stoics, it was the heart (the source of *pneuma*) and not the head that was the body's ultimate control center.

Galen disagreed with this, privileging the brain, and also brought breath back into the equation, suggesting that the creation of *pneuma* begins when air enters the lungs where it is altered into a "*pneuma*-like" substance by the body's innate heat. Galen also proposed the existence of three qualitatively different types of *pneuma*: psychic (or later, animal, as in *anima*, or soul), associated with sensation and voluntary motion in the brain; vital, associated with the heat of the heart; and natural, associated with the nutritive function of the liver. If we were looking for analogies, the Indian concepts to compare would be the *vāyus* (or *prāṇas*), *tejas*, and *ojas*. Finally, Galen is credited with elaborating the doctrine of the humors of the human body, which we earlier compared to the Āyurvedic *doṣas*. As we said then, the humors are the microcosmic bodily counterpart of the four macrocosmic elements: air, fire, earth, and water.

Well into the Renaissance, European theories of "internal" medicine thus came in two basic and often interacting varieties, the humoral (which described the internal workings of the body) and the astrological (which dealt with external influences). The theory of "spirits" ultimately served as a bridge between the two. On the one hand, Galenic thought came to maintain that the body's natural spirits (*pneuma physikon*) were infused, within their home in the liver, into the four humoral fluids. On the other hand, spirit as external ether served as the medium through which the celestial bodies could exert their influence upon the sublunar sphere, including upon the organs of the human microcosm. Health thus depended on a state of harmony, both among the elements of one's body, and with the forces of the universe.[31]

Now, we could argue that medicine in itself is a way of "perfecting" the body and its subtle inner workings. But these more-or-less natural ideas about the body also had implications for how people came to think about the ascent of the soul. Neo-Platonists used them to develop a mechanism for this ascent, which they called the *ochema pneuma*, literally the "pneumatic vehicle" that aids the soul in its ascent after the likes of Plato's allegorical chariot. This subtle body was called pneumatic (*pneumatikos*), that is made of the life force of *pneuma* or spirit, as well as etheric (*aitherodes*, referring to the macrocosmic equivalent of *pneuma*), and "astral" (*astroeides*, made of the stuff of heavenly bodies—the stars). The soul's ascent was conceived in spatial terms. It rose along the rays of the sun, following them like paths through the planetary spheres.[32]

Recall that when Plato gave us his chariot metaphor, he contrasted the gods' orderly vehicles, sailing through the heavens in their perfect circular orbits, with the human chariot, whose charioteer (reason) loses control of the unruly dark horse (appetite), causing it to be knocked from its path and fall to earth. Later Neo-Platonists, like Iamblichus or Chalsis, would write that by assimilating itself to the divine intellect, of which the sun is the cosmic manifestation, the soul's vehicle becomes perfectly spherical and moves once more in a perfect circle, just like the heavenly bodies of the gods.[33] Iamblichus explicitly considered this to be a way of becoming liberated from the limitation of matter while still embodied,[34] not so unlike the Indian ideal of *jīvanmukti*. In this sense, we would do well to remember that the heart was considered to be the bodily counterpart of the sun, so a journey up to the creative source of the cosmos could also very much be understood as a journey into the divine nature of one's soul.

A pilgrim's waystations

Both Aristotelian and Neo-Platonic ideas caught on quite readily in the Muslim world. In the four-fold scheme of cosmic emanation codified by Islamic thinkers, human beings are unique in that they combine attributes of both the higher and lower realms and so are most suited to be the mirror of God.[35] Within mystical Sufi Islam, one way of discussing this complex composition of the human being is through the idea of *laṭīfa*, which, depending on the context, can be translated as "subtle substance," "subtle center," or "subtle body."[36] The first translation is probably the most generic, whereas the latter two can show up in contexts where the *laṭīfa* is either a kind of localized organ or otherwise a layered sheath. In Chapter 2, we discussed the *maqāms* (places or stations), which in some contexts come to be understood as something akin to metaphysical waystations along a pilgrim's inward spiritual journey toward God. The *laṭīfa* are a related though not exactly identical concept. In general, all of these ideas build on earlier systems, especially Greek Neo-Platonic ones. However, in their particulars, they are pretty uniquely Islamic.

The models of *laṭīfas* developed gradually over time, with the earliest frameworks including only a triad of the soul, spirit, and mystery.[37] More elaborate later versions build up to a total of seven layers: body (*qālab*); soul (*nafs*); heart (*qalb*); spirit (*rūḥ*); inmost being (*sirr*); mystery (*khafī*); and supreme mystery (*akhfā*), the "real" (*ḥaqq*), or the *laṭīfa* of true "I-ness" (*al-laṭīfa al-anā'iyya*).[38] It's not uncommon to find frameworks that include either only the higher or the middle five, while still other systems may have six members and modify some of their relative positions. *Laṭīfas* were often associated with various parts of the body, colors, prophets, interpretations of the Qur'ān, elements of the cosmos, and the like, though how these are arranged can also vary.

In other words, as always, things are far from standard or consistent. But a good (and quite systematic) example can be found in the writings of the 13th-century Persian mystic 'Alā'-uddawla Simnānī, who associated the *laṭīfas* with seven prophets (from Adam up to Muhammad), seven colors (turbid black, blue, red, white, yellow, luminescent black, green),[39] and the seven spheres of the cosmos. The higher *laṭīfas* represent an "acquired body" that persists after the destruction of the physical body.[40] Simnānī prescribed recitation and breathing techniques, and explained that the colors associated with the *laṭīfa* signify the visions the mystic experiences along his path, until he finally reaches the state of pure I-ness, which alone is capable of perfectly reflecting God like a clear mirror.

Unsurprisingly, in the writings of some Indian Sufis, these ideas began to meld with analogous yogic and tantric concepts. Some of this happened in Arabic translations of *haṭha* yogic texts, where we can see gods replaced with prophets and the ascent of the *kuṇḍalinī* through the *cakras* becoming an ascent of the soul through the planetary spheres.[41] On the other hand, some Bengali Sufis composed novel texts representing what was essentially an Islamic yoga. Here we can find, for instance, *maqāms* (associated with the four cosmic spheres) represented in the manner of *cakras*, each correlated with an element, color, sound, and so on, and presided over by an archangel.[42] Notably, all of these specific elements are drawn from an Islamic framework rather than a Hindu or Buddhist one.

In the grand scheme of things, these kinds of substitutions are minor—after all, they happened all the time in South Asia between different tantric sects. But here's a more revolutionary move: the Sufi systems also modified the way the practitioner was to move through the *cakras*. The *maqām* of the lowest stage (*nāsūt*) was associated with the *mūlādhāra cakra* at the base of the spine, while the spiritual stage of Sovereignty (*malakūt*) corresponded to the *maṇipūra cakra* at the navel. So far, so good. Except then, as the practitioner reached the higher spiritual stage of Omnipotence (*jabarūt*), he jumped to the *amṛtakuṇḍa* (the pool of immortal nectar) in the head, before doubling back to end up at the ultimate divine stage (*lāhūt*) at the place of the *anāhata cakra* in the heart. Why? Well, because there's really no getting around the centrality of the heart in Sufism, even if it makes your subtle body journey a little bit circuitous. Of course, the heart is also an important feature of Indian thought in general and some yogic systems in particular. As we mentioned earlier, tantric systems might start their ascent at the heart (if that's where the *suṣumnā* opens and the *kuṇḍalinī* rests), but their goal is located higher, at the crown of the head or just beyond it. There are some systems, like Trika-Kaula Śaivism, that do really double down on the idea of the heart as the resting place of the divine, but even in those cases this kind of downward reversal through the *cakras* is fairly unprecedented. But, of course, like some of the other seemingly paradoxical things we discussed earlier, the contradiction makes sense in accordance with the context tradition's understanding of the subtle body, which is a Sufi and not a tantric one. So, the method being used (the actual physical practice) is yogic and Indian, but the framework to which it's applied and, therefore, the goal it ultimately seeks to accomplish, are Western and Islamic.

So, as we get closer to the modern synthesis of *haṭha* yoga with Western harmonial models, we can at least say: it's certainly not the first time something like this has happened in the history of yoga, and it will most likely not be the last.

Harmonious spheres

In contrast to Sufi Islam's complex system of *laṭīfas*, European understandings of the subtle body, evolving largely in the context of Christianity, tended to simplify the subtle body's schematics. At least this was true of primarily religious understandings. Notably, pre-modern European medicine, which was heavily astrological, retained a fairly complex framework of correlating the body's various organs to the heavenly bodies and their movements. When it came to matters of spiritual elevation, however, Europeans tended to think in threes. Man, like the cosmos, was recognized as possessing a physical body, a spiritual (or otherwise "astral" or "sidereal") body, and a soul. Man, like the cosmos, was also divided in a vertical and hierarchical fashion into lower physical (associated with the lower torso), middle ethereal (associated with the middle torso and especially the lungs and the heart), and higher empyrean (associated with the head) realms or principles[43] (Figure 3.3).

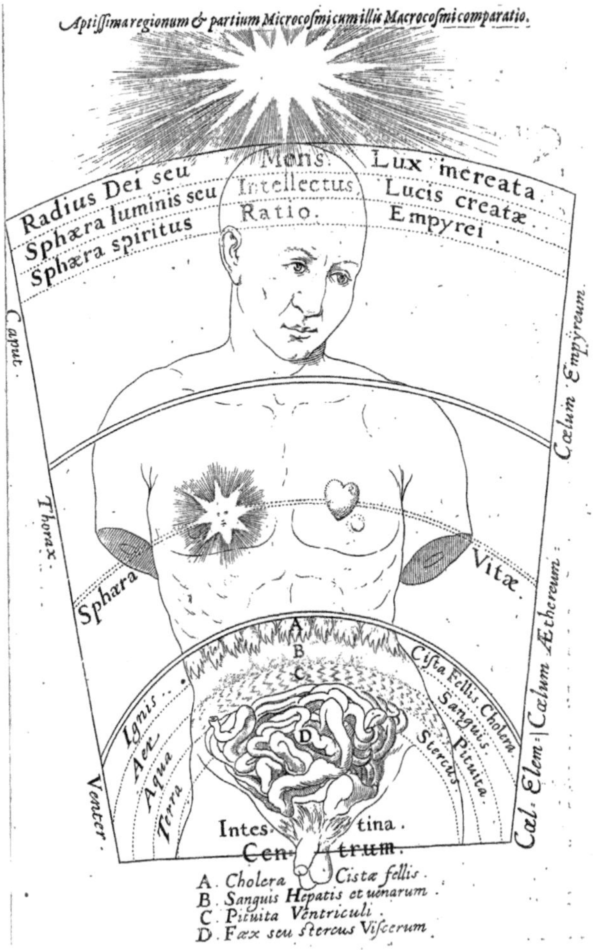

Figure 3.3 Diagram of the three spheres from Robert Fludd's *Utriusque cosmi maioris scilicet et minoris metaphysica, physica atqve technica historia* (1617).

During the Renaissance, Pythagorean ideas that the universe is ordered according to the same numerical proportions as those responsible for producing harmony in music led to the notion of a *musica mundana,* literally a "music of the world" that brought order to everything from actual music, to theater and dance, to architecture, literature, and medicine. The human pulse, for instance, was believed to be fundamentally musical.[44] And so, logically, the human body, spirit, and soul resonated with its own version of this same cosmic harmony, a *musica humana* or "music of humanity."[45] Above all, this was a highly optimistic vision of the material world. Man and nature—microcosm and macrocosm—alike were believed to have been masterfully wrought by their Creator according to a set of perfectly ordered proportions[46] (Figure 3.4).

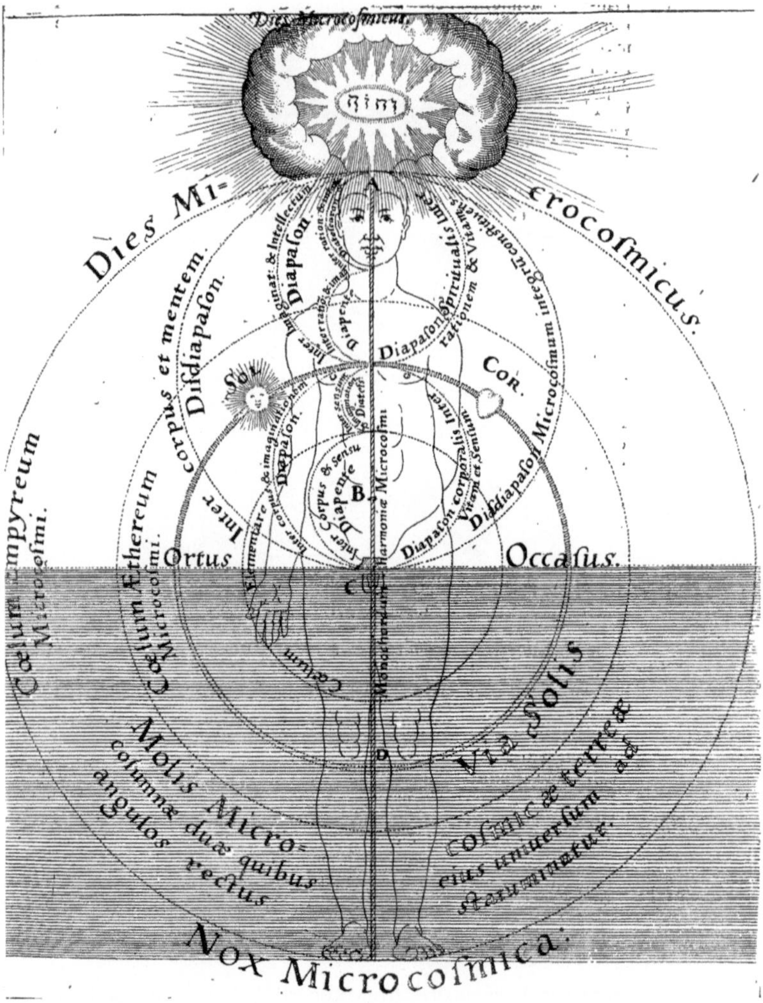

Figure 3.4 Diagram of the harmonic proportions of the human body and cosmos from Robert Fludd's *Utriusque cosmi maioris scilicet et minoris metaphysica, physica atqve technica historia* (1617).

Neo-Platonic thinkers like the Italian wizard Marsilio Ficino (1433–1499) suggested that we could literally draw life down from the heavens by "ingesting" or "absorbing" *spiritus* from the cosmos—as the quintessence or ether—into our own bodily *spiritus*. According to Ficino, you could to this in seven different ways: though well-composed images; medicines; pleasant odors; harmonious music (along with ritual movements, gestures, and dance); imagination; philosophy; and tranquil contemplation. Ficino even advised his readers to "exercise by keeping constantly in motion and make various circular movements like those of the heavenly bodies. Since by their movings and circlings you were engendered, by making similar motions you will be preserved."[47] And, according to Ficino, the best and most abundant spirit was a solar spirit and so we should strive to make our spirits as solar as possible with appropriate foods, timely rest, clean air, a joyful mood and, above all, by warming the heart. It is no coincidence that in Ficino's system we can find precedents for many of the practices that today's Western practitioners combine with the physical movements they call yoga: music, aromatherapy, the use of certain stones (crystals), and so forth.

Pulling it all together: how the *cakras* became a rainbow

The modern system of the seven "chakras," lined up vertically along the torso like a rainbow (Figure 3.5), is a perfect example of how different versions of the subtle body can blend to produce something at once old and entirely new. Notice that in the previous sentence we used an Anglicized spelling of this Sanskrit word that

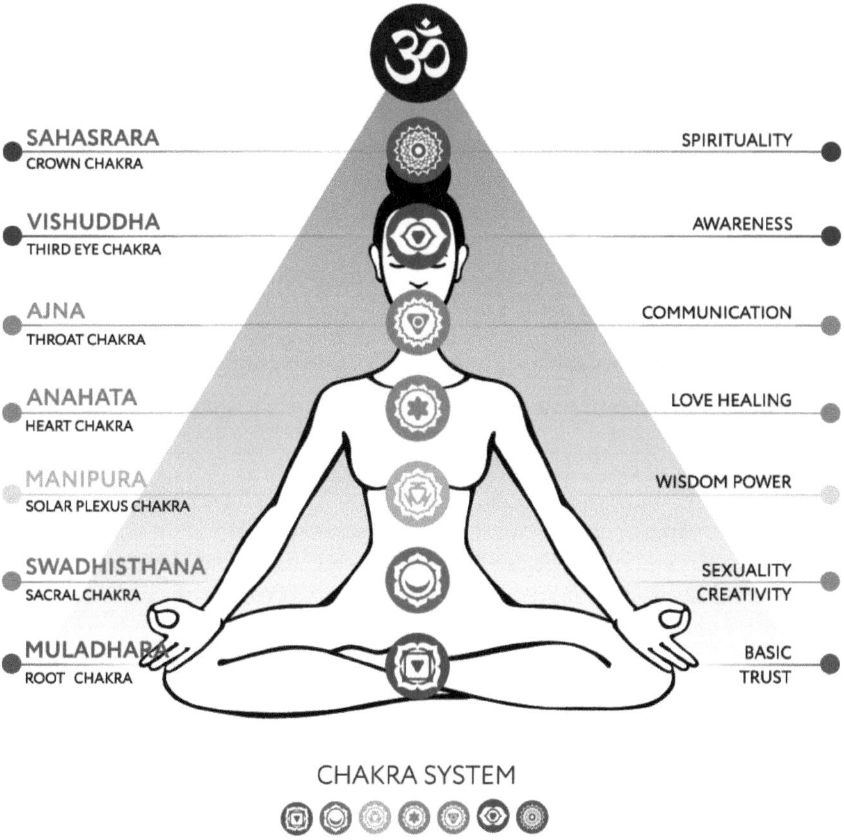

Figure 3.5 An example of a modern hybrid chakra system.

Source: Image by Olga Zelenkova.

we've already encountered multiple times over the course of this chapter. *Cakras* were already a complex concept in the evolving history of South Asian traditions. Chakras, though, are not exclusively South Asian. Like modern global yoga practices, they are a cultural blend. So, how did we go from *cakras* to chakras?

We've already mentioned that, in Indian tantric traditions, *cakras* were originally tools for visualization. Circles (*cakras*) of deities out there in the big world of the cosmos were ritually and contemplatively imposed as circles (*cakras*) of divine energy, often in the form of sound *mantras*, onto and into the little world of the human body. As we mentioned earlier, there are other ways of talking about the "contents" of the tantric subtle body. We might also talk about it as containing knots, or voids, or seasons, depending on the kinds of internal mechanics and analogies to the external worlds that we want to highlight. So, *cakras* are not always a standard feature of the tantric body, nor is there (at least not at the outset) a standard and universal way of describing the *cakras*. Instead, like a lot of things in tantra, they vary from sect to sect in their overall number as well as in individual details.

It's pretty common for a *cakra* to be associated with a "governing" deity (the one at the center), with a sound (usually a "seed" syllable belonging to the deity), with a color (or multiple colors, all variable), and located in some place along the body's torso (also variable). *Cakras* are often described as lotuses (*padmas*) and much attention is given to the number of their petals, which might be associated with lesser deities (the actual circle and the governing deity's entourage), with their specific syllables, and sometimes with abstract principles connected to the contemplative process.

By the 12th century or so, the most common consensus was that there are six *cakras* (Figure 3.6). This is the system we find in the *Kubjikāmata Tantra* (most likely dated to the 10th century), an influential text where we also encounter the idea of *kuṇḍalinī*. This text belonged to the Western Transmission (*paścimāmnāya*) of Kaula Śaivism, associated with goddess Kubjikā ("the Crooked One") but we also find its six-*cakra* framework in later texts from the Southern Transmission (*dakṣināmnāya*) of the Kaula tradition. This branch is associated with the goddess Tripurasundarī ("the Beautiful One of the Three Citadels") and comes to be called Śrīvidyā, the name under which it's still known today. These traditions, including their version of the *cakras*, endured because of their association with India's most prominent and still-active orders of ascetic yogis. However, in the early 20th century, their *cakra* model became a major ingredient of the global standard because of an English translation of the *Ṣaṭ Cakra Nirūpaṇa* ("The Description of the Six *Cakras*," a 16th-century text from the Southern Transmission), which appeared in 1919 as part of *The Serpent Power* by Arthur Avalon.[48]

As its title would suggest, the *Ṣaṭ Cakra Nirūpaṇa* describes six primary *cakras* or lotuses (*padmas*). It describes them in fairly great detail, focusing largely on inhabiting deities, syllables and metaphysical principles, but we'll instead list these *cakras* alongside some more minor features that are mentioned only in passing. Why? Because, on the one hand, these and not the more elaborate descriptions are the ones that stick. And because, on the other hand, one of these features, which

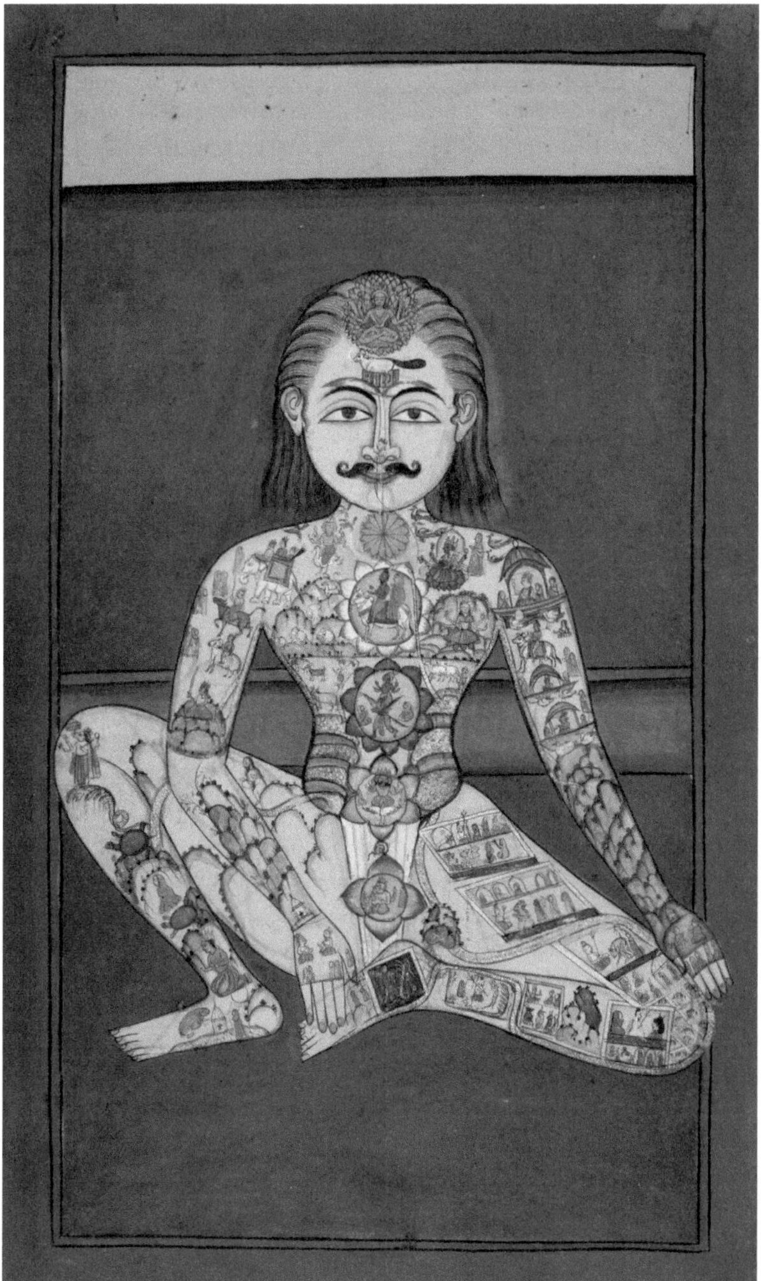

Figure 3.6 The subtle body and its six *cakras* represented as lotuses inhabited by deities. From an illustrated manuscript of the Jogapradīpakā. India, likely Punjab, ca. 1830.

Source: Courtesy of the British Library.

seems to translate—the idea that the lotuses have colors—is not so much translated as it is replaced. So, the lotuses described by the *Ṣaṭ Cakra Nirūpaṇa* are: the *mūlādhāra* (a crimson lotus with four petals); *svādhiṣṭhāna* (vermilion with six petals); *maṇipūra* (dark like rain-clouds, ten petals); *anāhata* (bright red like the *bandhūka* flower with twelve petals); the *viśuddha* (smoky purple with sixteen petals); and the *ājñā* (white like the moon with two petals). These are presumably the six *cakras* to which the text's title refers and are more or less consistent with those described in the *Kubjikāmata Tantra*. However, like some other texts in the Southern Transmission (but not the Western one), it also adds another lotus—the luminous and thousand-petaled inverted lotus of the *sahasrāra*, located at the cranial fontanelle or just above it.

As we already said, some elements of the *Ṣaṭ Cakra Nirūpaṇa*'s description go on to become standard features of modern chakras, while others fall by the wayside. For instance, the text goes on at length about the deities that inhabit each lotus, including their vehicles, the colors of their adornments, and so forth. This is pretty typical of sources that go into detail about the *cakras*, and it makes sense given the *cakras*' original nature specifically as circles of deities out there in the external world. But these culturally specific details don't usually make it into today's popular chakra models. On the other hand, modern models do generally preserve the names of the lotuses, the number of petals, and they pull in the additional lotus of the *sahasrāra* to bring the number up to seven. That last move is not entirely traditional, but it's not unprecedented either. But what don't we find in the *Ṣaṭ Cakra Nirūpaṇa*'s system? Certainly none of the more peripheral correspondences that are now commonplace in global chakra systems—no planets or astrological signs, no gemstones, no musical notes. But, most importantly, we don't find the one basic thing that served as an anchoring point for all these other connections. We don't find the seven colors of the rainbow.

To understand how the chakras became rainbow-colored is also to understand how they came to be decidedly seven and not six in number. In fact, the rainbow is a bit counterintuitive this way as well. To understand how "Roy G. Biv" (Red, Orange, Yellow, Green, Blue, Indigo, Violet) became the mnemonic device taught to every schoolchild, we have to understand why early modern physicists decided that there *had* to be seven colors in the spectrum of visible light. After all, we all know indigo is really just blue, which is why some modern chakra systems will do away with it in place of promoting white to the very top, and why modern scientists (if they divide the spectrum at all) would divide it into six basic colors. So why are there seven? Because it's not about the colors—it's about what the colors represent.

At least since the Renaissance, and arguably even much earlier, seven was the magical number in Western religion and spirituality. Because the mathematical proportions of music are foundational to Western harmonial logics, the whole world had to be subdivided into sevens, and specifically into the five full steps (whole tones) and two half steps (semitones) of the heptatonic (seven-tone) musical scale. In harmonial cosmologies, the entire universe was fitted together according to these mathematical proportions. This applied to the actual cosmos, where the solar system was subdivided into seven planetary spheres or cosmic layers through which the divine heavenly bodies traveled, and it applied to the human body, which was subdivided into seven corresponding segments (see again Figure 3.4). At the base of the torso was the earthly principle, represented by the sublunar sphere, which governed the vegetative functions of the "natural spirits," chiefly digestion and reproduction. The subdivisions then progressed through the standard old-school geocentric order, all the way up to the high intellectual capacities of Saturn up in the head. So, there are seven spheres, associated with seven planets (the Sun and Moon being considered planets in this case), seven musical notes, and seven intervals on the visible spectrum of electromagnetic energy (or, in other words, the rainbow—we can thank Isaac Newton for that one, see Figure 3.7).

It's important to keep in mind, though, that subtle body models sometimes combine and sometimes distinguish between metaphysical and physiological understandings of how the body is laid out and how it works. We've already seen this in the conflict between ascetic and tantric frameworks, in the Indian context. Is that fiery lower principle creative or destructive? Do we keep the immortal elixir in the head or do we flood it through the body? We find the same kind of contradictions here, in the Western context. Sometimes the planetary spheres are progressive heavens through which the spiritual aspirant must ascend, with the uppermost sphere representing the divine abode of God. But other times, especially if one is looking at astrology in more medical terms, that upper sphere is the sphere of Saturn, associated with the negative melancholy aspects of intellectual labor. Modern Western ideas of the chakras, incidentally, tend to lean more on the medical legacy. This is why we see a lot of talk of balancing the chakras, something that doesn't really make sense in the Indian *kuṇḍalinī*-based models, which still ultimately

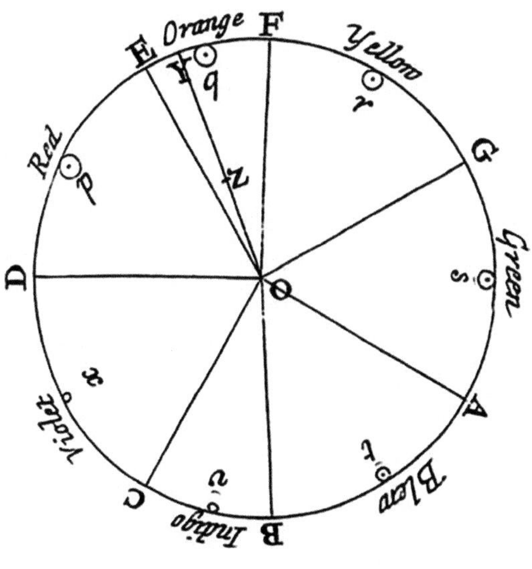

Figure 3.7 Newton's heptatonic color wheel, as found in his *Opticks* (1704).

focus on ascent to the very top. The idea of balance (of harmony), comes from the notion that you never want the influence of any single planetary principle to dominate. Too much Saturn leads to depression.

Along with the Charles Leadbeater's slightly later book, *The Chakras* (1927), Avalon's version of the *Ṣaṭ Cakra Nirūpaṇa* would go on to shape Western understandings of the chakras for the rest of the 20th century. Leadbeater was a member of the Theosophical Society, an organization whose bread and butter was the fusion of Eastern and Western mysticism, and his rendering of the chakras was more heavily influenced by Western harmonial ideas of psychic forces and various astrological ideas.[49] The notion of chakras would go through several stages of combinations and recombinations from the 1920s onwards, mostly by Western authors but a few by self-styled Indian yogis teaching in North America, featuring different associations with planets, astrological signs, nerve plexuses, endocrine glands, psychological and emotional principles, and colors.[50]

It's important to note that not all of these systems understood the chakras to be primary thing onto which all of these other principles were mapped. In fact, insofar as these systems of correspondences were first and foremost Western and harmonial in character, sometimes they didn't mention chakras at all. Instead, they talked about cosmic rays and auras (a word etymologically associated with sound) emanating from the ether, and advised readers on how to identify *Your Aura and Your Keynote* (a 1912 book by Julia Seton Sears) or *Just How to Wake the Solar Plexus* (a 1926 book by Elizabeth Towne).[51] Perhaps most important among these were the chromatotherapists, who paired scientific ideas about vibrational frequencies (color and sound) with older harmonial correspondences to other healing modalities such as aromas. It's here that the rainbow chakras begin to become standard.[52]

But here's one final but very crucial point: neither the Indian *cakras* nor the European planetary spheres were originally supposed to point to literal anatomical features of the human body. Both were a figurative imposition, working through different logics of correspondences between the microcosm and the macrocosm. Ultimately, the modern idea of locating chakras in the actual anatomy of the body as energetic points, represented by organs or by convergences of nerves, is a feature that's new to both systems. But, in another sense, it's a feature that becomes very important because it's precisely where these two otherwise culturally different systems find their least common denominator. And, from the standpoint of modernity, it corresponds to our privileging of science as a human universal and the proper basis for medicine and therapy.

Modernizing the yogic body

It's important to keep in mind that the yogic body has always been somewhat "medical." That is, if we're serious about understanding how concepts and practices change through time, we have to take seriously pre-modern understandings of the world, including pre-modern science, medicine, and the like. Yogic models of all varieties begin with the baseline of contemporary medical (let's say, at least shallowly Āyurvedic) knowledge about the body and its mechanics even as they purport to move beyond it to reach less mundane goals. The subtle body is not identical to the physical body, but it is nevertheless continuous with it.

There is a striking, though likely apocryphal story that Swami Dayānanda Saraswati, founder of the modern Hindu reformist group, the Ārya Samāj, once pulled a corpse out of the Ganga and dissected it in search of *cakras*. Upon failing to find any he chucked his Sanskrit texts on yoga, including the famous *Haṭha Pradīpikā*, into the river like so much dead weight.[53] But of course this would be akin to throwing out the whole of classical Greek philosophy on account of modern knowledge that the earth revolves around the sun and not the other way around. And so, other 19th- and 20th-century modernizers were not quite so brash. Modern Indian proponents of yoga freely blended older ascetic and tantric concepts and practices with contemporary biology, medicine, and physical culture. Key modernizers like Swami Kuvalayananda and Shri Yogendra sought to scientifically measure the effects of traditional yogic practices like *prāṇāyāma* on the body's biological processes.[54]

The work of global yoga guru B. K. S. Iyengar (1918–2014) is a good example of how modern yoga systems transition to a primarily bio-medical rather than metaphysical understanding of the yogic body. In his classic manual, *Light on Yoga* (1966), Iyengar occasionally refers to *haṭha* yoga's medieval literature, citing it on minor points in the introductory section. But little of the real substance of these texts, their methods, and less still their understanding of the goals of yoga practice make into the subsequent bulk of Iyengar's manual. The awakening of *kuṇḍalinī* is briefly mentioned as an effect of *padmāsana* (lotus pose), as described in the *Haṭha Pradīpikā*, on which point Iyengar advises the reader to consult Arthur Avalon's *The Serpent Power* (1919) and says no more.[55] The fullest treatment of such matters is found in the short section on *prāṇāyāma* under the subheader, "Bandhas, Nāḍis, and Chakras," which offers a very basic overview of these three concepts before concluding by speculating that the raising of the *kuṇḍalinī* is "perhaps an allegorical way of describing the tremendous vitality, especially sexual, which is obtained by the practice of *Uḍḍīyāna* and *Mūla Bandhas* described above. The arousing of *Kuṇḍalinī* and forcing it up is perhaps a symbolic way of describing the sublimation of sexual energy."[56]

Similarly, in his slightly later book, *Light on Pranayama* (1981), Iyengar asserts that "many people misconceive that *bhastrikā prāṇāyāma* awakens the *kuṇḍalinī śakti*. The authoritative books have said the same regarding many *Prāṇāyāmas* and *āsanas*, but this is far from true. There is no doubt that *bhastrikā* and *kapālabhāti* refresh the brain and stir it to activity, but if people perform them because they believe that they awaken the *kuṇḍalinī*, disaster to body, nerves, and brain may result."[57] If we look carefully, we might see an interesting history hidden in Iyengar's statement. Insofar as various technical modes of breath control were originally ascetic (rather than tantric) practices, Iyengar's entirely right. Awakening *kuṇḍalinī* would not have been their original goal. As we discussed, such uses would have only become common in the medieval *haṭha* literature, making them an example of a relatively novel repurposing. And so we might regard modern yoga practice in a similar way. In modern yoga, some of these physical techniques have been repurposed yet again, this time towards medical and fitness-oriented goals. Ancient ascetics might have wanted to shut down the brain—Iyengar wants to freshen it and stir it to activity.

Conclusions

- Many cultures have used ideas of a subtle body—that is, something that represents aspects of the body that are not immediately visible and tangible—to explain both biological and religious realities. From the biological perspective, such models could be used to explain the body's vital processes. From a religious one, they often provided a mechanism for linking up the body's microcosm to the macrocosm of the universe.
- In South Asia, ascetic traditions tended to take a negative position towards the body, viewing is as fundamentally corrupted and impure, and using techniques to control, purify (as much as possible), and ultimately to arrest the body's vital functions.
- Tantric traditions, on the other hand, often sought to perfect and transform the body into a perfect vehicle of the world's divine energy.
- A number of other systems such as that of Āyurvedic medicine, Vedāntic philosophy, and devotional *bhakti* traditions also made use of subtle body concepts.
- By the late 19th century, ascetic, tantric, and Vedāntic models of the yogic body had stacked on top of one another and blended together to produce a complex synthesis. This already layered model was further complicated by the addition of Western harmonial models and modern medical understandings.
- The modern hybrid chakra system is an example of this transcultural blending, combining Indian and European understandings of the body as a spiritual microcosm of the larger world and reinterpreting this idea in "universal" anatomically-grounded terms.

Notes

1 David Gordon White, *The Alchemical Body: Siddha Traditions in Medieval India* (Chicago: Chicago University Press, 1996), 15. White references Robert Isaac Levy, *Mesocosm: Hinduism and the Organization of the Traditional Newar City in Nepal* (Berkeley; Los Angeles; Oxford: University of California Press, 1990).

2 Barbara A. Holdrege, *Bhakti and Embodiment: Fashioning Divine Bodies and Devotional Bodies in Krsna Bhakti* (Abingdon: Routledge, 2015), 16–20.

3 *Caraka Saṃhitā* 4.5.5 and *Caraka Saṃhitā* 4.4.13 quoted in David Gordon White, "'Open' and 'Closed' Models of the Human Body in Indian Medical and Yogic Traditions," *Asian Medicine*, 2, no. 1 (2006): 3.

4 Dominik Wujastyk, *The Roots of Ayurveda: Selections from Sanskrit Medical Writings* (London: Penguin Books, 2003), 30–1.

5 Translation adapted from Patrick Olivelle, *The Early Upaniṣads: Annotated Text and Translation* (Oxford and New York: Oxford University Press, 1998), 279. See also David Gordon White, *Sinister Yogis* (Chicago: University of Chicago Press, 2009), 86.

6 Patrick Olivelle, *Ascetics and Brahmins: Studies in Ideologies and Institutions* (Cambridge: Cambridge University Press, 2013), 105.

7 Daniela Bevilacqua, "Let the Sādhus Talk: Ascetic Understanding of Haṭha Yoga and Yogāsanas," *Religions of South Asia*, 11, nos. 2–3 (2018): 182–206; James Mallinson

and Mark Singleton, *Roots of Yoga: A Sourcebook from the Indic Traditions* (London: Penguin Classics, 2017), 181.

8 David Gordon White, *Sinister Yogis* (Chicago: University of Chicago Press, 2009), 134–5.

9 Patrick Olivelle, *The Early Upaniṣads: Annotated Text and Translation* (Oxford and New York: Oxford University Press, 1998), 21.

10 James Mallinson, "Yoga and Yogis," *Nāmarūpa*, 3, no. 15 (2012): 10–12.

11 Mallinson and Singleton, *Roots of Yoga*, 182.

12 Quoted in Mallinson and Singleton, *Roots of Yoga*, 175.

13 David Gordon White, ed., *Tantra in Practice* (Princeton, NJ: Princeton University Press, 2000), 10.

14 Gavin D. Flood, *The Tantric Body: The Secret Tradition of Hindu Religion* (London and New York: I.B. Tauris, 2006), 110–13, 140–3.

15 Flood, *The Tantric Body*, 113.

16 Flood, *The Tantric Body*, 140–1.

17 Mallinson and Singleton, *Roots of Yoga*, 178.

18 Mallinson, "Yoga and Yogis," 6.

19 James Mallinson, "Hathayoga's Philosophy: A Fortuitous Union of Non-Dualities," *Journal of Indian Philosophy*, 42, no. 1 (2014): 225–47.

20 Mallinson and Singleton, *Roots of Yoga*, 182.

21 Jason Birch, "The Proliferation of Āsanas in Late-Mediaeval Yoga Texts," in *Yoga in Transformation: Historical and Contemporary Perspectives on a Global Phenomenon*, ed. Karl Baier, Philip A. Maas, and Karin Preisendanz (Göttingen: Vandenhoeck & Ruprecht Unipress, 2018), 135.

22 Hélène Brunner, "Le Sādhaka, Personnage Oublié Du Śivaïsme Du Sud," *Journal Asiatique* 263 (1975): 411–43 and Marion Rastelli, "The Religious Practice of the Sādhaka According to the Jayākhyasaṃhitā," *Indo-Iranian Journal* 43 (2000): 219–95.

23 Rastelli, "The Religious Practice of the Sādhaka," 356.

24 Holdrege, *Bhakti and Embodiment*, 363–5.

25 June MacDaniel, *Offering Flowers, Feeding Skulls: Popular Goddess Worship in West Bengal* (New York: Oxford University Press, 2004), 194.

26 Mallinson and Singleton, *Roots of Yoga*, 184.

27 Anya P. Foxen, *Biography of a Yogi: Paramahansa Yogananda and the Origins of Modern Yoga* (New York: Oxford University Press, 2017), 171–2.

28 Arthur F. Buehler, *Sufi Heirs of the Prophet: The Indian Naqshbandiyya and the Rise of the Mediating Sufi Shaykh* (Columbia: University of South Carolina Press, 1998), x–xx; Justin E. H. Smith, "Spirit as Intermediary in Post-Cartesian Natural Philosophy," in *Spirits Unseen: The Representation of Subtle Bodies in Early Modern European Culture*, ed. Christine Göttler and Wolfgang Neuber (Leiden and Boston: Brill, 2008), 274.

29 John M. Rist, "On Greek Biology, Greek Cosmology and Some Sources of Theological Pneuma," in *Man, Soul, and Body: Essays in Encient Thought from Plato to Dionysius*, ed. D. W. Dockrill and R. G. Tanner, Prudentia, Supplementary no. 1985 (Auckland, New Zealand: University of Auckland, 1985), 32.

30 Rist, "On Greek Biology," 27–32.

31 Anya P. Foxen, *Inhaling Spirit: Harmonialism, Orientalism, and the Western Roots of Modern Yoga* (New York: Oxford University Press, 2020), 66.

32 Ruth Majercik, ed., *The Chaldean Oracles. Text, Translation, and Commentary*, trans. Ruth Majercik (Leiden and New York: Brill, 1989), 38–9.

33 Gregory Shaw, "Theurgy and the Platonist's Luminous Body," in *Practicing Gnosis: Ritual, Magic, Theurgy, and Liturgy in Nag Hammadi, Manichaean and Other Ancient Literature: Essays in Honor of Birger A. Pearson*, ed. April D. De Conick, Gregory Shaw, and John Douglas Turner (Leiden: Brill, 2013), 545.

34 Gregory Shaw, *Theurgy and the Soul: The Neoplatonism of Iamblichus* (University Park: Pennsylvania State University Press, 1995), 26.
35 Jamal J. Elias, *The Throne Carrier of God: The Life and Thought of Ala Ad-Dawlah as-Simnani* (Albany: State University of New York Press, 1995), 79.
36 Buehler, *Sufi Heirs of the Prophet*, 103.
37 Buehler, *Sufi Heirs of the Prophet*, 107.
38 Buehler, *Sufi Heirs of the Prophet*, 105–6; Elias, *The Throne Carrier of God*, 81–3.
39 Elias, *The Throne Carrier of God*, 136.
40 Elias, *The Throne Carrier of God*, 81.
41 Carl W. Ernst, "The Islamization of Yoga in the 'Amrtakunda' Translations," *Journal of the Royal Asiatic Society*, series 3, 13, no. 2 (2003): 199–226.
42 Shaman Hatley, "Mapping the Esoteric Body in the Islamic Yoga of Bengal," *History of Religions*,46, no. 4 (2007): 351–68.
43 Foxen, *Inhaling Spirit*, 86.
44 Jacomien Prins, "The Music of the Pulse in Marsilio Ficino's Timaeus Commentary," in *Blood, Sweat, and Tears: The Changing Concepts of Physiology from Antiquity into Early Modern Europe*, ed. Manfred Horstmanshoff, Helen King, and Claus Zittel (Leiden and Boston: Brill, 2012), 393–441.
45 Jacomien Prins and Maude Vanhaelen, eds., *Sing Aloud Harmonious Spheres: Renaissance Conceptions of Cosmic Harmony* (London and New York: Routledge, 2017), 2.
46 Foxen, *Inhaling Spirit*, 74.
47 Marsilio Ficino, *Three Books on Life*, trans. Carol V. Kaske and John R. Clark (Binghamton, NY: Center for Medieval and Early Renaissance Studies, 1989), 373.
48 Mallinson and Singleton, *Roots of Yoga*, 176–7.
49 Kurt Leland, *Rainbow Body: A History of the Western Chakra System from Blavatsky to Brennan* (Lake Worth, FL: Ibis Press, 2016), 197–210.
50 Leland, *Rainbow Body*, 213–49.
51 Foxen, *Inhaling Spirit*, 246.
52 Leland, *Rainbow Body*, 254–94.
53 Mallinson, "Yoga and Yogis," 7.
54 Joseph S. Alter, *Yoga in Modern India: The Body Between Science and Philosophy* (Princeton, NJ: Princeton University Press, 2004).
55 B. K. S. Iyengar, *Light on Yoga: Yoga Dipika* (New York: Schocken Books, 1979), 130.
56 Iyengar, *Light on Yoga*, 440.
57 B. K. S. Iyengar, *Light on Prāṇāyāma: Prāṇāyāma Dīpikā* (London, Boston, and Sydney: Unwin Paperbacks, 1983), 179–80.

4 Mythologies

Yogic role models

We often structure and explain the big questions of human existence—who we are, why we are here, where we go when we die—through the concepts of myth and the actions of ritual. We experience ourselves and our bodies according to these myths and rituals through subjective and culturally-specific concepts of right thinking ("orthodoxy," which tells us which story is the correct story) and right practice (orthopraxy, which tells us how to correctly act out that story in the world). In other words, we forge a series of correspondences between the little world represented by our individual embodied experiences and the big world of our surrounding culture, history, and indeed our whole imagined universe. And the way that we do that is through acting out in miniature—often in a controlled environment called a "ritual"—the grander model of how we understand the world to function.

So, one way of understanding the practices of yoga is to look at the stories people have historically told about those practices and especially about those who engage in them. Like anything else about yoga, yogic myths and rituals are not monolithic. They draw on and get refracted through the cultural knowledge and embodied experiences of disparate geographic areas, numerous Dravidian and Sanskritic languages and literatures, Vedic Brahminical, Jain, Buddhist, Islamic and Sikh tellings and retellings, and of course European colonialism and global market culture. Even the myths themselves are often aware of this multiplicity, especially in in South Asia.

There is one version of the *Rāmāyaṇa*, one of India's two major classical epics (alongside the *Mahābhārata*) that asks and answers the question of how many *Rāmāyaṇas* there have been by telling a story about Hanumān, king Rāma's trusty sidekick after whom the yogic pose *hanumānāsana* is named. Hanumān goes down to the underworld to retrieve Rāma's ring, which has fallen there, but the King of Spirits presents him with a platter full of identical rings all belonging to different Rāmas who have lived and died throughout the ages of the universe. "'There have been as many Rāmas as there are rings on this platter," the King tells Hanumān[1]—as many Rāmas and therefore, the reader can surmise, as many *Rāmāyaṇas*. One scholar of the epic counted around 300 retellings.[2] All of this has happened before, and all of it will happen again. But also, stories never are the same from telling to telling.

Needless to say, then, this chapter is by no means a complete or exhaustive account. It would be impossible to collect all the stories about yoga and yogis, much less all the different versions of those stories. Because of the massive and contradictory undertaking of speaking to such diverse and colorful traditions, we're faced with an inevitable process of inclusion and exclusion. That being said, in this chapter, we selectively touch on the key narratives, figures, and themes that have shaped the historical South Asian as well as modern global understanding of yoga.

A quick note, before we begin: you'll notice that nearly every mythological figure mentioned in this chapter (and especially those meant to serve as "role models" for yogis) is male. This is of course not a coincidence. It's also not a coincidence that, throughout this book, when we talk about a yogic practitioner, we use male pronouns. Yogis have historically been men. While women almost certainly did practice yoga, the default point of view (as it often is in all sorts of publicly recorded and "universal" narratives) is masculine. There isn't much to be done about this—the historical sources are what they are—but it's worth acknowledging, if only as another facet of the ways in which myths often claim to tell universal stories in what are in reality very particular ways.

Myth as story

Our English word "myth" is derived from the Greek *mythos*, which means essentially something like "story." Even for the ancient Greeks, however, myth designated the kind of story that might not be literally true, not true in all times, or from all perspectives. At the same time, myths could be stories of gods and heroes that illustrated larger narrative themes or revealed deeper philosophical truths. Devdutt Pattanaik, a famous mythologist, has drawn a bridge to South Asian culture by cleverly stating that "myth = *mithya*."[3] To be fair, the relationship between the two words is more one of convenient homophones than true cognates. In Sanskrit, *mithya*, even more so than "myth," is a word that means "falsehood." But that direct translation is of course much too shallow, if not outright misleading.

Instead of understanding *mithya* (or myth) as simply untrue, we might think of a famous line attributed to the 8th-century Advaita Vedānta philosopher Śaṅkara, who was asked to summarize his entire (very complex) system in a single sentence. Śaṅkara replied: "*brahma-satyam, jagan-mithyā, jivo brahmaiva nāparaḥ*."[4] The *brahman* (the "expansion") is the truth, the world is false, and the individual Self is none other than the *brahman*. Now, without getting into the intricacies of Śaṅkara's philosophy, what does he mean when he says the world is *mithyā*? That it's false? According to Śaṅkara, the entire universe is nothing other than the singular, eternal, and undifferentiated essence of *brahman*, which is pure self-luminous consciousness. So, from this perspective, our ordinary world of rivers and mountains, plants and animals, pots and pans, and even gods and philosophers and yogi adepts, is one big fiction. But even Śaṅkara would have been hard-pressed to say that there's literally nothing to the world as we perceive it. The world of our senses still reveals something to us—most of us would probably even say it's a very useful something, depending on our circumstances.

So too with myth. As Pattanaik tells us

> everybody lives in myth. This idea disturbs most people. For conventionally myth means falsehood. Nobody likes to live in falsehood. Everybody believes they live in truth. But there are many types of truth. Some objective, some subjective. Some logical, some intuitive. Some cultural, some universal. Some are based on evidence; others depend on faith. Myth is truth which is subjective, intuitive, cultural and grounded in faith.[5]

When we encounter yoga or yogis through myth, we are encountering models that are at once very culturally specific but also often self-proclaimedly universal. Myths show us specific figures engaged in specific practices, but from these figures we are often meant to extrapolate something much broader. Something that, in a different time and place and way, might also apply to us. So, on the one hand, myths about yoga present us with role models that practitioners (past and present) might seek to emulate. On the other hand, examining the myth from the outside, especially from one retelling to another, allows us to track in a very profound way how the meaning of stories and practices changes over time and across space.

As Pattanaik suggested, myth is a subjective and a cultural truth. It might be reasonable to assume, then, that even though practices reflect and even transmit cultural understandings, such dimensions may not fully translate when practices move from one culture to another. A Western practitioner performing *agnistambhāsana* (which is usually translated as "fire log pose" but actually means something more like "fire-suppression pose") is likely not aware of the deep mythical significance of the god Agni, of historical understandings of the digestive fire. Or, even if she knows the stories, they almost certainly mean something different to her than they would to a person for whom they are a cultural home. But the global nature of modern yoga practice also means that it has become its own kind of culture, one where ancient myths have taken on new forms, and where new ones have emerged.

While myths often display what cultures find to be sacred, it's also true that the sacred does not necessarily have to be traditionally "religious" in nature. As David Chidester notes, the sacred is not only the province of religious institutions but of any generic activity that is engaged with the transcendent or with the ultimate concerns of human life. This can be Sunday mass, or it can be pop culture.[6] We bring this up specifically to note that even contexts where modern yoga functions largely as "fitness" are not closed off from myth and ritual. Similarly to Chidester, yoga scholar Andrea Jain has argued that it might be worthwhile to consider postural yoga as a body of religious practice, even though modern practitioners themselves might not use such terminology. For Jain, we should understand

> *body of religious practice* here to refer to a set of behaviors characterized by the following: They are treated as sacred, set apart from the ordinary or mundane; they are grounded in a shared ontology or worldview (although that ontology may or may not provide a metanarrative or all-encompassing worldview); they are grounded in a shared axiology or set of values or goals

> concerned with resolving weakness, suffering, or death; and the above qualities are reinforced through narrative and ritual.

Myth, in this sense, can work and be enacted on multiple levels, from the nitty-gritty of practice (like naming certain poses after exemplary yogis) to grand meta-narratives about how we should understand our practice as a whole. Some myths provide content for yoga traditions. In other chapters we have talked about how yoga practices, especially visionary and meditative ones, have been based on the ideas of going and knowing. In yoga, the mythological idea of going (that is, literally ascending) to some higher realm of existence—such as one inhabited by gods and perfected adepts—becomes an action of knowing, of raising consciousness, of experiencing that mythical reality in some way that is more immediate to one's immediate embodied being. And then there are all sorts of contemporary framing myths about yoga and its relationship to not only religious traditions but also nation states, economic systems, and bodies, for example. Take for instance the notion of yoga as a practice rooted in universal wisdom that transcends (and allows us to individually transcend) everything from national boundaries to the ills of our bodies and minds.

In many ways, the story of yoga—what yoga is, how it came to be, and what it's supposed to do for us—is one big myth, told over and over, in different ways and from different perspectives. This book is a collection of such myths, spun into one retelling.

Ritual as practice

Rituals can be seen as the acting out of stories of cosmic significance or what Adam Seligman has dubbed an "as if" or "could be" universe.[7] In an inherently fractured and chaotic world, ritual serves the purpose of providing a momentary semblance of order and control through action. It is also a space of potentiality as it lives outside of the normal rules of being and doing. Seligman suggests that "ritual practice becomes the arena where the dynamic of that third space, the potential space within which cultural creativity takes place, is worked out."[8] Like myths, rituals only really make sense within their specific cultural framework. They are a grammar of behavior through which the cultural narratives of myth can be spoken. If myth provides content for visionary yogas or going and knowing, then ritual structures the yoga of doing. If myth is the "what" and the "why," then ritual is the how.

Rituals can be mundane, like a handshake, or very obviously religious, like studying a sacred text or reciting a prayer or *mantra*. And in some cases, of course, they might be both—like breathing and putting the body through a specific set of poses or movements. When we talk about ritual in other sections of this book, we are usually referring to more formal, highly structured and regimented rituals. For instance, Vedic fire sacrifice or tantric deity worship must be performed in a very precise way, according to very specific parameters, and with no allowed deviation. Think about it as following a very complex recipe. Most yoga practices, however, have not necessarily been so strictly framed and in this chapter we're going to think about ritual in a much more generic way. Here ritual is more of a routine—a habitual performance that provides a common template or framework for action. Ritual is practice writ large.

For instance, yoga scholar Elizabeth De Michelis has proposed that we think of modern postural yoga as a healing ritual of secular religion.[9] Rituals tend to follow a fairly standard pattern that includes preparation, a leaving of the ordinary world or the crossing of a threshold into a special designated space, an encounter with the supra-ordinary or sacred, and the return to mundane life. In contemporary yoga practice, the ritual often begins with the act of changing into specific clothing, the laying out and crossing of the threshold onto a yoga mat, perhaps a period of "quieting" or conscious letting go of one's "to-do" list. The core of the ritual, of course, is the specific sequence of conscious breath and bodily movement. This ritual act then culminates in the final *śavāsana* ("corpse pose," incidentally originally a tantric practice meant to imitate the god Śiva),[10] which the modern practitioner might consider as a metaphoric death, fetal position as the liminal phase between, and the final set of words or bow as the reintegration out of the ritual or sacred space and back into mundane world where one goes about the rest of one's day.

Cosmic principles

Here is a story—

> In the beginning, there was neither something (*sat*) nor nothing (*asat*), neither atmosphere nor sky beyond, neither death nor immortality, neither day nor night. There was only that One, breathing breathlessly by virtue of its own inherent power, and beyond it there was nothing. Darkness enclosed darkness across great bottomless waters and that One arose through the power of brooding heat (*tapas*). It was desire that came upon that One in the beginning, and this was the first seed of mind. Poets, searching with wisdom within their hearts, discerned the correspondence (*bandhu*) between something and nothing and extended their cord across. In the beginning, there were those endowed with seed and those endowed with magnitude, there was inherent power below and intention above. But who really knows? Who will declare how and whence this creation was produced? (For even the gods came afterwards.) Maybe it produced itself, or maybe it did not. He who looks down from the highest heaven—only He knows ... or maybe he doesn't.[11]

This creation myth comprises one of the most famous sections of the *Ṛg Veda* (c. 1500 BCE), often called the "Nāsadīya Sūkta," literally the "Hymn of the Not-Non-Existent (*na-asat*)." The double negative is meant to hint at the hymn's essential paradox, the impossible nature of that which precedes creation itself. It is a challenging and highly abstract set of verses, which is of course the very thing that makes them so evocative. There is much more to Indian tradition than just the Vedas, but we chose to start with this hymn largely because its abstruse nature means that even themes that aren't Vedic in their origins can (and, more importantly, have been) read back onto it. So, that being said, let's use it to look at a handful of principles that run through the knot of Indian, including yogic, myth and ritual.

The cosmic power of sound

You have to squint a little bit to find the sound in our creation myth. Of course, in another sense, the whole thing is sound. The *Ṛg* is the oldest of the Vedic Saṃhitās, literally "compilations" of verses, which are largely hymns of one type or another. And it's only once we can wrap our heads around the cosmic importance of the Vedic verses that we can make sense of that reference to poets searching for wisdom within their hearts, which is sort of an odd interjection into a hymn that otherwise seems to be about a state of primordial reality where nothing (much less poets) can yet be said to really exist.

Vedic verses are also referred to as *mantras*, from the verbal root √*man*, "to think," combined with the suffix -tra, which designates the idea of an instrument or machine. So, a *mantra* is literally a mental machine, an instrument of thought. As the Vedic period (which runs approximately 1500–800 BCE) progresses, the notion of *brahman* emerges as the fundamental principle of cosmic power. Elsewhere in this book, we'll be translating *brahman* as the "expansion," which is both a more literal translation of the word itself and abstract enough to capture the term's larger meaning as "ultimate reality" in its various manifestations throughout history. Here, though, it's worth noting that *brahman* can also be translated as an utterance, an outpouring or speech, or "the Word."[12] In our hymn, we might connect it to "that One."

So what are those poets doing all the way back at the dawn of creation? One way we could interpret them is as representatives of the historical keepers of the Vedic verses, the *brāhmaṇa* priests whose primary social role it was to memorize and pass down the entirety of the Veda, as well as to recite it during the sacrificial ritual. But the Vedic verses aren't just words, they're *mantras*, and every syllable is imbued with the cosmic power that first set the universe into motion. To know and speak the *mantras* is to tap into that power, to experience its unfolding, and to wield its creative potential.

In the *Brāhmaṇa* priestly commentaries, the three regions of cosmic creation—the earth, the atmosphere, and the heavens—are reduced, in their essence to a single seed (*bīja*) syllable, *oṃ*, which consists of the three sounds: *a*, *u*, and *ṃ*.[13] Various seed mantras also become a key feature of later tantric traditions, where they often become the literal sonic embodiments of gods and goddesses. In the Vedic and the tantric world alike, sound is understood to be the substratum on which reality is woven. Tantric yoga is perhaps above all, *mantra* yoga, a yoga achieved through the ritual recitation of *mantras*.

Fire: creation and destruction

Fire (*agni*) and heat (*tapas*) are key motifs in Indian mythology from Vedic times onwards and so they become central to yoga traditions as well. It's no coincidence that in our creation myth the One arises through *tapas*—through brooding heat. The qualifier of brooding[14] is especially fitting here because it allows us to bridge the reproductive and psychological metaphors that are implicit in the hymn's abstract language. Elsewhere in the *Ṛg Veda*, the first being in the cosmos is explicitly called Hiraṇyagarbha, the Golden Egg, but even without this explicit gestational imagery, we can get the sense that this is a creative and generative kind of *tapas*. The One broods on Itself like a chicken broods over an egg. But of course to brood also means to dwell on mentally—to think in an intense and fixated sort of way. The One, by virtue of desire, also yields the first seed (literally *retas*, the same word used for semen) of mind.

Heat and fire can certainly be destructive. Fire, personified as the god Agni, effectively destroys the sacrifice on earth so that it can be carried up to the gods. In yogic traditions, *tapas* comes to refer primarily to the ascetic practice of austerities that are meant to bake, even scorch the body with their intensity. In tantric traditions, the fiery energy (*śakti*) of the divine feminine personified as Kuṇḍalinī (the Coiled One) or else, in Buddhist traditions, explicitly as Caṇḍalī (the Fiery One), blazes an electrifying trail through the body. In epic and Purāṇic mythology, the cosmic age ends in a grand conflagration that burns up the triple world until all that remains is ash.

But even in these cases, fire emerges as ultimately and primarily creative. In the *Ṛg Veda*, Agni is a paradoxical and mysterious god. Though he is, in essence, fire, he is the child of the primordial waters. And Agni loves to hide, sometimes retreating into the waters whence he came, and sometimes concealing himself in the transient vitality of living things.[15] And so too the power of Agni has an ambiguous and multilayered character. Sacrifice consumes the offering but brings boons to the sacrificer (and, in the greater Vedic framework, order to the cosmos). Austerities destroy the impure body but open the door to liberation, or else produce a more perfect body capable of immense, even superhuman power. This latter effect is even more true in tantric traditions where the practitioner's internal fiery energy, once ascended, often returns to flood the body with immortal nectar. Even the apocalyptic fire at the end of the cosmic age destroys only so that the universe can arise anew from the eternal ocean of milk.

The elixir of immortality

There is an old wisdom among ascetics: mind, breath, and semen are intrinsically related. You cannot control one without the others.[16] In the beginning, the One breathes without wind, entirely by its own impulse and, overcome with desire, it gestates the first seed of mind. But the *Ṛg Veda*'s mythology is full of intertwining themes and metaphors. Though Agni is the fire that lives within the waters, this paradoxical substance—this "fiery juice" that is at once fire and water—ultimately becomes *soma* (or "Soma," a god who, like Agni, is also a substance), the elixir of immortality.[17] *Soma* is brought down from the heavens, by Indra, the god of rain, thunder, and lightning, riding astride a great eagle. Rain begets plants, including the particular plant from which the vision-granting (that is, psycho-active) juice of *soma* would have been pressed. *Soma* is a magical, milky liquid and, true to its paradoxical nature, it brings both virility and worldly power, but also induces a trance-like otherworldly state of being.

In later Vedic times, it comes to be said that human souls go up to the moon as smoke or vapor, condense there, and come back down as rain. Rain once again begets plants, plants are consumed by male animals, and from the semen of males souls are then reborn into the wombs of females.[18] *Soma* thus becomes identified with another natural divinity—the Moon (Chandra).[19] But, as we've said in other chapters, the big world of the cosmos (the macrocosm, with its gods and natural forces) is mirrored within the little world of the human body. And this principle is most important here. The triad of fluid, fire, and wind becomes crucial to all sorts of physical models, from digestion and metabolism, to bodily health and regeneration, to conception and gestation, to the kind of internal alchemy that leads to yogic immortality.[20]

One of the clearest examples is the tantric one we have already mentioned, especially in the form which it takes in medieval *haṭha* yoga traditions, where it also blends with ascetic elements. In such contexts, we see the fiery feminine energy of *kuṇḍalinī*, awakened by the forceful manipulation of breath, shoot its way up the spine until it reaches the cranial vault. There, it breaks open the store of masculine seminal *amṛta* (immortal nectar), with which it then floods the body upon its return. Thus, the practitioner's ordinary body is effectively destroyed, to be replaced by a perfected immortal body, mirroring the new creation that follows cosmic dissolution.

Gods: the supreme yogis

As examples like Agni and Soma illustrate, Vedic gods are often, though not always, associated with natural and cosmic forces. The gods of later Indian tradition, including the supreme gods of Hinduism, take on a more personal and more explicitly embodied form. This is especially clear in the idea of the avatar (from the Sanskrit *avatāra*, literally something like "descent"), where the divine becomes incarnated in humanoid (if not strictly human) form. As avatars, gods take on earthly bodies and identities without being entirely subject to human limitations. In other words, they remain decidedly superhuman.

However, descended gods are not the only beings in the Indian cultural imagination who can claim superhuman status—so can yogis. In fact, the powers of yogis are often remarkably similar to those of avatars. In light of this, yoga historian David White suggests that we might consider the "deification" or "cosmi-fication" of human yogis as a parallel phenomenon to the "yogi-fication" of Indian deities.[21] On the one hand, yogis became an example of humans functioning like cosmic gods, while, on the other hand, the powers of gods are explained through the mechanics of yoga. Some yoga traditions are explicitly built on the idea that human practitioners should imitate God (often, the God in question is Śiva) so as to become exactly like him. But, if we wanted to speak more generally, we could say that gods who are portrayed as yogis work to illustrate the idea of yoga's cosmic significance, establishing that these are principles that apply at the highest levels of reality.

Śiva: erotic ascetic and Lord of the Dance

> Once upon a time, the great sage Dakṣa ordered a grand sacrifice. Dakṣa had a beautiful daughter named Satī and she, much against her father's wishes, had

> married the mountain-dweller, Śiva. Long ago, Śiva had cut off the head of Dakṣa's ancestor, Brahmā. (Brahmā had a few heads to spare, so he was actually fine.) All said, the action had been a valid one, for it was done to punish Brahmā for lusting after his own daughter. Still, shedding the blood of a pure Brahmin was a grave offense, and so Śiva was henceforth ostracized, condemned to dwell on the fringes of society, bathing in ashes, using Brahmā's skull as a begging bowl for his alms. Śiva, having thus embraced his life as an ascetic yogi, had not been interested in Satī, but she'd won him over with the power and commitment of her own *tapas*, her austerities. And so, when Dakṣa announced his sacrifice, Śiva found himself excluded as usual, which was nothing new as far as he was concerned. Satī, though, could not abide such an insult against her husband. She went to her father's house and, before all who were gathered there, set herself alight on the sacrificial altar through the sheer power of her yogic *tapas*. Hearing of his wife's death, Śiva was understandably enraged. He gathered his great horde of ghosts and ghouls, and he laid waste to Daṣka's sacrifice, killing all in attendance, and ultimately immolating the grounds altogether. And once it was over, Śiva took up Satī's charred corpse, and carried it all through the worlds, howling in wrathful agony. The god Viṣṇu grew concerned for the fate of the cosmos, and so he drew his discus and cut Satī's body into 108 pieces, and where each piece fell, there the goddess was to be always honored with offerings, and Śiva along with her.[22]

Like all Indian gods, Śiva has many names and even more epithets. He is Rudra, the Howler, the fierce Vedic deity who is banished from the sacrificial grounds. He is also Paśupati, the Lord of the Sacrificial Beasts, who ultimately restores the sacrifice. He is Naṭarāja, the Lord of the Dance, who whirls madly in the fires that immolate the three worlds, only to dance his blissful dance of creation so that all rises from the ashes once more (Figure 4.1). He is the Mahāyogi, the great ascetic who dwells in the cremation grounds or else high up in the mountains. He is Ardhanarīśvara, the Lord Who Is Half-Woman, embodying the ultimate creative union of masculine and feminine. Śiva thus unites the ascetic and the erotic, the creative and the destructive, masculine and feminine aspects of existence into a single divine reality.

The historical evolution of Śiva's mythology indicates that he was ultimately accepted into the sacrificial order and therefore into mainstream society. However, this idea of tension with or transgression of social norms, especially the norms of purity presided over by the priestly Brahmins, remains a key part of his image. This is also where we can find myth easily bleeding into practice. Early Śaiva sects, like the ascetic Pāśupatas, took this idea of enacting myth through ritual very seriously. In the Pāśupatas' origin myth, Śiva possesses the corpse of a young Brahmin on the cremation grounds. The revived body becomes Lakulīśa ("Lord of the Club"), who delivers the foundational teachings of the sect, eventually set down as the *Pāśupata Sūtras*. Pāśupatas would imitate this ghastly manifestation of Śiva by smearing their bodies with ashes, living in cremation grounds, and carrying a skull begging-bowl.[23] In later tantric forms of yoga, one way to dissolve the mind in Śiva (to attain what was called *laya* or the yoga of dissolution), was to lay on the ground in imitation of Śiva as the corpse.[24]

Figure 4.1 Śiva as Natarāja, the Lord of the Cosmic Dance. India, Tamil Nadu, 11th century.
Source: Courtesy of Metropolitan Museum of Art.

Kṛṣṇa: the pervading one

Once upon a time, there was a prince named Kṛṣṇa, who was a man but also a god come to Earth. Kṛṣṇa's cosmic form was that of the god Viṣṇu, the one who pervades all. To escape the wrath of his murderous uncle (who, to be fair, was only murderous because it was prophesized that his nephew would one day kill him), baby Kṛṣṇa was smuggled away in the dead of night to a neighboring village, where he was switched with a little girl, born at the exact same time. (The little girl, fortunately, happened to be the Goddess herself, so when the wicked king dashed her body upon the stones, she burst forth in all her fierce glory, once again prophesizing his demise.) Little Kṛṣṇa, meanwhile, grew up in a pastoral paradise, where he did mischievous things like slay demons and lift mountains. One time, when his mother was cleaning dirt out of his mouth, he opened up wide and showed her the whole universe. And when Kṛṣṇa grew into a young man his greatest devotees were the milkmaids, who loved him purely and unconditionally. There were over 16,000 of them, but this presented no problem for our hero, who used the supreme magic of his yoga—that is, his ability to pervade all—to reduplicate himself such that every maiden could whirl in the divine dance with her own personal Kṛṣṇa.[25]

And then there was another Kṛṣṇa—the grown Kṛṣṇa who had become a statesman and a kingmaker. This Kṛṣṇa served as his friend Arjuna's charioteer on the field of Kurukṣetra. And when Arjuna lost his nerve, unable to slay his family, members of which stood on the opposing side, Kṛṣṇa counseled him—right there on the battlefield—on the true nature of the Self and the many paths of yoga. This is the *Bhagavad Gītā*, where Kṛṣṇa reveals himself as Viṣṇu, the ultimate "Pervading One," with endless arms and legs and mouths, blazing with the brilliance of a thousand suns, containing all that ever was, is, and will be, and declares: "I am Time, the great destroyer of worlds"

(11.32)

Unlike Śiva, the boundary-crossing outcast, Kṛṣṇa tends to be found closer to the center of the action. He is a prince on earth and, in his cosmic form as Viṣṇu, he is kingly. The goddess who is his companion is called Śri, "Sovereignty" embodied. Though Kṛṣṇa comes to be identified as Viṣṇu's perhaps most important avatar, and certainly the one most clearly associated with yoga, all of Viṣṇu's descents to earth are undertaken for the sake of upholding *dharma*, or social and cosmic righteousness. Viṣṇu is the one who enters, who pervades. The hard kernel of Śiva's yoga is the destructive yet all-powerful notion of ascetic heat, which the practitioner can come to wield for himself through self-discipline, or else the idea of the individual practitioner's self-dissolution into Śiva's universal and unmanifest nature. But Viṣṇu-cum-Kṛṣṇa's yoga is one of entering, of possessing, of pervading the practitioner, who is ultimately a devotee, just as he pervades the whole world. But in this, the individual still remains, the world-order is preserved, and it is through understanding one's ultimate relationship to Viṣṇu, by giving oneself over, that liberation is most readily actualized. *Bhakta* (devotional) yogis dance and sing their praises to Kṛṣṇa, absorbed in the *bhāva*, the ecstatic mood of their connection with him, much as the mythical milkmaids must have been (Figure 4.2).

Śakti: fierce goddesses and disembodied energies

Once upon a time, when the gods (*devas*) still waged war with the demons (*asuras*), they entreated the great Goddess (Devī) for her aid. And so the Goddess, she who is eternal and whose form is the whole world, came forth. Her head appeared from the energy (*śakti*) of Śiva, and her two arms from the energy of Viṣṇu. Her feet were formed of the Brahmā's energy, her hair of Yama's (Death's) energy, her breasts of Candra's (the Moon's) energy, and so on. And so she stood, more dangerous than all the gods and demons together. As Durgā, with many arms wielding many weapons, riding a great lion as her mount, she slayed Mahiṣa, the Buffalo Demon. When time came to battle the demons Caṇḍa and Muṇḍa, she came forth in another form still, bursting from the radiant Goddesses's angry brow as the dark and fearsome Kālī, and cut off their heads. Then the demon Raktabīja challenged her, and Kālī came at him with her sword, but from every drop of his blood that hit the earth, Raktabīja would sprout anew, multiplying himself time and time again. So with her red, lolling tongue, Kālī lapped up the blood, and slayed the demon once and for all.[26]

Figure 4.2 Kṛṣṇa dances the *rasa līlā* with the *gopī* maidens, multiplying his form. India, Rajasthan, c. 1675–1700.

Source: Courtesy of the Los Angeles County Museum of Art.

More so than either Śiva or Viṣṇu, the Goddess is truly everywhere. Every feminine divinity, from minor village goddesses to the high forms of Lakṣmī or Parvatī, is ultimately just another manifestation of the supreme Devī. In traditions focused on male gods, the Goddess is usually depicted as their essential quality or power. Viṣṇu is the supreme holder Śrī ("Sovereignty"), Śiva has his Śakti ("Energy"). This of course makes her fundamental but also subordinate—she is something the male god possesses or wields. In Śākta (that is Śakti or Goddess-oriented traditions), it's this power itself and its pervading creative energy that becomes supreme (Figure 4.3). Relatedly, non-dual Śaiva–Śakta traditions ultimately view the masculine and feminine as two poles of the same divine principle.

The Goddess's role in yoga usually depends on the particular tradition's attitude towards material nature, which is gendered feminine, as opposed to consciousness, which is gendered masculine. Sometimes the feminine principle, such as *prakṛti* (nature, in dualistic Sāṅkhya philosophy and in Patañjali's *Yoga Sūtras*) or *māyā* (illusion in non-dual Advaita Vedānta philosophy), is something that must

Figure 4.3 The gods worshipping the Goddess in her form as Durgā after her victory over a demon. India, Madhya Pradesh, c. 1775.

Source: Courtesy of the Los Angeles County Museum of Art.

be transcended or otherwise left behind. In other, especially tantric schools, the feminine principle becomes essential to the practitioner's progress and ultimate goal. Because tantric traditions state that the human can, and indeed should, ultimately become divine, the practitioner's relationship to the Goddess is the same as that of a god. It's no coincidence that in premodern texts, "yogi" usually refers to a human practitioner of yoga, while "Yoginī" (the feminine form of the same noun) more often than not refers to one of the fierce goddesses whose power a yogi hopes to appropriate. For example, in medieval *haṭha* yoga traditions, which ultimately come to a non-dual perspective, imagine the masculine and feminine cosmic principles as both existing within the little world of the practitioner's own body. The feminine *kuṇḍalinī śakti* resides in the bottom of the torso, until yogic practice drives her to union with the masculine principle at the crown of the head—in their union, the practitioner comes to realize his own divinity.

Heroes and adepts

In this section, we'll examine a set of more human (or at least human-adjacent) figures who blur the lines between our ordinary mortal existence and something more transcendent or divine. In other words, if yogi gods are top-down models for the principles of yoga as cosmology, then these more human figures are bottom-up role models for how practitioners might fit into such a framework.

Ṛṣis, Siddhas, and other assorted demigods

Within Hindu traditions that define themselves with respect the Vedas, the principal role models for what a yogi looks like are the ancient Ṛṣis (seers), the quasi-mythical and semi-divine predecessors of the *brāhmaṇa* priests. It was the Ṛṣis who first intuited, in their states of mystical trance, the cosmic *mantras* that comprise the Vedas. As we saw in our creation hymn, the Ṛṣis perceive these primordial sounds in the heart, and it's in the heart that they "fashion" them from cognition into speech.[27] The heart continues to serve a crucial function, including within visionary forms of yogic practice, as the meeting place of the human and the divine, the juncture between the little world of the human body and the big world of the cosmos.

Tradition associates each of the *Ṛg Veda*'s 1,028 hymns with a particular Ṛṣi and subsequent members of his family. Later texts speak of a primeval set of seven families (*gotras*), stemming from a principal set of Ṛṣis, collectively known as the *saptārṣis* (seven Ṛṣis, though notably the actual members of the group tend to vary), who are said to be divine, immortal, and descended from the gods themselves.[28] Of these seven, one becomes particularly important to yogic traditions: Vasiṣṭha, also celebrated among other groups of significant Ṛṣis, such as the Brahmārṣis ("mind-born" sons of the creator god Brahmā) and Devārṣis (divine Ṛṣis).[29]

Vasiṣṭha, to whom a number of later Hindu texts and scriptures are attributed, is particularly known as the sage who delivers the discourses contained in the *Yoga Vāsiṣṭha*, a text likely compiled in multiple forms from the 6th to the 11th century CE. In it, Vasiṣṭha instructs prince Rāma, who is somewhat troubled by his task of chasing demons away from the hermitages of forest-dwelling sages. The dialogue with Vasiṣṭha, which contains, among other things, a non-dual philosophy and a seven-limb method of yoga, restores Rāma's resolve and empowers him to fulfill his *dharma*.[30] Vasiṣṭha, along with a couple of other famous Ṛṣis like Viśvāmitra and Marīci, survives in the time of modern yoga by lending his name to an *āsana*.

In the end, the yoga of the Ṛṣis is very much a visionary yoga, although, as time goes on, the Ṛṣis do also become associates with *tapas*[31] (remembering that the brooding heat of *tapas* can have both physical and mental dimensions). There is a later class of semi-divine superhumans that mirrors this dynamic, and these are the Siddhas, the "Accomplished" or "Perfected Ones." The Siddhas appear in both Hindu and Buddhist traditions, where it is not uncommon to find references to and canonical lists of 84 Siddhas (though, as with the Ṛṣis, the members of these lists vary). They dwell in

Figure 4.4 Hanumān making the great leap to Lanka. India, Gujarat, c. 1775–1800.
Source: Courtesy of the Los Angeles County Museum of Art.

the uppermost regions of the cosmos along with the gods and other divine beings and, like the Ṛṣis, the earliest Siddhas are somewhat ambiguous characters, in that it's not always clear whether they were born perfect (that is, divine) or made themselves that way.[32] Over time, however, and especially in tantric traditions, they become a model for "self-made gods."[33] We'll examine two such tantric Siddhas, who started out as human but became more-or-less divine, later in this section.

Our final example of a superhuman demigod isn't actually human at all. Hanumān, who is not only an epic hero but an extremely popular folk deity, is actually a monkey. Well, technically, he is one of the Vānaras, the mythical forest-dwelling monkey-people of the *Rāmāyaṇa* epic. And though Hanumān is the subject of many other stories, he is perhaps most famous for his role as the devoted companion to Rāma. Most modern yoga practitioners will be familiar with *hanumānāsana*, a pose that more or less amounts to the splits and is meant to evoke the monkey demigod's monumental leap from the subcontinent all the way to the island on Lanka (Figure 4.4). However, Hanumān's connection to yoga is arguably much more elaborate. If there is a type of yoga that Hanumān most powerfully exemplifies, then it is *bhakti* yoga, the yoga of devotion. But, even more importantly, Hanumān is, among other things, a sort of patron god of wrestlers. And wrestling, as a tradition, has fascinating areas of overlap with physical yoga practice.[34]

As scholar of Indian physical culture traditions Joseph Alter points out,

> one of the most striking features of Hanumān's character is that he appears to be the essence of all divine power manifest in one form. He has the speed of the wind, the radiance of fire and immunity from water. As the essence of virility, he is able to bestow fertility on barren women and potency on men.

> He can tell the future and cure diseases. He is a master musician, a sage interpreter of the *śāstras*, and a great grammarian. He is a warrior par excellence: immortal, tireless, and strong beyond compare. He is also capable of fervent and absolute devotion. Essentially he is all-powerful and all-loving.[35]

To the wrestlers who venerate him, Hanumān is a tangible embodiment of the divine *śakti* (energy) that pervades the whole cosmos and upon which they draw for their strength. But Hanumān's *śakti* is ultimately a product of his *bhakti*, his devotion to and love for Rāma. And so, in that sense Hanumān is a very simple but powerful role model—just as he draws *śakti* from his devotion to Rāma, so too the wrester can draw *śakti* from his devotion to Hanumān.[36]

However, there is another explanation for Hanumān's great power—one that is either alternative or complementary to the *bhakti* narrative, depending on how one looks at it. Hanumān is also the model for *brahmācarya*, or celibacy. This, of course is a common feature of asceticism and, insofar as wrestlers believe celibacy to be at the root of their physical strength,[37] they are perhaps really not so different from ascetic yogis. The common principle here is the power of *tapas*, the power generated by the internal heat of austerities, which, incidentally, is also where the villain of the *Rāmāyaṇa*—the demon king Rāvaṇa—draws his impressive abilities.

Thus, with all of these figures, we see a kind of back-and-forth between innate and acquired power. Celestial heritage and visionary inspiration suggest that the human (or, in Hanumān's case, the monkey) is in some sense already divine. On the other hand, where we see practice, especially evident in the form of *tapas*, we also see the evidence of a method that leads to this divinity and its gifts (Figure 4.5). It is this latter dimension that the next section emphasizes.

Ascetic princes

So, here is a story—

> Long ago, there was a prince named Siddhārtha Gautama. Upon the prince's birth, the priests read their omens and foretold that the child was destined to be extraordinary—either an Awakened Seer or a World Conqueror. The king, Siddhārtha's father, logically preferred the latter, and so he confined the boy to the lavish palace grounds where his every desire would be fulfilled and he would never come to witness suffering or hardship of the kind that drive men to seek spiritual release. But eventually the prince had occasion to venture out of the palace. On his first trip, his courtly entourage came upon an old man, on the second trip upon a sick man, and on the third trip upon a dead man. Young Siddhārtha returned from each outing more troubled than from the last. Finally, on a fourth journey outside the palace gates, he encountered a mendicant renouncer. That very night, disgusted by the sleeping bodies of the palace girls in whom he had previously delighted, he abandoned his family, fled the palace, and took up the life of a wandering ascetic.
>
> In his travels, Siddhārtha encountered many teachers and learned many techniques. He meditated to still his mind and performed such extreme

austerities that his body became emaciated and his hair began to fall out, but none of these eased the pain brought on by knowledge of disease, old age, and death. In the end, Siddhārtha concluded that the path to awakening and release could not be attained by one who was not sound of body. He accepted some milk rice offered to him by a simple milkmaid and, upon seeing this, his ascetic companions abandoned him, thinking that he had fallen from the righteous path. But Siddhārtha, his strength returned, took a seat at the root of a *bodhi* tree and determined not to rise until he attained his goal. Sensing danger, the demon Māra sent his sons and daughters born of desire to tempt Siddhārtha into earthly glory and sensual delights, and, when this proved ineffective, he sent his frightful armies to threaten Siddhārtha with violence, but Siddhārtha's resolve proved unshakeable. Throughout the watches of the night, Siddhārtha attained many visions and wondrous powers and, finally, meditating on the true nature of reality, he understood the truth of interdependent origination that leads to disease, old age, and death—that there is no center and no permanence to anything, that nothing in the world exists in itself. And at dawn, he woke to the cessation of suffering and resolved to pass his knowledge to others[38] … And they called him Buddha, the "Awakened One."

Figure 4.5 Kāraikkāl Ammaiyār, one of three women among the 63 Nāyaṉmārs ("hounds of Śiva"), South Indian ascetic poet-saints devoted to Śiva living between the 6th and 8th centuries. In her songs, Kāraikkāl Ammaiyār speaks of herself as a *pey*, a superhuman ghoul in Śiva's army. India, Tamil Nadu, late 13th century.

Source: Courtesy of the Metropolitan Museum of Art.

Here is another story—

> Long ago, there was a prince named Vardhamāna. Before the prince's birth, his mother had many auspicious dreams, and the priests and interpreters listened to them, and they declared that this meant the child was destined to be extraordinary—either an Awakened Seer or a World Conqueror. And the king was pleased and joyful to hear this, and accepted the meaning of the dreams, honored the interpreters, and dismissed them. While still in the womb, out of compassion for his mother, Vardhamāna remained so quiet and still that the queen feared her child had died. Intuiting his mother's pain, Vardhamāna quivered and this brought her such great joy that he resolved right then never to enter a life of renunciation while his parents still lived. But eventually the time came for Vardhamāna to cast off his worldly life. And so one day when he was out with his courtly retinue, he descended from his palanquin beneath an *aśoka* tree and took off his jewels, and his garlands, and his finery, and plucked out all of his hair in five handfuls.
>
> For twelve years, Vardhamāna wandered naked, abandoning all care of his body, indifferent to all attachments and earthly pleasures. Finally, in the thirteenth year, after taking neither food nor water for two days, he squatted down with his heels joined, exposing himself to the hot sun, and engaged in deep meditation, and he attained that ultimate state of supreme Isolation[39] … And they called him Mahāvīra, the "Great Hero."

The personal myths of the Buddha and Mahāvīra are, as scholar of religions Jeffrey Kripal has suggested, actually most effectively examined in comparison to one another. Both men are almost certainly actual historical figures, but they lived so long ago (both around the 6th century BCE) and became such important anchors for their respective traditions that their stories are better treated as hagiographies, a term medieval Christians used to label the lives of saints.[40] The two men's legendary lives share some remarkable similarities, including details which we've glossed over here. Both come into the world through miraculous births by mothers who experienced a series of auspicious visions. Both are born into great wealth and privilege and are members of the high (and relatively pure, but notably not priestly) *kṣatriya* Warrior class. Both, of course, also go on to renounce that worldly authority and privilege, undergoing a series of intense trials.[41] This final point is emblematic of their belonging to the contemporary fold of *śramaṇa* (literally "those who exert themselves") non-Vedic movements, which began to gain prominence around 500 BCE (Figure 4.6).

But it's really the differences that matter, because in them we can spot not only the philosophical assumptions that differentiate Buddhism from Jainism, but also the consequent methods that the two traditions prescribe in order to achieve what they view as the ultimate goal. As Kripal and his coauthors Andrea Jain and Erin Prophet point out,

Figure 4.6 The Buddha emaciated during his extreme ascetic period, pre-enlightenment. India, Kashmir, 8th century.

Source: Courtesy of the Cleveland Museum of Art.

> whereas the Buddha prescribed what is called in the Buddhist tradition 'the Middle Way'—a monastic lifestyle between the extremes of radical asceticism and worldly indulgence—Mahāvīra argued that radical asceticism was indeed necessary for advancement along the path toward enlightenment. Hence the Buddha achieved enlightenment under the shade of a tree, on some soft patch of grass, after taking nourishment from a young woman, whereas Mahāvīra achieves enlightenment while baking in the sun in the middle of a field, after thirteen years.[42]

In other words, ritual once again mirrors myth.

Tantric lords

Here is a different kind of story—

> Long ago, there was a fisherman named Mīna. One day, Mīna hooked a fish so large that the force of its thrashing threw him overboard. But, protected by his good *karma*, Mīna was swallowed by the fish and survived in its gargantuan stomach. And, after some time, it came to pass that the Lord Śiva had repaired to the bottom of the sea so that he could instruct his divine partner Umā in some secret teachings in a secluded spot where no one would overhear this esoteric discourse. At one point, the Goddess grew so tired of Śiva's instruction that she actually fell asleep. "Are you listening," asked Śiva. "Yes!" Mīna promptly replied from within the fish's belly. Spotting Mīna with the yogic sight of his third eye, Śiva was so pleased that he initiated the fisherman into his secret teachings on the spot. For twelve more years, Mīna lived in the fish's belly, engaging in the secret practices taught to him by Śiva with great dedication. Eventually, though, another fisherman caught the great fish and slit its gut, whence Mīna emerged as a fully realized Siddha[43] … And they called him Matsyendra, the "Lord of the Fishes."

And here is another—

> Long ago, there was a peasant woman who longed for a child. She implored the Lord Śiva to grant her a son and, eventually, he took pity on her and gave her some ash to eat. But the woman did not understand the gift she'd been given, and so she threw the ash onto a heap of cow dung. Twelve years passed and the great Matsyendra happened to overhear Śiva regaling his spouse with tales of this magical child. Curious, Matsyendra sought out the peasant woman only to have her confess that she had discarded Śiva's gift. "Go and search the dung heap," Matseyndra told her, for he wished to adopt the boy as his disciple. And so the woman went and dug through the dung heap, and from within it, emerged the one they called Goraksha, the "Protector of Cows."[44]

Unlike the Buddha and Mahāvīra, who start out as literal princes, these tantric masters are specifically said to hail from the lowest rungs of society. We might nevertheless talk about both sets of figures as challenging, transgressing, and breaking down social norms, so to find the crucial differences we have to dig a little bit deeper. Social class in South Asia is, of course, explicitly connected to purity and while not all tantric traditions upend purity codes, the Kaula traditions with which Gorakṣa and Matsyendra are associated are known for this. Matsyendra starts out as a fisherman, a fairly low-class and rather impure occupation. Goraksha, of course, is literally born from a dung heap. Even though they renounce worldly society, the ascetic practices of the Buddha and Mahāvīra nevertheless maintain (and indeed double down on) most traditional codes of purity. The practices of Matsyendra's Kaula tradition, on the other hand, are rooted rituals involving impure actions and substances, such as meat, alcohol, and sexual intercourse.

Despite their humble origins, figures like Gorakṣa and Matsyendra go on to be called Nāths ("Lords") and Siddhas ("Perfected Ones"). It's notable that the wisdom that allows them to reach this perfection does ultimately have a divine source—Śiva. This is common in tantric traditions, which are decidedly theistic. However, while Śiva may be the Ādi, the first or primordial, Nāth, his status is attainable to his human followers. Especially in the non-dual Kaula traditions with which Gorakṣa and Matsyendra are associated, the human is in the end fully divine.

But myths can also reveal the shifting identity of the group to whom they belong. There is a famous myth in which Gorakṣa rescues his guru Matsyendra from the Kingdom of Women where he had been ensnared by the queen and her 1,600 courtesans into being their lover. Matsyendra spends 12 years enjoying the kingdom's sensual pleasures before Gorakṣa extracts him and restores him to the proper life of an ascetic.[45] Matsyendra and Gorakṣa were probably historical figures, living sometime between the 9th and 12th centuries, though it's likely that they were separated by more than one lifetime. Though the historical Gorakṣa was in all likelihood a Kaula *tantrika* just like Matsyendra, he is associated the formation of the Nāth lineage as an order of celibate ascetics practicing the internal rituals of *haṭha* yoga rather than external tantric rites.[46] And thus, we find the *Gorakṣa Śataka*, a 13th-century Nāth *haṭha* text, declaring:

> We drink the dripping liquid called *bindu*, "the drop," not wine; we eat the rejection of the objects of the five senses, not meat; we do not embrace a sweetheart [but] the *suṣumnā nāḍī*, her body curved like *kuśa* grass; if we are to have intercourse, it takes place in a mind dissolved in the void, not in a vagina.[47]

Is Garuda your archetype?

As we noted earlier, much of this mythology, culturally-specific as it is to South Asia, does not fully translate into modern global or Western yoga practice. However, as these stories and the concepts and figures they represent have been incorporated into the universalist mindset of global yoga, they have taken on a new life.

Let's consider, for instance, Swami Sivananda Radha (1911–1995), who was born Sylvia Demitz in Germany, and was a concert dancer before she studied with Swami Sivananda in Rishikesh in the 1950s. In her book, *Hatha Yoga: The Hidden Language* (1987), Sivananda Radha dwells on Indian, but also Greek and Egyptian mythology. She grounds this interpretation in transpersonal psychology, referencing Abraham Maslow (a prominent psychologist) and Joseph Campbell (scholar of comparative mythology and author of the famous book, *The Hero with a Thousand Faces*). Sivananda Radha explains,

> To blend East and West, we can take what is valuable in the West and put it together with yogic philosophy and methods. Western psychology, particularly Transpersonal Psychology, is a stepping-stone to the analysis that is done by the Easterner through the application of Yoga Psychology.[48]

She thus argues that symbolism, which is ultimately transcultural, can be used to delve into hidden recesses of mind. What comes of evoking and imitating a mountain? A plough? Or a fish?

For Sivananda Radha, such practices can help one through the difficulty of transcending otherwise occluded aspects of personality. She explains, "Symbolism is very helpful for understanding these complexities; for example, in doing Garudāsana one's own aggressiveness may become apparent."[49] Though she never references him directly, Sivananda Radha is drawing on psychologist Carl Jung's notion of the archetype, which has its roots in Platonic ideas of ideal Forms. Jung's ideas, true to their harmonial roots, have been extremely popular in 20th-century Western spirituality. In the 21st century, they have been taken up (among others) by the global universalist guru Deepak Chopra, who has explicitly championed the idea of Indian deities like Śiva, Śakti, and Gaṇeśa as archetypes, explaining that

> archetypes can be a source of inspiration or act as a role model as you set out to achieve a particular goal or make a lifestyle change. You can call upon an archetype that you identify with or look up to in times of need or to help in your meditation or yoga practice.[50]

So, what does it mean to say that Garuḍa, the mythical fire-bird and Viṣṇu's customary mount, is your archetype? In the melting pot of global yoga, culturally-specific symbols become fodder for new myths used to ground practices, both physical and psychological. Durgā sits side-by-side with Demeter. *Mūrtis* (sacred icons) of Indian deities adorn altars next to tarot cards.[51] Is it cultural appropriation? Is it yoga?

Conclusions

- Myth provides a narrative framework that links cosmology (our model of the world and how it works) to practice.
- Mythic themes such as sound, fire, and the elixir of immortality appear as early as the hymns of the *Ṛg Veda* (c. 1500 BCE) and flow through both Vedic and non-Vedic South Asian traditions.
- The mythologies of Indian gods have historically included yogic themes, especially when it comes to understanding the mechanics of divine power.
- Myth also features yogic role models in the form of semidivine beings (like Ṛṣis and Siddhas) and perfected human adepts (like the Buddha and Mahāvīra).
- Global yoga culture includes some aspects of South Asian myth, but reinterprets them in more universalist (and often Western-influenced) ways.

Notes

1 A. K. Ramanujan, "Three Hundred *Rāmāyaṇas*: Five Examples and Three Thoughts on Translation," in *The Collected Essays of A. K. Ramanujan*, ed. Vinay Dharwadker (Oxford and New York: Oxford University Press, 1999), 133.

2 Ramanujan, "Three Hundred *Rāmāyaṇas*," 134.

3 Devdutt Pattanaik, *Myth = Mithya: A Handbook of Hindu Mythology* (New Delhi: Penguin Books, 2006).
4 Bina Gupta, *An Introduction to Indian Philosophy: Perspectives on Reality, Knowledge and Freedom* (New York: Routledge, 2012), 225.
5 Pattanaik, *Myth = Mithya*, 1.
6 David Chidester, *Authentic Fakes: Religion and American Popular Culture* (Berkeley: University of California Press, 2010), 13.
7 Adam B. Seligman, *Ritual and Its Consequences: An Essay on the Limits of Sincerity* (New York: Oxford University Press, 2008).
8 Seligman, *Ritual and Its Consequences*, 37.
9 Elizabeth De Michelis, *A History of Modern Yoga: Patañjali and Western Esoterism* (London: Continuum, 2004), 249–59.
10 James Mallinson, "Yoga and Yogis," *Nāmarūpa*, 3, no. 15 (2012): 7.
11 Adapted from Wendy Doniger, *The Rig Veda: An Anthology* (London: Penguin, 2005), 25–6.
12 Barbara A. Holdrege, *Veda and Torah: Transcending the Textuality of Scripture* (Albany: State University of New York Press, 1996), 33–4.
13 Holdrege, *Veda and Torah*, 57.
14 Walter O. Kaelber, *Tapta Mārga: Ascetism and Initiation in Vedic India* (Albany: State University of New York Press, 1989), 64.
15 Doniger, *The Rig Veda*, 104–9, 117.
16 James Mallinson and Mark Singleton, *Roots of Yoga: A Sourcebook from the Indic Traditions* (London: Penguin Classics, 2017), 181.
17 Doniger, *The Rig Veda*, 128.
18 Patrick Olivelle, *The Early Upaniṣads: Annotated Text and Translation* (Oxford and New York: Oxford University Press, 1998), 21.
19 David Gordon White, *The Alchemical Body: Siddha Traditions in Medieval India* (Chicago: Chicago University Press, 1996), 11.
20 White, *The Alchemical Body*, 29.
21 White, *Sinister Yogis*, 167.
22 Adapted from Wendy Doniger, *Hindu Myths: A Sourcebook Translated from the Sanskrit* (London and New York: Penguin, 2004), 116–25, 249–51 and Pattanaik, *Myth = Mithya*, 167–73.
23 Gavin D. Flood, *An Introduction to Hinduism* (Cambridge: Cambridge University Press, 2006), 156–7.
24 Mallinson, "Yoga and Yogis," 7.
25 Adapted from Doniger, *Hindu Myths*, 204–31.
26 Adapted from Doniger, *Hindu Myths*, 239–41 and Thomas B. Coburn, *Encountering the Goddess: A Translation of the Devi-Mahatmya and a Study of Its Interpretation* (Albany: State University of New York Press, 2000), 32–84.
27 Holdrege, *Veda and Torah*, 235.
28 Holdrege, *Veda and Torah*, 229–30.
29 Holdrege, *Veda and Torah*, 244.
30 Christopher Key Chapple, "The Sevenfold Yoga of the Yogavāsiṣṭha," in *Yoga in Practice*, ed. David Gordon White (Princeton, NJ: Princeton University Press, 2012), 117.
31 Holdrege, *Veda and Torah*, 240–1.
32 White, *The Alchemical Body*, 3.
33 White, *Sinister Yogis*, 195.
34 Joseph S. Alter, *The Wrestler's Body: Identity and Ideology in North India* (Berkeley: University of California Press, 1992).
35 Alter, *The Wrestler's Body*, 167.
36 Alter, *The Wrestler's Body*, 168–71.
37 Alter, *The Wrestler's Body*, 174.
38 Adapted from Patrick Olivelle, trans., *Life of the Buddha* (New York: New York University Press, 2009).

39 Adapted from Hermann Georg Jacobi, *Jaina Sutras: Translated from Prakrit* (New York: Dover Publications, 1968), 195–208.
40 Jeffrey J. Kripal, Andrea R. Jain, and Erin L. Prophet, *Comparing Religions: Coming to Terms* (Chichester: Wiley-Blackwell, 2014), 134–6.
41 Kripal et al., *Comparing Religions*, 134.
42 Kripal et al., *Comparing Religions*, 135–6.
43 Adapted from Georg Feuerstein, *The Yoga Tradition: Its History, Literature, Philosophy, and Practice* (Delhi: Motilal Banarsidass, 2002), 511–12.
44 Adapted from Feuerstein, *The Yoga Tradition*, 512.
45 Adrián Muñoz, "Matsyendra's 'Golden Legend': Yogi Tales and Nāth Ideology," in *Yogi Heroes and Poets: Histories and Legends of the Naths*, ed. David N. Lorenzen and Adrián Muñoz (Albany: State University of New York Press, 2011), 115–17.
46 James Mallinson, "Yoga and Yogis," *Nāmarūpa*, 3, no. 15 (2012): 7.
47 Mallinson, "Yoga and Yogis," 8.
48 Swami Sivananda Radha, *Hatha Yoga: The Hidden Language: Symbols, Secrets, and Metaphor* (Boston: Shambhala, 1987), 279.
49 Sivananda Radha, *Hatha Yoga*, 13.
50 "Exploring Vedic Archetypes: How to Get Started," Chopra.com, May 19, 2016, https://chopra.com/articles/exploring-vedic-archetypes-how-to-get-started
51 Drew Thomases, "Devotion in the Desert: Religion and Emotion on the Margins of Hindu and Hippie," *The Revealer*, November 7, 2016, https://therevealer.org/devotion-in-the-desert-religion-and-emotion-on-the-margins-of-hindu-and-hippie/

Part II

Histories

5 Ancient to classical yogas

Yoga practitioners routinely disagree about how old "yoga" actually is: 5,000 years? 10,000? 40,000? The lowest figure usually assumes yoga began with the Indus Valley Civilization. The higher numbers tend to rely on "insider" models of history, which are rooted in traditional Indian ideas of time, cosmic ages, and so on. But even conservative scholarly estimates are often ambiguous and difficult to substantiate. To some extent, many of the sources we'll refer to in this chapter cannot be dated with any great degree of precision. This is due to a number of factors, including a cultural emphasis on transmitting knowledge orally (rather than writing it down), a tendency to compile texts from parts of other texts, and the very basic fact that ancient history is precisely that—ancient, meaning our sources are often distant and limited. However, when it comes to yoga, we are also faced with the difficulty that a word and a concept are never precisely the same thing. On the one hand, "yoga" can historically mean a lot of things, some of which are entirely irrelevant to the practice we associate with that label today. On the other hand, there are ancient ideas and practices that we might associate with yoga for any number of reasons, but which would not have actually carried that label. The further back in time we go, the more tenuous all of these connections become.

And so, although we'll address their existence, we'll have to be very cautious about locating yoga in the most ancient layers of South Asian civilization like the material artifacts of the Indus Valley, or the hymns of the *Ṛg Veda*. To a large extent, we'll begin with South Asia's second wave of urbanization (the first being the Indus Valley Civilization) in approximately 500 BCE, which yields the ascetic movements that go on to birth traditions like Buddhism and Jainism as well as the "yogic" bridge between this asceticism and the sacrificial culture of the Vedas represented by the Upaniṣads. Along with this, we'll focus on South Asia's "classical" period, beginning approximately in the 3rd century BCE and running through the 6th century CE. This period is marked by the heyday of the Maurya Empire (322–185 BCE) on one end and the decline of the Gupta Empire (320–550 CE) on the other.

Not surprisingly, a lot can happen in the course of a millennium. As we already mentioned, Jainism and Buddhism have their origins in this period, and each enjoyed their time in the political spotlight. This is also the period to which we date the cornerstone texts of Hinduism, like the great epics of the *Mahābhārata* (and, more importantly for our intents and purposes, the *Bhagavad Gītā*, which appears inside it) and the *Rāmāyaṇa*, as well as the encyclopedic Purāṇas. Though, as we'll see, there are many places where we can find yoga during this time, and many forms which yoga takes; it's also the period during which the famous *Yoga Sūtras* of Patañjali were composed.

Ultimately, "yoga" is a Sanskrit word and so it should not be surprising that we first find it in the oldest Sanskrit texts to which we have access: the Vedic hymns. However, this does not mean that we should view yoga as originating exclusively (or even directly) from Vedic tradition. Instead, the takeaway from this chapter should be the ways in which different South Asian traditions—Vedic and otherwise—meet, respond to one another, combine, diverge, and recombine. And it's through this messy process that yoga emerges.

If it looks like a yogi ...

For a long time, we've told the story of yoga by starting with the Indus Valley Civilization, an apparently advanced and urban but still poorly understood Bronze Age society that flourished in the northwestern region of the Indian subcontinent from approximately 2500 to 1900 BCE. We do this for a couple of reasons. One reason is that this is usually our starting point for talking about South Asian history as a whole, though the age, origins, and character of the Indus Valley Civilization remain hotly contested topics among scholars, both Indian and Euro-American.[1]

The other reason is due to the existence of a particular image, inscribed on soapstone, among the artifacts that archeologists have uncovered as evidence of these early communities. The image in question is often called the "Paśupati Seal," after the god Paśupati, the "Lord of the Beasts" and a famous epithet of Śiva (Figure 5.1). The god Śiva eventually comes to be known as the prototypical ascetic and yogi. True to this narrative, the apparently male figure at the center of the seal seems to be seated in a traditional yogic meditative posture, bent knees apart and heels stacked or otherwise pressed together. However, things are not always what they seem.

There is, of course the general difficulty of interpreting an image—in this case, a very ancient and not overly clear one—out of context. What is the relationship between the central human figure and the surrounding animals? Does the figure have three faces or one? Is the figure, as some scholars have suggested, ithyphallic or is his purportedly erect penis actually a fancy belt? Is the figure even male? And then there's the pose. Identifications with Śiva aside, the figure's yogic identity has hinged on our assumption that it's seated in a yogic *āsana*. Does sitting with folded legs automatically make someone a yogi? And if so, then what do we do with the range of other archeological examples that feature figures in such poses, ranging over a variety of ancient cultures, including an image of the Celtic horned god Cernunnos?[2]

In the South Asian context, the Buddha and Mahāvīra (the founder of Jainism) are pictured in such poses some 2,000 years later, but so is the goddess Śrī, whose

Figure 5.1 The "Paśupati Seal," uncovered in the Mohenjo-Daro archeological site and dated to the late 3rd millennium BCE. The seal appears to show a human figure in a horned headdress, seated with folded legs upon a dais and surrounded by a variety of animals.

Source: Angelo Hornak/Alamy Stock Photo.

chief association is not with yoga but with sovereignty and prosperity. This has led historian of yoga, David Gordon White, to conclude that

> in the centuries around the beginning of the common era, the cross-legged "lotus position" was a mark of royal sovereignty: royal gods or goddesses, their priests, and kings sat enthroned in this posture atop a dais, lotus, or cushion. When Buddhas and Jīnas began to be represented anthropomorphically in Kushan-era sculpture and coinage, their cross-legged posture was originally an indication of their royal sovereignty, rather than of any meditative or yogic practice.[3]

As we will see shortly, however, the fact that both the Buddha and Mahāvīra were originally princes and therefore belonged to the *kṣatriya* or warrior class may well be important to their identity as yogis in a number of ways.

So, is the figure in the seal a yogi? The truth is, we may never know. But the complications that arise when we try to answer this question might be useful in and of themselves. If the figure's pose—and only its pose—marks it as a yogi, then we have to really consider what we mean by "yoga." Is there such a thing as Egyptian yoga? (After all, there's no shortage of ancient Egyptian imagery featuring human figures in very interesting bodily poses.) And is every form of bodily discipline automatically yoga, even if the people who practiced it would not have used that word?

Poets, ascetics, flying mystics, and chariots

The trickiest part of interpreting images from the Indus Valley Civilization is that its language remains undeciphered. This changes when we enter the Vedic period (roughly 1500–500 BCE), which gives us a body of literature composed in Vedic Sanskrit by a nomadic people who referred to themselves as the *ārya*s ("Aryans" to us), or the "noble ones." To what extent these people were continuous with the earlier Indus Valley inhabitants, or whether and how they displaced or blended with them, is another one of those hotly contested topics. We know that these nomads spoke a language that shares roots with others in what we call the Indo-European linguistic family, including ancient Greek and Latin, but also modern languages like Spanish, German, Russian, and English. We also know that their mythology and their pantheon are marked by close family resemblances to the ancient religions of these other cultures. Beyond that, the details are once again complex, messy, and contested.

The Vedic period takes its name from the Vedic corpus of texts (though all of these were originally transmitted orally), namely the four Vedas themselves (*Ṛg*, *Yajur*, *Sāma*, and *Atharva*) also known the *saṃhitās* or "compilations" of verses. These consist largely of hymns, evocations, and mythological narratives of the gods (*devas*) but also include ritual and some philosophical speculation. In addition to building on one another, with the *Ṛg Veda* being the foundational and most important composition, the Vedas support a further three layers of sacred texts: the Brāhmaṇa priestly commentaries, which deal heavily with ritual; the Āraṇyakas ("of the forest"), which combine ritual and philosophy; and the Upaniṣads ("Correspondences"), which venture most directly into philosophy and spirituality. While all parts of the Vedic corpus have proven very difficult to date, the four layers appear to have developed in a roughly chronological fashion, following the order we just listed.

The ancient Vedic religion, which shows significant linguistic affinity and even overlap with the Avestan traditions of ancient Persia that would give rise to Zoroastrianism, is based around the rites of a sacrificial fire. The *brāhmaṇa* ("Brahmin") or priestly class was responsible for administering the complex rituals on behalf of sacrificers looking to garner the goodwill of the gods. The role of the sacrificer would normally be occupied by a male member of the *kṣatriya* ruling and warrior or *vaiśya* farming and merchant classes. The fourth *śūdra* servant class was technically excluded from the sacrificial order. In their heyday, sacrificial rites were extremely elaborate and could take days, so they presented quite the material investment.

Though the rites of the fire were originally aimed at calling down the gods, or at least their favor, they eventually came to overshadow the gods to be an end in themselves. In this early context, *karma* signified ritual action and specifically the accrued merit that resulted from the sacrifice. Good *karma* was considered crucial for the sacrificer's own fortune, in this life and in the next, but also held a larger significance. The sacrificial order underpinned the whole of reality and the continued act of sacrifice was necessarily to keep the cosmic wheel turning. One's religious obligation was therefore also one's social obligation, and vice versa. From a conceptual perspective, this is an important development for us because it means that, through a series of correspondences, the sacrifice became homologized to the creation (and continuous re-creation or renewal) of the entire cosmos. As part of this, the body of the sacrificer in particular became correlated with the body of the "Cosmic Man" (Puruṣa) from whose sacrificial act the whole universe had first come into being. As such, it represented an early instance of the correspondences between the macrocosm of the world and the microcosm of the human body that would become key to certain strains of yoga.

If we are on the lookout for yogis, the most natural candidates in this early period would appear to be the Vedic Ṛṣis, "seers" and mystical poets, who are the quasi-mythical predecessors of the *brāhmaṇa* priests. The term "*veda*" comes from the Sanskrit root √*vid*, "to know." The Vedas, therefore, are literally that which is (or was) known. The Vedas are also traditionally described as *śruti*, "that which was heard" or something like "revelation." This is as opposed to the category of *smṛti*, or "that which is remembered," which is something like "tradition" and is used to describe a range of other important literature such as law codes and epics. The latter is of human origin, while the former is not. Instead, the Vedas are believed to have been "known"—or "heard," in a mystical synesthetic sort of way—by the ancient Ṛṣis.

It bears mentioning that, though they become firmly associated with the traditionalist and purity-oriented priestly class, the Ṛṣis did not attain their revelatory visions through contemplation alone. Exalted throughout the Vedas is the power of *soma*, a psychoactive substance derived from a now-unidentifiable plant, that was important enough to be deemed a deity in its own right. Nevertheless, in later Vedic tradition, the wisdom of the Ṛṣis did come to be imagined as more contemplative. Specifically, their mastery of the Vedic hymns, which would have been memorized and passed down orally from father to son within the Brahmin class, meant that they were masters of the hidden correspondences (*bandhus*) that governed the cosmos.

Another suggestive yogi-like character can be found in a Vedic hymn devoted to the *keśin* (*Ṛg Veda* 10.136), literally "the long-haired one." The *keśin* is a *muni*, or a silent ascetic, who rides on the rushing wind and drinks poison with the god Rudra himself. Taking on the voice of these mystics, the hymn declares: "Mad with asceticism, we have mounted the wind. You mortals see only our bodies."[4] Given this wording, it's tough to tell whether the *keśin*'s flight is literal or one of the mind. Perhaps it was meant to read as both. Likewise debatable is the *keśin*'s social status. His association with Rudra (later identified with Śiva), who often finds himself on the periphery of the Vedic social order, seems to differentiate him from the Ṛṣi, but perhaps not—both, after all, are visionary mystics who keep company with the gods.

Note, however, that the term "yoga" is not associated with either of these figures. Nor do we see description of the kind of systematic practice, either bodily or contemplative, that will characterize later yoga traditions. This is not to say that such techniques definitely did not exist, but they are not described in the texts to which we have access. Instead, what the texts show us are visionary experiences of gnosis. The fact that they likely involve psychoactive substances ("drugs") should not suggest to us that they are any less complex or authentic. Asceticism may also be important, but possibly more marginal, as represented by the *keśin* and his silent wandering.

This brings us to a Vedic term that might rival "yoga" in its complex history and multiplicity of meanings. This term is *tapas*—"heat," if translated literally. The non-literal translations of the word range rather widely. Most commonly, it might refer to natural heat in the form of the sun or fire, generative heat as associated with fertility and gestation, and finally—and perhaps most importantly, for our purposes—the heat of exertion and austerity.[5] In other words, one way to translate *tapas* is "austerities" or "asceticism." But, really, it's worth taking all of these meanings into account if we are to truly understand the significance of *tapas*, both on its own terms and in its later relationship to yoga. Heat can be creative as easily as it can be destructive. And if we really want to rope in the contemplative element that will eventually come to play a role in that aforementioned relationship, then perhaps the best translation is something like "brooding."[6] It's worth restating, however, that even though *tapas* is explicitly linked to the activities of the Vedic Ṛṣis in a way that evokes all of these meanings, it is not yet connected to yoga.

Where does the word "yoga" get used in this earlier Vedic period? Chariots. And other animal-driven wheeled conveyances. But most importantly, chariots. At least, this has been the argument of the aforementioned David Gordon White, who suggests that in addition to "yoke," other good translations for "yoga" would be words like "hitch" or "rig," which similarly function as both nouns and verbs.[7] Which brings us to yet another Vedic character, besides the Ṛṣi (or *kavi*, "poet") and the wandering *keśin* or *muni*, who got to hang out with the gods. White points us to a famous aphorism found across a variety of sources early in the first millennium of the Common Era: "These are the two people in this world who pierce the solar disk: the wanderer (*parivrāj*) and the *yogayukta* [warrior] who is slain [while] facing [his enemies] on the field of battle."[8] Thus, the sacrificer following the wisdom of the Ṛṣis, the wandering ascetic, and the warrior all had one thing in common. If they did their job right, they would be able to ascend to the celestial realm of the gods. But, in the beginning, only in the case of the warrior would this have had anything to do with "yoga" because this word was primarily associated with literal yoking and so, since it was on their glorious chariots that warriors would make their final ascent, the word was an appropriate one.

What happened next, White argues, was a series of metaphors. Specifically, Brahmin priests, who saw themselves as the earthly representatives of the semi-divine Ṛṣis of old, sought to weave themselves and their rituals into the system of political power controlled by the ruling warrior class. And so, they began talking about the ritual grounds of the fire sacrifice as a metaphorical field of battle—if you performed well, you would get to make your divine ascent. Mystical poets became metaphorical warriors and vice versa.

Why does this archaic use of the word "yoga" matter to us? For one, it shows the difficulty of assuming that words always mean the same thing. But, at the same time, the use of yoga as a literal yoking and its later meanings with regards to spiritual practice are also not unrelated. What's important about the warrior's ascent, and about the *keśin*'s flight, and even about the mystical knowledge of the Ṛṣis, is their generally worldly nature. These are not examples of transcendence as a dissolution or a cessation of the self. Instead, these are selves that ascended to become superhuman like the gods.

Finding your Self in the woods

It is not until the Upaniṣads—and even there comparatively late and inconsistently—that we see all of these concepts not only come together as associated with the word "yoga" but also with the kind of spiritual liberation that the word might entail today. This final layer of the Vedic textual corpus is typically associated with the late Vedic period, where we find the rise of renouncer traditions aimed at rejecting and even escaping the complementary social and cosmic orders that the Vedic ritual seeks to uphold. The Upaniṣads reflect Vedic culture, and today we would call them "Hindu" (though this label would not exist for many more centuries). In this sense we might say they teach a Brahminical (*brāhmaṇa*) style of renunciation that ultimately reinterprets but does not completely overturn the Vedic social and sacrificial order. Other contemporary renouncer movements, which we call *śramaṇa* ("exerting"), don't concern themselves much with the Vedas at all. The most famous and resilient of these would become what we today call Buddhism and Jainism.

There is debate among scholars as to which of the renouncer traditions emerged first. Certainly we might argue that all of them, regardless of their eventual sectarian affiliations, were responding to the same general social and cultural climate. Early Vedic culture had been nomadic but, from around 500 BCE onward, a second urbanization had begun to build. This occurred in a region referred to as Greater Magadha, located in the northeast of the South Asian subcontinent, actually apart from the heartland of Vedic society, which lay to the northwest of the convergence of the Ganges and Yamuna rivers. The historical Buddha Siddārtha Gautama and Vardhamāna Mahāvīra of Jainism are both thought to have lived in this region sometime in the 6th to 5th century BCE.

Emerging scholarship suggests that the non-Vedic culture of Magadha, marked by its own Indo-European dialect, is proof of a far more complicated dispersal of people and ideas across this area than previously imagined. Scholars have continuously cautioned us against linking language to ethnicity—the *āryas* of the Vedas are not, for instance, a "race" but only those who speak a certain language. Or, even more specifically, a certain variation of a certain language. The distinct culture of the Magadha region suggests that if there was a migration of Indo-European speakers that entered South Asia, this migration happened over a lengthy period of time, in several waves, and produced co-evolving cultures that were not only distinct but sometimes hostile to one another's ways of life.[9]

Most recently, the scholar Johannes Bronkhorst has argued that some of the most distinctive features that we now associate with Indic religions, namely the belief in a cycle of reincarnation (*saṃsāra*) and the role of actions and their effects to trap us in that cycle (*karma*), have their origins in the non-Vedic culture of Magadha. Past scholars have assumed that Buddhism and Jainism emerged as "protest movements" against the dominant norms of Vedic Brahminical sacrifice culture. Bronkhorst tells us that Buddhists and Jains were actually building on distinct features of belief current in Magadha at the time, and that Brahminical asceticism should be placed alongside these as another (specifically Vedic-based) way of solving the same problems.

In this context, if you believed that the never-ending cycle of *saṃsāra* was a problem and that worldly desire, action, and their results were its cause, then you had a couple of options. The first and most straightforward option was to simply stop acting. On the other hand, you could assert that the true Self was fundamentally inactive, and therefore beyond *karma* and the cycle of rebirth. In this case, it was necessary only to realize the nature of this true Self and your identity with it.[10] Early Jain texts suggest a preference for the first option. If one does not wish to be reborn, one must seek to bring an end to all activity, both physical and mental. This could be done through a variety of ascetic (keeping the body very still, abstaining from food, stilling the breath, and so on) and meditative (stilling the mind) practices, which would have the dual effect of not producing any further *karma* and of rendering any previously accrued *karma* ineffective.[11] Early Brahminical solutions likewise privilege inactivity when it comes to meditation, but do notably emphasize knowledge of the true Self in other contexts. James Mallinson, a philologist studying later, medieval traditions of yoga has also suggested that many of the techniques we associate with these traditions actually developed much earlier—in fact, precisely among these original *śramaṇa* renouncer movements—but were passed on orally, explaining why we don't find them in contemporary texts. These techniques include a variety of methods for building up *tapas*, including those specifically targeted towards preserving sexual energy by retaining the semen.[12]

And so, we have a mix of competing techniques, some quite physical (these usually being called "*tapas*" rather than "yoga"), others more psychological, clustering around two potential ways of viewing the world—again: one is either already free and must simply realize it, or else one must work very hard to become free. Buddhism presents an interesting case insofar as it takes these two solutions and uses them to reframe the problem. For Buddhists, it is not karmic action itself that is the problem, but the driving cause behind it. This cause is desire or "thirst" (*tṛṣṇā*) and one cannot be free until one eliminates it, regardless of how one acts (or doesn't act) or what one knows about one's Self (the Buddhists, in any case, do not believe that such an eternal and pure Self exists).[13] For this reason, early Buddhist meditation differed from what Bronkhorst has argued counted as "mainstream meditation." Whereas mainstream meditation, as it appears in early Jain and Brahminical sources, was aimed at a straightforward stilling of the mind (inactivity), Buddhist meditation depended on the cultivation of insight that led to a specific mental disposition. The Buddhist method eventually comes to integrate the ascetic and knowledge paths in its own distinct way, and one which would come to greatly influence the formulation of classical yoga.[14] Notably, though, neither the early Buddhists nor their Jain counterparts refer to their practice as "yoga." Insofar as the practice is meditative, the preferred word in Pāli is *jhāna* (Sanskrit: *dhyāna*). Buddhist texts frequently enumerate four meditative states or *jhānas*.

The renouncer traditions of the time are certainly a response to these existential concerns, but also to a novel social climate. The "going off into the forest" (*vanaprastha*, Figure 5.2) model of spiritual seeking, which is eventually incorporated as the final stage of a "proper" Brahminical social life, makes more sense in an urban society than it does in a pastoral one. Urbanization would have drastically changed the traditional

Figure 5.2 An ascetic and his forest hut. India, Mewar, ca. 1720.

Source: Courtesy of the Smithsonian Institute, Arthur M. Sackler Gallery, Catherine and Ralph Benkaim Collection.

way of life for many residents of Greater Magadha, and the neighboring Vedic culture with its nomadic roots appears to have been skeptical of city life from the start.[15]

It's tempting to view the renouncer movements as a sort of counterculture, and perhaps there is some truth to this. Amidst the growing chaos of urban life, it is not surprising that the forest is idealized as a place of escape. The life stories of sectarian founders such as the Buddha and Mahāvīra, both born into the wealthy ruling classes only to turn their backs on privilege and luxury to seek wisdom in the wilderness, certainly add to this narrative. At the same time, we should be cautious of taking the solitary hermit in the woods too literally. Even hermitages require resources. The monastic traditions of Buddhism and Jainism demonstrate the ultimately social and institutional nature of these movements. The support of kings, which was often predicated on what services (either literal or symbolic) ascetics could offer to the state in return, largely decided which renouncer communities would survive and thrive. This suggests that renouncer movements may have been seen not as countercultural, but as solving some of their culture's most pressing big-picture problems.

For Vedic society, a cultural climate where rebirth and karmic consequence were increasingly accepted realities meant that the old model of the sacrifice was now of limited use. Good ritual *karma* might win you a trip to the celestial realms but, in a cyclical model of rebirth, this sojourn was only temporary. Not all proponents of the Brahminical model immediately accepted this new vision, but the Upaniṣads are an example of how it was negotiated by those who did.

The *varṇa-āśrama-dharma* system

In ancient Vedic society, *dharma*, or one's rightful duty, was understood in social as well as in cosmic terms. Or, perhaps more accurately, the social was cosmic. In the grander sense, *dharma* is not only an individual duty, it's order in general. As we mentioned earlier, the Cosmic Man of the *Ṛg Veda* draws a direct correspondence between the human and the cosmic, and his story is that of primordial sacrifice. The ritual of sacrifice (*yajña*) was thus a way of mediating between these two levels of reality. On a fundamental level, one's *dharma* centered on one's role in this sacrificial order and, in practical terms, this translated to one's role in the resulting order of society.

Dharma is a complex topic, akin to something like "political philosophy," and there are entire bodies of literature dedicated to it throughout Indian history. For our purposes, though, it's enough to list a few of its major principles. As a man, your *dharma* was largely determined by two major aspects of your identity: your social class (*varṇa*) and the current stage of your life (*āśrama*). Women had their own *dharma*, which was largely centered on the idea of acting in service to the man on whom they were currently dependent: their father, husband, or son.

Varṇa, literally translated as "color" (though not to be confused with anything like our modern notion of race), referred to a person's inherent nature. But this, again, needs to be understood in "big picture" terms—one's individual nature is very much a function of one's place in the natural order, and vice versa. The four *varṇas* were understood to emerge from the various body parts of that same Cosmic Man: the *brāhmaṇas* or Priests emerged from his head; the *kṣatriyas* or ruling Warriors emerged from his arms; the *vaiśyas*, the People or the "productive" class, emerged from his thighs, and the *śūdras* or Servants emerged from his feet. In this sense, then, they were more or less sewn into the fabric of the universe. The first three classes were considered "twice-born," meaning they were born both in a literal sense and then, in adolescence, born into the world of *dharma* through ritual initiation. Meaning, they had a place in and a direct obligation to maintaining the cosmic sacrificial order. The Servants did not have a direct obligation to the *dharma* of sacrifice, but rather their duty was to serve the other classes in fulfilling theirs. It's worth noting that the *varṇa* system is related to but not identical with the idea of "caste." Caste, usually a translation of *jāti* (birth), is an incredibly complicated socio-economic framework that, among other things, also includes "untouchable" (*dalit*, "the oppressed") classes of people who would have been considered complete outsiders to the Vedic order, lower than even the Servants.

Āśrama represented a man's particular stage in life. First, there was that of the celibate student, or *brahmacarya*, where he acquired the training appropriate to his *varṇa*. Next came the life of a householder, or *gṛhastha*, defined by marriage, children, and the fulfillment of all other social obligations of his *varṇa*. Eventually, he entered *vānaprastha* or retirement into the woods, where, released from his social obligations, he could undertake the simple life of a hermit. And finally, at the very end of his days, he would enter *saṃnyāsa*, or a life of full renunciation, and become a wandering ascetic.

Now, it's worth noting that some scholars have suggested the *āśramas* were originally understood as alternatives for how to live one's life, rather than progressive lifestages.[16] This should be considered alongside the traditional goals of Vedic society where, along with *dharma*, a man would have also pursued *artha* (prosperity) and *kāma* (pleasure). Eventually, the ultimate goal of all human existence is declared to be liberation or *mokṣa*, to be pursued in earnest during the latter stages of one's life once all social obligations have been fulfilled. In this sense, we might consider how organizing the *aśramas* into progressive stages and relegating the pursuit of liberation from *karma* (which, in the Vedic order was primarily ritual action, but by extension also referred to all action that maintained the material world) to the end of one's life might have reflected an attempt to reconcile *brāhmaṇa* (Brahminical Vedic) and *śramaṇa* (non-Vedic renunciant) viewpoints.

Yoking in the Upaniṣads

The earliest Upaniṣads are thought to have been composed (not all at the same time) between the 5th century BCE and the 1st century CE. In them, we see the beginning of a worldview that bridges the old language of the sacrifice with the new concerns of liberation from *saṃsāra*. This happens primarily through knowledge of the true Self (*ātman*), which is in one way or another related to an ultimate and unchanging reality called either the *paramātman* ("highest Self") or *brahman* (literally translated, something like "the expansion"). Knowledge of this Self and its nature is revealed to be the true meaning of the sacrifice. If the priests of the past had made the sacrificial grounds a stand-in for the warrior's ascent into the realm of the gods, the composers of the Upaniṣads added yet another layer. The sacrificial rite of the fire was itself a metaphor for the internal recognition of the *ātman*. By the transitive property, then, this knowledge could be called "yoga."

The Upaniṣads in which this term appears make the connection between the old order of the sacrificial rite and the new path of ascetic practice and liberating insight quite explicitly. For example, the second section of the *Śvetāśvatara Upaniṣad* begins with Savitṛ, a Vedic god sometimes associated with the sun, yoking his mind and extending his thoughts to bring fire and light down to earth. It then proceeds to parallel this to human beings who yoke their minds to the gods to make their offering and identifies the sacrificial ground as the place where the mind is born. Finally, it brings in the physical practice of keeping the body straight and erect, while drawing the senses and the mind into the heart (established throughout the Upaniṣads as the dwelling place of *ātman*) and suppressing the breath along with all bodily movement. This is the activity of yoking. A body thus tempered by the "fire of yoga" (*yoga-agni*) is said to be beyond sickness, suffering, and old age and is instead endowed with health, lightness, and purity. But this is only the first step—once the "yoked one" (*yukta*) recognizes, by virtue of this own Self (*ātman*), the nature of *brahman*, then he is freed from all fetters.

Elsewhere in the Upaniṣads, we can locate concepts that eventually become central to yoga philosophy and practice. The *Kaṭha Upaniṣad*, for instance, introduces us to the famous chariot metaphor (discussed in Chapter 2) that reveals the inner workings of the mind. The *Śvetāśvatara Upaniṣad* (2.9) echoes this image when it declares that the practitioner should control his mind like he would a chariot yoked to unruly horses. The *Taittirīya Upaniṣad* largely consists of discussions of what will eventually become the five bodily frames (*kośas*; food, life-breath, mind, understanding, and bliss) of Vedānta philosophy, the role of the life-breath or *prāṇā*, and asceticism (*tapas*) as a means to the realization of *brahman* (see especially *Taittirīya Upaniṣad* 3.1–6). Finally, the *Chāndogya Upaniṣad* (8.6) discusses the correspondence between the channels (*nāḍīs*) of the heart and the rays of the sun, along which the mind can travel. At death, if one rises up along these rays with the sound of "*oṃ*" on his mind, he can pass all the way through the door of the sun to the hidden world. Here we meet with a verse that is also quoted in the *Kaṭha Upaniṣad* (6.16): "One hundred and one are the channels (*nāḍīs*) of the heart. One of them runs through the crown of the head. Going up by it, he reaches the immortal. The others, in their ascent, spread out in all directions."[17]

If this all seems rather complicated and full of mixed metaphors, then we're on the right track. In fact, an entire classical school of philosophy—Vedānta, which literally means the "end" or "culmination" (*anta*) of the Vedas—evolved to interpret and reconcile the seemingly diverse perspectives on reality that can be found in the Upaniṣads. For our purposes, it's enough to observe that the Upaniṣads really are trying to string together a lot of different things. And so, we begin to find some tenuous continuity emerging between the things that get called "yoga." Yoga, in one way or another, is about preparing oneself to go upwards and onwards—rising up, as through the rays of the sun, to reach the immortal. However, just like the rites of the fire, this journey is increasingly understood in a figurative rather than literal sense. To go upwards really means to go inwards.

It's important to remember that, insofar as we see any physical practices described with relation to yoga in the Upaniṣads, these practices are overwhelmingly of the ascetic variety. On this level, the yoga of the Upaniṣads is consistent with the *jhāna/dhyāna* meditation-oriented practices of contemporary non-Vedic *śramaṇa* movements (though these are, for the most part, not yet being called yoga). Moreover, diverse as they may be in their contents, the Upaniṣads do have an overarching theme. This theme is the exposition of the true nature of the Self (*ātman*) and its relationship to the eternal *brahman*. For this reason, they give us a fairly limited perspective on what yoga looks like at large.

Then there is the problem that, to the extent that we can date the Upaniṣads at all, even the oldest set crops up over the course of an entire millennium. For instance, the *Bṛhadāranyaka* and *Chāndogya Upaniṣads* are usually dated to somewhere between the 8th and 6th century BCE, and are therefore considered to possibly predate surviving *śramaṇa* schools such as Buddhism. On the other hand, the *Kaṭha Upaniṣad* is usually dated to the 3rd century BCE and the *Śvetaśvātara Upaniṣad* may be even later. Then there is the *Maitrī* (or *Maitrāyaṇīya*) *Upaniṣad*, which contains the most elaborate depiction of yoga, including a "six-limbed" method, but is dated well into the 1st millennium of the Common Era. In the next three sections, then, we will look at three "classical" examples that are all roughly contemporaneous with the Upaniṣadic period, representing the variety of approaches to yoga circulating around at this time.

Patañjali's threads of yoga

The first of these texts is usually referred to as the *Yoga Sūtras* and is attributed to a quasi-mythic sage named Patañjali. *Sūtra* translates to something like "string" or "thread" and describes a genre of South Asian literature that is written in the form of short aphoristic phrases. The *Yoga Sūtras* themselves are a composition of 195 such phrases, broken up into four sections. However, for their entire recorded history, the *Yoga Sūtras* have been part of a larger text called the *Yoga-Śāstra* ("The Treatise on Yoga"), which includes the *sūtras* as well as the *bhāṣya* ("Commentary") by another author named Vyāsa.

Vyāsa's commentary has profoundly shaped how the *Yoga Sūtras* have historically been understood, and with good reason. Imagine that, instead of being able to listen to a lecture, you were handed a set of "bullet point" notes the speaker made to keep herself on track. Now imagine having to reconstruct the lecture, which you never heard, from these notes. That's what reading the *Yoga Sūtras* would be like without Vyāsa's commentary. Vyāsa was not the last person to interpret the text but

Edwin Bryant, who has compiled the oldest and most influential commentaries, has described the situation this way:

> So when we speak of the philosophy of Patañjali, what we really mean (or should mean) is the understanding of Patañjali according to Vyāsa: It is Vyāsa who determined what Patañjali's abstruse sutras meant, and all subsequent commentators elaborated on Vyāsa. While, on occasion, modern scholarship has insightfully questioned whether Vyāsa has accurately represented Patañjali in all instances, for the Yoga tradition itself, his commentary becomes as canonical as Patañjali's (in fact, a number of traditional sources identify Vyāsa as none other than Patañjali himself). Indeed, the Vyāsa *bhāṣya* (commentary) becomes inseparable from the *sūtras*, an extension of it (such that on occasion commentators differ as to whether a line belongs to the commentary or the primary text). From one *sūtra* of a few words, Vyāsa might write several lines of comment without which the *sūtra* remains incomprehensible. It cannot be overstated that Yoga philosophy is Patañjali's philosophy as understood and articulated by Vyāsa.[18]

In fact, Vyāsa's role is so crucial that it has led modern scholars to likewise propose that the *sūtras* and the commentary are a unified work belonging to a single author, which should be dated sometime between 325 and 425 CE.[19]

In this context, it's worth considering the full title of this work: the *Pātañjala-Yoga-Śāstra-Sāṅkhya-Pravacana* ("the authoritative exposition of yoga that originates with Patañjali, the mandatory Sāṅkhya teaching").[20] The *Yoga Sūtras* are today frequently regarded as a practice manual. This is not entirely off-base since the text (especially when taken together with the commentary) does contain far more practical details than anything we're encountered so far. However, all in all, the *Yoga Sūtras* are a philosophical project and the philosophical vision they advance is that of the Sāṅkhya school.

The connection between the Yoga and Sāṅkhya, which are often regarded as sister schools among the six classical schools of Indian philosophy, is profound and long-standing. Sāṅkhya is the intellectual (knowledge-based) counterpart of the practical (asceticism and meditation-based) yoga, and vice versa. Technically, these are two independent paths and they roughly correspond to the two options for liberation that we discussed earlier. To rid yourself of *karma* and its effects, you can either cease to act, or you can realize that your true Self is fundamentally beyond action.[21] We might then regard the *Yoga Sūtras* as an attempt to combine these two ideas. You engage in ascetic practice—specifically in stilling the mind—precisely so that you *can* recognize your truly inactive Self.

The *Yoga Sūtras* also show us the fuller context in which such ascetic "yoking" practices existed. By this point in time, it is a well-known fact that asceticism potentially accomplishes two things: (1) it builds up heat (*tapas*) to power superhuman feats, up to and including complete mastery over the natural world; (2) it stops the building up of *karma* (the seeds of action) through inaction, the effort of which also destroys any that were previously accrued. Contemporary Indian literature (to say nothing of folklore) is full of ascetics, both heroic and sinister, performing acts of *tapas* to gain all sorts of superhuman abilities. Often these are rewards ("boons") from the gods, who are pleased by this effort. Other times, the powers seem to manifest on their own. Historians of yoga have typically focused on the second liberatory effect of yogic practice. However, the first effect, even when it is not the final goal, is an important and nearly universally accepted staple of what it means to be a yogi. For this reason, the entire third section of the *Yoga Sūtras* is devoted to a discussion of *vibhūti* (literally something like "omni-presencing"), which basically amounts to an impressive list of superpowers. These include everything from making oneself infinitely small or large, flight, and knowing (as well as influencing) the minds of others.

Such powers are in fact perfectly consistent with and indeed baked into the overall vision of the world upon which the *Yoga Sūtras* (and by extension Sāṅkhya philosophy) rely. In this case, the vision is fundamentally dualistic, which differentiates it from some other systems of yoga, but the effect with regards to powers is generally the same. The goal of the *Yoga Sūtras* is to extract the Self—which, following Sāṅkhya terminology it prefers to call *puruṣa* (person)—from *prakṛti* or nature. As *puruṣa*'s awareness moves through the various layers of *prakṛti*, the mind through which this awareness is reflected gains an understanding of the ultimate structure of reality, both gross and subtle, becoming ever more expansive until it eventually transcends the physical and psychological limitations of its individual identity.[22] Sort of like reverse-engineering and "hacking" the system. It's also worth pointing out that it is the mind and not *puruṣa* itself that is thus capable of (and interested in) pervading all of material reality and bending it to its will. The mind, however, like the rest of *prakṛti*, is ultimately inert. As we've said previously, if physical matter is the hardware, the mind is the software, but *puruṣa* is the ghost in the machine of *prakṛti*. It is the conscious observer, and *prakṛti* is only the object that is being observed. Once the mind traces *puruṣa*'s sentient awareness back to its true source, it separates *puruṣa* from its false identification with *prakṛti*, and the conscious Self emerges into isolation and complete freedom.

This journey to isolation is achieved by following a series of eight steps or "limbs," hence the reason this method is sometimes called *aṣṭāṅga* (*aṣṭa* [eight]-*aṅga* [limb]) yoga. The limbs, enumerated in *Yoga Sūtras* 2.29, are as follows:

(1) Rules (*yama*): non-violence (*ahimsā*); truthfulness (*satya*); not stealing (*asteya*); celibacy (*brahmacarya*); renunciation (*aparigraha*)
(2) Observances (*niyama*): cleanliness (*śauca*); contentment (*santoṣa*); austerities (*tapas*); scriptural study (*svādhyāya*); devotion to God (*īśvarapraṇidhāna*)
(3) Posture (*āsana*)
(4) Breath-control (*prāṇāyāma*)
(5) Withdrawal (*pratyāhāra*)
(6) Fixation (*dhāraṇa*)
(7) Meditation (*dhyāna*)
(8) Completion (*samādhi*)

A reasonable point of comparison for the rules (*yamas*) might be the vows (such as chastity, poverty, and obedience) taken by monastics in the Catholic tradition.

Meaning, although a couple of these, like telling the truth and not stealing other people's stuff are good advice for everyone, the others (like celibacy) are things that differentiate the yogi from a typical householder. These are strict rules that indicate dedication to a specific lifestyle, like the vows of a monk or a nun. The *Yoga Sūtras* basically label them as such, declaring that these are the "great vow" (*mahā-vrata*; *Yoga Sūtras* 2.31). Notably, the first *yama* of non-violence (*ahimsā*), which the commentators single out as the most important, forms the cornerstone of Jain monasticism and the Jains use precisely the same term, *mahā-vrata*, to refer to their vows . The original intent of the bodily practices, posture (*āsana*) and breath-control (*prāṇāyāma*), was most likely absolute stillness. Though the *sūtras* specify only that the posture should be steady and comfortable, Vyāsa names eleven different poses, with the suggestion that others exist. These, to the extent that they are described, are all seated postures suitable for meditation.[23] Withdrawal (*pratyāhāra*), which refers to the direction of the senses, caps off the "external" limbs. The final three steps are regarded as "internal," dealing with the processes of the mind.

In light of all this, another key feature of the *Yoga Sūtras* is the text's relationship to Buddhist theory and practice. Specifically, the *sūtras* show a high level of overlap with contemporary Buddhist sources when it comes to concepts and language, especially when discussing the prescribed meditative process itself.[24] Though Patañjali issues, at the very outset, a very simple definition of the ultimate state of yoga—*yogaś-citta-vṛtti-nirodhaḥ*, "yoga is the suppression of the fluctuations of the mind"—the process of getting to this state turns out to be far more complicated. This is in large part due to an attempt to integrate Buddhist theories of cognition (especially the notion of the four *jhānas/dhyānas*, or stages of meditation) with Sāṅkhyan philosophy of mind. An especially important point of contact is with the Yogācāra (literally "Yoga-Practice") school of Buddhism. Yogācāra is heavily invested in meditation and therefore the cognitive structure of the mind, and its origins fall into roughly the same time period as the composition of the *Yoga Sūtras*. In his analysis of Patañjali's *sūtras*, Pradeep Gokhale argues that Buddhism is in fact the primary influence behind the text's content, behind that of Sāṅkhya and Jainism.[25]

For a number of reasons, then, it's important to remember that the *Yoga Sūtras* never claim to be the original teaching on yoga. In its very first verse, the text declares itself as *anuśāsana*, a continuation of instruction. In order to better understand Patañjali's method, we need to put it in the context of the traditions that likely preceded it.

Epic heroes and "The Song of the Blessed One"

The other major place we see yoga (and Sāṅkhya) crop up during this time period is in the epic of the *Mahābhārata*, "The Great Tale of the Bhāratas." Along with the *Rāmāyaṇa* ("The Story of Rāma"), the *Mahābhārata* is one of the two principal Sanskrit epics. The *Rāmāyaṇa* does not feature as much in the way of yoga, though the villain of the piece, the demonic king Rāvaṇa, does acquire most of his superpowers by performing *tapas*. Likewise, some scholars have pointed to the epic's protagonist, Rāma, as balancing two types of ideal king, the warrior and the sagely renouncer.[26] The *Mahābhārata* is quite a bit longer than the *Rāmāyaṇa* and was likely compiled in parts over a considerable span of time. It's likely that both of the epics precede the *Yoga Sūtras*—they are generally thought to have reached their complete form by the 2nd to 3rd century CE.

All of this means that the varieties of yoga represented in the *Mahābhārata* are potentially quite diverse. The epic is, among other things, the story of a war between two sets of cousins, the Pāṇḍavas and the Kauravas, both belonging to the great dynasty of Bharata. In this martial context, it is not surprising that we see some of the oldest meanings of yoga re-emerge. In several places, the yoga of the *Mahābhārata* is very much a yoga of the dying chariot warrior's glorious ascent up through the disk of the sun.[27] However, the epic also includes accounts of yoga as *dhyāna*, and *tapas*,[28] as well as the yoga of superpowers that allows the practitioner to enter into or possess the bodies and minds of others.[29]

But arguably the most famous account of yoga in the *Mahābhārata* is the *Bhagavad Gītā*, or "The Song of the Blessed One." The *Gītā*, which is often extracted as a stand-alone text, occurs in the sixth section of the epic. It begins just as the two great armies have finally come to face off on the field of battle. Suddenly, the Pāṇḍava hero Arjuna, loses his nerve. Confronted with the prospect of fighting against his family members and his teachers, he despairs and turns to renunciation. Luckily, Arjuna's friend and charioteer, Kṛṣṇa is there to talk him through this moment of crisis. Arjuna doesn't know it yet, but his friend also happens to be an incarnation of the supreme god Viṣṇu and an embodiment of *brahman* itself. And so, in the midst of the battlefield, Kṛṣṇa launches into an explanation of the nature of the Self, of duty (*dharma*), and of the paths to liberation.

Key to Kṛṣṇa's message is the notion of the Self that does not act. In fact, this is his first pitch in answer to Arjuna's despair in the face of killing his family. The true Self neither kills nor is killed. Of course, in addition to finding the matter emotionally taxing, Arjuna's also concerned that killing his family might lead to some bad *karma*. On this count, Kṛṣṇa rejects the path of total inaction outright, declaring that it is not only inferior but actually impossible. Instead, the way to stop the buildup of *karma* is to acquire the proper mental disposition—an attitude of non-attachment to the fruits of one's actions. He identifies two ancient paths, the "yoga of knowing" (*jñāna* yoga) practiced by followers of Sāṅkhya and the "yoga of doing" (*karma* yoga) practiced by the yogis, declaring that Sāṅkhya and yoga ultimately amount to the same thing.

Here, the *Gītā*'s big transformative move is to argue that the yoga of doing does not actually amount to a cessation of action via austerities and renunciation. In fact, it is quite the opposite. To perform *karma* yoga is to act according to one's social *dharma*, but with the aforementioned cognitive shift to non-attachment. The method of achieving this equanimous state (which the text refers to as *dhyāna* yoga, or meditative yoga) is not so different from what we find in the *Yoga Sūtras* and certain sections of the Upaniṣads. One should observe certain basic vows and austerities and practice by remaining still, with the body erect, the senses drawn inwards, and work on focusing and quieting the mind to bring it to awareness of the Self (*ātman*).

However, it's worth noting that even as the *Gītā*'s project is religious, it is also somewhat political. Secure in the knowledge of the true Self, one's body and mind, which are not the Self, can continue on in discharging their social duties. There is no need to renounce society on a literal level, as the *śramaṇa* movements might argue. Instead, proper renunciation means that one "Selflessly" resigns one's body and mind to fulfill their proper roles.[30]

Furthermore, insofar as the *Gītā*'s project is religious, it is also theistic—that is, there's a personal God in the equation—and it's sectarian. The God in question is Kṛṣṇa (or Viṣṇu, as he reveals his universal form). And thus the path that the *Gītā* ultimately prescribes as superior to all others is devotion (*bhakti*). This path absorbs all others—you can devote yourself to Kṛṣṇa by fixing your mind and meditating on him or simply offering up the fruits of your actions to him. You can even choose the old-fashioned path of meditating on the unmanifest reality of *brahman*, though Kṛṣṇa warns this is more difficult, and still attain him as the ultimate goal. In all cases, the best yoga is the yoga that yokes you to Kṛṣṇa.

But this is where things get interesting. In establishing himself as the supreme *brahman*, Kṛṣṇa reveals that he has a special yoga of his own. He is the supreme Self who pervades and manifests (*vibhūti*) the entire cosmos, including all beings. The careful reader might have spotted that the Sanskrit word used here is the same one that the *Yoga Sūtras* use to describe the powers of yogis on their way to full Self-realization.

Here it's worth noting that the word *bhakti*, which we normally translate as "devotion," comes from the verbal root √*bhaj*, the primary sense of which is "to divide, distribute, or share." Taking this into account, the kind of attachment that *bhakti* signifies carries with it a sense of being a part of, being contained within, and partaking in. Kṛṣṇa's speech in the *Gītā* does not explicitly suggest the kind of full identification and oneness with the deity (in this case, himself) that we will see in the next chapter of this book. Indeed, Kṛṣṇa and Viṣṇu-focused traditions have been a bit more resistant to the idea of this kind of "merging" than some others. But historically the distance between traditions of devotion and traditions of possession (that is, the entering and taking over of a human body by some superhuman being, whether ghost, demon, or deity) has been smaller than one might think. And so has the distinction between both of these concepts and yoga.

Kṛṣṇa's cosmic form, which he reveals to Arjuna in the 11th section of the *Gītā* (Figure 5.3), is an example of what White has referred to as the parallel phenomena of the "deification" or "cosmi-fication" of Indic yogis one the one hand and the "yogi-fication" of Indic deities on the other.[31] Meaning, yogis became an example of humans functioning like cosmic gods and the powers of gods were explained through the mechanics of yoga. Which happened first is still up for debate and may in fact be somewhat of a "chicken and egg" question. We will see quite a bit more of this in Chapter 6, but for now it's worth remarking that this idea of humans being identified with or having influence over the cosmos is not entirely new, nor is it unique. We saw this same kind of logic at the height of the Vedic rites of fire, and the idea of the microcosm/macrocosm relationship, or the link between big and little worlds, is something that crops up across cultures (as we saw in Chapters 2

Figure 5.3 Kṛṣṇa's *viśvarūpa* or all-pervading form, evoking the idea of the Cosmic Man. India, Himachal Pradesh, Bilaspur, ca. 1740.

Source: Courtesy of the Smithsonian Institute, Arthur M. Sackler Gallery, Catherine and Ralph Benkaim Collection.

and 3). Nevertheless, especially when one gets into specifics, the version(s) of it that we see here is both particular to the Indic context and increasingly associated with the word yoga.

The four (?) yogas of the *Bhagavad Gītā*

It's commonly repeated today that in the *Bhagavad Gītā*, Kṛṣṇa teaches four yogas: *jñāna*, *karma*, *bhakti*, and *rāja*. In this context, *rāja* yoga is usually equated with the method of Patañjali's *Yoga Sūtras*. Unfortunately, this is somewhat of a misconception—Kṛṣṇa never actually prescribes a yoga he refers to as "rāja." The equivalency between *rāja* yoga and Pātañjala yoga was first hinted at by Western writers belonging to the Theosophical Society in the late 19th century and was finally cemented by Swami Vivekananda in his famous book *Rāja Yoga* (1896).[32] *Rāja* (literally, "kingly") yoga does not crop up as a distinct term until sometime during the 11th century and is then used to signify "the best yoga"—most often it refers directly to the final stage of yoga, that is *samādhi*.[33] So, what yogas does Kṛṣṇa teach in the *Gītā*? And why the confusion?

Here, it's important to remember that, aside from its theistic concerns (in the *Gītā*, *bhakti* yoga is definitely the best yoga), the *Bhagavad Gītā* is also very interested in upholding the social order of *dharma*. As we saw earlier, renunciatory traditions might have been seen as a threat to this order given that, by definition, they often advocated leaving behind society. The *Gītā* also finds itself somewhat at a crossroads when it comes to the shape of mainstream religious practice. Older Vedic *brāhmaṇa* religion was centered on the ritual of the fire sacrifice. The sacrifice, as we've seen, structured all of society, including social class. *Dharma*, or social duty, then meant playing one's proper role in the sacrificial culture. One did this through *karma*, which referred specifically to ritual action or *yajña*. In the *śramaṇa* traditions, whose goal was *mokṣa* or liberation from the cycle of *saṃsāra*, on the other hand, *karma* (that is, action of any kind) was a bad thing insofar as it kept you trapped in said cycle. The means for getting rid of *karma* was increasingly referred to as yoga. So, let's review:

	Brāhmaṇa	*Śramaṇa*
Goal	*dharma*	*mokṣa*
Mechanism	*karma*	*~~karma~~*
Method	*yajña* (sacrifice)	yoga

Now, consider the following lines from the *Gītā* (4.25–32), as delivered by Kṛṣṇa: "Some yogis sacrifice to a god, while others sacrifice through sacrifice itself in the fire of *brahman*. Others offer the senses, like hearing, in the fire of restrain, while still others offer the sense objects, like sound, into the fire of the senses." He goes on to enumerate many kinds of sacrifice—of material objects, of austerities, of knowledge, of offering breath into breath—before concluding that "thus, there are many kinds of sacrifice spread out before *brahman*. Know them all to be born of action (*karma*) and, so knowing, you'll be liberated."[34] Do you notice what Kṛṣṇa's done? All of these actions are sacrifice, and all of these sacrificers are yogis. And if, effectively, sacrifice = yoga, then there is no conflict between the *brāhmaṇa* and *śramaṇa* positions.

Through the act of sacrifice, *karma* (rather than being antithetical to yoga) becomes yoga. Specifically, Kṛṣṇa argues, offering the fruits of one's action as a sacrifice is a kind of yoga. *Karma* is good because it leads to *dharma*, but the yogic act of sacrifice frees you from *karma*'s effects, which leads to *mokṣa*. It's an ingenious way to yoke the Vedic ideology of sacrifice, the social interests of *dharma*, and the *śramaṇa* goals of liberation into a single team of concepts and then put Kṛṣṇa at the head. But of course there's quite a bit of ideological scaffolding that goes into this move, which is where the different types of yoga that the *Gītā* recognizes become relevant. In fact, the *Gītā* teaches a rather long list of yogas (remember, one of the main points is that nearly anything can be classified as yoga), but one 16th-century commentator named Madhusūdana Sarasvati subdivides the *Gītā*'s chapters into thirds, covering three types of yoga: *jñāna*, *karma*, and *bhakti*.[35] If we read the *Gītā* with this lens, we might say that the yogas break down as follows:

(1) *Jñāna* yoga: knowing that the true Self is inactive and therefore not subject to the effects of *karma*
(2) *Karma* yoga: performing one's *karma* with the mental attitude that its fruits do not belong to one's true Self
(3) *Bhakti* yoga: offering up oneself and the fruits of one's actions to Kṛṣṇa

Now, what's missing from this framework is how one gets from the first point, which entails a kind of intellectual knowing, to the second point where one must act with a disposition based on this knowledge. Recall that in order to achieve this disposition of detachment, Kṛṣṇa tells Arjuna to practice *dhyāna* or meditation. In fact, the more we read the *Gītā*, the more we realize that the practice of fixing the mind through *dhyāna* seems to underly Kṛṣṇa's argument that all of these things can function as yoga. Notably, it's still quite an interpretive leap to call this "*rāja* yoga" or to equate it fully with Patañjali's method.

So does the *Gītā* teach four yogas? Yes and no. No, in the sense that technically it teaches far more than four, and none of these are ever really grouped together or otherwise organized in a very systematic way. *Jñāna*, *karma*, and *bhakti* yoga do appear but not very often and never together. *Rāja* is absent completely. On the other hand, insofar as later commentators and interpreters (and we shouldn't dismiss Vivekananda as an interpreter just because he's a bit more modern) have read the text this way, the idea of the four yogas has become part of the *Gītā*'s tradition.

Yoga for God's sake

The Kṛṣṇa-oriented yoga of the *Bhagavad Gītā* is not a unique phenomenon. In the Upaniṣads, even if we're only looking at the ones that mention yoga, we can already find connections being made to one deity or another—usually either Viṣṇu (or Nārāyaṇa) or Śiva (or Rudra). Alongside these, of course, we also have the developing traditions of Jainism and Buddhism, with their Tīrthaṅkaras ("Ford-Makers") and their Bodhisattvas ("Awakened Beings"). The latter are not quite gods, but because of this are particularly good examples of the connection we made between the powers of gods and yogis at the end of the previous section. In any case, the language of yoga is increasingly in vogue here as well.

Within the Hindu fold, if we want to counterbalance the Viṣṇu-centric yoga of the *Bhagavad Gītā*, we might look to the doctrines and practices of the Pāśupatas. The Pāśupatas, ascetic devotees of Śiva, are mentioned in the *Mahābhārata* and therefore are at least as old if not older than the *bhakti* yoga of Kṛṣṇa. Both of these takes on yoga, therefore, notably precede Patañjali. Pāśupata-style renunciation was also quite a bit more antisocial than the duty-driven offering up of karmic fruits advocated by the *Gītā*. Following in Śiva's footsteps, Pāśupatas would adopt a lifestyle of wandering, smeared with ashes and carrying a skull begging bowl. This was supported by the origin myth of the sect, which tells of Śiva possessing the corpse of a young Brahmin in the cremation grounds. The revived body becomes Lakulīśa ("Lord of the Club"), who delivers the foundational teachings of the sect, eventually set down as the *Pāśupata Sūtras*.

The Pāśupata doctrine consisted of five basic elements: (1) *paśu*: beast/sacrificial victim, representing the individual soul; (2) *pati*: the Lord, specifically Śiva; (3) *yoga*: the union of *paśu* and *pati*; (4) *vidhi*: the prescribed method to attain this yoga; and (5) *duḥkhānta*: the end of suffering. Here, the state of yoga or union with Śiva meant that the practitioner became like Śiva himself, a master of the world—not only free but in possession of all the attendant powers, omnipresent, omniscient, and omnipotent.[36] And so, it was liberation that the Pāśupatas and their successors (such as the Lākulas and the Kālāmukhas) put forth as their goal, even though incredible power was certainly the happy side-effect of such a state. The method of their yoga was fundamentally ascetic, formulated in imitation of Śiva himself, as a form of worship. Theirs was the *atimārga*—the higher or outer path, existing outside of normative society but nevertheless concerned with purity and social hierarchy. For instance, only a male person of the Brahmin class, and one who had undergone the appropriate caste-based initiation ceremony, could become a Pāśupata.

Pāśupatas would engage in socially inappropriate behavior, purposefully presenting themselves as though crippled or deranged. However, while a Pāśupata might make lewd gestures at passing women as part of his performance, he was strictly celibate and was in fact instructed to otherwise avoid women's polluting and distracting company.[37] Importantly, this "bad behavior" on the part of the Pāśupatas was, at least at the outset, fundamentally different from the kind of transgressive behavior we find in later tantric traditions. There, a practitioner might engage with typically polluting substances to draw on their inherent power, or else as a demonstration of his spiritual transcendence (after all, to the enlightened mind, the pure and impure are one and the same). The Pāśupata's transgression is instead best understood as a kind of *tapas*. It purifies by way of karmic transference, passing the practitioner's *karma* on to those who mock and otherwise abuse him.

As far as more formal practice was concerned, a Pāśupata's daily regimen involved bathing in ashes—three times a day, and as needed for purification, in the event that he should gaze upon urine or feces, or speak to a woman or a low-caste man. He could also purify himself by means of breath-control and the repetition of certain *mantras*. Besides this, he was to live in or near a temple dedicated to Śiva, and worship Śiva regularly with song, dance, yells, laughter, bows, chants, and other offerings.[38] In addition to these preliminary observances, the Pāśupata method included a standard sort of meditative practice, similar in its general structure to the one we find in Patañjali. The *Vāyu Purāṇa* (dated 7th–10th century CE), for example, lists five "limbs" (though it actually calls them practices, or *dharmas*) of Pāśupata yoga: breath-control (*prāṇāyāma*); meditation (*dhyāna*); withdrawal (*pratyāhāra*); fixation (*dhāraṇa*); and recollection (*smaraṇa*).[39] Importantly, other later sources like the *Skanda Purāṇa* and the *Īśvara Gītā* (both also dated 7th–10th century) seem to describe not simply a stilling, controlling, or transformation of the mind, but the kind of visualization practice that we will see increasingly combined with older physical techniques for cultivating *tapas* by the rising tantric traditions. The practitioner is instructed to assume a seated *āsana* and, moving the breath through the channels of the body, to imagine Śiva, the Supreme Lord, as situated in his own Self. Common meditative imagery includes a light or flame and a lotus, usually located in the heart. The syllable "oṃ" also features prominently.[40]

The Pāśupatas, perhaps quite a bit more so than the *Bhagavad Gītā*, are a good signpost for the direction yoga would take over the course of the 2nd millennium CE. Famous Indologist Alexis Sanderson has gone so far as to dub the period stretching from the 5th to the 13th century of the Common Era the "Śaiva Age."[41] This same span of time would yield the eclectic body of traditions we usually refer to as "tantra," which would in turn prove to be a fertile breeding ground for yoga practice. Unlike the ascetic Pāśupatas, some tantric traditions were far less concerned with purity and far more comfortable with the pursuit of power as its own end. Like the Pāśupatas, however, the Tantras (which are, ultimately, texts) tend to be unapologetically theistic, though it's not always Śiva who winds up being the ultimate of ultimates. It might be Śiva, but it might just as easily be the Goddess, Viṣṇu, a Bodhisattva, or a Tīrthaṅkara (or else his goddess attendant) at the center of the tantric *maṇḍala*. In this sense, the Pāśupatas give us the first explicit instance of an important new meaning of yoga—one that will go on to become extremely popular. Yoga is the union of the individual soul with God.

Many yogas, many limbs

Though we've come to view Patañjali's *aṣṭāṅga* (eight-limbed) system as the golden standard of yoga, there have historically been a great many alternative arrangements. Historically, the auxiliaries of yoga (that is, those elements and practices that lead to the goal of yoga) have numbered everywhere from four to fifteen depending on the text. Alongside the eight-fold systems (of which there are also quite a few, including, for instance, the standard Buddhist "Noble Eight-fold Path"), six-fold systems are by far the most common.[42] *Ṣaḍaṅga* (six-limbed) yogas show up most frequently in Śaiva contexts, but are also found in Vaiṣṇava, Jain, and Buddhist sources.

Śaiva *ṣaḍaṅga* yogas typically include breath control (*prāṇāyāma*), withdrawal (*pratyāhāra*), fixation (*dhāraṇa*), meditation (*dhyāna*), and completion/absorption (*samādhi*), though the order may vary and the elements may be defined differently than in Patañjali's system. The behavioral codes Patañjali calls the *yamas* and *niyamas* usually appear as preliminary practices, while *āsana* is usually absent.[43] Most of these systems also include a limb that tends to be distinctive to the Śaiva context: *tarka*, which is best translated as something like judgement or discrimination. *Tarka* is a standard feature of Indian philosophy, where is it used as a method of deduction to justify certain assumptions and remove doubt. In the context of Śaiva yoga, *tarka* gives the practitioner a means to logically evaluate his progress against the standards established by scripture until he is certain that he has, in fact, arrived at the highest level of attainment.[44]

As we creep past the 7th century of the Common Era and into the new millennium, it is these *ṣaḍaṅga yogas* that arguably prove to be among the most influential. Such systems become a staple in Śaiva tantric texts, where they provide the scaffolding for complex visualizations and subtle body practices. However, we shouldn't underestimate the continuing diversity of yoga traditions nor the variety of contexts in which yogic innovation happens.

Conclusions

- We can find precedents for yogi-like figures in the older Vedic texts by looking at figures like the Ṛṣi poet-mystics or the silent and wandering *muni* ascetics, both of whom are associated with divine visionary experiences. Neither, however, is connected with the term "yoga," which the Vedic hymns tend to use to refer to horse-drawn conveyances, especially war chariots.
- Beginning in 500 BCE, the *śramaṇa* ascetic movements emerge in response to the existential problem of *saṃsāra*, the never-ending (and generally suffering-filled) cycle of rebirth. The fundamental problem is action (*karma*), and so the possible solutions include ceasing all action, realizing that one's true Self (as opposed to one's body and mind) is actually inactive, or else figuring out a way to nullify the effects of action.
- The Upaniṣads, a Vedic response to the problem of *saṃsāra*, attempt to reframe the sacrifice as a metaphor for an internal contemplative process that reveals the true immortal Self. Relying on pre-existing Vedic tropes of heat (the heat of the sacrificial fire, the heat of *tapas*, the heat of the sun), ascension to the heavens, and especially the ascension of divinized warriors on their well-controlled (yoked) war chariots, they call this process "yoga."

- Classical sources show a continuously expanding range of meanings when it comes to yoga, including a variety of elements (auxiliaries or "limbs," *aṅgas*) of which the practice might consist, how its ascetic tendencies might mesh with social concerns of *dharma*, and the role of God.
- We can increasingly associate "yoga" with two potentially (but not necessarily) overlapping terms: *dhyāna* or meditation, and *tapas* or asceticism. Both can be viewed as either cessative or transformative, reflecting either world-negative or world-positive attitudes. That is, *tapas* can be a way of mortifying the body and *dhyāna* can be a way of completely stilling the mind, in order to release the true Self from their bondage. However, *tapas* can also be a way of generating great bodily power, and *dhyāna* can be a visionary practice in which the human becomes divine.

Notes

1 Edwin F. Bryant and Laurie L. Patton, *The Indo-Aryan Controversy: Evidence and Inference in Indian History* (London and New York: Routledge, 2005).
2 David Gordon White, *Sinister Yogis* (Chicago: University of Chicago Press, 2009), 49–54.
3 White, *Sinister Yogis*, 56.
4 *Ṛgveda* 10.136.3; Wendy Doniger, *The Rig Veda: An Anthology* (London: Penguin, 2005), 138 and Karel Werner, "The Longhaired Sage of Rv 10, 136: A Shaman, a Mystic or a Yogi?," in *The Yogi and the Mystic: Studies in Indian and Comparative Mysticism* (London: Curzon, 1989), 143, offer a couple of different translations.
5 Walter O. Kaelber, *Tapta Mārga: Ascetism and Initiation in Vedic India* (Albany: State University of New York Press, 1989), 15–20.
6 Kaelber, *Tapta Mārga*, 64.
7 White, *Sinister Yogis*, 63.
8 White, *Sinister Yogis*, 33, 60.
9 Johannes Bronkhorst, *Greater Magadha: Studies in the Culture of Early India* (Leiden and Boston: Brill, 2007), 265–7.
10 Johannes Bronkhorst, *How the Brahmins Won: From Alexander to the Guptas* (Leiden and Boston: Brill, 2016), 249–50.
11 Bronkhorst, *Greater Magadha*, 24.
12 James Mallinson, "Yoga and Yogis," *Nāmarūpa*, 3, no. 15 (2012): 10–12.
13 Bronkhorst, *Greater Magadha*, 52.
14 Johannes Bronkhorst, *The Two Traditions of Meditation in Ancient India* (Delhi: Motilal Banarsidass Publishers, 2000), 43–50.
15 Bronkhorst, *Greater Magadha*, 251.
16 Johannes Bronkhorst, *The Two Sources of Indian Asceticism* (Delhi: Motilal Banarsidass Publishers, 1998), 21–34.
17 Translation adapted from Patrick Olivelle, *The Early Upaniṣads: Annotated Text and Translation* (Oxford and New York: Oxford University Press, 1998), 279.
18 Edwin F. Bryant, *The Yoga Sutras of Patañjali: A New Edition, Translation, and Commentary: With Insights from the Traditional Commentators* (New York: North Point Press, 2009), xxxviii.
19 Philip A. Maas, "A Concise Historiography of Classical Yoga Philosophy," in *Periodization and Historiography of Indian Philosophy*, ed. Eli Franco, Publications of the De Nobili Research Library 37 (Vienna: Sammlung De Nobili, 2013), 61.
20 Maas, "A Concise Historiography," 58; James Mallinson and Mark Singleton, *Roots of Yoga: A Sourcebook from the Indic Traditions* (London: Penguin Classics, 2017), xvii.

21 Bronkhorst, *How the Brahmins Won*, 250–1.
22 Bryant, *The Yoga Sutras of Patañjali*, 713–14.
23 Bryant, *The Yoga Sutras of Patañjali*, 285–6.
24 Knut A. Jacobsen, ed., *Theory and Practice of Yoga: Essays in Honour of Gerald James Larson* (Boston: Brill, 2005), 12–13.
25 Pradeep P. Gokhale, *The Yogasutra of Patañjali: A New Introduction to the Buddhist Roots of the Yoga System*. (New York and London: Routledge, 2020).
26 Geoffrey Samuel, *The Origins of Yoga and Tantra: Indic Religions to the Thirteenth Century* (Cambridge and New York: Cambridge University Press, 2008), 69.
27 White, *Sinister Yogis*, 67–71.
28 John Brockington, "Yoga in the Mahābhārata," in *Yoga: The Indian Tradition*, ed. Ian Whicher and David Carpenter (London: RoutledgeCurzon, 2003), 13–25.
29 White, *Sinister Yogis*, 141–5.
30 Bronkhorst, *How the Brahmins Won*, 253.
31 White, *Sinister Yogis*, 167.
32 Elizabeth De Michelis, *A History of Modern Yoga: Patañjali and Western Esoterism* (London: Continuum, 2004), 178.
33 Jason Birch, "Rājayoga: The Reincarnations of the King of All Yogas," *International Journal of Hindu Studies*, 17, no. 3 (2013): 399–442.
34 Translation adapted from Winthrop Sargeant, trans., *The Bhagavad Gītā* (Albany: State University of New York Press, 2009), 225–32.
35 Dermot Killingley, "Manufacturing Yogis: Swami Vivekananda as a Yoga Teacher," in *Gurus of Modern Yoga*, ed. Mark Singleton and Ellen Goldberg (New York: Oxford University Press, 2014), 37n22.
36 White, *Sinister Yogis*, 105.
37 Gavin D. Flood, *An Introduction to Hinduism* (Cambridge: Cambridge University Press, 2006), 156–7.
38 Mallinson and Singleton, *Roots of Yoga*, 66.
39 Mallinson and Singleton, *Roots of Yoga*, 37.
40 Mallinson and Singleton, *Roots of Yoga*, 312–13; Hans T. Bakker, *The World of the Skandapurāṇa: Northern India in the Sixth and Seventh Centuries* (Leiden and Boston: Brill, 2016), 141.
41 Alexis Sanderson, "The Śaiva Age: The Rise and Dominance of Śaivism during the Early Medieval Period," in *Genesis and Development of Tantrism*, ed. Shingo Einoo, Institute of Oriental Culture Special Series 23 (Tokyo: Institute of Oriental Culture, University of Tokyo, 2009), 41–350.
42 Mallinson and Singleton, *Roots of Yoga*, 8.
43 Somadeva Vasudeva, "The Śaiva Yogas and Their Relation to Other Systems of Yoga," *RINDAS Series of Working Papers: Traditional Indian Thoughts*, 26 (2017): 3–5.
44 Vasudeva, "The Śaiva Yogas," 6.

6 Medieval to early modern yogas

So far, most of the yoga techniques we've discussed (with the exception of the ones involving chariots) can be loosely clustered around the idea of *tapas*. However, between the 6th and 13th centuries of the Common Era, the period that has been dubbed the "Śaiva Age,"[1] there developed a new method of self-cultivation for the attainment of both worldly superpower (*siddhi*) and liberation. This method, arising most prominently within Śaiva and Śaiva-adjacent Śākta groups, lay at the core of traditions we now refer to as "tantric," and it arose out of a worldview that regards the universe as a manifestation of divine energy. Relying again on the idea that the universe was the macrocosmic ("big world") equivalent of the microcosmic ("little world") human being, tantric traditions sought to use this relationship to bridge the gap between human and divine. Not all tantra is yogic and not all yoga is tantric. But, that being said, tantric traditions often incorporated yogic techniques in novel and innovative ways. To this day, traces of tantra are easily found in modern forms of yoga.

India's classical period, culminating in the Gupta and Vākāṭaka empires (320–550 CE), was a period of unification and relative stability. The early medieval period, starting in the 6th century, on the other hand, was more fragmented and decentralized. There we see different smaller kingdoms emerge as regional centers of power, each with their own local identity, all vying for dominance. Power, however, is never simply military—it's also cultural. A grand kingdom needs a grand court, and so rulers sponsored architects, artists, and religious specialists who in turn developed rich cultural networks that sought to place their particular kingdom at the center of the world.[2]

Against this background, tantra emerged as a new system of institutional ritual to compete with, add to, and ultimately blend with the older *brāhmaṇa* (Brahminical priestly) framework. Tantric texts were considered revelation in the literal sense of the word. That is, they were spoken by a deity (the deity varies depending on the context) or else a divinized figure like a Bodhisattva and thus could overwrite the older authority of Vedic scripture. In this sense, tantric traditions pitched themselves as an updated version or a "new testament" on the nature of the cosmos.

Like Vedic ritual, tantric ritual relied on the logic of big and little worlds, but it updated this logic to fit the feudal structure of medieval kingdoms. The tantric ritual diagram, the *maṇḍala* (circle) or *yantra* (instrument) was a multipurpose map—it was the little world of the human body and the big world of the universe, but it was also a sort of symbolic geography of the state. Insofar as tantric systems are centered on the idea of the human becoming divine, this narrative would have been especially attractive for a king looking to establish himself as the absolute master of his realm.[3]

In this sense, tantric systems were very much at the social and political center of medieval India. However, like the earlier renouncer movements, they also established an interesting back-and-forth between the center and the periphery, culture and counterculture. On the periphery we find a variety of independent adepts, primarily the Śaiva-Śākta and Buddhist (Mahā)Siddhas or the "(Great) Perfected Ones," who model themselves on quasi-mythical ideas of divine sages and other ascended beings. Though more rare, there were also some Vaiṣṇavas and the occasional Jain (Jains tended to avoid outright transgression, but did still deal in some dangerous substances). For many such figures, power and transgression went hand in hand. They existed on the margins of society, by virtue of either being or holding congress with outcaste people. They hung out in the wilderness or, worse yet, on cremation grounds, where they were thought to transact with frightful superhuman beings (Figure 6.1). And they engaged practices involving all sorts of polluting substances, from flesh and intoxicants, to illicit sexual rites. Whether they obtained their power from these dangerous behaviors, or whether such habits were themselves a marker of their power and transcendence is a bit of a chicken-or-egg question.

Figure 6.1 The Goddess Bhairavi and Śiva on the cremation grounds. India, Mughal dynasty, ca. 1630–35.

Source: Courtesy of the Metropolitan Museum of Art.

In both the normative and the transgressive varieties of tantra, we find practices, some physical ascetic and some contemplative or visionary, that would have been called yoga. It's important to emphasize that tantric traditions, even when they are about liberation, are also very much about worldly power. As we saw in Chapter 5, the pursuit of power is not necessarily an unusual thing in the context of yoga, even in its ascetic varieties. However, the tantric idea of an embodied divinity takes this to a new level. It is in the context of tantric traditions, for instance, that we see the full development of *jīvanmukti*, "liberation while living," which allows the yogi to reach his highest goal while still remaining in the world.

It is also in the context of tantra that we find the closest precedent to modern forms of yoga—*haṭha* yoga. In the later medieval period, starting in the 13th century with the rise of the Delhi Sultanate, *haṭha* yogic texts emerged as a set of cosmopolitan manuals that synthesized a variety of ascetic and tantric practices in a non-sectarian fashion. Their yoga was explicitly meant to be a universal yoga, accessible to householders and transferrable across religious boundaries. It was a yoga based on a method, which itself was a kind of medley of methods, that yielded the intended goal (power or liberation, and ideally both) regardless of the practitioner's identity or ideological commitments.

The way of the mantra

Tantric traditions, and the texts from which they get their name, are diverse and incredibly complex. Because this book is about yoga and not tantra, we won't be able to cover them in detail here. However, there is one aspect that is shared by most if not all early tantric traditions that becomes extremely important if we want to understand later developments in yoga. This aspect is the use of *mantras*. *Mantra* was so important that the tantric form of Śaivism is referred to as the *mantramārga*, or "The Path of *Mantra*." Unlike the ascetic *atimārga* ("Highest Path") of the Pāśupatas, this path was open to ascetics and householders alike. Likewise, tantric Vajrayāna ("The Adamantine Vehicle") Buddhism is also called the Mantranaya ("The *Mantra* Method"). It's worth mentioning that followers of the *mantramārga* do generally consider their own path to in fact be the highest, or at least to lead to the highest goal.

When we use the term "tantra," we're generally talking about the types of concepts and practices that are grounded in a set of texts that begin to crop up from around the 6th century onwards. Not all tantric texts are called "Tantras," some are called "Āgamas" or "Samhitās." One thing that they all tend to have in common, however, is their self-professed status as divine revelation or scripture. Tantric texts tend to take the shape of a dialogue between the deity—a god in Hindu traditions, or a perfected being in Buddhism and Jainism—and either their divine consort or else a human sage. So, though tantric texts share a tendency towards theism (allowing that a divinized human like the Bodhisattva is a sort of deity), this theism means that they're sectarian and therefore don't form a single unified tradition. That is, it really matters who the deity revealing the text ultimately is.

At the same time, although the specifics of tantric ritual practice can vary quite a bit as one hops between the various Śaiva, Śākta, Buddhist, Vaiṣṇava, and Jain forms, its overall basic structure remains fairly standard. The fundamental goal of tantric ritual is to transform the human being into something more than simply human—a perfected being in a perfected body. The first step in this process in one of purification, often called *bhūtaśuddhi* ("purification of the elements"). At this stage, the practitioner, either with the aid of some external ritual or by way of meditative visualization, dissolves the material elements that constitute his human body. As we discussed in Chapters 2 and 3, this usually involves working one's way through the body as a microcosm, continuous with the universe at large, following the same framework as the one found in earlier systems like Sāṅkhya. The second step is *nyāsa*, literally something like "imposition," where the practitioner (again either externally or internally) assigns deities or divine energies, usually represented by their special *mantras*, to the various parts of his body. In doing so, he essentially reassembles himself as a perfected cosmic being made up not of ordinary matter but of subtle powers.

The practitioner then proceeds to worship the chief deity who is the target of his ritual. Like the previous steps, this can be done either externally through the use of *mudrās* ("gestures," notably different from the ascetic *mudrās* or bodily "seals" that become common in later *haṭha* yoga traditions), the recitation of *mantras*, the making of oblations and offerings and so on, or internally by means of meditation and visualization. The end result of this process may be liberation, if that is the practitioner's goal, and if the invoked deity is so inclined. Otherwise, the practitioner can expect to gain not only his newly perfected immortal body, but also the potentially dazzling array of superpowers this body possesses.

As we've mentioned previously, the typical practitioner of the tantric traditions was not usually referred to as a yogi, but as a *sādhaka*, an "aspirant," engaged in a *sādhana* or a "means for accomplishment." The accomplishment, or *siddhi*, points to the refinement, perfection, and even divinization of the human body through practice.[4] When we say that certain practices prescribed by the tantric texts are "yogic" in nature, this usually means they include visualization-based *dhyānas* or meditations. However, when it comes to most tantric texts, such practices account for only a minority of the text's overall content. The texts in question generally deal with four types of topics: *jñāna*, or knowledge, including philosophy, cosmology and the like; yoga, or contemplative and visionary practices; *kriyā,* or ritual; and *caryā*, or behavior and codes of conduct. Most tantric texts overwhelmingly privilege the latter two subjects, *kriyā* and *caryā*, devoting most of their effort to describing rituals, outlining proper practices concerning temples and images of deities, and so forth.[5]

Mantras are central in many of the above practices, whether they be formal ritual or meditation. They're also intimately connected to the undeniably theistic nature of tantric traditions. *Mantras* are a way of interacting with, coopting, and controlling divine powers. The *mantra* that the *sādhaka* incorporates into his practice is not simply a verbal utterance, or even a "magical spell," but the literal sonic form of a superhuman being or deity.[6] When the tantric practitioner receives his initiation, he is given the *mantra* of a chosen deity, which he then uses in his practice. This is where things begin to diverge, depending on the particular tradition to which the practitioner belongs. In some traditions, deities are worshipped, in others they are conquered. In dualistic schools such as the Śaiva Siddhānta or Vaiṣṇava Pañcarātra, the practitioner remains distinct from the ultimate godhead, while partaking in its power. In monistic systems like the Kaula, the practitioner literally becomes one with the ultimate divine. In a qualified sort of way, this is also true in the tantric Buddhist tradition. It is in the latter sort of context that we find some of the more interesting (and currently persistent) developments, as far as yoga is concerned—and so, it's to the origins of these traditions that we will now turn.

Circles of goddesses, without

The aspirants who set off into the woods in search of knowledge and power were not out there on their own. Yogic traditions have always been home to a wide variety of superhuman beings, some who started out as human and others who did not. We finished the previous chapter by discussing the ways in which the gods who would come to dominate Hinduism, such as Śiva and Viṣṇu/Kṛṣṇa, fit into the idea of yogic practice, whether of the ascetic or devotion-driven variety. We also briefly mentioned the *śramana* adepts, including Buddhists and Jains, whose ascetic practices may have ultimately been geared at shutting down the mind-body machine, but nevertheless produced along the way an array of powers that basically rendered such practitioners nothing short of superhuman. There is another piece we need to add to this picture: the wide world of intermediary deities (minor gods, demons, nature spirits, and the like) who did not represent divinity in the highest sense, but who were also definitively not human. Such beings are a staple of religious traditions the world over and are an especially important feature of folk religion—that is, everyday religion practiced by everyday people.

This is important for us because it turns out that certain of these beings could be co-opted for the purposes of yoga, both in terms of worldly power and in terms of liberation. These "helpful" beings were female and came to be referred to as Yoginīs or, in the Buddhist context, Ḍākinīs. To call them helpful is perhaps a bit misleading because they were generally a frightful and fierce lot. These female divinities have their roots in a number of earlier beings, who often come in groups, such as Sylphs (*apsarasas*), Dryads (*yakṣiṇīs*), and especially the various Mother-goddesses (*mātṛs* or *mātṛkās*) or Seizers (*grahīs*). Yoginīs were frequently depicted as having animal characteristics, especially animal heads, and possessed the ability to shape-shift (Figure 6.2). They inhabited (or at least frequented) remote, liminal, and often dangerous locations such as caves, forests, crossroads, and especially mountain tops and cremation grounds. They also had a predilection for arranging themselves in circles and so, when temples were built to worship them, these temples were generally circular, with representations of the female divinities in question being arranged around the periphery. Sometimes, they were understood to be the entourage of a male god (often a form of Śiva), in which case this male god would be placed at the center.[7]

Though there are *bhucarī* (literally, "earth-going" or terrestrial) varieties of Yoginīs, the prototypical Yoginī is a *khecharī* ("air-going"—that is, she flies through the air with the greatest of ease) and she is therefore a guardian of the most coveted of yogic superpowers, flight. Accordingly, Yoginī temples are not only circular, but also roofless, allowing any interested Yoginīs to swoop in as

Figure 6.2 A horse-headed Yoginī. India, Madhya Pradesh, 11th century.
Source: Courtesy of the Los Angeles County Museum of Art.

they desire. If you happened to come across one or more of these beings, they were likely to possess you, or else simply eat you alive. Unless, that is, you were sufficiently virile—a *vīra* (hero) rather than a *paśu* (victim)—in which case the Yoginīs rewarded your sacrifice with either splendid powers (flight, but also so much more) or otherwise liberation, depending on which you were after.[8]

The primal version of this encounter calls up the vision of the tantric practitioner, alone amidst the ashes of the cremation ground, offering his own body as a sacrifice to the horde of Yoginīs, who descend upon him and threaten to devour him with their gnarly gnashing mouths. However, because he is a proper *vīra* (a hero, and not a victim), the Yoginīs are subdued by his virile virtuosity and instead offer him power by way of their other (nether) mouths, accepting him into their clan (*kula*).[9] Yoginīs were thought to be particularly fond of human flesh, which helped fuel their flight, but they could also be propitiated with offerings of meat (which replaced the supplicant's own flesh and blood), alcohol, and noxious incense.[10]

In the most extreme scenario, though, getting torn apart and consumed by the Yoginīs is exactly what one wants. The Yoginīs destroy the practitioner's mortal body so that he may be reconstituted as their superhuman counterpart, a Siddha.[11] We can see a symbolic version of this idea enacted in the typical tantric practice of *bhūtaśuddhi*, where the practitioner's bodily constituents are ritually dissolved so that his body can be reconstituted as a perfected body made up of *mantra* powers. It also sheds some light on why the Yoginīs are called "Yoginīs," which might be translated as something like "Joiners." As the scholar David Gordon White explains,

> Śiva created human sacrificial victims (*paśus*) precisely in order that they might be liberated from suffering existence. This the Yoginīs effect by killing them, since all they are killing, in truth, are the bonds that trap said victims in suffering existence. So it is that they join the souls of these *paśus* to their lord (*pati*), Śiva.[12]

Yoginīs and Ḍākinīs were superhuman beings, but they could also manifest as human women. Indeed, the idea that it was possible for a woman to become one of these beings is one of the few hints we have of the existence of a female practice—the idea that human women, as well as men, could aspire to become something like divine.[13] In any case, Yoginīs, whether human or divine, played a crucial role in initiation and the transmission of clan (*kula*) esoteric knowledge. Some scholars, especially White, have argued that the nature of this transmission is primarily and fundamentally sexual. According to White, the Yoginī's power rests specifically in her ability to "insanguinate" the initiate with her sexual fluids, thereby transmitting the "gnosis" of the *kula* as a kind of transformative substance that spontaneously bestows knowledge and therefore power[14]—like a spiritual mutagen of sorts. Or perhaps we could call it sexually transmitted enlightenment.

This kind of practice forms the bedrock of the Śākta and non-Siddhānta Śaiva tantric schools, represented especially by the Kaula Tantras ("kaula" being derived from "kula" or the idea of the clan), as well as the Buddhist Mahāyoga- and Yoginī Tantras, which began to emerge from the 8th century onwards. In these texts, the quasi-mythical encounters of lone aspirants and fierce goddesses are transformed into group rituals performed by human men and women.

Circles of goddesses, within

By the end of the this section, we will see a similar kind of "internalization" of ritual—that is, taking something that was once literally done in the outside world and imagining it happening within the mind and body of the practitioner—as occurred with the Vedic fire sacrifice in Chapter 5. In the beginning, the practices in question were quite external and literal, including in their sexual dimensions and other interactions with impure substances.[15] However, over time, the external circular arrangements of Yoginīs and other female deities become visualized as internal *cakras* located within the practitioner's own body. The female ritual partner becomes the feminine *kuṇḍalinī* energy resting at the base of the spine. These are the goddesses within.

In the early Kaula ("of the clan") rituals the quasi-mythical exchange between the *vīra* and the Yoginīs is translated into the initiatory encounter with a human partner, mediated by the clan's guru. In this context, the female partner might be referred to as a *dūtī*—a messenger—who conveys the knowledge contained within her sexual fluid as a representative of the superhuman Yoginī.[16] The divine Yoginīs of the clan would be ritually worshipped with a formalized set of impure substances, which became known as the *pañca-makāra*, or the "Five M-words." These included: *māṃsa* (meat); *matsya* (fish); *madya* (liquor); *mudrā* (an ambiguous term that eventually comes to signify an aphrodisiac sort of grain, but which White argues originally referred to the vulva of the female ritual partner);[17] and *maithuna* (mixed sexual fluids, usually of the guru and his partner). At the highest stages of practice, the practitioner would ritually consume these substances as an offering to the circles of deities that were now located within his own body (Figure 6.3).

Figure 6.3 A tantric Buddhist *maṇḍala* featuring the goddess Vajraḍākinī at the center, flanked by circles (*cakras*) of attendant Ḍākinīs. The outermost ring depicts the cremation grounds where ritual occurs, including offerings of liquor, flesh, sexual ritual, and so on. Further out still are depictions of various yogis and Siddhas. Central Tibet, ca. 1375.

Source: Courtesy of the Cleveland Museum of Art.

Some of the most interesting testaments we have to this kind of practice are found in the enigmatic verses of the *Caryāgīti*. These "Wanderer-Songs" are esoteric poems generally dated from the 8th to the 12th century CE. They are attributed to various Buddhist Siddhas and would have been sung by orderless Buddhist (though they could have just as easily been Śaiva or Vaiṣṇava) practitioners—wandering yogi minstrels of a sort, who would have perhaps earned their offerings by singing as they roamed village to village.[18] Scholar and novelist Lee Siegel has rather accurately described the *Caryāgīti* as "mysterious and rude, compelling and vulgar, sometimes playful and sometimes dreadful."[19] Taken literally, the songs can indeed be both colorful and challenging, but their most important function is perhaps symbolic and therefore esoteric. Read this way, they offer hints of a sexual yoga that functions on an external ritual, but also on an internal metaphysical level.[20] Rejecting social and religious distinctions as well as taboos, they advocated a *sahaja*—innate, spontaneous, and natural—approach to liberation, which they understood to be worldly and embodied.

Such practices, in their original form, were by definition marginal. Even once they were formalized into clan ritual, they tended to be understandably esoteric with practitioners meeting in secret and under the cover of night. How clandestine these later meetings actually were, however, really depended on the socio-political context. If the king happened to be a *sādhaka*, then the clan's rituals tended to be the worst kept secret in the municipality.[21] Presumably, though, the closer they got to the era's major centers or power, both political and intellectual, the less countercultural these rituals became. Transgressive practices involving contact with impure substances and the violation of caste and other social norms were gradually naturalized into the tantric mainstream, where they were cleaned up with high-brow philosophy, symbolism, and ritual substitutions.[22]

For our purposes, the Kaula tradition is worth singling out for a couple of specific reasons. The purportedly first human gurus of *haṭha* yoga, the Nāths Matsyendra and Gorakṣa (whose stories we reviewed in Chapter 4) belonged to the Kaula's Western Transmission (*paścimāmnāya*). It is also within this school, belonging to the Crooked Goddess, Kubjikā, that we find the *Kubjikāmata Tantra*. This circa 10th-century text is the first to describe the six-*cakra* system that would eventually become the gold standard, surpassing a number of competing frameworks. What's more, this is a major place where we meet the goddess Kuṇḍalinī (the "Coiled One").[23]

(Re)Absorption of the mind

Before we zoom in on the Nāths and their *haṭha* yoga synthesis, it would be helpful to elaborate on an important idea that arises out of Śākta-Śaiva tantras such as the *Kubjikāmata*. This is the goal of *cittalaya*, or the "dissolution" or more literally "absorption of the mind." *Cittalaya* is both similar to and different from the kind of stilling of the mind we've previously seen referred to as *citta(vṛtti)nirodhaḥ*. On the one hand, both concepts share the idea of transcending the ordinary human mind, as well as the way in which one might do this, at least if we're thinking specifically about the Patañjali's yoga model. *Cittalaya* often involves a progressive movement upwards through and conquest of the constituents of reality, which, at least at the outset, are identical to those found in Sāṅkhya.[24]

The goal of *cittalaya*, however, is not isolation (*kaivalya* in Patañjali, or *ayoga* as we saw in some Jain systems) but reabsorption of the mind into the singular reality that is God, usually Śiva. Śaiva tantric texts prescribe a variety of specific techniques (called *saṃketas* or "methods") for how to achieve this goal, many of which have to do with the cultivation of internal sounds (*nāda*) that act as a sort of meditative tuning device. The most popular of these methods, however, is precisely the raising of the divine feminine Kuṇḍalinī through the six *cakras* of deities.[25] Within the body, the *cakras* become associated with various anatomical points and the Goddess Kuṇḍalinī manifests as the *kuṇḍalinī śakti* ("coiled energy") at the base of the torso. Similar techniques could be found in tantric Buddhist texts, except that here it was not the coiled *kuṇḍalinī* but *caṇḍalī* (the "Fiery One") that made the journey through the inner microcosm of the practitioner's body. Taken together, these kinds of practices may be referred to as *laya* yoga.[26]

The idea of *laya*, like everything else in this system, operates according to a micro–macro kind of tantric correspondence. As we discussed in Chapter 3, *kuṇḍalinī* represents undifferentiated creative energy and her original descent is the process of cosmic emanation. Her upward return thus signals the reverse process of cosmic reabsorption. Within the body, her reunion with the masculine principle at the crown of the head, which correlates to the summit of the cosmos, results in the singularity of liberation. However, things don't end there. This is all part of a cycle, after all, and destruction begets creation. And so, the *kuṇḍalinī* not only frees the mind by drowning it in the pool of immortal oneness that is the divine, but she releases that pool back downwards, flooding the body with the nectar of immortality (*amṛta*) and resulting in a state of embodied liberation for the *sādhaka*.

Positioning *haṭha* yoga

Over the first half of the 2nd millennium, we witness the gradual emergence of something called "*haṭha* yoga," sometimes translated as "the yoga of force." Though medieval, *haṭha* practice is still a far cry from what one can expect to find at a modern yoga studio, there are elements of it that have survived to become important features of today's global yoga. The term "*haṭha*" is usually translated as "forceful," though it is not always clear where this force is to be found within the practice. One hypothesis is that the practice itself requires a sort of forceful effort, though historical sources suggest that this is often not understood to be the case. Another, more likely possibility is that the qualifier refers to the force the practice applies to the body's vital energies—for instance, forcefully moving the *bindu* upwards through the body's central channel. There is yet another, so called esoteric definition, which breaks up the syllables *ha* and *ṭha* as corresponding to the sun and moon.[27] *Haṭha* yoga is their union. This correspondence is linked up with a number of other such pairs, such as the in- and out-breaths, the *īḍā* and *piṅgalā* channels of the body, and so on.

As we mentioned earlier, the system of *haṭha* yoga has traditionally been credited to the teachings of the Nāth yogis, especially Gorakṣa and Matsyendra. The best known account of this yoga is found in a 15th-century text called the *Haṭha Pradīpikā* ("The Little Lamp on Haṭha"). The central method taught in this text involves using a variety of physical techniques to awaken the *kuṇḍalinī* energy in her resting place at the base of the spine, and to raise her upwards until she unites with the masculine principle at the crown of the head. The *Haṭha Pradīpikā* turns out to be a compiled text, one that quotes from a number of earlier sources and synthesizes their teachings. When examined closely, however, the synthesis begins to splinter—not only does the text's picture of *haṭha* yoga include a rather complicated mish-mash of ideas and practices, but some of these ideas and practices actually turn out to be mutually contradictory.[28] We'll come back to the contents of the *Haṭha Pradīpikā* shortly but, before we do so, we'll need to trace how this synthesis occurred and why the word "*haṭha*" was applied to it.

So, what is—or was—*haṭha* yoga? Together with another now very famous term (*rāja* or "royal" yoga), *mantra*, *laya*, and *haṭha* make up a common set of yoga terminology floating around over the first half of the 2nd millennium CE. While *mantra* and *laya* yoga refer fairly clearly to practices found in the Śaiva-Śākta and Buddhist tantras, which we just reviewed, *rāja* is a bit more of a floating signifier. Most often, it refers simply to the state of *samādhi* or "completion," the goal more so than the practice. In other words, *rāja* yoga is a common summit that can be attained via a variety of techniques, such as the aforementioned *mantra*, *laya*, and *haṭha*. Other times, it might refer either explicitly or implicitly to "the best yoga," whatever that may be.[29] The *Dattātreya Yoga Śāstra*, for instance, ranks the yogas hierarchically from *mantra* being the lowest, followed by *laya*, then *haṭha*, up to *rāja* as the highest. Another text, the *Amaraugha Prabodha*, clarifies that this ranking corresponds to the kind of student for whom each yoga is most appropriate. *Mantra* yoga is for the weak student, *laya* for the average, *haṭha* for the above average, and *rāja* for the extremely above average.[30] *Haṭha Pradīpikā*, on the other hand, resolves this proliferation of yogas by ignoring *mantra* yoga altogether and merging (in an interesting way we'll examine momentarily) *laya* yoga with *haṭha* yoga, and declaring *haṭha* to be the supreme ladder towards *rāja*, or *samādhi*.[31]

In other words, the terminology is far from precise, and there's often a fair amount of crossover between one kind of practice and another. So the question becomes not so much, what is *haṭha* yoga, but: how do we identify *haṭha* yoga as its own thing?

Ascetic techniques, tantric goals

According to yoga scholar and philologist James Mallinson, the distinguishing feature of *haṭha* yoga is the use of physical techniques like *mudrās* and *bandhas* ("seals" and "locks," respectively). These mark *haṭha* practice as different from *laya* yoga, which is characterized by the visionary *saṃketas*, or from *mantra* yoga, which relies on (not surprisingly) *mantras*. Mallinson traces these techniques to earlier forms of ascetic practice, grounded in the idea of *tapas*, and geared at keeping the body's vital constituents where they belong—inside the body, and not leaking out into the world. In other words, though it may seem like these are newer practices that emerge for the first time in the literature of medieval *haṭha* yoga, they are in fact much older techniques that have been passed down by ascetics for centuries but not written down.[32]

The first text to describe the core techniques and concepts of *haṭha* yoga is the 12th-century Vājrayana Buddhist *Amṛta Siddhi*. Here we find for the first time, fully formed, the association of semen or *bindu* with the immortal nectar, *amṛita*, which drips down from the moon, and likewise the association of the sun with the consuming fire in the stomach. We also find descriptions of the three *granthis* ("knots") in the body and several techniques that use bodily postures and breath control to pierce those knots and raise the breath up the body's central channel. These features all become standard in later texts on *haṭha* yoga, which often quote from the *Amṛta Siddhi* extensively, suggesting that it is the original written source of such teachings.[33]

The term "*haṭha* yoga" does first appear in Buddhist tantras, where it pops up as early as the 8th-century *Guhya Samāja tantra*, though it is not described there.[34] Notably, however, the *Amṛta Siddhi* does not itself use the word "*haṭha*" for any of the techniques we just mentioned. This happens for the first time in the 13th-century *Dattātreya Yoga Śāstra*, likely written by predecessors of the Daśanāmī ("Ten Names") Saṃnyāsīs, and especially their Giri and Puri subdivisions. Together with the Rāmānandīs, the Daśanāmīs persist today as India's largest monastic orders and the principal ascetic practitioners of *haṭha* yoga.[35] The Daśanāmīs are generally considered to be Śaivas, but it is likely that some of them (particularly the ones responsible for the *Dattātreya Yoga Śāstra*) were originally Vaiṣṇava in their sympathies.[36] This, together with the Buddhist slant of the *Amṛta Siddhi*, shows not only the generally fluid nature of religious boundaries in premodern South Asia, but the impossibility of locating even specific forms of yoga practice within any one sect or religion.

So, this is where things get very messy. If we look at the *Dattātreya Yoga Śāstra*, we find core *haṭha* yogic practices, like the aforementioned *mudrās* and *bandhas*, that are now being explicitly called *haṭha* yoga. So far, so good. What we don't find, however, are any references to *cakras* or *kuṇḍalinī*, which are now often treated as hallmarks of "*haṭha* yoga," as defined by the cornerstone of the *Haṭha Pradīpikā*. The same goes for the earlier *Amṛta Siddhi*—nothing about *cakras* or *kuṇḍalinī* in there. Instead, these texts teach techniques geared at keeping the immortal *bindu* trapped in its proper place in the head. On the other hand, there are other 13th-century texts, mostly attributed to the Nāth gurus, that teach these *mudrās* and *bandhas* for the purpose of raising the *kuṇḍalinī*. Some of them quote verses from the *Amṛta Siddhi* and the *Dattātreya Yoga Śāstra*, but they do not call their yoga "*haṭha*." Some of these texts still say that the physical techniques are meant for the preservation of *bindu* (even though they're otherwise about *kuṇḍalinī*), while others say that the same techniques are to be used for raising the *kuṇḍalinī* directly.[37] See? A mess.

The famous *Haṭha Pradīpikā* is a particularly good example of this confusion. For example, it teaches one specific *mudrā*, the *khecarī mudrā*, where the practitioner folds back and presses the tip of his tongue over the cavity in the soft palate, in one place as sealing the *bindu* in the head, and then in a different place as releasing the *amṛta* from the cranial vault. Why is this a problem? These two goals represent two different and competing models of the body, which we have already discussed to a greater extent in Chapter 3—one ascetic, the other tantric.

The first is concerned with the preservation of sexual fluids (*bindu*/semen or, nominally, *rajas*/menstrual blood), hence the use of physical techniques to keep the *bindu* sealed in the head, where it is produced, and to raise it back up if it should happen to fall. Keeping the *bindu* from falling into the lower digestive fires or, even worse, being ejaculated, helps to prevent weakness, disease, and old age. In this model, the intent would actually be to *separate* the moon (or its seminal droppings) from the sun.

The second is centered on the idea of *amṛta*, or the nectar of immortality, which is usually equated with that same *bindu*, and the raising of the *kuṇḍalinī* energy. If the *kuṇḍalinī* can be raised to the crown of the head, where the *amṛta* is stored, then it can flood the body with this nectar on its return journey, rendering the body perfectly strong, healthy, and immortal. This is the union of sun and moon.

By now, it should be obvious these models are not only different but competing—they advise the practitioner to do completely opposite things. One says that the thing in the cranium should stay there at all costs, while the other wants to let it loose throughout the whole body.

Again, a mess.

But why is it a mess? Well, if we follow Mallinson's argument, it's because we're actually seeing an evolving attempt to combine these two separate systems. The physical techniques of *haṭha* yoga, a kind of forceful yoga of doing, originated amongst celibate renouncers for the purpose of preserving the semen or *bindu*, presumably beyond the default level that celibacy could account for. These techniques, along with other forms of asceticism, were geared at building up *tapas*. Between the 13th and 15th centuries, however, they were increasingly co-opted by certain tantric groups to add physical scaffolding to transform the external rituals that imitated their mythic yoga of going—one where the practitioner would interact with actual divine Yoginīs who would transform his mortal body into that of a celestial Siddha—to an embodied yoga of knowing, where that transformation happened internally, on the level of subtle energies. And so, these groups produce texts that adopt the techniques used to for the preservation of *bindu*, and retool them instead for the awakening and raising of *kuṇḍalinī*.

There's a sort of social, human element to this as well. It reflects an effort on the part of the Nāths to become a formal, celibate ascetic order by cleaning up their act, so to say. After all, the legendary founders of the Nāths—the same Gorakṣa and Matsyendra—weren't celibate ascetics, they were out-and-out Kaula tantrics, complete with all the impure substances and sexual rituals that this entailed.[38] We see this transition from one to the other expressed rather explicitly in the *Gorakṣa Śataka*, a 13th-century Nāth *haṭha* text, which ends by declaring:

> We drink the dripping liquid called *bindu*, "the drop", not wine; we eat the rejection of the objects of the five senses, not meat; we do not embrace a sweetheart [but] the *suṣumnā nāḍī*, her body curved like *kuśa* grass; if we are to have intercourse, it takes place in a mind dissolved in the void, not in a vagina.[39]

(See Figure 6.4). And so, the Nāth texts lift the techniques of the ascetic Daśanāmīs (or at least their predecessors), but never mention their names. A perfectly logical move, Mallinson points out, given that the Nāths and the Daśanāmīs have been longtime rivals.[40]

The *Haṭha Pradīpikā*, to which we will now turn, is the culmination of these efforts. Despite the text's long shadow, however, Mallinson argues that this type of yoga was not really taken up in the long-term by the Nāths, who have for the most part remained true to their roots as experts in tantric meditation, magic, and goddess worship.[41] This is supported by the fact that modern ascetic practitioners

Figure 6.4 A Nāth yogi and the divine energies of his body. The lowest *padma* (lotus, another way of representing *cakras*) contains an inverted triangle symbolizing the yoni (vulva) and therefore the feminine principle. A coiled spiral within the triangle may be a representation of the *kuṇḍalinī* in her typical resting place, where she is wrapped around Śiva's *liṅgam* (symbolic phallus). A goddess presides over the heart and the same goddess is shown in union with Śiva in the cranial vault where the crescent moon holds the nectar of *amṛta* like a bowl. India, Himchal Pradesh, Mandi, 19th century.

Source: Courtesy of the Los Angeles County Museum of Art.

of yoga usually associate the term *haṭha* specifically with *tapas* rather than *kuṇḍalinī*.[42] Likewise, early international yogis who taught *kuṇḍalinī-* or *nāda-*oriented techniques, like Swami Vivekananda or Paramahansa Yogananda, did not usually refer to their yoga as *haṭha*. So, it would be a stretch to say that there was ever a coherent tradition of *haṭha* yoga that led directly to modern physical yoga practices. Instead, the impact of the *Haṭha Pradīpikā*, and other such texts, ended up being something much broader.

The first popularization

Haṭha yoga emerged in the 13th century, just as the Śaiva Age was coming to a close. From a philosophical perspective, this meant that the Śaiva framework was giving way to that of Vedānta. The Upaniṣads were making a comeback. From a religious perspective, tantra was beginning to cede space to—and, in important ways, to merge with—*bhakti*, or devotion. Amidst this sea-change, texts on yoga find new and creative ways to parse, compare, rank, and synthesize these various perspectives. As we saw, the *Haṭha Pradīpikā* teaches a range of yogic practices but can't quite decide on their goal. Conflicting models and goals are not uncommon feature of *haṭha* texts. Conceptually speaking, though literature on *haṭha* generally refrains from expressing loyalties to any religious sect or philosophical school, it often draws on both Śaiva and Vedānta versions of non-dualism.[43]

This balancing act is important, as is the fact that it happens implicitly and below the surface. Even Svātmārāma, the compiler of the *Haṭha Pradīpikā* who ultimately wanted to claim *haṭha* yoga for the Nāths, went to great lengths to avoid any sign of sectarian bias by stripping out deity-specific *mantras* and *maṇḍalas*, even in borrowed verses that contained such features in their original sources.[44] Other texts go even further in proclaiming the universality of their methods. For example, the *Dattātreya Yoga Śāstra* explicitly says:

> Whether a Brahmin, an ascetic, a Buddhist, a Jain, a Skull-Bearer or a materialist, the wise man who is endowed with faith and constantly devoted to the practice of [*haṭha*] yoga will attain complete success. Success happens for one who performs the practices. How could it happen for one who does not?[45]

In other words, it doesn't matter who you are. There's no need or complex philosophy or theology. No need for harsh asceticism or elaborate rituals of initiation. No need for secrecy and no need or priests. Just practice, and you will succeed.

Mallinson has argued that what we're seeing here is a kind of democratization of religion, akin to that found in the devotional *bhakti* traditions that begin to pop up around the same time. For the first time, the higher fruits of religious practice—from superpowers to liberation—are available to ordinary individuals outside of either an esoteric or renunciatory lineage. This also explains why, for the first time, we see some of these much older techniques set down in writing. Lineages can pass down teachings orally, guru to disciple. Once you bring in regular householders, you need texts. Of course to produce texts you need funding, leading Mallinson to speculate that this process was underpinned by a system of patronage from these new "bourgeois" practitioners, who enlisted learned pandits to collect, codify, and reproduce the teachings of various gurus.[46]

This may have also expanded the scope of what yoga practice was traditionally used to accomplish. In the *haṭha* texts, we see for the first time the idea that *āsanas* and methods of *prāṇāyāma* can be used for practical, therapeutic ends. The *Haṭha Pradīpikā* informs us that *āsanas* can be used to cultivate steadiness, health, and suppleness in the body. Specific *āsanas* are recommended as a means to destroy disease as well as to strengthen the digestive fire.[47] Such therapeutic uses also appear in other earlier *haṭha* and *haṭha*-adjacent texts, which indicate that both *āsana* and *prāṇāyāma* have the effect of purifying the body of imbalance and disease.[48] For instance, the *Yoga Śastra* of Hemacandra, an 11th-century Jain text, tells us: "A person should continuously hold *prāṇa* and the other breaths wherever they have a painful disease in order to cure it."[49]

The core techniques of *haṭha* yoga

Haṭha yoga is a system fundamentally grounded in the body, though, as we noted earlier, whether its approach to the body is ascetic or tantric is up for debate and differs from text to text. *Haṭha* texts frequently include cleansing techniques (the *ṣaṭ karmāni* or the "six actions"), bodily postures (*āsanas*), and breathing exercises (*prāṇāyāma* or *kumbhaka*). On the one hand, these can and have been used in an ascetic context to discipline and mortify the body, to mop up its unclean fluids, and ultimately to shut down its vital processes. On the other hand, they can be used to purify, strengthen, and perfect the body. The same can be said for the practice's core and defining techniques, the physical locks (*bandhas*) and seals (*mudrās*) that manipulate the body's vital forces and subtle energies. Nearly every one of the following practices is prescribed by medieval *haṭha* texts as being either for preserving *bindu* or for raising the *kuṇḍalinī*, depending on the particular text and context:[50]

- *Mahāmudrā* ("great seal"): Seated, the practitioner presses the heel of one foot into the perineum and extends the other foot away from the body while holding it with both hands. He draws in the abdomen, presses his chin down to his chest, inhales, and exhales. He swaps the position of the feet and repeats. Note that this includes the three basic *bandhas* described below (*jālandhara*, *uḍḍīyāna*, and *mūla*).
- *Mahāvedha* ("great piercing"): Seated, knees bent, the practitioner places the soles of his feet together and presses the heels into the perineum. Alternatively, he may place one heel under the perineum, lift himself up with the hands, and drop the perineum down onto the heel. This makes the breath enter the central channel.

- *Mahābandha* ("great lock"): Initially, the same as *mūlabandha*. Later, the same as the *mahāmudrā* position, but with the outstretched foot placed on the opposite thigh.
- *Khecarīmudra* "sky-going seal"): The tongue is lengthened, folded back, and inserted into the cavity above the soft palate.
- *Jālandharabandha* ("net-bearing lock"): The chin is pressed down into the chest, constricting the throat.
- *Uḍḍīyānabandha* ("upward-flying lock"): The abdomen is drawn up and in.
- *Mūlabandha* ("root lock"): The perineal region is engaged and contracted.
- *Viparītakaraṇi* ("inversion"): The body is inverted, via headstand, shoulderstand, or similar.
- *Vajrolī* (not translatable, but probably meant to evoke the various meanings of *vajra*): Semen or commingled sexual fluids are drawn back up through the urethra.
- *Śakticālanī* ("*śakti* stimulator"): The tongue is wrapped in cloth and pulled.
- *Yonimudrā* ("origin seal"): The same as *mūlabandha*.

But what about the poses?

Notably, it is at the culmination of medieval *haṭha* yoga's burgeoning popularity that we find a proliferation of physical poses, or *āsanas*. The important thing to remember is this: yoga has never existed in a vacuum. As we discussed in the earlier chapters, it is impossible to make sense of yoga—much less of the different types of yoga—without some general knowledge of South Asian culture, be that religion, philosophy, medicine, martial arts, and so forth. This is crucial when one is thinking about yoga's physical practices, including *āsanas*, which may very well have first emerged in contexts that were not strictly speaking yogic, and may have been instead used for other purposes.

As we've seen, earlier yoga texts don't tend to make a big to-do about *āsana*. We first find complex and sometimes non-seated *āsanas* being discussed as an element of yoga in Vaiṣṇava texts, including the tantric Pañcarātra school, beginning in the 9th and 10th centuries.[51] Here we see elaborate poses like *mayūrāsana*, or peacock pose, which requires the practitioner to balance on the hands, elbows bent under the body while holding it up parallel to the ground. Many earlier *haṭha* texts, however, name or describe one or two *āsanas*, and often none at all. As best, they signal the existence of a multitude of *āsanas* before reducing them down to a single essential one, such as the *Dattātreya Yoga Śāstra* does when it says, "Among the eight million four hundred thousand *āsana*-s, listen to [my description of] the best one. In this system it is called lotus pose, [which] was taught by Śiva."[52] The takeaway, therefore, seems to be that there is nothing to be gained from these innumerable *āsanas* that cannot be accomplished by sitting with the legs crossed.

The *Haṭha Pradīpikā*, includes a higher number of *āsanas* than its predecessors, clocking in at 15 in total and gesturing at the existence of more. Most of these can be found scattered across the various sources that Svātmārāma used to compile his text.[53] However, as we just mentioned, the *Haṭha Pradīpikā* also expands on the potential usefulness of *āsana* practice. It also begins the trend of referring to other sorts of yogic techniques as *āsanas*. For instance, the practice of lying supine on the ground like a corpse first appears as one of the *saṃketas* of *laya* yoga. In the *Haṭha Pradīpikā* this is called *śavāsana* ("corpse pose").[54] Later texts take this idea further, and we see the inverted poses that were originally practiced as a *mudrā* called *viparītakaraṇī* now being referred to as *āsanas*, like *viparītakaraṇāsana* and *kapālāsana*, which become the equivalents of the "shoulderstand" and "headstand" postures we know today[55] (Figure 6.5).

By the 17th century, the number of *āsanas* being either named or fully described jumps into the hundreds. Texts dated to this period and into the 18th century feature hundreds of complex *āsanas*, sometimes involving the use of props like ropes, which may or may not have been performed as sequences. For instance, the (likely 18th-century) *Haṭha Abhyāsa Paddhati* subdivides its 112 poses into 6 categories: supine *āsanas*; prone *āsanas*; stationary *āsanas*; standing *āsanas*; rope *āsanas*; and *āsanas* that pierce the sun and moon. Other texts specifically claim to present what they understand to be the 84 *āsanas* taught by Śiva himself—a canonical number that is repeated by yoga schools to this day. The purpose of these poses, ostensibly, was bodily strength and fitness.[56]

Ultimately, it's impossible to say exactly how these *āsanas* would have been practiced prior to the modern period. For instance, were they held for some amount of time, or were they performed in rapid succession? Nor, aside from a very specific few described in earlier texts, do we have a very clear idea as to how much these *āsanas* correspond to the ones we see in postural yoga systems today. At the very least, however, we know that some of the innovators of modern postural yoga in the 20th century were aware of these texts and therefore of the poses contained within them. It seems more than likely, therefore, that they are one significant ingredient among others in the development of modern postural yoga.

Yoga without borders

As we've already seen, sectarian boundaries—be they between Śaivas and Vaiṣṇavas or Hindus and Buddhists—are not necessarily absolute, stationary, or particularly useful in tracking the development of yoga. Perhaps more important than *which* religion a group was practicing, is the question of *how* they were practicing it. Is the nature of the practice ascetic? Tantric? Devotional? Possibly all of the above? And, again, all of these approaches might well include a type of yoga.

One major development we haven't mentioned yet, but which will become crucial as yoga moves into the modern period, is the role of Advaita Vedānta. Vedānta, literally the end (*ānta*) or the final part of the Veda, is a philosophical tradition devoted to examining the Upaniṣads. Advaita or "Non-Dual" Vedānta is a specific school within this stream that has its origins in the thought of an 8th-century theologian

Figure 6.5 *Viparītakaraṇāsana* ("inversion pose") practiced by an ascetic. From an illustrated manuscript of the Jogapradīpakā. India, likely Punjab, ca. 1830.

Source: Courtesy of the British Library.

named Śaṅkara. According to Śaṅkara, *brahman* is the only true reality, while the material world and the notion of individual Selves (*ātman*) are ultimately illusions born of ignorance (*avidyā*). Liberation in this system entails realizing the true nature of *brahman*, and the means to doing this is *jñāna*, knowledge or gnosis. Traditionally, Advaita Vedāntins did not think very highly of yogic methods, which they believed to depend on ultimately inferior cognitive mechanisms. Beginning in the 13th century, however, this began to change. For instance, the Yoga Upaniṣads, written largely in this medieval period, borrow from *haṭha* materials and integrate them with Advaita Vedānta.[57] Drawing on Advaita-friendly yogic texts such as the circa 10th-century *Yoga Vāsiṣṭha*, medieval Advaita Vedāntins gradually transformed their tradition in concert with the times.[58] By the early modern period, the situation was the reverse of what it had once been: authority in Advaita Vedānta had become associated with meditative yogic attainment rather than purely philosophical *jñāna*.[59] This would prove crucial for colonial understandings of what counted as "real" yoga.

The 2nd millennium of the Common Era also marks the arrival and gradual suffusion of Islam through the South Asian continent. The Delhi Sultanate rose as a center of power throughout much of the subcontinent between the 13th and 16th centuries, after which the Mughal empire dominated the political landscape into the 18th century. As early as the 12th century, the Sufis of northern India were readily translating and absorbing tantric (and therefore yogic) ideas, practices, and models of the body,[60] resulting in the synthesis we briefly examined in Chapters 2 and 3. In their works, *cakras* became cosmological spheres and waystations on the mystic's path. The deities formerly inhabiting the *cakras* gave way to archangels. Some scholars have proposed that it was as a response to this new religious atmosphere that *bhakti* devotionalism may have come to overtake tantric ritualism.[61] The true reality is probably quite a bit messier and more complicated and yoga, of course, has historically taken root with equal ease within both frameworks.

One example of a fruitful crosspollination between tantric and *bhakti* practices can be found in the Gauḍīya Vaiṣṇava tradition that is today globally represented by the International Society for Krishna Consciousness. The movement began in 16th-century Bengal, based on the teachings of a guru named Caitanya, who, in a rather tantric fashion, was believed by later devotees to be an incarnational of both of the male god Kṛṣṇa and his female partner Radhā in a single body. Caitanya's teachings were codified by six of his followers known collectively as the Gosvāmins. In their hands, Gauḍīya Vaiṣṇava practice became a path known as *rāgānugā* (passionate) *bhakti*, a complex *sādhana* through which the practitioner meditatively constructs a perfected body (*siddha rūpa*) that allows them to inhabit Kṛṣṇa's eternal divine play (*līlā*) as one of its stock characters.[62] The dramatic metaphor is very intentional here. The Gosvāmins relied heavily on aesthetics and drama theory to fashion their framework. Using the traditional narrative of Kṛṣṇa's time in the idyllic pastoral setting on Vṛndāvana (a holy site found in modern Uttar Pradesh) as a template, the practitioner uses tantric ritual and visualization techniques to construct their ideal devotional persona. It is important to note, however (and it is a point that the Gosvāmins emphasize again and again), that although one can become one of Kṛṣṇa's eternal entourage, one cannot and should never identify oneself with Kṛṣṇa, nor Radhā for that matter. The attitude of *bhakti* demands that the devotee remain different from their object of their devotion. God is supreme.

Within the *bhakti* devotional traditions we also find the songs of Mīrābāī, a woman from 16th-century Rajasthan whose voice has become one of the most famous expressions of devotion to Kṛṣṇa. Mīrā often speaks of Kṛṣṇa as a husband and lover, an erotic mode of devotion that also represents the highest form of Gauḍīya Vaiṣṇava *rāgānugā bhakti*. However, she often combines her romantic longing for Kṛṣṇa with ascetic imagery. She sings:

> Oh, the yogi—
> my friend, that clever one
> whose mind is on Shiva and the Snake,
> that all-knowing yogi—tell him this:
> "I'm not staying here, not staying where
> the land's grown strange without you, my dear
> But coming home, coming to where your place is;
> take me, guard me with your guardian mercy,
> please
> I'll take up your yogic garb—
> your prayer beads,
> earrings,
> begging-bowl skull,
> tattered yogic cloth—
> I'll take them all
> And search through the world as a yogi does
> with you—yogi and yoginī, side by side."[63]

Mīrā's vision of yoga suggests something of the more ascetic variety, but among the Vaiṣṇava Sahajiyās, we find a devotional tantric yoga that also carries echoes of the older Buddhist *Caryagītī*. Evolving side-by-side with the Gaudīya Vaiṣṇavas, the Sahajiyās relied on many of the same devotional and aesthetic tropes but embraced a fuller range of tantric practices including sexual rituals, *haṭha* yogic and alchemical techniques, and strived for ultimate identity with the divine.[64] Today, we can still see this kind of itinerant yogic eclecticism carried on by the Bauls of Bengal and modern-day Bangladesh, who still sing of a natural mysticism grounded in the body. The songs of the Bauls blend Hindu, Buddhist, and Muslim ideas to light an esoteric path that transcends the distinctions and strictures of ordinary society.[65]

Conclusions

- After 500 CE, tantra emerged as the mainstream form of religion in South Asia. Tantra was, overall, heavily ritualistic but it also included certain visionary practices associated with yoga, which were used to perfect and even divinize the human body so that it was more suitable to worship the supreme deity.

- One specific type of tantra, its origins based in transgressive interactions with wrathful goddesses, evolved across Buddhist and Śaiva contexts. These traditions originally organized their goddesses into clans or *kulas*, and so they were called Kaula. Over time, the norm-defying rituals of these groups became cleaned up, philosophized, and internalized, giving us yogic concepts like the *cakras* of the subtle body and the internal energy of *kuṇḍalinī śakti*.
- The physical practices associated with premodern *haṭha* yoga originally began among celibate ascetics and were used to preserve *bindu*. Passed down orally from guru to disciple, these various *bandhas* (locks) and *mudrās* (seals) were practiced alongside other forms of asceticism such as immobilizing the body to the point that limbs would atrophy, or sitting in a circle of fires under the hot sun. All of these were originally geared at mortifying the body and cultivating the energy of *tapas*.
- From the 13th century onwards, we see a blending of these two streams as texts purporting to teach *haṭha* yoga and instruct the use of ascetic techniques alongside tantric visionary methods in order to awaken and raise the energy of *kuṇḍalinī* so as to achieve a state of perfected embodied liberation.
- Yoga continually drifted between the ascetic and the tantric, the bodily and the visionary. As cultural winds shifted, it was also used to achieve a devotional connection with the supreme Gods of *bhakti* traditions, to realize the philosophical truths of non-dual Vedānta, and even to chart the way back to Allāh in Sufi mysticism.

Notes

1 Alexis Sanderson, "The Śaiva Age: The Rise and Dominance of Śaivism during the Early Medieval Period," in *Genesis and Development of Tantrism*, ed. Shingo Einoo, Institute of Oriental Culture Special Series 23 (Tokyo: Institute of Oriental Culture, University of Tokyo, 2009), 41–350.

2 Ronald M. Davidson, *Indian Esoteric Buddhism: Social History of the Tantric Movement* (Delhi: Motilal Banarsidass, 2004), 25–30.

3 David Gordon White, ed., *Tantra in Practice* (Princeton, NJ: Princeton University Press, 2000), 25–8.

4 Hélène Brunner, "Le Sādhaka, Personnage Oublié Du Śivaïsme Du Sud," *Journal Asiatique*, 263 (1975): 411–43.

5 Gavin D. Flood, *The Tantric Body: The Secret Tradition of Hindu Religion* (London and New York: I. B. Tauris, 2006), 53.

6 André Padoux, *The Hindu Tantric World: An Overview* (Chicago: University of Chicago Press, 2017), 105–9.

7 David Gordon White, *The Kiss of the Yoginī: "Tantric Sex" in Its South Asian Contexts* (Chicago: University of Chicago Press, 2002), 27; Shaman Hatley, "What Is a Yoginī? Towards a Polythetic Definition," in *"Yogini" in South Asia: Interdisciplinary Approaches*, ed. István Keul (Abingdon and New York: Routledge, 2013), 21–31.

8 White, *The Kiss of the Yoginī*, 61–3.

9 Alexis Sanderson, "Purity and Power among the Brahmans of Kashmir," in *The Category of the Person: Anthropology, Philosophy, History*, ed. Michael Carrithers, Steven Collins, and Steven Lukes (Cambridge: Cambridge University Press, 1985), 190–216, and White, *The Kiss of the Yoginī*, 188–218.

10 Hatley, "What Is a Yoginī?," 28.

11 White, *The Kiss of the Yoginī*, 160–87.
12 White, *The Kiss of the Yoginī*, 195.
13 Hatley, "What Is a Yoginī?," 23–4.
14 White, *The Kiss of the Yoginī*, 106–12.
15 White, *The Kiss of the Yoginī*, 234–5.
16 White, *The Kiss of the Yoginī*, 109–12.
17 White, *The Kiss of the Yoginī*, 83.
18 Roger R. Jackson, *Tantric Treasures: Three Collections of Mystical Verse from Buddhist India* (New York: Oxford University Press, 2004).
19 Lee Siegel, "Bengal Blackie and the Sacred Slut: A Sahajayāna Buddhist Song," *Buddhist-Christian Studies Buddhist-Christian Studies*, 1 (1981): 51, and Lee Siegel, "Bengal Blackie Rides Again," *Buddhist-Christian Studies*, 5 (1985): 191–2.
20 Jackson Stephenson, "Love Me for the Sake of the World: 'Goddess Songs' in Tantric Buddhist Maṇḍala Rituals," *Religions*, 11, no. 3 (2020).
21 White, *Tantra in Practice*, 32.
22 White, *The Kiss of the Yoginī*, 219–57.
23 James Mallinson and Mark Singleton, *Roots of Yoga: A Sourcebook from the Indic Traditions* (London: Penguin Classics, 2017), 179.
24 Somadeva Vasudeva, *The Yoga of the Mālinīvijayottaratantra: Chapters 1–4, 7, 11–17* (Pondichery: Institut français de Pondichéry, Ecole française d'Extrême-Orient, 2004), 434–6.
25 James Mallinson, "Yoga and Yogis," *Nāmarūpa*, 3, no. 15 (2012): 7.
26 Mallinson, "Yoga and Yogis," 7.
27 Jason Birch, "The Meaning of Haṭha in Early Haṭhayoga," *Journal of the American Oriental Society*, 131, no. 4 (2011): 527–54.
28 James Mallinson, "Hathayoga's Philosophy: A Fortuitous Union of Non-Dualities," *Journal of Indian Philosophy*, 42, no. 1 (2014): 225–47.
29 Jason Birch, "Rājayoga: The Reincarnations of the King of All Yogas," *International Journal of Hindu Studies*, 17, no. 3 (2013): 399–442.
30 Birch, "The Meaning of Haṭha in Early Haṭhayoga," 546.
31 Birch, "Rājayoga," 408.
32 Mallinson, "Yoga and Yogis," 11–12.
33 James Mallinson, "The Amṛtasiddhi: Haṭhayoga's Tantric Buddhist Source Text," in *Śaivism and the Tantric Traditions: A Festschrift for Alexis Sanderson*, ed. Dominic Goodall, Shaman Hatley, and Harunaga Isaacson (Leiden: Brill, forthcoming).
34 Birch, "The Meaning of Haṭha in Early Haṭhayoga," 535.
35 Mallinson, "Yoga and Yogis," 12.
36 Mallinson, "Yoga and Yogis," 20.
37 Mallinson, "Yoga and Yogis," 6.
38 Mallinson, "Yoga and Yogis," 7.
39 Mallinson, "Yoga and Yogis," 8.
40 Mallinson, "Yoga and Yogis," 9.
41 Mallinson, "Yoga and Yogis," 8.
42 Daniela Bevilacqua, "Let the Sādhus Talk: Ascetic Understanding of Haṭha Yoga and Yogāsanas," *Religions of South Asia*, 11, nos. 2–3 (2017): 182–206.
43 James Mallinson, "*Hathayoga*'s Philosophy: A Fortuitous Union of Non-Dualities," *Journal of Indian Philosophy*, 42, no. 1 (2014): 225–47.
44 Mallinson, "*Hathayoga*'s Philosophy," 229.
45 Mallinson, "*Hathayoga*'s Philosophy," 230.
46 Mallinson, "Yoga and Yogis," 27.
47 James Mallinson, "Haṭha Yoga," in *Brill's Encyclopedia of Hinduism: Volume III, Society, Religious Specialists, Religious Traditions, Philosophy*, ed. Knut A. Jacobsen et al. (Leiden; Boston: Brill, 2011), 776.

48 Jason Birch, "Premodern Yoga Traditions and Ayurveda: Preliminary Remarks on Shared Terminology, Theory, and Praxis," *History of Science in South Asia*, 6 (2018): 1–83.
49 Mallinson and Singleton, *Roots of Yoga*, 154.
50 This list is directly adapted from Mallinson, "Haṭha Yoga," 778.
51 Mallinson, "*Hathayoga*'s Philosophy," 227–8.
52 Jason Birch, "The Proliferation of *Āsana*-s in Late-Mediaeval Yoga Texts," in *Yoga in Transformation: Historical and Contemporary Perspectives on a Global Phenomenon*, ed. Karl Baier, Philip A. Maas, and Karin Preisendanz (Göttingen, The Netherlands: Vandenhoeck & Ruprecht Unipress, 2018), 107.
53 Mallinson, "*Hathayoga*'s Philosophy," 227.
54 Mallinson, "Haṭha Yoga," 776.
55 Birch, "The Proliferation of *Āsana*-s," 139–40.
56 Birch, "The Proliferation of *Āsana*-s," 135 and Jason Birch and Mark Singleton, "The Yoga of the Haṭhābhyāsapaddhati: Haṭhayoga on the Cusp of Modernity," *Journal of Yoga Studies*, 2 (2019): 3–70.
57 Christian Bouy, *Les Nātha-yogin et les Upaniṣads: étude d'histoire de la littérature hindoue* (Paris: Diffusion de Boccard, 1994), and Jeffrey Clark Ruff, "Yoga in the Yoga Upaniṣads: Disciplines of the Mystical OṂ Sound," in *Yoga in Practice*, ed. David Gordon White (Princeton, NJ: Princeton University Press, 2012), 97–116.
58 James Madaio, "Rethinking Neo-Vedānta: Swami Vivekananda and the Selective Historiography of Advaita Vedānta," *Religions*, 8, no. 6 (2017): 1–12.
59 Jason Schwartz, "Parabrahman Among the Yogins," *International Journal of Hindu Studies*, 21, no. 3 (2017): 345–89.
60 Carl W. Ernst, "The Islamization of Yoga in the 'Amrtakunda' Translations," *Journal of the Royal Asiatic Society*, 3, 13, no. 2 (2003): 199–226, and Shaman Hatley, "Mapping the Esoteric Body in the Islamic Yoga of Bengal," *History of Religions*, 46, no. 4 (2007): 351–68.
61 For instance, William R. Pinch, *Warrior Ascetics and Indian Empires* (New York: Cambridge University Press, 2006), 31, and White, *Sinister Yogis*, 241.
62 David Haberman, *Acting as a Way to Salvation: A Study of Rāgānugā Bhakti Sādhana* (New York: Oxford University Press, 1988).
63 John Stratton Hawley, *Three Bhakti Voices: Mirabai, Surdas, and Kabir in Their Time and Ours* (New Delhi: Oxford University Press, 2005), 255.
64 Glen A. Hayes, "The Necklace of Immortality: A Seventeenth-Century Vaiṣṇava Sahajiyā Text," in *Tantra in Practice*, ed. David Gordon White (Princeton, NJ: Princeton University Press, 2000), 308–25.
65 Rahul Peter Das, "Problematic Aspects of the Sexual Rituals of the Bauls of Bengal," *Jameroriesoci Journal of the American Oriental Society*, 112, no. 3 (1992): 388–432, and Keith E. Cantú, "Islamic Esotericism in the Bengali Bāul Songs of Lālan Fakir," *Correspondences*, 7, no. 1 (2019): 109–65.

7 The rise of modern postural yoga

In the previous two chapters we have kept our focus entirely on the South Asian subcontinent. In this chapter, on the other hand, we will spend a good portion of our time in Europe and North America, and especially in the United States. This should not be taken to suggest that modern yoga developed in the West. We've seen, however, the way in which shifts in what yoga looks like have historically corresponded to shifts in its surrounding culture. Evolution is often a response to something. The case with modern postural yoga—the kind of yoga you'll find when you walk into your average yoga studio or a yoga class at the local gym—is even more complicated. This is because modern postural yoga is global. Meaning, it developed and continues to exist in multiple cultural contexts, literally on different sides of the globe.

It's tempting to think of this notion of yoga as something like an export. As though yoga is a thing, produced in India, and then brought over to the West in a kind of one-directional movement. Another, slightly more complex way of thinking about this is what's known as the "pizza effect."[1] This model says that yoga (like pizza!) started out in one culture, was exported to another culture where it was transformed in some way, and then was re-imported back to its place of origin in this new form, where it now enjoys an unprecedented level of popularity. This is a slightly better metaphor because it, at least, acknowledges the kind of bi-directional back-and-forth that takes place when two cultures interact. But this is still a little too neat.

Instead, we propose returning to the metaphor we raised in the first section of this book: plants. Yoga (or, really any complex cultural thing) is like a rhizomatic plant—hops, water lilies, lotuses, or bamboo—pick your favorite. Rhizomes spread via a subterranean tangle of roots and shoots. Each plant is a little bit different, springing up here and there, but they're all connected as part of the same network. Just so, every manifestation of yoga is its own unique tradition, but all spring from the same deep cultural consciousness.

Now, what might happen if you were to take such a plant to the other side of the world? (Since we're talking about yoga, let's stick with lotuses.) Well, you're not going to dump your lotus in just any old patch of dirt. If you want it to take root in this new environment, you might look for the places where similar plants have thrived. If you've got a lotus on your hands, you might plant it in a pond of water lilies. A few years later, you've got a big tangle on your hands. You'll hardly be able to tell where the water lilies end and the lotuses begin, or even which is which. Who knows, your little experiment might even produce some wild new lotus–water lily hybrid!

So how is this metaphor different from the others? There are two things involved. The place you brought your lotus already had water lilies. What you did with the lotus was influenced by your understanding of water lilies, and vice versa. A person from that other culture who's never seen a lotus before would likely go, "Oh, it's basically a water lily." They might even like the word lotus and what it represents so much that they start going around and calling water lilies lotuses. And, of course, now that they've grown together, just try and pull them apart!

Modern postural yoga is one big lotus–water lily exchange program.

So why are we spending a lot of this chapter talking about Europe and North America? In order to understand what happens to the lotus, we need to understand the water lily. In order to understand what happens to yoga, we need to understand Western harmonialism.

The other central question of this chapter is more or less: how did popular global yoga come to function primarily as exercise? There, the answer is twofold. On the one hand, it has to do with the fact that the men who modernized and popularized Indian yoga in the 20th century were deeply interested in physical culture. In fact, they saw strong (specifically male) bodies as the cornerstone of India's fight for independence from colonial rule. On the other hand, it has to do with the fact that this fitness-oriented yoga happened to closely resemble the light, dance-like gymnastics that were at that very moment rapidly gaining in popularity among Western women. In Part III of this book, we will grapple with yoga in the context of modern capitalism. For now, then, let's borrow some language from that world to explain what's going on here. In the West, yoga holds a specific (niche feminine) market-share of physical culture. In India, the market is different, and yoga occupies a different (and far more mainstream masculine) place in it. There's no essential reason, other than the seemingly accidental winds of cultural norms, why it should have been men in one case and women in the other. We might only suggest that these two groups did share something in the way of reasons when they chose to adopt yoga—they were both looking to tap into a history (whether real or imagined) and a set of meanings that "regular" exercise did not seem to have.

Indian modernizers who chose to engage in yoga did so for a reason. For them, yoga and especially yogis had a culturally specific history that grounded the practice in strength, discipline, and most importantly in India and increasingly in Hinduism. Western women who chose to engage in yoga also did so for a reason. For them, yoga and to some extent yogis evoked an exotic timelessness that grounded the practice in spirituality, and in an ancient and ultimately universal wisdom. Both counterbalanced these claims to history with an insistence that the exercises of yoga were medically sound and supported by the understandings of modern science. Given all this, it's important to note that neither of these groups viewed their activities as precisely "secular." Meaning, yoga was exercise but that did not mean that it was without metaphysical import. As we saw in Chapter 3, another thing that the two groups shared was a cultural history of viewing the body as integrally connected to a spiritual reality, where bodily perfection was directly related to spiritual accomplishment.

Colonialism and yogis

The definitive history of yoga and yogis under European colonialism has not yet been written. Modern scholars of yoga who deal with this time period have tended to focus on colonial perceptions of yogis, which of course tells us very little about what yoga practice would have actually looked like during this time. However, on second glance, the gap is smaller than it may seem. Some of the major texts of classical *haṭha* yoga, such as the *Gheraṇḍa Saṃhitā*, were written as late as the 18th century. Add to this the fact that the yoga practice we find among early international yogis like Paramahansa Yogananda still looks, at its core, very much like classical *haṭha* yoga, and we can perhaps conclude that many of the ideas and practices we described at the end of Chapter 6 persisted and continued to evolve without much interruption.

There is a standard narrative that by the 19th century, yoga had fallen into deep disrepute in Indian society. If one looks at such arguments a bit closer, it becomes clear that here yoga really means *haṭha* yoga, and this in turn refers more to the kinds of physical techniques normally practiced by ascetics rather than the tantric synthesis of the medieval texts. As a result, Swami Vivekananda, who is often credited with singlehandedly introducing yoga to the West, can totally dismiss "*haṭha* yoga" while teaching a yoga consisting of using *prāṇāyāma* and visualization techniques to raise the *kuṇḍalinī*.

But what gave ascetics such a bad reputation? Granted, itinerant yogis have always been rather ambiguous figures in Indian folklore—they might just as easily use the powers they gained from their *tapas* to curse you as to bless you.[2] The rising popularity of devotional *bhakti* traditions against the backdrop of Muslim rule from the 13th century onwards didn't help matters. Devotional literature is full of puffed up and power-hungry yogis, both ascetic and tantric, who are routinely humiliated by the superior miracles of God-loving *bhaktas* and Sufis[3] (Figure 7.1). And of course there was never any shortage of beggars and swindlers who would pose as yogis in order to garner alms. But there is a much more specific historical reason at work here, too. As historian William R. Pinch has demonstrated, the formal ascetic orders had once been some of India's fiercest military contractors.[4] Under colonial rule, however, their power became an issue as it never had been before.

From the 17th century onwards, European nations began to extend their influence into India, primarily by way to trade. Over the following two centuries, Great Britain and its East India Company would emerge as the dominant player. After the decline of the Mughal Empire in the early 18th century and the subsequent defeat of the Maratha Empire in the Second (1803–1805) and Third (1817–1818) Anglo-Maratha Wars, the East India Company became the dominant power on the subcontinent. By the beginning of the 19th century, the Company had already become an arm of the British government. In 1857, a major uprising against Company

Figure 7.1 A pilgrim meeting a yogi ascetic. India, Mughal dynasty, ca. 1600.
Source: Courtesy of the Smithsonian Institute, Freer Gallery of Art and Arthur M. Sackler Gallery.

rule led to its dissolution by the British Crown. It was replaced by the British Raj, which ruled over a large portion of the subcontinent until the region's independence in 1947 and its subsequent partition into the modern-day republics of India, Pakistan, and eventually Bangladesh.

It's uncertain when and why ascetics first took up arms but, by the 18th century, the declining Mughal Empire left a power vacuum that allowed them to become major players in warfare and trade alike.[5] In this sense, they were the British East India Company's chief rivals. Rather than availing themselves of the armed yogi's services as contractors, the British chose instead to oppose and suppress them, first via military action and later via legislation.[6] As historian of yoga David Gordon White has summarized the situation, "With a stroke of the pen in 1773, Warren Hastings transformed the yogis entering or traversing Company-controlled territories from members of religious orders to vagrants and criminals."[7] Pinch and White both suggest that this criminalization of martial ascetics contributed to the poor perception of yogis in colonial India and, combined with the ongoing influence of *bhakti* and Muslim devotionalism, yielded the more contemplative, inwardly oriented ideal of the monk, uninterested in worldly power, which was far from the historical norm.[8] As we'll see shortly, however, it is precisely this kind of worldly yogic power that scholars of modern yoga like Joseph Alter and Mark Singleton have argued is behind the association of yoga with masculine physical culture.[9]

On the other hand, while ascetic yogis were likely to be treated with disdain, British and German Orientalists—that is, early scholars of Asian traditions—were busy sifting through the rich heritage of India's philosophic traditions, which they interpreted and misinterpreted based on their own priorities, interests, and agendas. By the end of the 18th century, the philosophical tradition of Vedānta and specifically Advaita (Non-dual) Vedānta, had come to dominate the Indian philosophic arena. And so, along with Vaiṣṇava *bhakti*, which the famous philologist Sir Monier Monier-Williams once declared, "notwithstanding the gross polytheistic superstitions and hideous idolatry to which it gives rise, is the only Hindū system worthy of being called a religion,"[10] it was Vedānta that Europeans came to deem most worthy.

However, while Orientalist philosophers were mostly concerned with what they perceived to the be the pure and original Vedānta found in pre-modern texts, on the ground in India Vedānta was a living tradition. One significant way that Advaita Vedānta had evolved since its inception in the 9th century was to absorb and incorporate a number of tantric and yogic concepts and practices. Consequently, when reformist groups began to formulate their agendas to uplift and modernize Hinduism, their predilection for Vedāntic philosophy opened up a back door for the concurrent modernization and popularization of yoga. This yoga was in their eyes, as in the eyes of colonial authorities, distinctly different from the "false" yoga of the maligned and ragged ascetics. "True" yoga was philosophical, contemplative, and—above all—universal.

It would be inaccurate to say that this yoga wasn't physical. Vedāntic tradition had by this time absorbed a considerable amount of *haṭha* yoga and, with it, all manner of breathwork and bodily practices. However, it would not have historically involved the severe kinds of bodily discipline practiced by ascetic yogis. By the end of the 19th century, as the tensions of colonialism mounted, things would begin to shift. In the hands of a new wave of reformers, ascetic methods that promoted power and virility were married with this philosophical synthesis to produce an ideal of yoga that was at once physical and metaphysical. By this time, though, Indian frameworks—whether the philosophies of Advaita Vedānta or the physical sciences of the body—had melded significantly with analogous Western imports. Water lilies had begun to take root among lotuses. And so understanding what happens next is going to require a shift in perspective.

Enter Western harmonialism

This is where we must make a bit of a cultural leap. Because this book is written for a primarily Western audience, familiar with the modern Western manifestations of yoga (specifically those currently popular in North America and Europe), we need to fill in a bit of the history that precedes Indian yoga's arrival in the West. We've already hinted at some of this history in our first section, when we reviewed a number of concepts that cannot historically be considered "yogic" prior to the 19th century or so. Now, we'll need to return to those concepts and place them in their proper context.

As we've previously mentioned, if there's anything like yoga to be found in pre-modern Europe, it's the cluster of ideas and practices that we can loosely identify as "harmonial." Allowing that both terms have a wide and historically variable range of meanings, if Indian spiritual practices have often strived for "yoga" (translated as "union," "yoking," or a bit more technically, "rigging"), Western ones have strived for "harmony" (from the ancient Greek *harmonia*, which should be understood as carrying both its technical musical and more generic meanings).

Like yoga, harmonialism straddles the divides between religion, magic, alchemy, medicine, and aesthetics. Like Sāṅkhyan and tantric systems, harmonial systems tend to view reality as a hierarchical emanation from the subtle to the gross, and possibly all stemming from the divine itself. Matter is therefore not only suffused with spirit, but ultimately reducible to it, and the world operates according to a series of correspondences that allow all of reality to function as an interconnected whole. Grounded in ancient Greek thought, harmonialism makes a comeback during the European Renaissance, when it begins to take on some of the forms we're most familiar with today. Since we've already reviewed some of the central concepts of harmonialism in Chapters 2 and 3, at least where it comes to things like the body, the soul, and the nature of the universe, we won't do so again here. For our current purposes, it suffices to know that by the 19th century harmonial ideas were still alive and well.

In the sphere of religion and spirituality, they were birthing a number of new movements, some of which looked like slightly less conventional Christian Churches (like the New Church, influenced by Emanuel Swedenborg) and some of which were more like the equivalent of today's "spiritual but not religious" crowd (like the New Thought movement). Closer to the fringes, we see secret societies, such as the Theosophical Society founded by the Russian expat Helena Blavatsky and her American colleague Henry Steel Olcott, that double down on the historically "esoteric" or secret aspect of harmonialism. In a different arena, though science and religion were increasingly coming to be viewed as separate domains, physicists were still entertaining the idea of a luminiferous ether, which served as a medium for transmitting not only electromagnetism but also spirit. Likewise, truly modern medicine was still a way's off (even by the late 19th century, medical professionals were often liable to do more harm than good), leaving room for competing methods ranging from "Mind Cure," which advocated healing by putting mind over matter, to "Movement Cure," which was something like an all-purpose form of physical therapy.

At the juncture of all these things, we find 19th-century Westerners engaging in breathing exercises—sometimes for spiritual, sometimes for healing purposes, and sometimes for both—which are not the same as yogic *prāṇāyāma*, but which would shortly become conflated with it. We also see these breathing practices occasionally accompanied by physical exercises, sometimes simple arm movements and shifts of weight and sometimes more dynamic gymnastics, that are not yet called yoga, but which soon will be.

Like Indian yoga, harmonial ways of connecting the physical and the spiritual are historically diverse and conceptually multifaceted. Since we don't have the time or space to go all the way back to the beginning, we'll skip ahead and introduce this equally complex tradition by way of two key exemplary figures, both of whom just happen to be men from Sweden. The first is Emanuel Swedenborg (1688–1772), a scientist and mystic who best embodies the sort of harmonial contemplative practice that comes closest to yogic notions of *dhyāna*. The second is Pehr Henrik Ling (1776–1839), a poet, physical culturalist, and physician whose system of harmonial gymnastics would go on to indirectly influence the Indian innovators of postural yoga as well as serve as a crucial ingredient for Western notions of spiritual exercise. We'll also briefly discuss a few of the people they influenced, who would then go on to advocate the practice of something that looks and sounds a lot like postural yoga in the West.

Inhaling spirit

Swedenborg had been enjoying a fairly prolific scientific career when, just as he was preparing a project that sought to explain the soul from an anatomical point of view, his own soul began to take periodic journeys to places seemingly far from his earthly anatomy. In 1743, during a trip abroad, Swedenborg began to have strange dreams that by the end of the following year had made it clear to him that his path had now crossed solidly into the sphere of theology. This shift, and the non-traditional direction that Swedenborg's Christianity then took, elicited a self-distancing work of satire from the famous Enlightenment philosopher Immanuel Kant (1724–1804) as well as censorship and whispers of heresy. Swedenborg's spiritual writings are voluminous, and the metaphysics revealed therein are complex. Likewise, his influences must have been diverse and, for lack of specific documentation, are difficult to pinpoint. He certainly had much in common with the Neo-Platonists, and it's possible that he drew to some extent on Kabbalah.[11]

God, in Swedenborg's view, manifests as the "Divine Human," out of which flows heaven as the "Grand Man." Here we have again the logic of the micro- and macrocosms, the little world of the human body homologized to the big world of the universe. The body of the Grand Man is the totality of angels and their intricate communities. Swedenborg affirms, again and again, that man is essentially spirit and all spirits and angels belong to the human race. Thus, "man was created that he might come into heaven and become an angel" and, insofar as man is spiritual he serves as the link between the spiritual and natural worlds.[12] And, insofar as man's destiny is to become an angel, this entails the transition to a fully spiritual or "internal" existence in heaven—something that he can experience even while ensconced in his "external" natural body. Here we see something of a parallel to the yogic notion of *jīvanmukti*. Here is the idea of an embodied, living liberation.

At the crux of this process is Swedenborg's notion of "respiration" (*respiratio*) which can likewise be either internal or external. Through the motion of the breath, the human body is continuous with the celestial and spiritual worlds and thus it is through the breath—and specifically by physically stilling and internalizing the breath—that one can come to exist in these worlds, achieving a state of mystical absorption in the divine.

Though his work received limited positive attention during his own lifetime, societies for the dissemination of his writings, and eventually a number of church-like groups, began popping up after his death in the 1780s. Such groups spread throughout Europe and, by the first half of the 19th century, hopped the Atlantic Ocean to North America. There, they influenced other harmonial thinkers, like Warren Felt Evans (1817–1889), who left the Methodist Church where he was ordained as a minister in 1863 to join the Swedenborgian New Church after having read some of Swedenborg's writings.[13] Evans, also influenced by Theosophy, would emerge as an eclectic thinker and major advocate of what was becoming known as "Mind Cure." However, while most proponents of this kind of therapy stuck to the idea that disease was ultimately in the mind and could therefore be cured thought positive affirmations and correct thinking, Evans seemed to have really taken Swedenborg's ideas about the breath to heart. Breath drew in the inexhaustible energies of universal spirit into the human body. Deep full breathing, in Evans's view, was therefore crucial not only to bodily health but to a healthy state of mind and spirit. In turn, as the best means of cultivating proper breath he prescribed a system he called the "Swedish Movement Cure."[14]

The gymnastics of a Swedish poet

Pehr Ling received his degree in theology from Uppsala University in 1797, after which time he traveled throughout Europe for roughly a decade, mainly stopping in Germany, Denmark, and France. During this time, he made a meager living as a tutor, studied and wrote poetry on the subject of Norse mythology, and held several minor military appointments. It was also in this period that he became seriously interested in physical culture. In 1805, Ling was appointed as professor of fencing at Lund University and, in addition to his teaching duties, began to study anatomy, physiology, and other natural sciences, which he viewed as essential to gymnastics. Based on this work, Ling developed a system of holistic physical culture aimed chiefly at military training on the one hand and medical therapeutics on the other.

In 1812, he became an instructor at the Military Academy at Carlsberg, meanwhile making appeals for support for his system to the Swedish government. Though he had been initially rebuffed, being informed that "there are enough of jugglers and ropedancers, without exacting any further charge from the public treasury," his appointment at Carlsberg must have raised his level of credibility. He became founding head of the Royal Gymnastic Central Institute in Stockholm in 1813, which from that point onward served as his base of operations. Despite meeting with initial resistance, the adoption and dissemination of Ling's system by medical professionals across Sweden, Germany, and France bolstered his prestige, and in 1831 he was elected to the Swedish General Medical Association. By the middle of the 19th century, his system was well known in North America, where it was being touted by some as the "Movement Cure." Proponents of Ling's system, even in so-called secular contexts, hailed it as a complete regimen that addressed the "whole organism"—mind, body, and soul.[15]

Ling believed the human organism to be composed of three fundamental principles: the dynamic phenomena of the mental and moral faculties, the chemical phenomena of the body's internal processes, and the mechanical phenomena of the body's internal and external processes. The unified harmony of these vital orders signified a state of health and the necessary condition for an organism's development. The military and medical branches of Ling's system were by far both the most developed and most widely disseminated, which is unsurprising given his military background and medical training. However, Ling's system as he conceptualized it was actually divided into four branches: (1) pedagogical gymnastics, through which one learns to bring one's body under one's own will, developing unity among the parts of the organism; (2) military gymnastics, through which one seeks to subject the will of another person to one's own by means of one's bodily power, with or without the aid of a weapon; (3) medical gymnastics, through which one seeks either through one's own effort or with the help of another person to restore unity between the parts of one's body; and (4) aesthetic gymnastics, through which one seeks to express the unity of one's mental and bodily being.[16]

In contrast to the medical and gymnastic divisions, the last category—aesthetic gymnastics—remained the least developed and elaborated by Ling's immediate advocates (Ling himself never published much). This is unfortunate because this is the part of his system that is the most obviously harmonial in character, and arguably the most influential when it comes to what mainstream yoga looks like in North America today. Ling's own account of aesthetic gymnastics is extremely brief and unsystematic, focusing largely on abstract statements about the relationship between body and soul. He does, however, rather suggestively state that while in pedagogical gymnastics the body acts on the soul, in aesthetic gymnastics it is the soul that acts on the body.[17]

From aesthetic gymnastics to Oriental dance

The notion of aesthetic gymnastics would eventually gain in popularity, but when it did so, some half a century later, it would be associated with another man's name—Delsarte. François Alexandre Nicolas Chéri Delsarte (1811–1871) was a French composer and musical instructor. During his time studying at the prestigious Paris Conservatory, Delsarte became frustrated that the training of the students seemed not to be following any set of systematic aesthetic principles, and thus set out to develop his own. Ironically, very few of the practices that turned Delsarte into a household name were part of his original system, which was designed specifically for artists, actors, and orators. Delsarte's system, which was grounded in Christian harmonial principles, was above all a theory of aesthetics governing expression that, in its highest form, becomes a sort of body language for the soul. Much of Delsarte's system was actually focused on oratory and dramatic speech, which necessitated the inclusion of fairly complex breathing exercises to develop the vocal apparatus.

When it came to motion, Delsarte believed that gesture, like music (which, in harmonialism, is the true language of the soul) is rhythmic, inflective, and harmonic.

While Delsarte taught some physical exercises, there is no evidence that he ever advocated gymnastics for its own sake. The development of "aesthetic gymnastics" based on Delsarte's principles, with a generous infusion of Ling, was pioneered by Steele Mackaye (1842–1894), an American student of Delsarte. Mackaye's combination of the two systems is not unexpected. There is no known record of Ling and Delsarte ever meeting, nor any direct evidence (aside from some evocatively similar terminology) that Delsarte was familiar with Ling's work. But, regardless of whether there was any link between the two men, the similarities of their systems are undeniable. More importantly, these similarities were not lost on Mackaye, whose own work inextricably fused them into one coherent whole.

Delsarte—or "American Delsarteism," as it's sometimes more formally called—would emerge over the last three decades of the 19th century as the first fully modern wellness brand. Delsarte's name was pinned on everything from fitness classes, to "healthful" corsets, to home décor. And, not surprisingly, the Delsarte phenomenon was not only wildly popular but incredibly gender-specific. Between 1870 and 1900, over 400 active American teachers and performers identified as Delsarteans or expressed a significant debt to the system, 85 percent of whom were women.[18] The composition of students skewed even more drastically female.

This is important insofar as it was fairly revolutionary. The 19th century was a peak time for the ideology of the "separate spheres," which doubled down on the "natural" differences between men and women and insisted that women were inherently delicate and frail beings that needed to be sheltered in the home, unsuited to both intellectual and physical labor. So, one the one hand, a gymnastics designed specifically for women, and often taught at newly chartered women's colleges, flouted some core cultural norms. On the other hand, there is a reason that Delsarteism is an aesthetic style of gymnastics—this is an appropriately feminine style of physical culture. As popular wisdom declared, if the exercises were not sufficiently attractive and graceful, women simply wouldn't do them.[19]

Appropriately then, it's also in the hands of a woman, namely Genevieve Stebbins, that the fusion of Ling and Delsarte would reach its next level. Born in San Francisco in 1857, Stebbins spent most of her life in the United States, though she made several important trips to Europe. Stebbins began her career as a stage actress before meeting Steele Mackaye and being introduced to Delsarteism. She was also well-read and deeply embedded in the era's fashionable esoteric societies. Stebbins largely stripped out the explicitly Christian elements that lingered in Delsarteism in favor of the same kind of occult universalism favored by the Theosophists. She ultimately came to call her system "psycho-physical culture," which she defined as "the perfect unison of harmonic gymnastics and dynamic breathing, during the formulation of noble ideals in the mind." In other words, Stebbins was teaching a meditative way of synchronizing breath with movement.[20]

Stebbins, like most of her contemporaries, liked to claim that the exercises she was teaching were universal (that is, found in every culture) and as old as humanity itself. By the standards of her time, this signaled that her system was authoritative not only because it was supported by tradition (being ancient), but also because it was scientific (being universal). As part of this, she incorporated sequences of moving poses that she claimed were "Oriental"—though she appealed to Egypt and the Middle East more frequently than she did to India.

In the more formal of Stebbins' "drills," we can easily see the seeds of modern dance. In fact, many of the women who would go on to become the mothers of modern dance at the start of the 20th century were influenced by Stebbins. However, Stebbins' standard "home drill" could easily be taught today as a basic yoga class without raising a single eyebrow (Figure 7.2). Arguably, however, this is less due to any influence Stebbins may have received from Indian systems of yoga (a close look at her work shows that her understanding of any Indian movement

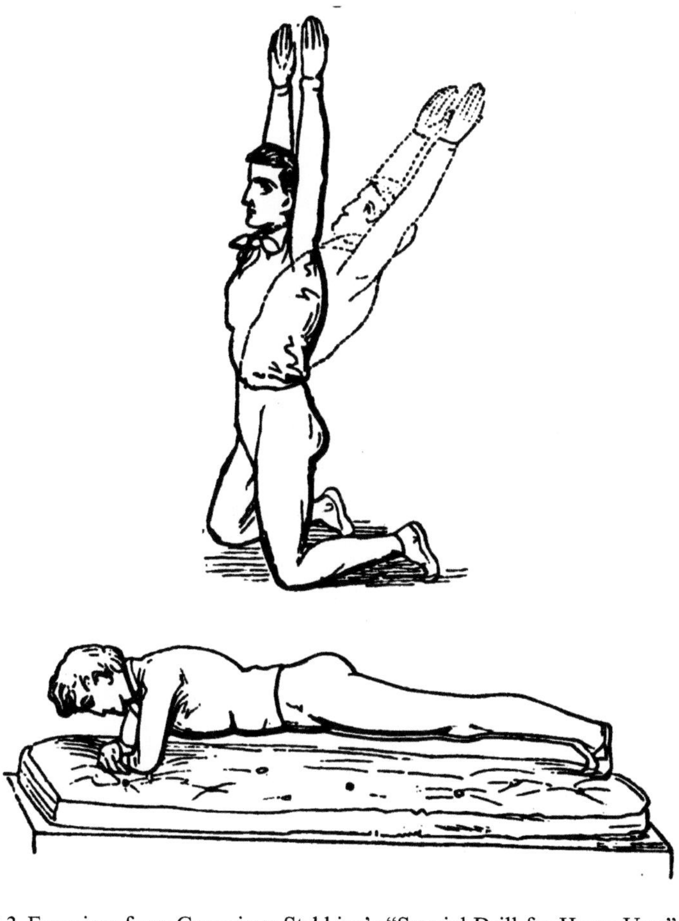

Figure 7.2 Exercises from Genevieve Stebbins's "Special Drill for Home Use," as illustrated in George Herbert Taylor's *An Exposition of the Swedish Movement Cure* (1860). Stebbins adapted exercises from masculine physical culture and built them into aesthetic routines that were at once gymnastics and theatrical dance.

practice, whether yoga or dance, was basically non-existent), than the other way around. At the very least, the same Ling movements that Stebbins strung together in her sequences had already made their way to India, seeding the ground there to intermingle with indigenous forms of physical culture. Even more significantly, we have evidence of Indian innovators of yoga, such as Shri Yogendra, explicitly quoting Stebbins' work and incorporating her techniques into their own systems.[21]

We'll turn back to India momentarily but, before we do so, one final question remains: how did all this stuff come to be called yoga? Some of the answer lies in the connections made by contemporary Indian yogis. But some of it is also due to the next American fitness craze to overtake Delsarte during the first decade of the 20th century: "Oriental dance." Spurred on by the general interest in anything Eastern and therefore exotic, several young female dancers who had been influenced by Delsarteism generally and Stebbins particularly, began performing choreography based on Delsartean movements in increasingly elaborate costumes and settings, evoking everything from Egypt, to India, to Japan (Figure 7.3).

Figure 7.3 Marguerite Agniel performing the "dervish-roll-around," which she describes, in her book *The Art of the Body* (1931), as an exercise for the digestive organs, whose "circular motion provides an effective climax for an Oriental dance." Unlike similar seated *āsanas* performed by yogis, this pose was built on Ling and Delsarte principles and made for movement.

Source: Photographed by J. de Mirjian, c. 1929. Courtesy of the Wellcome Collection, London.

Let's point out that there is a clear colonial dynamic of Orientalism (that is, erasing the actual cultural realities of Asia in favor of Western fantasy) and appropriation at work here. What makes the case of Oriental dance and its offshoots more interesting, however, is that the practice itself is by no means shallow. The women who developed and performed it often saw themselves as engaging in a spiritual practice that yoked body and soul together (or perhaps we should rather say harmonized them) through expressive movement. And, in truth, insofar as this practice was based on a fundamentally harmonial worldview, it had a depth and history on par with that of any of the "Oriental" traditions they imagined themselves to be emulating (including yoga)—the only problem was that what they were doing didn't actually have many Asian roots. They had a water-lily in their hands, but they insisted on imagining it as a lotus, largely because their universalist understanding of spirituality had convinced them that the two were ultimately the same thing.

Scholars of modern yoga such as Andrea Jain have argued that yoga, in the early 20th-century United States, was reserved for the minority of "those who could afford to be eccentric."[22] This was undoubtedly true of anything that actually got labeled "yoga"—a term that carried the colonial aura of something foreign and vaguely scandalous. "Yoga" was often taught by Indian men, who were subject to racism and xenophobia regardless of whether they were actually doing anything nefarious. "Oriental dance," on the other hand, was performed and taught by unthreatening white women, and newspapers vocally assured the public:

> The women who have gone into it [i.e. the dance] are not sensational seekers of novelties, they are not appealed to by the mysterious and heavily perfumed Orient. They have been practical women who believed this dance was the best beauty exercise they could undertake, and they have taken the healthful features of it and left the much criticised phases of it alone.[23]

And so, in the hands of dancing starlets and media darlings like Ruth St. Denis (1879–1968), Oriental dance became the favorite mode of fitness for "respectable" middle-class housewives. It would be a while before such exercises would become associated with yoga rather than with dance, but their supposedly "Oriental" pedigree meant that the transition was an easy one. Just as Delsarte before them, and yoga after them, by the 1920s the dance-like exercises that white female dancers claimed were inspired by the practices of the Orient were used by regular women in private, alongside breathwork and other fitness techniques, to cultivate a holistic, lightly-spiritual sense of wellness.

Yogis go West

The first famous yogi to go West, Swami Vivekananda (1863–1902), arrived in the United States right at the crest of the Delsarte craze. In reality, Vivekananda was not actually the first—men teaching Hindu philosophy and demonstrating yogic practices traveled with some frequency to England, though more rarely to the United States. Vivekananda was an educated man, and by all accounts a charismatic speaker, but likely he was also in the right place at the right time. His now celebrated appearance at the World Parliament of Religions, part of the World's Fair in Chicago in 1893, launched him on a meteoric rise to fame that no other yogi before him had managed to achieve.

All said, Vivekananda spent much less time in the West than some of the other famous (and quite a few of the more obscure) yogis who followed him. He toured the United States and England from 1893 to 1897, and then again briefly between 1899 and 1900. He died, in poor health, soon thereafter. In addition to his widely circulated publications, however, his legacy was cemented by two factors. The first was the organization he founded upon his return to India in 1897, the Ramakrishna Mission. Other monks from the Mission would travel westward to found a number of Vedanta Societies, quite a few of which survive to this day. The second, less obvious marker of Vivekananda's legacy was the influence he had on other proponents of yoga, both Indian yogis as well as Euro-American men and women who saw the novel concept as either a calling or an opportunity.

Vivekananda himself was born Narendranath Datta in Calcutta, India. In his youth, he became a frequent visitor of an *āśram* at Dakshineshwar, led by the famous mystic Ramakrishna Paramahansa (1836–1886). Ramakrishna was a yogi in the Śākta tantric mold, but his practice was eclectic and likewise incorporated *bhakti*-style devotionalism and a philosophical bend towards Advaita Vedānta. The young Vivekananda never quite became a *bhakta*, but the tantric understanding of yoga combined with Vedānta clearly left a mark on him.

It has become commonly accepted that Vivekananda did not teach, and indeed was rather contemptuous of physical yoga. This can be superficially substantiated by the dismissive statements he issues with regards to the category of *haṭha* yoga which he equates with placing the body in various postures and other bodily methods that he associated primarily with absolute control of the body and the attainment of bodily health. Interestingly, though, the other thing that Vivekananda says about this kind of yoga is that it is more or less identical to the "practices you will find in Delsarte, and other teachers, such as placing the body in different postures. The object of these is physical, not psychological."[24] On the one hand, such statements would have given credence to those who were trying to establish an equivalency between Delsartean exercises and Indian traditions, such as the Oriental dancers we discussed above. (Vivekananda, of course, is basically saying, "Why would I give you lotuses when you've already got water-lilies? And anyway, neither one is that useful …") On the other hand, it's another example of the curious distinction between popular (and probably more ancient) conceptions of *haṭha* yoga as *tapas*, or physical ascetic techniques, and the classical *haṭha* yoga found in medieval sources.

This latter point is crucial to understanding Vivekananda and his relationship to yoga. Vivekananda did not teach many of the strictly physical techniques of *haṭha* yoga, though other Vedanta Society swamis did. A good example is Swami Abhedananda (1866–1939), who took over the first Vedanta Society that Vivekananda founded in New York in 1897, where he taught a number of traditional *āsanas* and had no qualms about prescribing them for purely health-related purposes. By classical standards, however, what Vivekananda taught was exactly *haṭha* yoga. He taught basic seated postures, which one assumed in order to practice *prāṇāyāma* and visualization techniques, which were meant to forcefully awaken the *kuṇḍalinī* energy at the base of the spine and drive it upwards, piercing the body's major nerve centers. If successful, the practitioner would become an all-powerful yogi, enlightened and perfectly free. Vivekananda uses the language of electricity, nerves, and plexuses more often than he uses that of *prāṇā*, *nāḍīs*, and *cakras*, but the general framework is still the same.

Yogi impostors

Yogi Ramacharaka wasn't a real yogi. In fact, he wasn't even a real person. Yogi Ramacharaka was one of the many pseudonyms used by the American New Thought author William Walker Atkinson. This matters because the "yoga" that he described in most of his very popular publications, like his identity, was yoga in name only. However, in terms of consistent references it is not Vivekananda (or any other Indian yogi) but Ramacharaka who emerges as the popular authority on yoga over the first two decades of the 20th century. This is true of newspaper columns extolling the virtues of the "yogi breath" and it is true of major international figures who have famously been influenced by yoga.

For instance, historians of dance and drama have written excitedly of how Russian modernist Konstantin Stanislavsky revolutionized theatrical training through his incorporation of yogic techniques. The yoga books on Stanislavsky's bookshelf were penned by Ramacharaka.[25] Likewise, Eugenia Vasilyevna Peterson (1899–2002), who would go on to become Indra Devi, the first Western woman to study with modern yoga guru Tirumalai Krishnamacharya, first encountered yoga as a young girl in Moscow when she read Ramacharaka's *Fourteen Lessons in Yoga Philosophy and Oriental Occultism* (1905). Her original big hit, and one of the very first mainstream American yoga manuals, *Forever Young, Forever Healthy* (1953) begins with an ironic anecdote. During her stay in Bombay, Devi is put off by an encounter with a group of ascetic yogis, scoffing at the notion that one might stand on one's head to please God. A bystander—presumably a local—shares her rebuke, condemning the "sadhus" as charlatans whose antics only serve ruin India's good name with foreign visitors. The next day, someone hands her a book by Yogi Ramacharaka. Even in India, an American man from Baltimore had somehow become the model of an authentic yogi.[26]

Why is this important? Because, beyond a few Sanskrit terms, Ramacharaka's books tended to contain very little yoga or indeed anything else of Indian origin. His two most famous publications on the subject are *Hatha Yoga* (1904) and *Science of Breath* (1904). The first is largely an overview of contemporary understandings of human health, diet, and other related topics with sections devoted to basic breathing exercises (the kind one would find in contemporary Western manuals on oratory) and some minor Ling-style calisthenics. The second is a more thorough examination of said basic breathing exercises and some minor calisthenics, all of which can be readily found in contemporary physical culture and popular medical literature, including most Delsartean manuals. To go back to our metaphor, this is a man who sold tickets to a pond of water-lilies by advertising it as a lotus exhibit.

Yoga and physical culture

On the other side of the world, meanwhile, water lilies were likewise taking root amidst the lotuses. Though Vivekananda was generally dismissive of physical practice as yoga when speaking to his Western audiences, this did not necessarily mean that he did not support physical culture in general. Though Vivekananda is often remembered as a mystic, he was actually a passionate nationalist and Neo-Hindu reformer. In fact, he was occasionally quite pessimistic when it came to his spiritual project in the West. Toward the end of his first American sojourn, for instance, he declared to an inquiring woman in San Francisco: "Madam, I am not teaching religion. I am selling my own brain for money to help my people."[27] At home, Vivekananda was adamant about the importance of physical development for Indian youth and even reportedly claimed that one can get closer to God through football than through the *Bhagavad Gītā*.[28]

Others were of the opinion that maybe football and the *Gītā* were not so apart. Over the first few decades of the 20th century, a group of men (and some women) set about developing a modern regimen of physical culture that was fundamentally grounded in Hinduism. Such efforts often ended up somewhere between what Joseph Alter has called a "'hard-core' scientific nationalism"[29] on the one hand and what Mark Singleton has called "nationalist man-building"[30] on the other. This wasn't the first time that yoga had been used to build powerful, healthy, perfected bodies. It's just that now these bodies were being viewed through an updated lens. Aiming to prove the superior wisdom of yogic tradition, innovators appealed to modern understandings of anatomy and physiology, even attempting to put certain yogic techniques like *prāṇāyāma* to the test via the scientific method.[31]

When modern *akhāṛas* (physical culture clubs or gymnasiums) emerged in India in the first decade of the 20th century, they came to function as ad hoc centers of political resistance to British colonialism. Drawing on the existing legacy of yogis as militant ascetics, yoga practice became associated with the cultivation of the kind of masculine strength to combat India's (implicitly feminine) subjugation under British rule. As Singleton has put it,

> yoga as physical culture would have entered the sociocultural vocabulary of India partly as a specific signifier of violent, physical resistance to British rule. To "do yoga" or to be a yogi in this sense meant to train oneself as a guerilla, using whichever martial and body-strengthening techniques were to hand.[32]

Associating physical culture with yoga, which was at this same time being "rehabilitated" as major cornerstone of Indian philosophy thanks to colonial interest in the *Yoga Sūtras*, must have carried the added appeal of triangulating masculinity and strength with ancient (especially Hindu) wisdom.

Scholars of modern yoga have singled out men like Swami Kuvalayananda (born Jagannatha Ganesa Gune, 1883–1966), Swami Sivananda (born Kuppuswami Iyer, 1887–1963), Shri Yogendra (born Manibhai Haribhai Desai, 1897–1989), Tirumalai Krishnamacharya (1888–1989), and Bishnu Charan Ghosh (1903–1970) as being among the most influential anglophone innovators.[33] If one were casting a broader net, the list would be much longer. Looking only at the names above, all are clearly men of a single generation, born within a span of 20 years. The latter two would become far more famous, at least by proxy, due to the global popularity of their students—B. K. S. Iyengar and K. Pattabhi Jois on the side of Krishnamacharya and Bikram Choudhury on the side of Ghosh. All were responsible, however, for publishing either in English or in their native languages some of the first manuals that teach something fully recognizable as modern yoga. All had a background in physical culture as well as some contact with teachers of traditional *haṭha* yoga. Thus, ultimately, there is good reason to believe that all of the above drew on a range of physical cultural systems in formulating their yogic frameworks, including traditional *haṭha*-yogic *āsanas*, Indian wrestling practices including *daṇḍ-baiṭhak* (a kind of "burpee" exercise, combining push-ups and squats) and other indigenous exercises,[34] but also certainly Western gymnastics.

It's important to understand that the line between yoga and physical culture was uniquely blurry during this time. Not all physical culture was yoga and not all yoga was physical culture, but the two were increasingly practiced in the same places, and elements of one were actively being absorbed into the other.

There are a few common trends observable across these early manuals of postural yoga practice. As dynamic standing *āsanas* are incorporated, they are often distinguished from the more static seated *āsanas* that are meant to be combined with *prāṇāyāma* practice (Figure 7.4). Kuvalayananda, for instance,

Figure 7.4 Shri Yogendra sitting in *siddhāsana*. Yogendra also developed a method of dynamic poses, which he called the "Yogendra Rhythm."

Source: Courtesy of the Yoga Institute.

goes so far as to split the two into completely different sections under the headers of "Meditative Poses" versus "Cultural Poses."[35] Holistic manuals would typically include *āsana* and *prāṇāyāma* along with a varying range of other *haṭha*-yogic practices such as *bandhas*, *mudrās*, and various purifying techniques, which often blend into more generic hygienic advice. There is frequently talk of diet and, somewhat less frequently though still regularly, a section devoted to sexual continence. To the extent that goals of such practices are discussed, they include glancing references to the *kuṇḍalinī*. Likewise, insofar as a larger framework for yoga practice beyond *āsana* and *prāṇāyāma* is established, it invariably follows the eight-fold *Pātañjala* structure. In this sense, there is some continuity with the classical *haṭha* yogic tradition. On the whole, however, these manuals were less concerned with metaphysical goals than with physical ones.

As mentioned earlier, we know that more traditional forms of classical *haṭha* yoga practice persisted alongside such innovations. A good example of this is the "Kriya Yoga" system belonging to the lineage of yogis—some monks, some householders—that produced the aforementioned Yogananda. Kriya Yoga, so called after the *kriyās* (here best translated as "exercises") of which it is composed, as we already mentioned, is a fairly standard form of tantric *haṭha* yoga. It combines bodily techniques with the kind of standard tantric *sādhana* we reviewed in previous chapters, including a form of *bhūtaśuddhi* (purification of the body's gross elements), and the imposition of *mantras* onto the body through the practice of *nyāsa*. The practice culminates when, having established the inner divine sound, the practitioner uses advanced breathing techniques to consecutively raise and lower energy within his body in order to break through the *mūlādhāra granthi* (root knot) and release the *kuṇḍalinī*, leading to an embodied state of liberation and immortality.

But when Yogananda arrived in the United States and began disseminating pamphlets on a system he called "Yogoda," this is not the practice he taught. Instead, Yogoda consisted largely of Swedish calisthenics and basic concentration techniques. Kriya Yoga, on the other hand, continued to be passed down by initiation to his closer disciples. Notably, Yogananda also only taught *āsanas* only to his close, and specifically male, disciples—everyone else got the Swedish calisthenics (Figure 7.5).

Gendered yogas

Singleton has proposed explaining the diversity of today's yoga landscape by thinking about "gendered yogas." In other words, postural yoga's historical development mirrors "a gender division formalized in the earliest expressions of modern European gymnastics, in which men are primarily concerned with strength and vigor while women are expected to cultivate physical attractiveness and graceful movement."[36] This is almost certainly accurate, although we might refine Singleton's point just a bit. The formal differences in global yoga practice, after all, are not so great. It would be inaccurate to say that the styles of yoga developed by

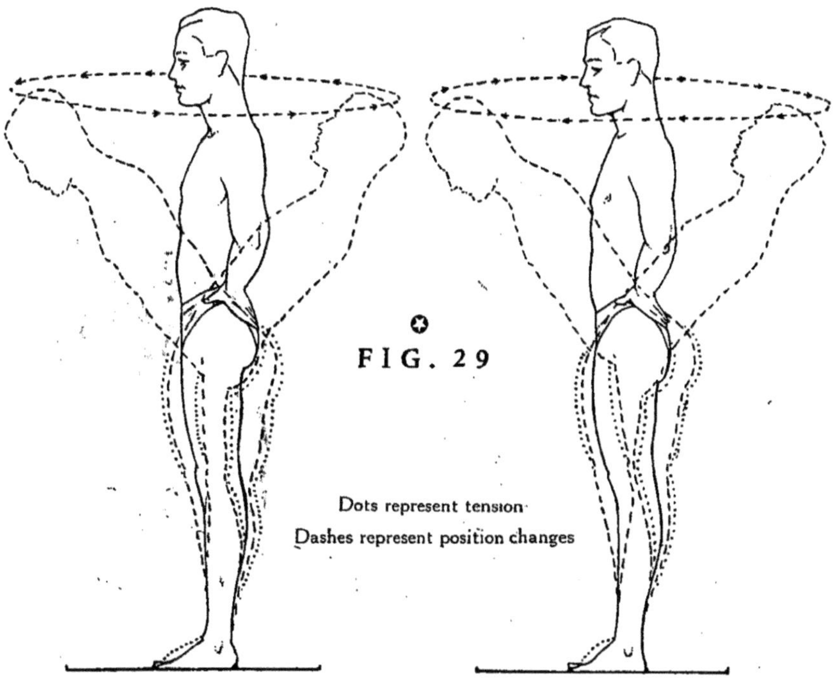

Figure 7.5 Yogananda's "Exercise for Waist" from his *Yogoda or Tissue-Will System of Physical Perfection* (1925), modeled on Ling.

Indian men were objectively more likely to develop muscular strength than those developed by Western women. If anything, today, it is the latter demographic that is more likely to incorporate weights into their yoga practice. And yet, the notion of gendered yoga is borne out by demographics. India is the only place where provisional studies have found a majority of yoga practitioners self-identifying as men. Everywhere else, women dominate.[37] So, the real question is why did these two demographics, Indian men on the one hand and Western women on the other, both take to calling their preferred style of physical culture yoga?

For the Indian innovators of yoga, the answer is simple, at least on the surface. As we've argued above, yoga was uniquely positioned as triangulating physical techniques (not only as *āsana* but, more importantly, as powerful ascetic *tapas*), masculinity, and Hindu identity. Insofar as the Euro-American physical culture movement of the 19th century was a movement—that is, something *new*—it began as a masculine movement. Exercise for the sake of general wellness, after all, was hardly a new idea nor was it the province of men alone. The new thing, as Singleton and Alter have shown us, was the way in which physical culture was getting linked up with nationalism and scientific modernity. This was true for men in Europe and North America, just as it was true for men in India, especially given the pressures of colonialism.

When Eugen Sandow (1867–1925), one of the first "iron men," went on his international tour in 1905, he was already incredibly popular in India and was met with great fanfare. Many of the men who would go on to revolutionize Indian postural yoga recalled seeing Sandow as a formative moment.[38] This has led Alter to go so far as saying: "At the risk of sounding heretical, I think Eugene Sandow, the father of modern body building, has had a greater influence on the form and practice of modern Yoga—and most certainly modern Haṭha Yoga—than either Aurobindo or Vivekananda."[39] This might well be true. Even more true, however, is that there simply is no one single father (or mother) of modern yoga, largely because there is no one single modern yoga.

This brings us back to our Western women. The important thing to remember here is that women like Stebbins were not practicing yoga, they were practicing Delsarte, psycho-physical culture, or aesthetic gymnastics. In this sense, they were practicing a subset of Western physical culture that was deemed to be especially appropriate for women. That they eventually began to call this kind of activity "yoga," was at least partially an accident of branding. "Delsarte" morphed into "Oriental dance" morphed into "yoga." The real story is not quite so tidy, of course. But a single look at the major figures of North American yoga over the course of the 20th century demonstrates the centrality of dance. Blanche DeVries, wife of the Orientalist playboy Pierre "the Omnipotent Oom" Bernard, and possibly the first American woman to make teaching yoga a lifelong career, got her start doing Oriental dance.[40] Indra Devi's earliest training was likewise in theater and modern dance. Magaña Baptiste, an Oriental dancer (and mother of "Power Yoga guru" Baron Baptiste) together with her body-builder husband, Walt Baptiste, opened a major yoga studio in downtown San Francisco in 1955—she learned from Indra Devi. Sharon Gannon, co-founder of the now-global Jivamukti Yoga, first established in 1984 in the East Village of New York City, has a bachelor's degree in dance. The famous "trance dance" yogini Shiva Rea has a master's degree, which she got studying dance anthropology. The list goes on.

The connection to yoga was somewhat of a historical accident but, in a larger way, perhaps it wasn't. Dance, after all, was not always women's domain. It became feminized because graceful movement and embodied aesthetics became feminized, but this is a relatively new phenomenon. The spiritual (and harmonial) dimensions of dance, on the other hand, have a much longer history. Guglielmo Ebreo da Pesaro (c. 1420–1484), a Jewish-Italian dance master who was one of the three men responsible for the style of Italian court dance that eventually evolved into ballet, once wrote:

> Dancing is nothing other than an action that shows outwardly the spiritual movements, which must agree with the measures and perfect concords of harmony. These descend into our intellect through our hearing and to the senses of the heart with delight. There, they produce sweet commotions, which are against their nature imprisoned and endeavour as much as possible to escape and to reveal themselves. This act draws to the outside this sweetness and melody and expresses them through our dancing body.[41]

In other words, in dance the harmonic principles that structure the universe descend through the medium of musical sound (which, recall, is the true language of the soul), into both head and heart, and thence seek to express themselves back out into the world. In this sense, we might make the argument that dance (and therefore dance-like gymnastics) was the Western style of physical culture that was most similar to Indian yoga insofar as it had a long history of built-in spiritual and metaphysical significance.

So much, then, for our lotuses and water lilies.

What happens when we breathe? Four modern harmonial and yogic perspectives

Genevieve Stebbins, in *Dynamic Breathing and Harmonic Gymnastics* (1892):

> Deep, rhythmic breathing combined with a clearly formulated image or idea in the mind produces a sensitive, magnetic condition of the brain and lungs, which attracts the finer ethereal essence from the atmosphere with every breath, and stores up this essence in the lung-cells and brain-convolutions in almost the same way that a storage battery stores up the electricity from the dynamo or other source of supply, and is held in suspension amid the molecules forming the cellular tissue as a dynamic energy, possessing both mental and magnetic powers, always ready for use whenever required. . . . the art of being able to always express the true self; to elevate the soul to its highest aspiration and the mind to express its highest possible plane of thought; and last, but not least, to concentrate the whole vital energy at a moment''s notice to any portion of the body for the immediate execution of the behests of the will. It is the art of graceful dynamic presentation of self under all possible circumstances, and an increase of life by increasing the capacity for the reception, storage and utilization of the vital power.[42]

Swami Vivekananda, in *Rāja Yoga* (1896):

> In the first place, from rhythmical breathing comes a tendency of all the molecules in the body to move in the same direction. When mind changes into will, the nerve currents change into a motion similar to electricity, because the nerves have been proved to show polarity under the action of electric currents. This shows that when the will is transformed into the nerve currents, it is changed into something like electricity. When all the motions of the body have become perfectly rhythmical, the body has, as it were, become a gigantic battery of will. This tremendous will is exactly what the Yogi wants. This is, therefore, a physiological explanation of the breathing exercise. It tends to bring a rhythmic action in the body, and helps us, through the respiratory centre, to control the other centres. The aim of *Prāṇāyāma* here is to rouse the coiled-up power in the *Mulādhāra*, called the *Kuṇḍalinī*.[43]

Ramacharaka (aka William Walker Atkinson), in *Science of Breath* (1904):

> All is in vibration. . . . In all vibration is to be found a certain rhythm. Rhythm pervades the universe. The swing of the planets around the sun; the rise and fall of the sea; the beating of the heart; the ebb and flow of the tide; all follow rhythmic laws. The rays of the sun reach us; the rain descends upon us, in obedience to the same law. All growth is but an exhibition of this law. All motion is a manifestation of the law of rhythm. Our bodies are as much subject to rhythmic laws as is the planet in its revolution around the sun. Much of the esoteric side of the Yogi Science of Breath is based upon this known principle of nature. By falling in with the rhythm of the body, the Yogi manages to absorb a great amount of Prana, which he disposes of to bring about results desired by him.[44]

Paramahansa Yogananda in *Yogoda, or Tissue-Will System of Physical Perfection* (1925):

> An automobile battery needs to be recharged once in a while when run down. So the battery of the body parts, exhausted by physical work and brain labor, requires to be recharged by fresh nerve current send down by Will. You will immediately get over fatigue by performing YOGODA exercises. You will also feel wonderful freshness, and your muscles will become more and more powerful. . . . With open ears you will be able to hear the vibrations at any time, especially at night, and will be in time intuitionally in tune with the Cosmic Vibration (or Rolling Om). This cosmic vibration is not only inside you but everywhere in the universe. . . . Remember the practice of the technique will give you command over your mind. It will enable you to focus your mind quickly on any object of thought—physical, intellectual, or spiritual. This is as true as the sun's rising in the east. It will also produce in you tremendous power of doing active works in life. Above all, it will bring you in touch with the Superconscious (the soul and the Great Spirit), giving you wonderful peace, harmony and poise of mind so essential to the higher living of life.[45]

Conclusions

- In colonial India, ascetic styles of yoga increasingly became denigrated in favor of the fusion between visionary tantric and contemplative Vedāntic practices. These practices were not always called *haṭha* yoga, a label that was sometimes marred by its associations with asceticism, but they retained the practical scaffolding that emerged out of the late medieval *haṭha* literature, as far as technique was concerned.
- Beginning in the later 18th century, harmonial spirituality and gymnastics contributed to a modern physical culture movement in Europe and North

America. A specific branch of this movement, occupied with aesthetic gymnastics, was particularly popular among women and led to the development of a dance-like style of feminine exercise.

- Harmonial gymnastics, touted as at once spiritually elevating and scientifically therapeutic, were believed to be based on an ancient and universal system of physical culture, setting the stage for an easy link to yoga.
- Indian physical culture modernizers blended Western gymnastics with an existing corpus of *haṭha* yogic *āsanas* and other indigenous physical culture practices to produce a parallel system of spiritualized exercise. International Indian yogis and authors of English-language yoga manuals consciously drew on both Western and Indian physical practices, sometimes differentiating and sometimes fully blending the two.
- Western practitioners, whether women practicing something increasingly called "Oriental dance" or male authors looking to market their spiritual gymnastics as something more ancient and exotic, selectively drew from elements of yoga made available by international yogis and incorporated them into their own harmonial systems.
- Eventually, all of this comes to be called "yoga."

Notes

1 Agehananda Bharati, "The Hindu Renaissance and Its Apologetic Patterns," *The Journal of Asian Studies*, 29, no. 2 (1970): 267–87.
2 David Gordon White, *Sinister Yogis* (Chicago: University of Chicago Press, 2009).
3 William R. Pinch, *Warrior Ascetics and Indian Empires* (New York: Cambridge University Press, 2006), 211–19. Patton Burchett, "My Miracle Trumps Your Magic: Encounters with Yogīs in Sufi and Bhakti Hagiograpical Literature," in *Yoga Powers: Extraordinary Capacities Attained Through Meditation and Concentration*, ed. Knut A. Jacobsen (Leiden: Brill, 2012), 345–80.
4 Pinch, *Warrior Ascetics and Indian Empires*.
5 Christopher A. Bayly, *Rulers, Townsmen and Bazaars: North Indian Society in the Age of British Expansion 1770–1870*, 3rd ed. (Oxford: Oxford University Press, 2012), 142–3.
6 Pinch, *Warrior Ascetics and Indian Empires*, 84–101.
7 White, *Sinister Yogis*, 240.
8 Pinch, *Warrior Ascetics and Indian Empires*, 31. White, *Sinister Yogis*, 241.
9 Joseph S. Alter, *Yoga in Modern India: The Body Between Science and Philosophy* (Princeton, NJ: Princeton University Press, 2004), and Mark Singleton, *Yoga Body: The Origins of Modern Posture Practice* (New York: Oxford University Press, 2010).
10 Monier Monier-Williams, *Brāhmanism and Hindūism: Or, Religious Thought and Life in India, as Based on the Veda and Other Sacred Books of the Hindūs*, 4th ed. (New York: Macmillan, 1891), 96.
11 Wouter J. Hanegraaff, "Swedenborg, the Jews, and Jewish Traditions," in *Reuchlin und seine Erben: Forscher, Denker, Ideologen und Spinner*, ed. Peter Schäfer and Irina Wandrey (Ostfildern, Germany: Jan Thorbecke Verlag, 2005), 135–54, and Jane Williams-Hogan, "Emanuel Swedenborg and the Kabbalistic Tradition," in *Esotérisme, gnoses et imaginaire symbolique: mélanges offerts à Antoine Faivre*, ed. Richard Caron et al. (Leuven, Belgium: Peeters, 2001), 343–60.
12 Anya P. Foxen, *Inhaling Spirit: Harmonialism, Orientalism, and the Western Roots of Modern Yoga* (New York: Oxford University Press, 2020), 94.

13 Catherine L. Albanese, ed., *The Spiritual Journals of Warren Felt Evans: From Methodism to Mind Cure* (Bloomington: Indiana University Press, 2016), 1–45.
14 Foxen, *Inhaling Spirit*, 104–5.
15 Foxen, *Inhaling Spirit*, 116.
16 Foxen, *Inhaling Spirit*, 117.
17 Foxen, *Inhaling Spirit*, 117.
18 Nancy Lee Chalfa Ruyter, *The Cultivation of Body and Mind in Nineteenth-Century American Delsartism* (Westport, CT: Greenwood Press, 1999), 57–8.
19 Foxen, *Inhaling Spirit*, 126–9 and Jan Todd, *Physical Culture and the Body Beautiful: Purposive Exercise in the Lives of American Women, 1800–1870* (Macon, GA: Mercer University Press, 1998), 90.
20 Genevieve Stebbins, *Dynamic Breathing and Harmonic Gymnastics: A Complete System of Psychical, Aesthetic and Physical Culture* (New York: Edgar S. Werner, 1892), 66, and Foxen, *Inhaling Spirit*, 139.
21 Foxen, *Inhaling Spirit*, 164, 241–2.
22 Andrea R. Jain, *Selling Yoga: From Counterculture to Pop Culture* (New York: Oxford University Press, 2014), 42.
23 Foxen, *Inhaling Spirit*, 208–9.
24 Swami Vivekananda, *The Complete Works of Swami Vivekananda*, vol. 1 (Calcutta: Advaita Ashrama, 1915), 158.
25 R. Andrew White, "Stanislavsky and Ramacharaka: The Influence of Yoga and Turn-of-the-Century Occultism on the System," *Theatre Survey*, 47, no. 1 (2006): 82.
26 Foxen, *Inhaling Spirit*, 252.
27 Narasingha Prosad Sil, *Swami Vivekananda: A Reassessment* (Selinsgrove, PA: Susquehanna University Press, 1997), 169.
28 Singleton, *Yoga Body*, 100.
29 Alter, *Yoga in Modern India*, 76.
30 Singleton, *Yoga Body*, 22.
31 Alter, *Yoga in Modern India*, 73–108.
32 Singleton, *Yoga Body*, 104.
33 Alter, *Yoga in Modern India*; Singleton, *Yoga Body*; Elliott Goldberg, *The Path of Modern Yoga: The History of an Embodied Spiritual Practice* (Rochester, VT: Inner Traditions, 2016).
34 Alter, *Yoga in Modern India*; Jerome Armstrong, *Calcutta Yoga: Buddha Bose and the Yoga Family of Bishnu Ghosh and Yogananda* (Alexandria, VA: Webstrong llc, 2018).
35 Foxen, *Inhaling Spirit*, 239.
36 Singleton, *Yoga Body*, 160.
37 Crystal Park, Tosca Braun, and Tamar Siegel, "Who Practices Yoga? A Systematic Review of Demographic, Health-Related, and Psychosocial Factors Associated with Yoga Practice," *Journal of Behavioral Medicine*, 38, no. 3 (2015): 460–71.
38 Singleton, *Yoga Body*, 89.
39 Alter, *Yoga in Modern India*, 28.
40 Robert Love, *The Great Oom: The Improbable Birth of Yoga in America* (New York: Viking, 2010), 88–9.
41 Günter Berghaus, "Neoplatonic and Pythagorean Notions of World Harmony and Unity and Their Influence on Renaissance Dance Theory," *Dance Research: The Journal of the Society for Dance Research*, 10, no. 2 (1992): 63.
42 Genevieve Stebbins, *Dynamic Breathing and Harmonic Gymnastics: A Complete System of Psychical, Aesthetic and Physical Culture* (New York: Edgar S. Werner, 1892), 52, 70.
43 Vivekananda, *The Complete Works*, 182.
44 Yogi Ramacharaka, *Science of Breath: A Complete Manual of the Oriental Breathing Philosophy of Physical, Mental, Psychic and Spiritual Development* (Chicago: Yogi Publication Society, 1904), 60–1.
45 Swami Yogananda, *Yogoda or Tissue-Will System of Physical Perfection*, 5th ed. (Boston: Sat-Sanga, 1925), 1, 20.

Part III

Modern practice

8 Gurus, lineages, and yogic authority

When we think about the different "types" of yoga that define the landscape of modern practice, we do this in one of two ways: we either talk about the teachings of a specific guru or master (amounting to a "school" or "lineage"), or we talk about brands. Ultimately, of course, these two categories may not be all that different. The first model appeals to more traditional notions of authority and transmission of knowledge but, in a global capitalist context, it often ends up looking and functioning very much like the second more modern and explicitly market-driven framework.

Consequently, we've chosen to focus this chapter on gurus both because of the paramount place that the guru has historically held in yogic traditions and because of the ways in which the rupture of this relationship is frequently used to explain the deep anxiety over authority, authenticity, and proper modes of transmission that permeates modern yoga practice. For instance, within modern postural yoga, where legitimacy and authenticity are especially fraught due to the perceived novelty of a purely physical and fitness-oriented style of practice, Tirumalai Krishnamacharya has come to be hailed as the "father of modern yoga." However, as we've seen in other chapters, modern yoga's paternity is a much more complicated matter. Even if we consider only global movements, the influence of others—such as for instance, Bishnu Ghosh, but also any number of earlier and lesser-known yogis—is difficult to deny. Krishnamacharya's title, then, is less tied to historical fact than it is to his particular placement as the guru of global gurus.

In fact, the history of modern yoga is difficult to penetrate specifically because messy and complex historical interactions are often obscured by the charismatic personas of globally famous gurus. Yoga's tantric and meditative heritage is far more obvious in the pre-modern timeline and so, in this sense, the "metaphysical" gurus we feature in this chapter are a useful point of comparison for the "physical" ones. Tantra and Vedānta are much larger bodies of practice, the modern histories of which are clearly not limited to the global presence of gurus like Swami Muktananda or Maharishi Mahesh. In the same way, we should not view physical yoga practice as restricted to the lineages of Tirumalai Krishnamacharya or Bishnu Ghosh, who are foregrounded in this chapter. Our division of "physical" and "metaphysical" gurus draws on the work of Elizabeth De Michelis, who was perhaps the first scholar to undertake a serious historical study of modern yoga. De Michelis differentiated between what she called "Modern Postural" and "Modern Meditational" (focusing on physical and mental practices, respectively, without much engagement with religious or philosophical claims) versus "Modern Denominational" (more tied to traditional and sectarian doctrines) yogas.[1] Ultimately, however, the lines between the two prove to be extremely blurry.

In addition to a several global gurus hailing from India, we'll also examine two offshoot schools ("Power Yoga" and "Hot Yoga") that serve as umbrella labels for a number of related styles. Both have roots in Indian lineages of postural yoga, but ultimately depart from and innovate on their parent styles, incorporating teachings from multiple sources. While such re-mixing might seem at first glance like a modern phenomenon, an earnest look at the historical landscape of yoga yields many such instances of practices that drift from one tradition to another, as well as countless moments of reinterpretation, recombination, and synthesis. The biographies of modern Indian gurus (such as, for instance, Paramahansa Yogananda or Swami Muktananda) often include periods of wandering and eclectic spiritual exploration that preceded their relationship with the men into whose lineages they'd ultimately fall. If we really wanted to push things into the past, we might think of the Buddha's hagiography, wherein he explores several methods and studies under several teachers before finally settling on his own "Middle Way." The difference, perhaps, is that modern Western innovators do not usually appeal to scriptural authority or divine revelation to justify what seem like otherwise novel systems. Instead, the system becomes self-justifying—it becomes a brand.

We'll also briefly address the potentially problematic nature of a guru's power. Most (though not all) of the figures mentioned in this chapter have been embroiled in sex scandals and other accusations of abuses of power at one point or another. On the one hand, one might be inclined to be skeptical, given the virulent racism that early global yogis often faced when they traveled to the West. For instance, in 1912 the *Washington Post* decried "the Hindu problem" presented by

> the presence of the swamis, or teachers, educated and able men, who with their swarthy faces and dreamy-looking eyes stand in themselves symbolic of the mystery of the Orient. It is [through] their teachings, their appeals for their disciples to try to attain impossible goals by unaccustomed paths that they are largely responsible for the deluded women who give away fortunes to "the cause," who give up home and children, and who, breaking down under the strain become hopeless lunatics.[2]

Upon examination, the prominent cases that flooded the media, some of which involved (for instance) contested wills in which wealthy widows had bestowed their fortunes upon their favorite spiritual centers, quickly prove to be unfounded.

On the other hand, many of the modern cases are extremely well documented and supported by large numbers of witness and survivor accounts. Moreover, there is something to be said for the ways in which the potential for abuse present in any hierarchical system of authority is exacerbated by the deep intimacy, vulnerability, and unconditional surrender required by the traditional guru–disciple relationship.

Amanda Lucia, a scholar of modern guru traditions and spirituality, has suggested that the problem lies not only in the transgressions of individual gurus, but in the very nature of the framework where they happen. The power attributed to the guru, his personal presence, and especially his touch, create

> conditions wherein physical contact with the guru becomes a sacred opportunity, but also the high spiritual value placed on physical proximity to the guru has social ramifications. Special audiences, private meetings, and unconventional intimacies between guru and disciple are communally lauded as sacred. Such events are communally envisioned as a blessing for any devotee, and to reject an offering of proximity to the guru constitutes a radical social breach.[3]

However, as both a complement and a counterpoint to Lucia's position, the scholar Andrea Jain has argued that expanding the lens from individual gurus as perpetrators to the larger power structures of the guru–disciple model still does not go quite far enough. Jain suggests that if we want to understand abuse specifically in modern yoga, we must also consider the ways in which our culture places a value on bodily control and autonomy while making these matters of personal responsibility.[4] So, just shifting our emphasis to the individual empowerment of the practitioner is not enough to dismantle the guru's power. Focusing on empowering individual victims is no more useful than focusing on taking down individual abusers. Change must be communal and structural.

What is a guru?

Given the oral quality of South Asian tradition, the student–teacher relationship would have historically been a ubiquitous central feature of how knowledge was passed down. This order of transmission is known as *paramparā*, "succession" or "lineage." In the original Sanskrit, *guru* means literally "heavy," and it is one of several terms that one might use to address a teacher (some others being *ācārya* or *śāstrin*, both of which translate more-or-less as "teacher"). Traditionally, such terms are in fact titles that are granted to very advanced individuals through an established system of hierarchy. For instance, within the Southern Indian Śaiva Siddhānta and Vaiṣṇava Pāñcarātra tantric traditions, the *ācārya* is the highest of four possible stages in a hierarchy of initiated practitioners and the only one who has the authority to initiate others. The very nature of the word "guru" is meant to signify the weighty and authoritative character of the role it represents. The traditional relationship between guru and disciple is indeed intensely hierarchical, requiring absolute commitment, obedience, and surrender. In other words, the relationship between a disciple and a guru is ultimately not so different from the relationship between a devotee and God—over time, it becomes understood as *bhakti*, absolute interpenetrating dependence and devotion.

Though there is much precedent for it in earlier traditions, the role of the guru as a figure of religious authority matures into its prime during India's early medieval period (500–1200 CE). In contrast to the preceding age of sprawling empires, this historical period was characterized by smaller regional kingdoms vying for power. Rulers invested in building up rich cultural networks of architects, artists, scholars, and religious specialists, all of whom sought to elevate their particular kingdom and position it at the center of the civilized world.[5] In this context, individual holy men who could be directly accessible to their disciples—including their royal disciples-cum-patrons—became the chief preceptors of religion.[6]

Such a direct relationship is especially crucial in tantric traditions, which usually require the practitioner to be initiated into the secret ritual knowledge of their particular sect. Because tantric practice often works on the premise of transforming and perfecting the human body—rooted in the idea that in order to worship a god, you must first become one yourself[7]—the initiation is not a matter of simple intellectual teaching. Instead, it is an embodied ritual in which the guru spiritually penetrates and enters the body of the disciple, clearing it of impurities and imbuing it with the divine cosmic energy (*śakti*) that his status allows him to wield.[8] Tantric philosophy maintains that because the material world is either woven from or permeated by this divine energy, human beings are capable (through practice) of becoming divine themselves. In such a framework, it becomes all the more reasonable that the student should approach the guru (who is, after all, the most accomplished kind of practitioner) as a god in human form.

This phenomenon of energetic possession by the guru, which survives in less ritually-elaborate and more spontaneous forms into the modern day, is often referred to as *śakti-pāta* (a descent or a casting down of energy). As Amanda Lucia has suggested, this belief in the guru as a conduit of divine energy accounts for the guru's powerful personal charisma. According to Lucia, charisma is the "It-effect," the socially constructed manifestation of a public figure's "personal magnetism, effervescent energetic power, and their physical attractiveness."[9] Such an effect may of course be the product of a number of intertwining and interdependent factors, from a guru's individual personality and charm, to the cultural narrative that surrounds them, to some actual experiential reality (what this energy "feels like" in the body) of the practitioner.

Early modern gurus and the universalization of yoga

Historians have suggested that, by the 19th century, colonial criminalization of ascetic yogis combined with the ongoing influence of *bhakti* and Muslim devotionalism to transform the image of the ideal yogi into the more contemplative, inwardly oriented ideal of the monk.[10] It is this ideal that was ultimately presented to Western audiences as Indian spiritual leaders began to travel and spread their teachings abroad.

Notably, before the first of them arrived, Western imaginations had already been primed for a "Mystic from the East" by sources like Edwin Arnold's wildly popular *Light of Asia* (1876), a novella-length narrative poem recounting the life of the historical Buddha in florid detail. Arnold depicts the Buddha as a Christ-like sage, "Sitting serene, with perfect virtue walled/As is a stronghold by its gates and ramps."[11] This ideal was further reinforced by the teachings of the Theosophical

Society, founded in New York in 1875 by American Spiritualist leader Henry Steel Olcott (1832–1907) and a Russian expatriate esotericist named Helena Petrovna Blavatsky (1831–1891). Blavatsky left her home country at the age of 18, abandoning a recent marriage to a man more than twice her age. Her biography over the succeeding decades is spotty, but in 1873 she resurfaced in New York as a most unusual medium to the spirits. Her unique powers, she claimed, stemmed from ancient secrets she had learned from a group of Masters—later called Mahatmas, after the Sanskrit term meaning "Great Self"—residing in the snowy ranges of the Himalayas. All of this confirmed an Orientalist fantasy of India as a place of magic, mysticism, and ancient universal wisdom—a narrative into which the guru easily fell.

Consequently, when Swami Vivekananda (1863–1902) arrived in the United States in 1893, the response his lectures received had been at least a few decades in the making. Cornelius Johannes Heijblom, a Dutch immigrant who would go on to become Swami Atulananda, saw Vivekananda in New York in 1899, about which he reminisced:

> What a giant, what strength, what manliness, what a personality! Everyone near him looks so insignificant in comparison. . . . What was it that gave Swamiji his distinction? Was it his height? No, there were gentlemen there taller than he was. Was it his build? No, there were near him some very fine specimens of American manhood. It seemed to be more in the expression of the face than anything else. Was it his purity? What was it? … I remember what had been said of Lord Buddha—"a lion amongst men."[12]

Josephine MacLeod, who would become an ardent admirer, described him in 1895 as "the fiery missionary whose physique was like a wrestler's and whose eyes were deep black."[13] Transfixed, she further recalled: "I saw with these very eyes . . . Krishna himself standing there and preaching the Gita. That was my first wonderful vision. I stared and stared . . . I saw only the figure and all else vanished."[14]

Vivekananda toured the United States and Europe from 1893 to 1897, and then again from 1899 to 1902. He established the first Vedanta Society center in New York, where he was succeeded by another monk from his order, Swami Abhedananda. Other monks from the Ramakrishna Math, founded by Vivekananda and several of his fellow disciples in honor of their own guru in 1886, followed Vivekananda abroad and established a number of other such Vedanta centers. Between 1900 and 1920, they were joined by a handful of other spiritual teachers—the most prominent being Swami Rama Tirtha and Paramahansa Yogananda—as well as a much larger number of non-monastic immigrants who nevertheless came to style themselves as spiritual entrepreneurs.[15]

One particularly interesting member of this early cohort of global gurus is Jiddu Krishnamurti (1895–1986), a boy from South India who was adopted by leaders of the Theosophical society and styled by them as the next "World Teacher." In 1929, Krishnamurti rejected this story and his role within it, declaring that "Truth is a pathless land" and that "because I am free, unconditioned, whole—not the part, not the relative but the whole Truth that is eternal—I desire those who seek to understand me to be free; not to follow me, not to make out of me a cage which will become a religion, a sect."[16] He spent the rest of his days teaching this message of unconditional freedom, becoming in essence a guru whose message was based on the rejection of his own authority.

Even gurus who didn't reject all notions of "path" or "sect," however, emphasized the idea that their teachings were not religious dogma but universal, even scientific truth. Vivekananda named yoga "one of the grandest of sciences" and advised his audiences that

> it is wrong to blindly believe. You must exercise your own reason and judgment; you must practice and see whether these things happen or not. Just as you would take up any other science, exactly in the same manner you should take up this science for study.[17]

On the other side of the globe, innovators of *haṭha* yoga like Swami Kuvalayananda were attempting to scientifically measure the biological effects of *prāṇāyāma* breathing exercises, while others like Shri Yogendra actively insisted in their yoga practice manuals that "yoga breathing" was scientifically superior to the varieties of deep breathing prescribed by other systems of physical culture on account of its optimal use of oxygen, obtained by exerting minimal effort. According to these gurus, yoga's true authority lay not so much in ancient tradition (though tradition still mattered) but in that it could be proven as a universally superior system of both physical and spiritual advancement by the objective methods of modern science.

Physical gurus

Tirumalai Krishnamacharya (1888–1989)

In writing about Krishnamacharya's status as a guru, Mark Singleton and Tara Fraser have observed that Krishnamacharya's biography is difficult to pin down, often by virtue of his own design. He was loath to talk about himself, and accounts given by disciples unsurprisingly trail into fanciful hagiography. Singleton and Fraser ultimately conclude that "Krishnamacharya is complicit in the creation of his own myth."[18] The myth, such as it is, follows a standard narrative of yogic transmission. Krishnamacharya was born in Karnataka as the eldest child of a prominent Brahmin family. His father instructed him in the practices of his native South Indian Śrī Vaiṣṇava tradition from an early age, but his chief yoga guru was a man named Rammohan Brahmacari with whom he studied for seven years in a cave either in Tibet[19] or Nepal.[20] Krishnamacharya's guru taught from and made his student memorize a text called the *Yoga Koruṇṭa*, a Gurkhali-language manuscript to which Krishnamacharya credits his dynamic postural sequencing. Mystically, Krishnamacharya claimed inspiration from the Āḻvār poet saints of the South Indian Śrī Vaiṣṇava tradition.[21] In fact, at the age of 16, even before his studies with Rammohan Brahmacari, he received the wisdom of another ancient yogic text, one he would call the *Yoga Rahasya* ("The Secret Yoga"). The long-lost text was dictated to Krishnamacharya in a vision by Nāthamuni,[22] a 10th-century theologian who collected the teachings of the Āḻvārs and founded the Śrī Vaiṣṇava community.[23]

Historical reality may be somewhat different. The current scholarly consensus on the *Yoga Rahasya* is that its verses are "likely a patchwork of other, better known texts plus Krishnamacharya's own additions"[24] and that, on the whole, "it might be harsh to call [the *Yoga Rahasya*] spurious, but it is written in rather unfortunate Sanskrit and is little more than a projection into antiquity of a modern description of and justification for the primacy of *āsana* practice."[25] All in all, it seems likely that Krishnamacharya did not travel all the way to the northern reaches of the subcontinent to study with his guru, but instead met him in northern Karnataka.[26] The *Yoga Koruṇṭa*, the manuscript of which was supposedly eaten by ants, might have a similarly oblique basis in reality. As Jason Birch and Mark Singleton have suggested, it may in fact be a version of the *Haṭha Abhyāsa Paddhati*, an 18th-century text authored by Kapālakuraṇṭaka, which, though it does not support the entirety of Krishnamacharya's method, does contain the sequencing of *āsanas*.[27] None of this should be understood as making Krishnamacharya's yoga any less legitimate, only a bit less ancient and a great deal more innovative than traditional narrative would have it.

Krishnamacharya developed the most influential iteration of his postural yoga (and taught it to his most prominent students) during his tenure as a chief preceptor of the physical culture program at the Jaganmohan Palace at Mysore. Under the auspices of the Maharaja Krishnaraja Wodiyar IV, the Mysore program was indeed innovative and eclectic, combining yogic *āsanas* with a number of indigenous physical culture styles.[28] Here, Krishnamacharya devised what he referred to as his *vinyāsa krama* ("specially ordered steps") style of practice, now simply called vinyasa, referring to a flowing progression of movements and poses.

Early versions of the *vinyāsa krama* centered specifically around the repeated "jump back" and "jump forward" sequence known as *sūryanamaskār* ("sun salutation") interspersed with postures. The more mature version of Krishnamacarya's method, as recorded by his son, T. K. V. Desikachar (1938–2016) focuses on linking breath with movement and adapting the sequence of poses to the needs of each individual practitioner.[29]

Iyengar yoga: B. K. S. Iyengar (1918–2014)

Iyengar, like his guru Krishnamacharya, was born into a highly respected family of Śri Vaiṣṇava Brahmins in Karnataka. Fittingly, then, he likewise evoked Nāthamuni as a spiritual ancestor, but furthermore considered himself to be both a yogi (in the vein of Patañjali, the author of the *Yoga Sūtras*) and a Vedāntin, following the qualified non-dual theism of the 12th-century Śri Vaiṣṇava philosopher Rāmānuja.[30] Iyengar studied directly with Krishnamacharya for only a year and a half, between 1935 and 1937. The apprenticeship effectively ended when Krishnamacharya sent Iyengar, at the age of 18, to teach yoga in Pune, Maharashtra.

Though Iyengar's early years in Pune were characterized by personal and economic hardship, he eventually gained prominence as a master in "medical" yoga, famous for his attention to the minute details of *āsana* practice.[31] A famous student, the American violinist Yehudi Menuhin, was instrumental in first introducing Iyengar to European circles of cultural elites, though always in the context of small private gatherings.[32] Iyengar later recounted that it took him nearly a decade of visits to the West to build any interest, noting that only "after 1961, I started treating some of the students who have been ailing for a very long period, and that boosted fast, so I think that the credit goes on the healing section of yoga, which took the West by storm."[33] However, it was the popularity of his now-classic practice manual, *Light on Yoga* (1966), that truly cemented his status as a global guru.

Beyond Iyengar himself, Iyengar Yoga became a worldwide brand, in part because of its notoriously stringent model of teacher training, which stressed extensive knowledge of bodily alignment and multiple levels of certification. In 1970, the Inner London Education Authority (ILEA) sanctioned the first official Iyengar teacher-training program. The ILEA also shaped the character of global Iyengar Yoga in that it required that the teachings be focused on the physical aspects of yoga rather than religion and spirituality, as well as that they foreground emphasis on safety and the health benefits of fitness and flexibility.[34] Iyengar's authority as a global guru was thus revolutionary in the sense that his teacher training model allowed for the dissemination of his system without the necessity of his personal presence. True to its founder's vision, however, the global manifestations of Iyengar Yoga have maintained their focus on therapeutic practice, a fact evidenced by their extensive use of props (such as straps, blocks, and chairs) and their focus on meticulous anatomical alignment.

Ashtanga yoga: K. Pattabhi Jois (1915–2009)

In contrast to Iyengar's detail-oriented, therapeutic style, the system K. Pattabhi Jois would come to call "Ashtanga Yoga" (often popularly understood to reference Patañjali's eight-fold system in the *Yoga Sūtras*) is arguably much closer to the kind of rapid, vinyasa-based practice their mutual guru Krishnamacharya taught during his tenure at the Mysore palace. Jois was another Karnataka Brahmin by birth and he ultimately spent about 25 years of his life working under Krishnamacharya, chiefly at Mysore.

Ashtanga Yoga is a highly regimented practice, consisting of non-varying sets of poses arranged into increasingly difficult sequences known as the Primary Series, Intermediate Series, and Advanced Series A/B/C/D. In these sequences poses follow one another without interruption and are to be performed in concert with the breath. The system is also known for its "Mysore Style" practice, in which the poses are performed in silence (that is, without instruction) by the students, while the teacher offers individual corrections.

Perhaps more so than any of its global contemporaries, Jois's system retains the traditional emphasis on direct contact with the guru. In the 1960s, Jois's earliest Western students sought him out, initially receiving resistance from Jois himself, in order to study with him in India. Jois's global fame and influence grew in large part because of these students, who returned home and taught students of their own. To this day, the idea of lineage remains extremely important in the Ashtanga community, and having studied with one of Jois's original students presents a great honor. Likewise, Ashtanga practitioners from all over the world have been encouraged to make the pilgrimage to Mysore—then, to study directly with Jois, and now with his grandson. Against this backdrop, in 2018, Jois was credibly accused of sexual abuse by a number of his female students.[35]

Power Yoga gurus

The shifting nature of yogic authority is nowhere more evident than under the umbrella label of Power Yoga. The term emerged during the 1990s, generally coined by teachers in the Ashtanga Yoga lineage. Specifically, two prominent second-generation Ashtanga teachers, each of whom had studied with one of Jois's first Western disciples, had begun using the term as a way of positioning their particular method on the existing North American yoga landscape. Beryl Bender Birch, based in New York, had studied with Norman Allen. On the other side of the country, there was Bryan Kest, based in Los Angeles and a student of David Williams. Both Williams and Allen had studied under Jois in India in the early 1970s.

The rationale for using a novel label was multifold. On the one hand, it allowed for a break with the rigid structure of Ashtanga's series. "Power Vinyasa" now signifies any number of intensely gymnastic and creatively choreographed—that is, a teacher may well teach a different sequence of poses in every class—varieties of yoga where breath is linked with flowing movement. On the other hand, and perhaps more importantly at the time, the label differentiated Birch's and Kest's physically demanding classes from the previous iterations of yoga that had already taken root in North America. Such forms of practice, as we reviewed in Chapter 7, would have drawn both on traditional *haṭha* yogic postures but even more importantly on harmonial gymnastics, specifically the flowing and dance-like but relatively non-strenuous varieties that had been deemed appropriate for women. Even when more physically (rather than meditatively) based, these styles of yoga would have been relatively gentle and would have incorporated much dedicated attention to deep breathing and relaxation. In contrast, the kind of practice that Birch and Kest were offering was sweaty, physically demanding, and relaxation was to be saved for after the hard work was done.

This very American redefinition of his yoga style was not well received by Jois, who wrote a letter to the popular publication *Yoga Journal* stating:

> I was disappointed to find that so many novice students have taken Ashtanga yoga and have turned it into a circus for their own fame and profit. . . . The title "Power Yoga" itself degrades the depth, purpose and method of the yoga system that I received from my guru, Sri T. Krishnamacharya. Power is the property of God. It is not something to be collected for one's ego. . . . The Ashtanga yoga system should never be confused with "power yoga" or any

> whimsical creation which goes against the tradition of the many types of yoga *shastras* (scriptures). It would be a shame to lose the precious jewel of liberation in the mud of ignorant body-building.[36]

Though it is tempting to view Jois's reprimand as evidence of Power Yoga's inauthenticity and superficiality, the accusations of "ego" and links to "body-building" may be a bit of a red herring. After all, Krishnamacarya's own yoga likely borrowed heavily from "secular" physical culture practices such as wrestling techniques, and not all traditional Indian yoga has been devotional in nature. On the other hand, Jois is of course accurately perceiving the ongoing delinking of yoga practice from specifically Indian models of tradition and spirituality. As it is practiced today, Power Yoga is often at least somewhat spiritual, but largely in a Western harmonial rather than Indian yogic or devotional way.

Though Birch and Kest may not be gurus in the traditional sense of the word, they exhibit a similar style of charismatic authority that is characteristic of the modern guru model. Where they and others like them diverge, however, is in decentralizing a single lineage of transmission. A prime example of this tendency is another contemporary Power Yoga innovator, Baron Baptiste, who developed his style of yoga after studying not only with Krishnamacharya disciples Iyengar and Jois, but also with Bikram Choudhury, who represents a different lineage and style altogether. Baptiste's parents Walt (1917–2001) and Magaña (1921–2016), a bodybuilder and an Oriental dancer, respectively, opened their yoga studio in San Francisco in 1955. Walt was first exposed to yoga by his uncle, who was a disciple of Paramahansa Yogananda. Magaña learned it from Indra Devi[37] (born Eugenia Vasilyevna Peterson 1899–1902), who had studied with Krishnamacarya and authored one of the first mainstream Western yoga manuals, *Forever Young, Forever Healthy* (1953). Baron, however, wanted something more vigorously physical than his parents' yoga. His style of yoga ultimately became centered on a Power style of vinyasa, performed in a heated room.

Bishnu Ghosh (1903–1970)

As we mentioned earlier, if we were to call Krishnamacharya the father of global yoga, this would be on the basis of his students' impact. By this metric, global yoga has another father—Bishnu Ghosh. Examining Ghosh's story, however, sets up an interesting contrast to the seeming coherence of the Krishnamacharya tradition. Though historical research has shown that Krishnamacharya's yoga was far more of a synthesis than the traditional story would claim, he and his major disciples (Iyengar and Jois) were all Karnataka Brahmins. All remained grounded in their native Śri Vaiṣṇava tradition and this was reflected in their approach to yoga, which combined (in a more-or-less dualistic fashion) postural practice as therapy and physical culture with devotional spirituality. Ghosh's lineage, if we can speak of such a thing, is much more diverse and indeed fully shows the complex interactions that resulted in modern yoga.

Bishnu Ghosh, the younger brother of Paramahansa Yogananda, was born in Lahore (now in Pakistan, but then still part of colonial India) into the clerical *kāyastha* caste. He was ten years younger than Yogananda and so his brother had a formative impact on him. The Kriya Yoga lineage to which Yogananda's family belonged was only one part of this influence. Ghosh was not formally initiated into the tantric Kriya practices until Yogananda briefly returned to India from the United States in 1935. However, at the school for boys which Yogananda had helped found before his departure to the West, Ghosh received an initial exposure to a variety of yoga practices.

The School of Divinity, as it was called, was first founded in 1917, with the support of the Maharaja Manindra Chandra Nandi of Kasimbazar. It offered lessons in the basic meditative techniques of Kriya Yoga, *prāṇāyāma*, and devotional chanting but also distinctly *haṭha*-yogic techniques such as *āsana*, *mudrā*, *bandha*, and *nauli* (which Ghosh would refer to as "muscle control"). The school's *haṭha* program was taught by a number of different yogis who were likely local and were brought in specifically for this purpose.[38] However, as he entered adulthood, Ghosh first went on to excel in a number of non-yogic physical disciplines, including wrestling, *vyāyāma* exercises, Western gymnastics, and jiu jitsu. He opened a gymnasium where he developed a program of physical culture with his student, close friend, and eventual son-in-law Buddha Bose. Having immersed themselves in Western systems of exercise, yoga proved to be somewhat of a rediscovery for the two men. Ghosh, of course, had learned it in his youth, while Bose began studying the written works of Kuvalayananda.[39]

The system that Ghosh and Bose ultimately formalized together drew on all of these sources. In the United States, Yogananda (who had also had a youthful interest in other brands of physical culture) was teaching his own style of spiritual fitness under the label of Yogoda. The two brothers found much in common at their reunion in 1935. In 1938, Ghosh and Bose departed on a world tour that featured their system of 84 *āsanas*, traveling to Europe as well as the United States, where they once again connected with Yogananda.[40] In 1953, together with their wives, Ashalata and Ava Rani, they founded the Yoga Cure Institute in Calcutta, today known as Ghosh's Yoga College.[41] Their teachings have also had a longstanding presence in Japan.

Historically, then, Ghosh and Bose share the paternity of this particular school of practice. So why is this section titled after Ghosh? Largely because lineage survives when someone goes on to propagate it, and the man who took upon himself the mantle of this particular lineage advertised Ghosh (and not Bose) as his guru.

Bikram Yoga: Bikram Choudhury (1944–)

The next, and best known link in the chain of "Calcutta Yoga" is Bikram Choudhury. Choudhury made famous the postural style called "Bikram Yoga," which is a sequence consisting of 26 poses and two breathing exercises, invariably performed over 90 minutes in a heated room. More than anyone in this chapter, Choudhury (or Bikram, as he is popularly called) is a self-styled guru. His biography has been repeated verbatim, as has the "script" of his classes, by the thousands of teachers he has trained.

It goes like this: Choudhury was handed over to his guru, Ghosh, by his parents at the tender age of six, in 1952, the same year that Yogananda left this earth. He won the Indian National Yoga Competition at the age of 13 and held the title, undefeated, for three years until he retired at the request of none other than the legendary B. K. S. Iyengar himself. When he was about 18, he dropped a 380-pound weight on his knee, shattering the patella. Doctors declared that he would never walk again, but Choudhury returned to his guru and Ghosh cured him with a miraculous regimen of yoga. After his rehabilitation, Choudhury left Calcutta to become the Yogiraj of Bollywood. When Ghosh died in 1970, he charged Choudhury with finishing the work his brother Yogananda had started in bringing yoga to the West.

All of this is fiction. Or rather, as Jerome Armstrong, who has meticulously documented the history of the Calcutta yoga lineage, has pointed out, "everything happened, just not to Bikram."[42] In reality, Choudhury began studying at Ghosh's gymnasium in 1962 when he was 18, where he befriended Ghosh's son Bishwanath. There, he specialized in body-building and Swedish massage. He did spend 1966–1969 in Bollywood, where he was primarily a masseur (rather than yoga teacher) to the stars. He returned to study under Ghosh in 1969, during which time he was also recuperating from a relatively minor knee injury, and it was then that he spent about six months studying yoga before departing for Japan. It was there, to compensate for Tokyo's cold winters that Choudhury began to introduce heat into his classes, and it was there that he adopted the sequence that would become "Bikram Yoga." Ghosh died shortly after Choudhury's departure and so, rather than returning to India, Choudhury went on to Hawaii and eventually the United States mainland.[43]

There, Choudhury settled in Beverly Hills, where he eventually did fulfill his claim of becoming a yoga teacher to the stars. In 1994 Choudhury held his first open teacher training program at his Los Angeles location. At their peak in the early 2000s, his training programs would regularly boast upwards of 300 registrants. All the meanwhile, Choudhury became famous for his diamond Rolexes and his fleet of Rolls-Royces. In 2013 Choudhury was sued by multiple women for sexual harassment and sexual assault, among other charges. He fled the United States in 2016 to escape prosecution.

Hot Yoga

Like students of Ashtanga developed styles beyond the framework of Jois's formal series of poses, students of Bikram Yoga too ultimately sought to move beyond Choudhury's trademark 26-posture sequence. This was exacerbated by the idea that Choudhury took the idea of a trademark on his yoga quite literally. In order to operate a studio under the Bikram Yoga name, teachers not only had to precisely adhere to Choudhury's sequence and script (in addition to other requirements for the studio space), but they were also prohibited from teaching any other style of yoga.

While these requirements were typically enforced through intimidation, in 2002 Choudhury filed a formal copyright infringement lawsuit against a group of yoga studios that were offering "Bikram Yoga" classes despite employing some teachers lacking formal certification from his organization. Choudhury's lawsuit, which was challenged by a consortium of schools (several led by former senior teachers) under the title of Open Source Yoga Unity, was settled out of court under a non-disclosure agreement.[44] Choudhury was ultimately unsuccessful in copyrighting his sequence. However, in 2012 the U.S. Copyright Office conclusively invalidated his copyright claims. As Jordan Susman has observed at the culmination of a lengthy legal analysis of Choudhury's copyright claims,

> had Bikram been more modest in his assertions and in his ambitions, he would have claimed that his sequence was an expressive dance and accentuated its aesthetic value. Although this might not have attracted huge throngs of followers, it would have afforded him maximum possible copyright protection. However, Bikram chose to be a savior—the man who developed the cure for all known illness.[45]

In other words, for Choudhury, it had to be both ways. He was both the owner of a commodity (and brand) and a guru propagating an ancient and universal system of salvific healing.

When Choudhury's former students did establish their own systems, they largely did so under the label of "Hot Yoga." For many, this came to signify not only the distinctive element of heating the room that Choudhury had introduced into his style of practice, but also the distinctive elements of the Calcutta postural system. These include certain poses not found in Krishnamacharya's lineage as well as, for some teachers, metaphysical elements that ground the practice in the early synthesis of tantric Kriya yoga with modern physical culture that arose out of Ghosh's time with his brother Yogananda. For instance, James Barkan was one of the first Americans to seriously study with Choudhury in the 1980s, as well as a devotee of Yogananda through the Self-Realization Fellowship and therefore an initiate of Kriya Yoga. Barkan's method of Hot Yoga consciously resynthesizes these elements into what is understood to be a distinct and traditional lineage of practice.

Metaphysical gurus

Transcendental Meditation (TM): Maharishi Mahesh Yogi (1918–2008)

In 1967, the Beatles went to Rishikesh, India and came back singing "Jai Guru Deva." A major impetus for the rock band's spiritual adventure was their desire to participate in Maharishi Mahesh Yogi's Spiritual Regeneration Movement. As Cynthia Humes explains,

> Maharishi Mahesh Yogi has crafted what many would identify as a highly influential Hindu global theological perspective through his Transcendental Meditation Movement. In the West, he has achieved this influence in part

> by denying the "Hindu-ness" of his teachings, and at least for a time, their religiosity as well. In so doing, he thrust the reach of his Advaita Vedantin interpretations and many standard cultural markers of Hinduism into a global context.[46]

Maharishi was born Mahesh Prasad Varma in Jabalpur, and in 1940, while he was still a college student, he met the man who would become his guru, Swami Brahamananda Saraswati, the Shankaracharya of Jyotir Math.[47] Maharishi ultimately called the meditation technique he learned from his guru, Transcendental Deep Meditation, later Transcendental Meditation (TM), which he linked via his guru's lineage directly to the traditional Advaita Vedānta philosophy of the 8th-century theologian Śaṅkara. The method was based in *mantra*-repetition, which he originally explained in a traditional fashion as working to harness the power of the *mantra* and of the deity that it embodied. Eventually, however, Maharishi would develop a more "scientific" mechanism for the *mantras*, through which they could work automatically. By 1959, he resolved to train a group of teachers in his method, who could then be qualified to further initiate their own students, effectively instituting a model of teacher training. It was precisely such a training that the Beatles attended, though it should be noted that Maharishi's center had by this time already acquired international fame and was especially popular among college students.[48]

Scientific language remained important to Maharishi's system. Maharishi certainly claimed that practitioners of TM would gain both physical and psychological health and generally improve all dimensions of their lives. However, extrapolating from a Vedāntic understanding of non-dual reality, he also came to claim that while TM practice could de-stress the individual, it also produced a more diffuse calming effect on all of society. Based on this logic, as well as a somewhat dubious study linking meditation and crime rates, he stated in 1974 that this "Maharishi Effect" was both predictable and scientific. In 1976, Maharishi introduced the TM-Sidhi program, in which he claimed that *mantra* repetition could result in "Yogic Flying."[49] Such claims are of course very common in traditional yogic systems, but less accepted according to the standards of modern science. In practice, all of this seemed to amount to the idea that the practitioner could briefly levitate via a series of concerted "hops."

Interestingly, unlike most global gurus who tended to move from the culturally specific to the universal, Maharishi ultimately took the opposite path, continually imbuing his system with layers of traditional Hindu cultural scaffolding, which was made available to advanced teachers and practitioners. In other words, for Maharishi, universal truth was ultimately affirmed to be Vedic and he emerged as the arbiter of its authority.[50]

Siddha Yoga: Swami Muktananda (1908–1982)

Most modern gurus draw in one way of another on the link between social charisma and the metaphysical energy of *śakti*, but one guru in particular made the transmission of this energy a hallmark of his image. Muktananda was born Krishna Rai in Karnataka. After a long period of spiritual exploration, he became the disciple of a man named Nityananda at an ashram in Ganeshpuri. Muktananda's chief philosophical influences were Advaita Vedānta and Kaula Śaivism, both non-dual schools of thought that ultimately maintain the oneness of all reality. However, it is ultimately from the tantric Śaiva school that Muktananda appears to have drawn his understandings of innate human divinity, the role of the guru, and the means of transcending all duality.[51] His method would come to be known as Siddha Yoga, after the "Perfected Ones," the tantric adepts who had started out as human but had become gods.

His own experience of receiving *śakti-pāta* from his guru was foundational to Muktananda's spiritual life. He sought to offer this same experience to others, first at the ashram at Ganeshpuri and then, and then through a series of weekend "Intensives," which he would conduct during his global tours. At these Intensives Muktananda would tap seekers with a peacock feather, awaken the dormant energy within them, and cause a fundamental shift in consciousness. The spectrum of reported experiences ranged from blissful to terrifying.[52] As scholar and practitioner Paul Muller-Ortega has observed, this global dissemination of *śakti-pāta* was a radical move in accessibility:

> Because of [*śakti-pāta*'s] historical rarity and relative unavailability, the notion that Swami Muktananda should have made [*śakti-pāta*] attainable on a wide scale around the world is quite noteworthy. After many centuries of barely being available even in India, its sudden and relatively easy accessibility marks an unprecedented and significant historical shift. It is only when we fathom the rarity of what Swami Muktananda professed to be offering to the world that we can begin to appreciate the boldness and genius of his decision to bring [*śakti-pāta*] out of its millennial obscurity.[53]

Notably, the Kaula tantric schools by which Muktananda was inspired have historically incorporated a number of socially and ethically transgressive practices, including the imbibing of impure substances and ritualized sexual intercourse. Over time and centuries before tantra's introduction into the West, such practices became domesticated (an effect of pre-modern popularization), ritual substitutions were made, and the ritual generally became abstracted and internalized with (for instance) literal sex being replaced with the visionary union of masculine and feminine principles within the practitioner's body.[54] As another scholar-practitioner, Douglas Brooks, has noted, when it came to appeals to tradition in the form of tantric scripture, Muktananda and his successors would "cite frequently but selectively,"[55] carefully conforming to normative social ethics. However, as Andrea Jain points out, Muktananda did engage in these more esoteric dimensions of tantric practice, especially towards the end of his life. After Muktananda's death in 1982, the ashram temporarily erupted with sex scandals and general disarray before being reined back in.[56] Such crises are common in new movements after the original founder's passing, but were perhaps exacerbated by the unique nature of Muktananda's authority as well as his late experimentation with more socially transgressive practices.

Osho (1931–1990)

Before Osho was Osho (as he rebranded himself towards the end of his life), he was Bhagwan Sree Rajneesh, and before that he was Rajneesh Chandra Mohan, born into a wealthy Jain family in a village in Madhya Pradesh. He ultimately received a master's degree and for nine years taught philosophy at the University of Jabalpur. However, having achieved a state of self-proclaimed full enlightenment by age 21, in 1967 Rajneesh decided that the time had come to spread his wisdom to the community. In the early 1970s, he began calling himself Bhagwan (from Bhagavan, or "Blessed One," an epithet for God) and built an ashram in Pune. By 1981, however, legal and financial trouble forced him and his devotees to flee India. He ultimately settled at a large ranch in Oregon. Under the leadership of senior administrators, Rajneeshpuram ("Rajneesh's Town"), as the community dubbed itself, evolved into a highly authoritarian institution. What's more, their large numbers allowed them to orchestrate a virtual political takeover of the neighboring town's local government. By 1986, a laundry list of criminal charges resulted in Rajneesh's deportation from the United States, upon which he returned to Pune.[57] Not to be undone, he became Osho, cosmic trickster and "spiritually incorrect mystic." He spent the final four years of his life preaching what he called a universal message, grounded in a variety of neo-esoteric techniques, and the center he founded only continued to grow in popularity following his death.[58]

Hugh Urban has described Rajneesh's radically subversive and ever-shifting teachings as a "postmodern pastiche" stitched together from "a remarkable range of sources, from Plato to Śaṅkara to Lao Tzu to Sartre," with "a special fondness for the more radical figures such as Nietzche, Gurdjieff, and Crowley."[59] Rajneesh taught a religion of antireligion, rejecting every norm, every boundary, and every metanarrative. His meditative techniques were similarly iconoclastic and unstructured, emphasizing spontaneity, and including music, uncontrolled breathing, free movement, dancing, and vocalization. He took explicit inspiration from tantric traditions but reinterpreted them into his own brand of "Neo-Tantra," glorifying transgression, personal (including material and sexual) gratification, and absolute individualism all premised on the innate divinity and perfection of human (and, indeed, of all) nature.[60] In practice, for Rajneesh this looked like group sex and a fleet of 93 Rolls-Royces.

Rajneesh, who freely embraced capitalism and branded himself as a "guru to the rich" saw his ideal as "Zorba the Buddha," declaring,

> My concept of the new man is that he will be Zorba the Greek and he will also be Gautama the Buddha. … He will be sensuous and spiritual—physical … in the senses, enjoying the body … and still a great consciousness. He will be Christ and Epicurus together.[61]

Urban has argued that tantric traditions provide a conveniently fitting metaphysics for the individualistic logics of late-stage capitalism, which effectively treats material goods as sacred and the self as divine. For Urban, Osho-Rajneesh embodies this dynamic.

Post-lineage and non-lineage yoga

Charismatic authority is notoriously difficult to pass down unless it manifests in a pre-established institutional context. For instance, while a new pope may be less personally charismatic than his predecessor, this is unlikely to bring an end to the Catholic Church. On the other hand, a guru's authority is often tied to that specific individual, and so his specific movement and organization may struggle to survive his death (or downfall in a scandal), especially on a global level. For this reason, modern guru-led movements represent a fascinating data point in the transmission of yogic knowledge. On the one hand, they tend to ground themselves in traditions that have survived for centuries (Śrī Vaiṣṇava, Advaita Vedānta, Kaula tantra, and so on) and will continue to do so regardless of the fate of any one ancillary movement. On the other hand, such gurus have built specific organizations, and arguably "brands" (Ashtanga Yoga, Bikram Yoga, Siddha Yoga, and so on), that are more-or-less tied to each guru's authority as a founder and innovator. However, when a guru exits the stage, the knowledge he transmitted and the practitioners who have come to embody it don't simply disappear. Indeed, in the modern global marketplace of ideas and practices, the natural mixing and mingling that has always characterized how traditions evolve and interact has only become more fluid and unconstrained.

In other chapters of this book we've compared yoga's sprawling diversity, as well as its ability to tangle and hybridize across cultures with other similar traditions, to webs of rhizomatic plants, like lotuses and water lilies. Yoga scholar Theodora Wildcroft adopts a similar metaphor when she speaks of dandelions (which are also rhizomatic). Wildcroft has proposed that we might use this more diffuse and potentially democratic model of tradition and authority to think about how yoga practitioners and the communities they comprise transition into what she calls a "post-lineage model." Wildcroft explains that post-lineage does not necessarily mean non-lineage or anti-lineage. Instead, she says that

> post-lineage yoga describes a shift that many yoga teachers and practitioners go through—they might start out only learning from one teacher, and never questioning their authority. But at some point, many look beyond the lineage teachings to expand their understanding of how yoga works in practice. They might or might not maintain a strong respect for their original teachers, but they might read books from other lineages, or be fascinated by the latest neuroscience research, or share a practice with peers or go to workshops with other teachers.[62]

In other words, transmission never flows in a single line (this is true even in a premodern context) for very long—it's always a web. We can see a very clear instance of this dynamic in the Power Yoga and Hot Yoga labels.

Going even further, we might indeed think of a non-lineage yoga. Global gurus represent in their own modern way a traditional, direct and oral mode or transmission. This kind of transmission happens between two human beings, with the guru acting as a central hub in a larger network. However, there are other modes of transmission—textual transmission, for instance, which by now has a long history of its own—that place more emphasis on the individual student and their agency in procuring, selecting, and adopting knowledge. For instance, historian of Western esotericism Arthur Versluis has argued that, within the tradition that we've been referring to as harmonialism, the mode of transmission and initiation has been primarily literary.[63] Of course individual teachers, including some incredibly charismatic ones, have certainly existed in the Western harmonial tradition. However, Versluis's evaluation is largely accurate and it becomes even more so as harmonial spiritual and wellness practices enter the prolific print culture of the 19th century and onwards. And so, when yogic knowledge is introduced and blends into this context—that is, when lotuses begin to take root among water lilies—it too begins to travel in this manner. We might think of Iyengar's *Light on Yoga*, a book used by many students and teachers who have never visited an Iyengar Yoga studio, as a prime example of this.

And so, to which lineage would we assign a practitioner who first begins attending yoga classes at a local gym, picks up *Light on Yoga* along with a few manuals by mostly Western teachers, and then largely practices at home using virtual instruction or else at a corporate gym? What if many of the physical and metaphysical practices this person engage in are actually harmonial? Such a person may have a committed, deep, and even spiritual practice but, if we call their practice yoga (as they themselves likely would), then it might be useful to think of it as a non-lineage yoga. In such a case, the individual practitioner becomes their own hub in the rhizomatic web of multiple traditions. And suddenly, Osho's radical pastiche doesn't seem so unusual—individuals stitch together their personal worldviews in this way all the time, just with fewer Rolls-Royces.

Conclusions

- Gurus have played a key role in the transmission of global yoga, both as individually charismatic figures of authority and as the originators of their own global brands.
- The figure of the guru has a long history in South Asian tradition, where the guru–disciple relationship has evolved in ways that include a high degree of hierarchy, intimacy, devotion, and surrender. Metaphysically, this is represented by the role of *śakti-pāta*, a practice (historically used in initiation rituals) in which the guru penetrates the disciple with an energetic influx of *śakti*, purifying his body and opening the door to enlightenment. In the modern context, this system represents a potentially problematic framework that can exacerbate possibilities of sexual assault and other abuses of power.
- Gurus became popular in the West in part because they fulfilled Western fantasies of the "mystic from the East," seen as a carrier of ancient and universal wisdom. Global gurus often played to such stereotypes, further

enhancing yoga's claims to universality by connecting it to the objective standards of modern science.

- Gurus of physical yoga, such as Tirumalai Krishnamacharya and Bishnu Ghosh, developed methods that drew on *haṭha* yoga, indigenous Indian physical culture, as well as Western gymnastics and body building. This eclecticism is mirrored in further innovations by Western teachers under labels such as "Power Yoga" and "Hot Yoga."
- Metaphysical gurus such as Maharishi Mahesh, Muktananda, and Osho-Rajneesh built on traditional Vedāntic and tantric frameworks but likewise adapted them to a global audience through mass teacher trainings and intensives, claims to scientific authority, and eclectic universalist blending.

Notes

1 Elizabeth De Michelis, *A History of Modern Yoga: Patañjali and Western Esoterism* (London: Continuum, 2004).
2 Anya P. Foxen, *Biography of a Yogi: Paramahansa Yogananda and the Origins of Modern Yoga* (New York: Oxford University Press, 2017), 50.
3 Amanda Lucia, "Guru Sex: Charisma, Proxemic Desire, and the Haptic Logics of the Guru–Disciple Relationship," *Journal of the American Academy of Religion*, 86, no. 4 (2018): 953–88. The yoga community has begun to take up and grapple with these complex issues, as for instance in a conference held at the Loyola Marymouth University Yoga Studies program: "Abuse in Yoga and Beyond: Cultural Logics and Pathways for the Future," Loyola Marymount University, June 13, 2020, https://bellarmine.lmu.edu/yoga/events/conferencesandpastevents/yogavcon/
4 Andrea R. Jain, *Peace, Love, Yoga: The Politics of Global Spirituality* (New York: Oxford University Press, 2020), 105.
5 Ronald M. Davidson, *Indian Esoteric Buddhism: Social History of the Tantric Movement* (Delhi: Motilal Banarsidass, 2004), 25–30.
6 Daniel Gold, *The Lord as Guru: Hindi Sants in North Indian Tradition* (New York; Oxford: Oxford University Press, 1987), 4.
7 Gavin D. Flood, *The Tantric Body: The Secret Tradition of Hindu Religion* (London and New York: I. B. Tauris, 2006), 11.
8 David Gordon White, *Sinister Yogis* (Chicago: University of Chicago Press, 2009), 140.
9 Lucia, "Guru Sex," 960.
10 Pinch, *Warrior Ascetics and Indian Empires*, 31. White, *Sinister Yogis*, 241.
11 Edwin Arnold, *Light of Asia: Or, The Great Renunciation* (New York: A. L. Burt, 1879), 119.
12 Quoted in Anya P. Foxen, *Biography of a Yogi: Paramahansa Yogananda and the Origins of Modern Yoga* (New York: Oxford University Press, 2017), 42.
13 Narasingha Prosad Sil, *Swami Vivekananda: A Reassessment* (Selinsgrove, PA: Susquehanna University Press, 1997), 129.
14 Sil, *Swami Vivekananda*, 93.
15 Philip Deslippe, "The Swami Circuit: Mapping the Terrain of Early American Yoga," *Journal of Yoga Studies*, 1 (2018): 5–44.
16 Roland Vernon, *Star in the East: Krishnamurti, the Invention of a Messiah* (New York: Palgrave for St. Martin's Press, 2001), 182.
17 Swami Vivekananda, *The Complete of Swami Vivekananda*, vol. 1 (Calcutta: Advaita Ashrama, 1915), 154.
18 Mark Singleton and Tara Fraser, "T. Krishnamacharya, Father of Modern Yoga," in *Gurus of Modern Yoga*, ed. Mark Singleton and Ellen Goldberg (New York: Oxford University Press, 2014), 85.

19 Singleton and Fraser, "T. Krishnamacharya," 86.
20 Jason Birch and Mark Singleton, "The Yoga of the *Haṭhābhyāsapaddhati*: Haṭhayoga on the Cusp of Modernity," *Journal of Yoga Studies*, 2 (2019): 50.
21 Singleton and Fraser, "T. Krishnamacharya," 93.
22 Singleton, *Yoga Body*, 185.
23 Gavin D. Flood, *An Introduction to Hinduism* (Cambridge: Cambridge University Press, 2006), 132.
24 Singleton, *Yoga Body*, 185.
25 Frederick M. Smith and Joan White, "Becoming an Icon: B. K. S. Iyengar as a Yoga Teacher and a Yoga Guru," in *Gurus of Modern Yoga*, ed. Mark Singleton and Ellen Goldberg (New York: Oxford University Press, 2014), 140n6.
26 Singleton and Fraser, "T. Krishnamacharya," 92.
27 Birch and Singleton, "The Yoga of the *Haṭhābhyāsapaddhati*," 51.
28 Singleton, *Yoga Body*, 178–84.
29 Singleton and Fraser, "T. Krishnamacharya," 87–8.
30 Smith and White, "Becoming an Icon," 134–5.
31 Smith and White, "Becoming an Icon," 128–9.
32 De Michelis, *A History of Modern Yoga*, 198.
33 "Interview with B. K. S. Iyengar," *CNN: Talk Asia*, October 24, 2007, http://edition.cnn.com/2007/WORLD/asiapcf/10/02/talkasia.iyengar/index.html
34 Smith and White, "Becoming an Icon," 157–9. See also Suzanne Newcombe, *Yoga in Britain: Stretching Spirituality and Educating Yogis* (Sheffield: Equinox, 2019).
35 "#TimesUp: Ending Sexual Abuse in the Yoga Community," *Yoga Journal*, February 12, 2018, https://www.yogajournal.com/lifestyle/timesup-metoo-ending-sexual-abuse-in-the-yoga-community.
36 K. Pattabhi Jois, "Ashtanga vs. Power Yoga," *Yoga Journal*, November/December 1995, 6.
37 Marianne Costantinou, "San Francisco's Yoga Pioneer Magaña Baptiste, at 84, Can Still Bend over Backward for Health," *SFGate*, August 15, 2005, https://www.sfgate.com/entertainment/article/San-Francisco-s-yoga-pioneer-Maga-a-Baptiste-at-2647599.php; Richard Rosen, "Walt Baptiste," *Yoga Journal*, April 5, 2007, https://www.yogajournal.com/yoga-101/walt-baptiste
38 Jerome Armstrong, *Calcutta Yoga: How Modern Yoga Travelled to the World from the Streets of Calcutta* (New Delhi: Macmillan, 2020), 42–3.
39 Armstrong, *Calcutta Yoga*, 93.
40 Armstrong, *Calcutta Yoga*, 189–215
41 Armstrong, *Calcutta Yoga*, 345.
42 Armstrong, *Calcutta Yoga*, 411.
43 Armstrong, *Calcutta Yoga*, 377–95.
44 Allison Fish, "The Commodification and Exchange of Knowledge in the Case of Transnational Commercial Yoga," *International Journal of Cultural Property*, 13 (2006): 189–206.
45 Jordan Susman, "Your Karma Ran Over My Dogma: Bikram Yoga and the (IM)Possibilities of Copyrighting Yoga," *Loyola of Los Angeles Entertainment Law Review*, 25, no. 2 (2005): 245–74.
46 Cynthia Ann Humes, "Maharishi Mahesh Yogi: Beyond the TM Technique," in *Gurus in America*, ed. Thomas A. Forsthoefel and Cynthia Ann Humes (Albany: State University of New York Press, 2005), 57.
47 Humes, "Maharishi Mahesh Yogi," 59.
48 Humes, "Maharishi Mahesh Yogi," 63–4.
49 Humes, "Maharishi Mahesh Yogi," 65–6.
50 Humes, "Maharishi Mahesh Yogi," 72–3.
51 Andrea R. Jain, "Muktananda: Entrepreneurial Godman, Tantric Hero," in *Gurus of Modern Yoga*, ed. Mark Singleton and Ellen Goldberg (New York: Oxford University Press, 2014), 193.

52 Lola Williamson, "The Perfectibility of Perfection: Siddha Yoga as a Global Movement," in *Gurus in America*, ed. Thomas A. Forsthoefel and Cynthia Ann Humes (Albany: State University of New York Press, 2005), 151–2; Jain, "Muktananda," 195, 199–201.
53 Paul E. Muller-Ortega, "Shaktipat: The Initiatory Descent of Power," in *Meditation Revolutions: A History and Theology of the Siddha Yoga Lineage*, ed. Douglas Renfrew Brooks et al. (South Fallsburg, NY: Agama Press, 1997), 410.
54 David Gordon White, *The Kiss of the Yoginī: "Tantric Sex" in Its South Asian Contexts* (Chicago: University of Chicago Press, 2002), 219–57.
55 Douglas Renfrew Brooks, "The Canons of Siddha Yoga: The Body of Scripture and the Form of the Guru," in *Meditation Revolutions: A History and Theology of the Siddha Yoga Lineage*, ed. Douglas Renfrew Brooks et al. (South Fallsburg, NY: Agama Press, 1997), 334.
56 Jain, "Muktananda," 204–5. See also Sarah Caldwell, "The Heart of the Secret: A Personal and Scholarly Encounter with Shakta Tantrism in Siddha Yoga," *Nova Religio*, 5, no. 1 (2001): 9–51.
57 Hugh B. Urban, "Osho, from Sex Guru to Guru of the Rich: The Spiritual Logic of Late Capitalism," in *Gurus in America*, ed. Thomas A. Forsthoefel and Cynthia Ann Humes (Albany: State University of New York Press, 2005), 172–3.
58 Urban, "Osho, from Sex Guru to Guru of the Rich," 181–2.
59 Urban, "Osho, from Sex Guru to Guru of the Rich," 173–4.
60 Urban, "Osho, from Sex Guru to Guru of the Rich," 174–6.
61 Quoted in Urban, "Osho, from Sex Guru to Guru of the Rich," 178.
62 Theodora Wildcroft, "Post-Lineage Yoga and Dandelions: What Dandelions Have to Teach Us about 'Post-Lineage Yoga,'" *The Luminescent*, September 12, 2019, https://www.theluminescent.org/2019/09/post-lineage-yoga-dandelions.html. See also Theodora Wildcroft, *Post-Lineage Yoga: From Guru to #metoo* (Sheffield: Equinox, 2020).
63 Arthur Versluis, *Restoring Paradise: Western Esotericism, Literature, Art, and Consciousness* (Albany: State University of New York Press, 2004), 10–15.

9 Liberating the modern self through the business of yoga

What does it mean to be free?

Are we talking about freedom from suffering? Absolute freedom of choice? Do we mean individual or collective freedom? Is my freedom helped or hampered by yours? All of these questions are as eminently relevant in modern political philosophy as they have been in historical yoga traditions. And what's more, the answers (complicated and contradictory as they are) might show quite a bit of overlap.

Yoga has always been both political and commercial. When the god Kṛṣṇa instructs the hero Arjuna on the battlefield—this is the context of the *Bhagavad Gītā*, a classical piece of scripture with much to say about the multiplicity of yogas—he isn't only concerned with Arjuna's spiritual liberation. He's also very insistent that the key to this liberation is nothing other than the fulfillment of Arjuna's social and political duty, his *dharma* as a warrior fighting a war. As scholars like David Gordon White and William Pinch have demonstrated, yogis have historically appeared not only as spiritual ascetics but as soldiers, political powerbrokers, and peddlers of everything from alchemical elixirs of immortality to aphrodisiacs. Pre-modern yogis, even those who were ultimately after enlightenment and liberation from the cycle of rebirth, were still embedded in the social, economic, and political institutions of their day.

Accordingly, pre-modern yoga traditions in India were never uniformly focused on a kind of disembodied spiritual liberation. Yoga practices, even ascetic ones that applied severe discipline to the body and mind, were often understood to yield not only a variety of physical benefits but also an array of fantastic abilities (essentially "superpowers" such as flight, the ability to bend others to one's will, and so forth) known as *siddhis* or "accomplishments." Some yoga traditions acknowledged such worldly benefits but ultimately viewed them as obstacles to true liberation. However, other schools of thought, and especially tantric traditions, understood them as an alternative goal or even a feature of liberation itself. Thus a premodern yogi could be what's called a *mumukṣu* (that is, one striving for liberation or *mukti* above all else), or he could be a *bubhukṣu* (one who is after enjoyment, or *bhukti*).[1] And, even in light of their potentially diverging goals, we might think about the ways that both positions nevertheless reflect an individualistic and progress-driven model of practice that we sometimes falsely imagine to be unique to our modern mindset. As scholar of Hinduism and modern spirituality

Amanda Lucia has pointed out, this self-optimizing "striving subject has been read by numerous critics as a neoliberal subject, but it is also the striving subject of romanticism and thousands of years of ascetic and mystic religious engagement."[2]

So, as we begin this chapter on the ways in which yoga has been commodified, politicized, and otherwise transformed in the modern global context (through mixing with Western physical culture and spirituality, for instance), we should be careful to remember that none of this is exactly unprecedented. It's a mistake to imagine that, once upon a time in India, there was a "pure" and "authentic" tradition of yoga that was somehow immune to disagreement, to change, and above all to economic and political interests. However, it's also important to acknowledge that our current economic and political climate is in many ways unique to our own specific cultural situation and historical moment. This becomes especially important when we consider yoga in a global context. The way that yoga functions in North America may well be different from the way it functions in Asia. Indian politics are different from those of the United States.

One key way in which modern global culture does differ from previous historical moments is an unprecedented degree of global connectivity that allows for the movement of both ideas and people. This results in a radically expanded access to a plurality of cultures, along with their attendant viewpoints, concepts, practices, and material goods. In the sphere of religion and spirituality, especially, such an expansion of possibilities can be transformative. The sociologist Peter Berger has described this modern phenomenon as "the heretical imperative." Heretic, from the Greek word *hairetikos* or "able to choose," was once the designation of an outsider and a deviant. Heretics who chose to diverge from proper (that is, institutionally sanctioned) doctrine and practice were seen as committing a criminal offense, the kind that could easily get them burned at the stake. But modernity has fractured religious authority, and globalization has created a climate where individuals have access to a wide variety of religious systems. By presenting us with options, modernity forces us to choose. "Thus heresy," Berger tells us, "once the occupation of marginal and eccentric types, has become a much more general condition; indeed, heresy has become universalized."[3]

On the one hand, such an emphasis on self-determination and choice can seem marvelously liberating. On the other hand, of course, complete autonomy and unsupported personal responsibility can prove disorienting, alienating, and taxing for the individual. Even more importantly, globalization does not necessarily mean democratization, in the sense of equality of access, opportunity, or resources. Power dynamics, both historical and current, represented by inequitable social and political institutions, determine who is really free to choose. None of this is unique to yoga, of course, but even a superficial look at global yoga culture quickly reveals traces of both of these potential pitfalls. For instance, a study analyzing nearly 50 years of cover images from the popular publication *Yoga Journal* found that, at its inception, the magazine featured more men than women, with a majority of them being famous Indian gurus and teachers of yoga. Later covers feature almost exclusively thin, white women to the exclusion of both men and women of color, as well as any diverse body types.[4] Notably, both trends are problematic in their own ways. The earlier covers presented Indian men as exotic representatives of a kind of timeless "fantasy culture," which is informed by a history of Western colonialism. The later covers not only exclude people of color, but also establish a standard ideal of health and beauty, to which can prove unattainable to the individual practitioner even if she is lucky enough to fall into the target demographic. Such messaging contributes to a self-perpetuating force of exclusion. As of the early 2000s, approximately 85 percent of American yoga practitioners have identified as Caucasian[5] and approximately 72–82 percent identified as women.[6]

However, commodifying and ideologically-loaded understandings of yoga are not exclusive to the West, but are just as easily found in global, including Indian, contexts. If there's a problem to be found in modern "Yogaland," that problem may not really be the "Westernization" of yoga. Instead, as Hugh Urban has suggested,

> the real threat today is the spread of consumer capitalism and the domination of the global marketplace over all local economies, polities, and cultural forms—a process that is no longer dominated by the West, no longer a matter of either "occidentalization" or "orientalization," but a far more complex product of transnational capitalism.[7]

Individualism, neoliberalism, and collage spirituality

Scholars have argued that modern Western culture—to a greater or lesser extent, depending on the country—is governed by the logic of neoliberalism. Neoliberalism has its roots in Enlightenment Era political philosophy, where "liberalism" came to signify the idea of individual rights (like the natural rights to life, liberty, and property identified by John Locke), which then became tied to a number of diverse and sometimes contradictory social principles like egalitarianism, democracy, secularism, and free markets. Neoliberalism is a term that emerged in the first half of the 20th century, mostly in the context of economics, but it was popularized in the 1980s by French philosopher Michel Foucault, who used it to talk about a much broader range of social phenomena. Modern scholars, following Foucault, describe neoliberalism as an ideology of radical individualism in which "nothing imposes an obligation, and everything, including one's own mind, body, and emotional state is a resource, a force to be excited, an opportunity to be developed, exploited, or leveraged for advantage in a world of competitive actors."[8] Neoliberal individuals are supremely free in the sense that they are utterly autonomous—self-governing, self-cultivating, and self-helping. Neoliberalism is capitalism writ large, in that every individual becomes the entrepreneurial manager of their own existence.

In such a context, postural yoga classes are only one aspect of a broader regimen of "self-care" in which the notion of yoga becomes associated with proper (because "healthy") behaviors of exercise, eating, stress-management, grooming choices, and so on.[9] But it's important to note that yoga's ethic of individual choice in the spirit of self-optimization is not only physical, it's also metaphysical. It's no coincidence that staples of the "self-help" genre like holistic wellness and positive thinking were a major feature of the pop spiritual movements of the 19th century, loosely grouped under the label of "New Thought." In fact, New Thought was rather old insofar as its ideological scaffolding was formed from notions of harmonial correspondence (for example, "like attracts like") that can be traced all the way back to the ancient Greek world. However, at the dawn of the Gilded Age, industrialization drastically transformed the social and economic landscape on which these ideas operated. The ethics of hard work and personal responsibility (rather than hereditary status) were used to justify the new forms of wealth inequality that arose from this modern capitalist and increasingly neoliberal economy. In other words, poverty became understood not as a natural condition, but as a matter of personal responsibility. From a spiritual perspective, this often entailed a radically optimistic view of the world. The divine order was one of bliss and bounty. If your life didn't reflect this reality, then it could only be a matter of personal fault—laziness, bad thoughts, and not being, as New Thought author Ralph Waldo Trine put it, properly "in tune with the Infinite."

"The optimist," Trine wrote, "by his superior wisdom and insight, is making his own heaven, and in the degree that he makes his own heaven is he helping to make one for all the world beside."[10] Interestingly, in her ethnographic research among modern practitioners of spirituality, Amanda Lucia found that the more a spiritual context centers around the idea of yoga, the more its likely to foreground internal self-transformation as the primary vehicle of social activism and change.[11] This correlation might derive from the commonality that many historical Indian yoga traditions share with this strand of Western harmonial spirituality—the logic of the macro- and microcosms, or the correspondence between the "big world" of the universe and the "little world" of the human self. But, while the core principles of this idea are quite ancient, they manifest today in distinctly modern ways. Under the ideology of neoliberal capitalism, even communal relationships are understood through the lens of the individual. On a social level, we are not to ask what society can do for us, but instead how we can be the most efficient, productive, and self-supporting members of society. On a spiritual level, this fits quite nicely with the logic of cosmic correspondence. Each individual is affirmed as a world unto themselves. Failure to care for oneself implies a failure to care for the world, not only because one risks being a burden on society, but because one is literally failing to fulfill one's role as a conduit of the universe's blissful oneness. This can lead to a phenomenon known as "spiritual bypassing," in which individuals may refuse to engage with ideas they view as breeding negative or unpleasant thoughts and emotions. As a result, yoga practitioners may use a stated focus on "light and love" to avoid contentious and otherwise difficult topics such as politics and social justice activism (especially serious anti-racism work).[12]

The ideal neoliberal individual is an entrepreneur, but also a consumer. In a world where everyone is selling something, consumption becomes the primary mode of social engagement. And so, "buying good is being good."[13] Yoga-adjacent brands thus often champion neoliberal versions of progressive ideals, like "conscious capitalism" that offers the consumer more ethical choices but doesn't fundamentally question the resulting distribution of wealth, or feminism that focuses on individual women's empowerment but does little to effect structural change. Andrea Jain suggests that these aspects of the modern yoga lifestyle serve as gestures to express resistance to the status quo, but ultimately end up structurally reinforcing the very systems they outwardly claim to subvert. In particular, according to Jain, "in the case of global spirituality, dissent is domesticated through commodification. In the forms these commodities take, a liberal-individualist understanding of 'progress' largely stands in place of socialist understandings of revolution."[14]

In fact, the idea of spirituality, which doesn't have the confining institutional valences of a term like "religion," seems ideally suited for the market-driven, individualist logics of neoliberalism. Religious blending, eclecticism, and a focus on individual experience are also not uniquely modern phenomena, of course. There is a long history of concepts like *prisca theologia* ("ancient theology") or *philosophia perennis* ("perennial philosophy")[15] that posit a sort of least common denominator at the root of all the world's religious traditions. And, in theory, if all religions contain the same kernel of ancient and universal truth, then it stands to reason that their individual concepts and practices are more-or-less analogous and interchangeable. They can be picked through, combined, and recombined to form a single unitary vision. Of course, in practice, this single and unitary universal truth often ends up looking a whole lot like *our* truth, into which other cultures' specific visions are naturalized by reducing them to a set of resemblances.

Modern technology, globalization, and the power structures of imperialism and colonialism did not create this dynamic, but they have certainly intensified it. Sociologists sometimes refer to "cafeteria" or "salad bar" religion, where each practitioner can take some of whatever she likes and leave the rest—a literal spiritual marketplace.[16] Another popular term is bricolage, an originally French word that means something along the same lines as the English expression DIY, "do it yourself." Again, the focus is on the individual, who picks and chooses, mixes and remixes to produce their own unique blend of ideas and practices. A more quotidian (though also French) term for this is "collage"—an art form with which every schoolchild is likely familiar. The idea of collage is especially fitting insofar as it resonates with a common contemporary practice shared by both spiritual seekers and capitalist consumers: the vision or inspiration board, a type of collage in which images, text, and other objects are collected as a representation of an individual's desires or ambitions. In its most earnest form, the collage of a vision board represents the practitioner's ideal self and reality, created piecemeal out of the cultural artifacts (ideas or objects), sourced from wherever they may be found.

How white women became yogis

In 1892, just a year before Swami Vivekananda would make his debut at the World's Parliament of Religions in Chicago as the prototypical image of the Indian mystic-cum-global yogi, an American woman named Genevieve Stebbins (1857–1934) published a book called *Dynamic Breathing and Harmonic Gymnastics: A Complete System of Psychical, Aesthetic and Physical Culture*. In this book,

Stebbins would advocate for her system of "psycho-physical culture," which she described as "the perfect unison of harmonic gymnastics and dynamic breathing, during the formulation of noble ideals in the mind."[17] To our eyes, this might look very much like Stebbins was teaching yogic *āsana* (posture), *prāṇāyāma* (breath-control), and *dhyāna* (meditation)—in other words, "yoga." But, actually, though Stebbins (being a well-educated and cultured woman) had probably heard of yoga, she was not deeply familiar with any of its practices. And so, although Stebbins did make some universalistic statements about the role of breath and movement in the "charmingly beautiful motions of sacred dance and prayer practiced by various oriental nations for certain religious and metaphysical effects," her chief points of reference when it comes to what physical practice should look like were Neo-classical (that is, Greek) aesthetic ideals and Pehr Henrik Ling's (1776–1839) system of Swedish gymnastics.

In other words, Stebbins wasn't teaching yoga. She was teaching a kind of spiritual (specifically harmonial) physical culture that has its own very long history spanning the ancient Mediterranean, medieval Islamic, and Renaissance and early modern European, and modern North American contexts. Specifically, the "Harmonic" label that Stebbins attached to her style of gymnastics derives from the Greek philosophical idea of *harmonia*, "fitting together" or "union," not unlike one possible translation of the Sanskrit word "yoga." And so, it's not surprising that Stebbins's system might sound like yoga to us. Though it's difficult to pinpoint pre-modern influence or common roots, we can certainly say that, in this case, the Indian yogic and the Western harmonial tradition share key similarities and that they evolved in analogous ways. In fact, as Mark Singleton has argued, "postural modern yoga displaced—or was the cultural successor of—the established methods of stretching and relaxing that had already become commonplace in the West, through harmonial gymnastics and female physical culture."[18] Anya Foxen has extended this argument to explain that these systems represent "a Western history of practice here that was overwritten by the imported language of yoga, thereby becoming invisible. In this form, it has continually been used to inform and occasionally to colonize the category of Indian yoga."[19]

Physical culture—the idea that one might engage in physical activity for the sole purpose of developing one's body and, more broadly, one's self—has always been a somewhat class-specific phenomenon. For instance, the ancient Greek physician Galen (129–210 CE) defined exercise as any movement that was vigorous, swift, or both, and that caused an acceleration of the breath. His rubric thus explicitly included wrestling, racing, hunting, and various ball games as well as a range of agricultural and artisanal activities such as ploughing, reaping, and building ships and houses. On the other hand, the Islamic philosopher Ibn Sīnā (aka Avicenna, 980–1037 CE), who played a major role in bridging ancient Greek and early modern medicine, declared that exercise should be "voluntary" and "undertaken for its own sake"[20]—in other words, exercise was not the same as physical labor. Historically, there would have been a few "occupations" that necessitated specific forms of bodily, mental, and spiritual discipline: soldiers, performers, athletes (which might significantly overlap with one of the previous two categories), and religious specialists might represent the most prominent examples. Besides these sorts of specialized groups, we can imagine that few people in a pre-industrial society, especially outside the aristocracy, would have had either the time or the necessity to purposefully exercise their bodies. To a large extent, intentional exercise became necessary for the general population over the course of the 18th and 19th centuries, when urbanization, industrialization, and the increasingly sedentary nature of middle-class labor limited both the need and the opportunity for incidental bodily activity.

Early modern physical culture was men's domain. In fact, many 19th-century physicians believed that women were inherently frail, largely due to the inordinate influence that their sexual biology exercised over their bodies. A whole slew of literature insisted that all female ailments—which were indeed both dire and numerous—arose from an undue strain placed on a woman's bodily resources, which were barely sufficient to sustain her fragile and tempestuous reproductive system. Any added exertion in the form of indulgences such as dancing, novel reading, higher education, exercise, or strong foods would inevitably prove deleterious not only to her own health but that of her children.[21] As a response to this, reformers concerned with women's wellness began devising systems of physical culture that would be appropriate for women's specialized needs. However, even those radical reformers who championed physical fitness as a pathway to women's "liberation" emphasized the notion that these systems needed to be appropriately feminine, graceful, and aesthetically pleasing. The reasoning was a practical one—if the exercises were not deemed attractive and if they didn't cultivate beauty, then women simply wouldn't do them.

And so, the transition between harmonial gymnastics and postural yoga is attributable to two historical factors: Victorian understandings of femininity and Victorian women's engagement with Orientalism. On the one hand, postural yoga as it was developing in India was genuinely closest to specifically the kind of light, equipment-free gymnastics that were becoming popular among economically privileged (so, generally, white) Western women. On the other hand, these same Western women—over and above Western men—were increasingly attracted to the novel and exotic aesthetics of the "Orient" (the imagined mystical land that encompassed any area eastward of Western Europe). As Mari Yoshihara has argued, performing imagined Asian versions of femininity allowed white women to ease their way into new identities. She observes that "white women often used Orientalism not only to make their interventions in American ideas about Asia per se but also to assert, address, and/or challenge women's roles in American society."[22]In doing so, white middle-class American women ultimately enacted a set of tropes and behaviors that became associated with the New Woman, who was beautifully fit, independent, worldly, and in touch with her sexuality.[23] In other words, she was liberated. Labeling their gymnastics as "yoga" thus catered to white women's desires on two levels. Socially, it provided an exotic sophistication and even a mildly risqué sensuality. Spiritually, it gestured towards the idea of an ancient and universal wisdom that rendered the practice something more than just physical exercise.

The commodification of yoga and the "East" is crucial here, both as a feature of modern (non-institutional) spirituality in general, and of white women's role in it in particular. For instance, feminist scholar Karlyn Crowley, has pointed to the feminine gendering of Western spirituality's major distinguishing features. Crowley asks, "Why did I always know someone who was into crystals or Reiki or Goddess worship? And what was the appeal of these practices for white women, especially, and why were they turning to crystals when they could just as easily enact public forms of feminist protest? Where does a crystal get you?"[24] It turns out that a crystal gets you quite a ways. Labeling modern spirituality narcissistic, consumeristic (and therefore materialistic and superficial), and irrational is easily construed as a gendered dog-whistle. Crowley points out, however, that these often-criticized qualities turn out to be the very same ones that offer female practitioners a sense of empowerment.

Spirituality grounded in the affirmation and in the ultimately divine nature of the self is bound to appeal to those whose selves have been historically denied. Consumerism and purchasing power can signal agency for those who have historically lacked a sense of self-determination. Finally, the irrational (which is really the mystical) seems to give meaning, purpose, and even sanctity to devalued "feminine" qualities such as intuition, emotion, and receptivity.[25] Postural yoga, as well as other such body-oriented systems, add yet another crucial dimension—they place value upon and give women a sense of control over their bodies. This, of course, speaks not only to the ways in which women have historically lacked this point of connection and control, but also reiterates the ongoing social pressures of femininity to be thin and beautiful, explaining modern yoga's sometimes regressive approach to body acceptance. However, the underlying assumptions regarding class, culture, and privilege also help explain why, for all of its progressive aspirations, Western yoga culture so easily slips into exclusivism and a tacit white supremacy.

"Playing Indian"—exoticism and appropriation

As Véronique Altglas demonstrates in her study of religious exoticism among practitioners of Kabbalah and various forms of Indian meditation, "otherness matters."[26] Class, but especially race and ethnicity determine "who can appropriate culture for self-making, and who can be appropriated."[27] To some extent, the deeper question might be: who gets to be the protagonist of their own story? If collage spirituality is a kind of quest of self-discovery, it's most available to those whose selves are most comfortably situated in the cultural mainstream. From this central position, everything else looks like a potentially more exciting alternative—a way to explore or to rebel. And, more importantly, everything seems available and free for the taking. The privileged individual is an entitled one.

Cultural appropriation is a broad and ambiguous label, applied to a range of behaviors, the interpretation of which might be subject to disagreement by individual members of a community. However, when we come to a consensus that something constitutes a problematic or downright unethical instance of cultural appropriation, our reasons for doing so might be either substantive or functional (though often they are both). Substantive problems with appropriation are usually easier to spot. They arise when the content of a cultural element, whether an object, a practice, or a concept, is poorly understood or improperly represented. Functional problems, on the other hand, arise from the effects that the act of appropriation produces. Looking at an instance of appropriation functionally can, for instance, help us understand why it's a problem to represent something in a way that isn't faithful to its traditional meaning. This is especially important if we're going to simultaneously insist that concepts and practices are diverse and historically variable—in other words, that tradition itself changes—as we've done here with yoga. It seems straightforward to say that when a cultural element is taken out of its proper context and misrepresented or misused, this reflects a problematic lack of knowledge, understanding, or respect. A straightforward but ubiquitous example might be a young white person wearing an imitation of a Native war bonnet at a music festival. But functional issues can also be structural, giving little regard to individual circumstances or intent. In the example of the war bonnet, it isn't only the lack of understanding that's a problem, but also the history of colonialism and the continued injustices committed against North America's Indigenous populations that loom in the background of the action. Similarly, even if the cultural artifact in question is respectfully and faithfully adopted, this might still be considered unethical due to such contextual concerns. Functional reasons are inevitably bound up in power dynamics, both historical and ongoing.

Paying attention to these structural elements is especially important when an individual's intent appears to be positive. For instance, in studying participants of various transformational festivals—some ostensibly associated with Indian culture, such as Bhakti Fest, and others not, like Burning Man—Amanda Lucia found that "in their critique of the existing status quo, participants turn to Indigenous and Indic religious forms because they imagine them to be expressions of alternative life ways existing outside of modernity."[28] Lucia points out that this follows a longstanding trend in which Americans have coopted the (real or imagined) features of these same cultures as "a means to protest and reject Euro American culture. By adopting exoticized practices of marginalized religious minorities, they have offered critiques of industrialization, consumerism, rationality, violence, sexual repression, and the devastation of nature."[29] We see this tendency in the 20th-century popularity of South Asian gurus, but we might also consider the fact that 19th-century Spiritualist séances were often visited by the ghosts of Indigenous tribal chiefs, whose spiritual guidance was used to call for reforms in this world as well as to light a path to the next.[30] In such cases, however, positive depictions or good intentions do little to negate the tokenism, exoticism, and historical inequality and even violence by which the relationships in question are inescapably defined. Along these lines, Deepak Sarma argues that white converts to Hinduism (such as, for instance, devotees within the global devotional guru-movement, the International Society for Krishna Consciousness or ISKCON) "mimic their imaginary (and often Orientalist) archetypal 'Hindu' in order to reverse-assimilate, to deny their colonial histories, to (futilely) color their lives, and, paradoxically, to be marginalized," but points out that "surely such an imagined transformation is only available to those who are privileged in the first place."[31] In other words, joining the counterculture is not the same as being a colonized subject or part of a racial minority group.

In yoga, the issue may be even more complex. As we noted above, there is a history to Western spiritual fitness practices that precedes the importation and popularization of yoga. Thus, much of what is practiced in Western corporate yoga studios might in fact not be specifically South Asian in its character or origins. White American women were doing lunges while breathing deeply even before they began calling this *virabhadrāsana*. In this case, it's not the act of doing a lunge itself that is appropriated, but the "brand"—that is, all of the associated implications that arise when we call the lunge "yoga." A lunge is just a lunge, but yoga is ancient, and spiritual, and exotic. Notably, 19th-century innovators of spiritual fitness like Stebbins also made these kinds of claims to ancient tradition, it's just that for them this "other" more enlightened culture was that of the ancient Greeks. As the 19th century drew to a close, Neo-classicism was all the rage and women practiced the spiritual gymnastics of "Delsarte" (arguably the first lifestyle brand) while wearing flowing Greek tunics. But as media and travel began to literally expand the horizons of middle-class Western culture, tastes turned eastward. The early decades of the 20th century brought a number of Indian gurus to the United States, where they readily made connections between yoga and the various domestic ideas and practices, both physical and spiritual, with which their audiences were already familiar. This, along with the modernizing efforts of yogis on the other side of the globe in colonial India, helped fuel the blending between Indian yoga and Western harmonial "psychophysical culture."

However, at this point it's worth reminding ourselves that it's not necessarily the content that is the problem when it comes to cultural appropriation—though certainly the label of "yoga" is itself a kind of content. In this case, it's the functional dimensions that pose the greatest concern. That is, we have to pay attention to what our use of the label "yoga" *does* to the social dynamics of the practice. On the one hand, this exoticizes Indian culture and individual yoga gurus. India is seen as a fantasy land, a static ancient repository of mystical wisdom, rather than a dynamic and diverse modern culture. On a social level, people of South Asian heritage become one-dimensional representatives of this imaginary place, expected to act out its attendant stereotypes even as, due to their minority status, they're often penalized for doing so. In a connected way, then, the complexity of actual South Asian culture (and of the people who embody it) is effectively contained, excluded, and even erased. As Roopa Singh, an Indian American woman and co-founder of the South Asian American Peoples Yoga Alliance (SAAPYA) and the Critical Yoga Studies forum, declared in an address to an audience of white yoga teachers: "As you fill that space, teach in that space, know that there is someone, who looks very much like my mother and looks very much like my father, who is not there, who doesn't feel as confident to integrate, to be in public in this country—just know that you are taking a space that is precious."[32]

Owning yoga

Yoga scholar Christopher Miller has argued that colonial India produced two approaches to modern yoga. On the one hand, "highly educated Indian elites sharing a universalistic vision of religion and spirituality produced and diplomatically disseminated universal yoga teachings internationally."[33] These figures included some of the first gurus who traveled to the West (such as Swami Vivekananda) and, in some cases, spent the majority of their lives in the United States (such as Paramahansa Yogananda), as well as other innovators (such as Swami Kuvalayananda, Shri Yogendra, and Sivananda Saraswati) who devised modern postural styles of yoga that appealed to the universal standards of modern science and wrote English-language practice manuals. On the other hand, Miller tells us,

> a number of other prominent nationalists opposed to the dissemination of Indian culture to a global audience sought to develop exclusively nationalist (and sometimes violent) forms of yoga on the home front in order to strengthen and inspire Indian citizens in their struggle against British imperial rule.[34]

However, as Miller points out, even the universalist presentations of yoga often tended to be culturally-specific and occasionally nationalist in character insofar as they have appealed to traditional scriptural sources and elevated Hindu philosophical frameworks as superior to all others.

Similar methods have been adopted by 21st-century political figures such as Prime Minister Narendra Modi and his Bharatiya Janata Party (BJP), who have touted yoga as a universal solution to any number of global ills and India's gift to the world while maintaining a clear Hindu Nationalist political position. Echoing Jain's argument regarding the ways in which neoliberal spirituality seems to offer solutions to social and political inequality while actually reinforcing its root causes, Miller points to Modi's claim of yoga as India's universal solution to climate change by creating more conscious and enlightened global citizens. However, Modi's domestic program of promoting yoga positions it as a form of neoliberal self-care—that is, exercise and stress-relief—geared at producing better, more efficient workers for India's industries, thereby driving an ultimately environmentally destructive capitalist agenda.[35] But for better or for worse, yoga has become the calling card of global Hinduism. In late 2014, the United Nations General Assembly declared an International Yoga Day to be marked every June 21, and Modi inaugurated the event in Delhi by leading 35,000 schoolchildren and civil servants through a series of yoga poses.[36] As part of Modi's International Yoga Day campaign, Indian officials weighed the idea of applying a "geographical indication" label or trade protection to yoga, similar to other regionally-specific goods such as French Champagne. Shripad Yesso Naik, BJP leader of India's Ministry in charge of yoga and traditional medicine, noted: "There is little doubt about yoga being an Indian art form, we're trying to establish to the world that it's ours."[37] Thus yoga continues to toe the line between a universal health regimen and a marker of Indian—and specifically Hindu—heritage.

On the other side of the globe, parallel logics underpinned the "Take Back Yoga" campaign launched by the Hindu American Foundation (HAF), a non-profit advocacy group headquartered in Washington DC. The matter began as a dispute over the popular *Yoga Journal*'s alleged resistance to explicitly associating yoga with Hinduism. In 2010, the HAF issued a position paper elaborating on what it perceived to be yoga's irrefutably Hindu origins. That same year, HAF co-founder Aseem Shukla published an opinion piece in the *Washington Post*'s "On Faith" blog, titled "The Theft of Yoga," in which he condemned the separation of yoga and Hinduism in American pop culture. Just a few days later, global guru Deepak Chopra issued a response on the same blog under the title of "Sorry, Your Patent on Yoga Has Run Out." The conversation went through a series of subsequent responses from both Shukla and Chopra: Shukla's "Dr. Chopra, Honor Thy Heritage"; Chopra's "Yoga Belongs to All of Us"; and Shukla's "Hinduism and Sanatana Dharma: One and the Same," the titles of which effectively capture both the direction and the tone of the exchange.

On the one hand, Chopra's argument was that of a universalist, as he stated, "Christians can claim prayer as their invention if they want to. It wouldn't make the claim less false—sensible people accept that prayer is universal."[38] On the other hand, though, Chopra doesn't dispute that the consciousness-raising techniques of yoga originated on South Asian soil, what he takes issue with are the institutional and ultimately "tribal" implications of labeling this ancient human knowledge as "Hindu." At this point, it might be useful to acknowledge that Chopra was born, raised, and educated in India, but has made his fortune as a global guru, bridging Indian and Western esoteric systems of thought. Shukla, on the other hand, is Indian American, born and raised in the United States. As such, Shukla's position is self-admittedly colored by having to restlessly defend his Hindu identity against gross misconceptions and outright attacks of the kind often leveled at religious and cultural minorities.[39] Of course, all of this is further complicated by the way that implicitly equating "Indian" with "Hindu" also affects the experience of religious minorities, including but certainly not limited to Muslims, in India.

And yet, though such positions might depict yoga as a cultural commodity, they also appear to resist the notion that it can be an individual one. One of the earliest claims to legal ownership in modern yoga can be traced to 2002 when Bikram Choudhury, of "Bikram Yoga," attempted to establish and enforce a legal copyright on his sequence of 26 yogic postures. Choudhury's initial lawsuits, largely leveled at his own students, were settled under non-disclosure agreements, but in 2012 the U.S. Copyright Office conclusively invalidated his copyright claims. As Jordan Susman has observed at the culmination of a lengthy legal analysis of Choudhury's case,

> had Bikram been more modest in his assertions and in his ambitions, he would have claimed that his sequence was an expressive dance and accentuated its aesthetic value. Although this might not have attracted huge throngs of followers, it would have afforded him maximum possible copyright protection. However, Bikram chose to be a savior—the man who developed the cure for all known illness.[40]

And so, Choudhury's attempts to position his yoga as a universal system of healing were counterproductive to his claims of individual ownership. However, his original attempts to patent the sequence did partially motivate the Indian government to launch its Traditional Knowledge Digital Library. The database is meant to serve as a resource for patent offices worldwide in addressing claims such as Choudhury's.

Ultimately, of course, the claim to cultural ownership is also deeply tied up with religious affiliation. The HAF didn't only want to claim yoga as Indian, it specifically wanted to establish it as Hindu. Such were the stakes in another legal case, *Sedlock v. Baird* (2013), wherein a group of parents objected to a yoga program offered within the Encinitas School District in California. The program was sponsored by a grant from the Jois Foundation, established by an American practitioner of Pattabhi Jois's (1915–2009) style of Ashtanga Yoga. Though Jois's system does make some appeals to select Hindu scriptures, these elements were not included in the school's curriculum, which instead focused on a "holistic" and "mind-body" approach to health.[41] In the course of the lawsuit, the plaintiff's expert witness, religious studies scholar Candy Gunther Brown, argued that even the purely physical elements of yoga could not be separated from the practice's religious, and specifically Hindu nature. According to Brown, every *āsana* is indelibly infused with the essence of Hindu religiosity.[42] Historically, yogic practices in South Asia can be found across a number of ancient traditions, including Hindu, Buddhist and Jain groups. However, although this diversity of origins might refute the claim that yoga is the method of one single religion, it does not do much to address whether yoga is "religious" in general. In *Sedlock v. Baird*, for instance, though Judge John S. Meyer ultimately ruled that the school's program didn't set out to propagate or denigrate any specific religious belief and therefore didn't violate U.S. law, he did agree with Brown that yoga practice is inherently religious.[43]

In some sense, then, such disputes highlight the difficulty of delineating between the culturally particular and the universal. For instance, conservative Christian leaders have likewise encouraged their flock to engage in non-yoga stretching and other forms of exercise.[44] But what is meant in this context by "non-yoga stretching"? Should one simply avoid things that look like yoga poses? One look at PraiseMoves, a system taught by Laurette Willis as a "Christian alternative to yoga," quickly casts doubt on this proposition. Willis's non-yoga poses look suspiciously just like yoga poses, a fact that Willis herself acknowledges.[45] In the end, there are only so many ways to move the human body. So, what makes something yoga? At this point, we might also recall Genevieve Stebbins's system of psycho-physical culture, which is historically and culturally not directly tied to South Asian yogic practices, but certainly looks like yoga to the modern eye.

It's impossible to say that a squat, or a lunge, or deep breathing is the traditional knowledge of one single culture. Though of course one might nevertheless say it's equally, if not more preposterous for a single individual to patent such a basic and universal movement. But we might also ask: when does a lunge or a deep breath become religious, or at least spiritual? And is this negated by the fact that you might have paid someone to tell you how to do it?

Selling yoga

The thing is, it turns out that the mechanics of marketing are not so different from those of religion. In order to successfully brand something, you have to associate it with a name, a symbol, and identity. You have to invest it with meaning, to tell a story—in other words, to mythologize it in a way that brings value to the customer that goes far beyond the product itself.[46] A successful brand is the aspirational symbol of an entire lifestyle. On some level, every practitioner has an image in their mind of what it means to be "the kind of person who does yoga." The same can be said for all sorts of yoga-adjacent products. "The kind of person who does yoga" easily becomes "the kind of person who wears Lululemon," "the kind of person who shops at Whole Foods," and so on. And, like religions, brands exhibit social dimensions as well. For example, fitness-centric Lululemon creates a health-and-wellness focused brand community by sponsoring yoga classes, providing product and a platform to brand ambassadors, and offering free yoga classes in its stores. The company engages and expands its brand community by participating in and sponsoring major yoga festivals. It signals its identity and values through elements like its social impact program, "Here to Be," which seeks to "disrupt inequity in wellbeing through movement, mindfulness, and advocacy."[47]

Religion is never an abstract, free-floating entity that simply materializes out of thin air, fully-formed, whenever it is called upon. Religions are social institutions that must be maintained by living and breathing people in order to survive. This means not only practitioners, but specialists (priests, monastics, scholars, and teachers) who devote themselves "full-time" to shaping and passing along the tradition's teachings, building and supporting its communities, and so forth. However, religious specialists are people too, and they require food, shelter, and other human necessities and perhaps even a few luxuries. And so, religions cannot exist—and historically have not existed—without funding. This means there are essentially two options: a religious institution can act like a government and collect "taxes" (or tithes) from its community, or it can act like a business and directly represent itself as providing certain goods and services in exchange for monetary support. When there is no link between religion and the state (that is, the actual government), then even "traditional" religious institutions such as churches have to act a little bit like businesses, attracting and retaining congregants in order to survive. In this sense, there is perhaps not so much difference between a mega-church and a national yoga studio brand. And, as Jain explains

> yoga brands, whether they signify a particular teacher, style, or product, signify more than just the fulfillment of utilitarian needs; rather, the fulfillment of religious needs becomes contained in the brand. Put more simply, postural yoga's rituals and narratives reflect yogis' deepest values and most sacred goals.[48]

On the extreme end, a brand might leave this creation of meaning completely open to the individual practitioner, allowing it to be anything to any yogi. By using carefully curated messaging that foregrounds the individual and their personal journey, a yoga brand can float between the deeply spiritual and the purely material in the space of a single tagline. A prime example of this kind of spiritually ambiguous corporate model is CorePower Yoga. Founded in Colorado in 2002, the CorePower brand has expanded across the United States to encompass 200 studios in 23 different states as of 2019. CorePower classes frequently utilize exclusively English terminology for their poses and exclude overtly religious practices such as devotional chanting. Though its marketing materials may occasionally use lightly spiritual language such as "soul-rocking" and "transformational" to describe its classes, the company's website works hard to signal a kind of non-specific inclusivity, encouraging practitioners to "discover the magic that happens when physical meets mindful. The power of practice is yours—wherever you are."[49] Trevor Tice, tech entrepreneur and one of the company's co-founders, once expressed a goal of turning the brand into the "Starbucks [coffee] of yoga"—an accessible nation-wide chain that customers would come to identify as the gold standard of the industry. CorePower has been embroiled in multiple lawsuits over its labor practices and its massive teacher training program has been compared to a multi-level marketing scheme.[50]

This kind of commodification is not a uniquely Western phenomenon. In fact, while a company like CorePower works hard to divest its version of yoga of culturally specific markers through a modern, secular branding focused on personal empowerment, its strategies are not so different from a more tradition-focused approach. Claiming a practice for a specific culture—as the Modi administration or the HAF's "Take Back Yoga" campaign have done, for instance—requires a similar exercise in branding. Even if the goal isn't to sell yoga, per se, establishing a cultural claim to origination or ownership means that yoga must be given a coherent identity, scope, and story. A successful brand has no room for historical complexity, multiple meanings, or other messiness. For instance, let's consider the information provided by India's Ministry of Ayurveda, Yoga and Naturopathy, Unani, Siddha and Homeopathy (AYUSH):

> Yoga is one of the six systems of Vedic philosophy. Maharishi Patanjali, rightly called "The Father of Yoga" compiled and refined various aspects of Yoga systematically in his "Yoga Sutras" (aphorisms). He advocated the eight folds [sic] path of Yoga, popularly known as "Ashtanga Yoga" for all-round development of human beings. They are: Yama, Niyama, Asana, Pranayama, Pratyahara, Dharana, Dhyana and Samadhi. These components advocate certain restraints and observances, physical discipline, breath regulations, restraining the sense organs, contemplation, meditation and samadhi. These steps are believed to have a potential for improvement of physical health by enhancing circulation of oxygenated blood in the body, retraining the sense organs thereby inducing tranquility and serenity of mind. The practice of Yoga prevents psychosomatic disorders and improves an individual's resistance and ability to endure stressful situations.[51]

In reality, yoga has many more meanings in South Asian culture, beyond the classical *darśana* (philosophical school) rooted in Patañjali's *Yoga Sūtras* (c. 325–425

CE). Such a narrative ignores the multiplicity of different yoga systems (including non-Vedic, Buddhist, and Jain systems), not all of which have eight components, some of which precede Patañjali, and many of which (even if they do come after) pay no attention to the *Yoga Sūtras*. And of course Patañjali says nothing about oxygenating the blood. Instead, what we can see in AYUSH's statement is a clear example of Jain's description of modern yoga branding. As she states, "in the postural yoga world, branding and mythologizing simultaneously involve validating yoga based on its ties to both ancient origins and modern science."[52]

Such branding of yoga has been used, for instance, by the famous Indian yoga guru, Baba Ramdev (1965–). Ramdev started his flagship institute, the Patanjali Yogpeeth, together with his partner, billionaire businessman Balkrishna Suvedi, in 2006. The Patanjali Yogpeeth is a large complex, which includes an Āyurvedic hospital, an Āyurvedic college called Patanjali University, and multiple large auditoriums used for various *haṭha* yoga and Āyurvedic activities, meditation, as well as social welfare programs, health care, and education. Ramdev's Yogpeeth Trust is also the umbrella organization for numerous other business ventures, including Divya Prakashan Books, Divya Yoga Sadhana videos, Yog Sandesh Magazine, Divya Pharmacy, Patañjali Ayurved Ltd., and Patañjali Food and Herbal Ltd.[53] A 2015 report by an equity research firm found that the Patañjali Ayurved brand alone had 200,000 outlets, most of them small, unofficial vendors selling everything from spices to instant noodles to clarified butter.[54] AYUSH and the Modi administration have been prime advocates for both Ramdev and the Yogpeeth. Minister Naik has stated that AYUSH would provide "all possible support" for the Ramdev's propagation of yoga.[55] Modi has echoed this endorsement, noting, "Swami Ramdev's herbs help you overcome all problems."[56] Notably, Ramdev is seen as a controversial figure due to, among other things, his Islamophobic statements and claims that he can cure the disease of homosexuality through yoga.[57]

In their own ways, both Indian and Western messaging on yoga does often work to highlight the practice's uniquely spiritual character, which is implicitly tied to its commercial desirability (despite, as we mentioned, outward condemnations of yoga's commercialization). Even CorePower describes its style of practice as a "juxtaposition of a really unique, kickass physical workout and the mindfulness of yoga—intensity with intention."[58] All this holds true, of course, until claims to spirituality become a liability rather than an asset. This is precisely the case when we examine yoga in China, for instance.

When China opened its doors to foreign investment and trade in 1979, the country experienced incredible economic growth. The government has since continued to focus its future economic expansion on services, experiences, individual consumption and personal development. Even in the early 2000s, both personal fitness gyms and yoga studios were nearly non-existent within China. Twenty years later, gyms, yoga studios, and a variety of fitness- and health-based products have become increasingly common. The government has supported this trend by promoting a nationalized fitness plan to mobilize citizens to participate in sports activities with an aim to improving overall health.[59] In 2016, the government established the China Yoga Sport Commission to oversee all standardized exercise programming, thereby including yoga alongside a range of other athletic activities ranging from table tennis to basketball. The commission is centrally administered but expands its reach and impact through the appointment of localized experts to oversee the execution of regional events and competitions.

In 2017, a government-funded "China Yoga Industry Development Report"[60] surveyed the current state of yoga in the country, as well as plans for including yoga as a focal point in a nationalized health and wellness initiative. The report's stated goal was to integrate the sport of yoga with Chinese culture, education, tourism, and the medical industry. The report specifically noted a connection between the popularity of yoga within a particular city and the city's overall level of economic prosperity, concluding that yoga may help lead to the betterment of China as a nation. Due to the size of its population and economy, China already represents a considerable presence on the landscape of global yoga. The 2017 report documented over 14,000 dedicated yoga schools and over 30,000 gyms and studios where yoga is taught, projecting that these number would grow exponentially. The report stated that in order for yoga to play a positive role in the Healthy China 2030 Plan, the government must look to introduce foreign advanced management concepts, construct standardized rules and regulations, and conduct management oversight for yoga's future development.[61] Notably, however, the report also implied that any foreign involvement in standardization should cater to China's secular national culture and the particular outcomes of nationalized health and wellness laid out by the governmental agenda. Thus, in China, it is yoga's potential as a holistic but decidedly secular regimen of wellness that emerges as its most valuable asset.

In the end, it is perhaps more helpful to ask not whether yoga is being commodified—this is clearly the case nearly universally in the modern world—but how and why this commodification happens. Examining examples from different cultural and political contexts can help shed light of the various styles of branding that are used to "sell" yoga. Indian appeals to yoga's traditional and religious character—it's monolithic Hindutva or "Hinduness"—stand in contrast to the highly individualistic but still generically spiritual character of American corporate yoga. Different still, is the state-sanctioned standardized and staunchly secular vision presented by China. Yet, in every case there appears to be something that nevertheless translates. Yoga is seen as a method for modern individuals to become better versions of themselves, in whatever manner their cultural context understands such improvement.

Conclusions

- Modern yoga follows a neoliberal logic in which every individual is viewed as an autonomous agent that is self-governing, self-cultivating, and self-helping. Both physically and metaphysically, self-care becomes the primary way of caring for the world. Neoliberal commercial spirituality can produce a number of issues, including: "spiritual bypassing" that ignores social justice efforts in favor of self-comfort, gestures of ethical consumption ("conscious capitalism") that don't ultimately question unethical systems, and an individualistic "collage spirituality" that can easily turn appropriative.

- Physical culture, which has always been a class-specific pursuit, evolved in ways that resulted in 19th-century middle-class women practicing a very specific style of light, dance-like (that is, flowing) gymnastics. At their outset, these gymnastics were Neo-classical in their aesthetics and drew on harmonial spiritual principles. However, combined with white women's consumptive use of "Oriental" products, tropes, and identities as stepping-stones to their own liberation, these styles of practice gradually became associated with and subsumed under the label of "yoga." This accounts for Western yoga's overwhelmingly white, female demographics. It also underpins logics of cultural appropriation that capitalize on yoga's exotic Indian character while simultaneously excluding actual South Asian people from global yoga culture.
- Both Western practitioners and Indian disseminators of yoga have tended to treat the concept as at once culturally specific and universal. This dual character can result in complex disputes when it comes to ownership. Treating yoga as the "intellectual property" of Indian (and specifically Hindu) culture is itself a form of commodification, but it has been used as a form of resistance against those who have sought to lay individual claim to yoga's methods.
- Yoga's character and status as a commodity is context-specific, often following national social and political interests. In the United States, yoga is exotic and spiritual when marketed, but also mainstream and secular when taught in public schools. In India, yoga can be tied to the interests of Hindu nationalism and support from the state is linked to its implicitly religious character. In China, yoga is seen as a public good that can be standardized, secularized, and integrated into a state-sponsored program of wellness.

Notes

1 Knut A. Jacobsen, ed., *Yoga Powers: Extraordinary Capacities Attained Through Meditation and Concentration* (Leiden: Brill, 2011), 10.
2 Amanda J. Lucia, *White Utopias: The Religious Exoticism of Transformational Festivals* (Oakland: University of California Press, 2020), 109.
3 Peter L. Berger, *The Heretical Imperative: Contemporary Possibilities of Religious Affirmation* (New York: Anchor Press, 1979), 30–1; Andrea R. Jain, *Selling Yoga: From Counterculture to Pop Culture* (New York: Oxford University Press, 2014), 44.
4 Agi Wittich and Patrick McCartney, "The Changing Face of the Yoga Industry, Its Dharmic Roots and the Message to Women: Analysis of Yoga Journal Magazine Covers 1975–2020," *Journal of Dharma Studies*, 3 (2020): 31–44.
5 Lucia, *White Utopias*, 241n47.
6 "Yoga in America Study," *Yoga Journal*, 2016, http://media.yogajour- nal.com/wp-content/uploads/2016-Yoga-in-America-Study-Comprehensive-RESULTS.pdf; "Yoga Journal Releases 2012 Yoga in America Market Study," *Yoga Journal*, December 5, 2012, https://www.yogajournal.com/press-releases/yoga-journal-releases-2012-yoga-in-america-market-study
7 Hugh B. Urban, "Osho, from Sex Guru to Guru of the Rich: The Spiritual Logic of Late Capitalism," in *Gurus in America*, ed. Thomas A. Forsthoefel and Cynthia Ann Humes (Albany: State University of New York Press, 2005), 187.

8 Sam Binkley, *Happiness as Enterprise: An Essay on Neoliberal Life* (Albany: State University of New York Press, 2014), 4. See also Wendy Brown, *Undoing the Demos: Neoliberalism's Stealth Revolution* (Cambridge, MA: MIT Press, 2015).

9 Farah Godrej, "The Neoliberal Yogi and the Politics of Yoga," *Political Theory*, 45, no. 6 (2017): 785–6.

10 Ralph Waldo Trine, *In Tune with the Infinite or, Fullness of Peace, Power, and Plenty* (New York: Thomas Y. Crowell and Company, 1897), 9–10.

11 Lucia, *White Utopias*, 5.

12 Patrick McCartney, "Spiritual Bypass and Entanglement in Yogaland (योगस्तान): How Neoliberalism, Soft Hindutva and Banal Nationalism Facilitate Yoga Fundamentalism," *Politics and Religion Journal*, 13, no. 1 (2019): 137–75.

13 Sarah Banet-Weiser, *Authentic TM: The Politics of Ambivalence in a Brand Culture* (New York: New York University Press, 2012), 176.

14 Andrea R. Jain, "Namaste All Day: Containing Dissent in Commercial Spirituality," *Harvard Divinity Bulletin*, 2019, https://bulletin.hds.harvard.edu/namaste-all-day/. See also Andrea R. Jain, *Peace, Love, Yoga: The Politics of Global Spirituality* (New York: Oxford University Press, 2020).

15 Wouter J. Hanegraaff, "Tradition," in *Dictionary of Gnosis and Western Esotericism*, ed. Wouter J. Hanegraaff et al. (Leiden and Boston: Brill, 2006), 1125–35.

16 Wade Clark Roof, *Spiritual Marketplace: Baby Boomers and the Remaking of American Religion* (Princeton, NJ: Princeton University Press, 2001).

17 Genevieve Stebbins, *Dynamic Breathing and Harmonic Gymnastics: A Complete System of Psychical, Aesthetic and Physical Culture* (New York: Edgar S. Werner, 1892), 66.

18 Mark Singleton, *Yoga Body: The Origins of Modern Posture Practice* (New York: Oxford University Press, 2010), 154.

19 Anya P. Foxen, *Inhaling Spirit: Harmonialism, Orientalism, and the Western Roots of Modern Yoga* (New York: Oxford University Press, 2020), 2.

20 Sandra Cavallo and Tessa Storey, *Healthy Living in Late Renaissance Italy* (New York and London: Oxford University Press, 2013), 146.

21 Diane Price Herndl, *Invalid Women: Figuring Feminine Illness in American Fiction and Culture, 1840–1940* (Chapel Hill: University of North Carolina Press, 1993), 34.

22 Mari Yoshihara, *Embracing the East: White Women and American Orientalism* (Oxford: Oxford University Press, 2003), 8.

23 Yoshihara, *Embracing the East*, 78.

24 Karlyn Crowley, *Feminism's New Age: Gender, Appropriation, and the Afterlife of Essentialism* (Albany: State University of New York Press, 2011), 1.

25 Crowley, *Feminism's New Age*, 32–54.

26 Véronique Altglas, *From Yoga to Kabbalah: Religious Exoticism and the Logics of Bricolage* (New York: Oxford University Press, 2014), 329.

27 Altglas, *From Yoga to Kabbalah*, 322.

28 Lucia, *White Utopias*, 4.

29 Lucia, *White Utopias*, 6.

30 Molly McGarry, *Ghosts of Futures Past: Spiritualism and the Cultural Politics of Nineteenth-Century America* (Berkeley: University of California Press, 2008), 66–93.

31 Deepak Sarma, "White Hindu Converts: Mimicry Or Mockery?" *Huffington Post*, November 15, 2012, https://www.huffpost.com/entry/mimicry-or-mockery-white-_b_2131329

32 Roopa Singh, "SAAPYA Unedited," YouTube, August 13, 2013, https://www.youtube.com/watch?v=901d1NbKa3c. Also quoted in Lucia, *White Utopias*, 54.

33 Christopher Patrick Miller, "Soft Power and Biopower: Narendra Modi's 'Double Discourse' Concerning Yoga for Climate Change and Self-Care," *Journal of Dharma Studies*, 3, no. 1 (2020): 94.

34 Miller, "Soft Power and Biopower," 94.

35 Miller, "Soft Power and Biopower," and Christopher Patrick Miller, "Modi-Fying Patañjali: Biopolitics and the 'Hostile Takeover of Bodies' in an Aspiring Neoliberal Nation

State," in *Contemporary Yoga and Sacred Texts*, ed. Susanne Scholtz and Caroline Vander Stichele (New York: Routledge, forthcoming 2021).

36 "India Yoga: PM Narendra Modi Leads Thousands in Celebration," *BBC News*, June 21, 2015, www.bbc.com/news/world-asia-india-33212949

37 Annie Gowen, "India's New Prime Minister, Narendra Modi, Aims to Rebrand and Promote Yoga in India," *Washington Post*, December 2, 2014, https://www.washingtonpost.com/world/asia_pacific/indias-new-prime-minister-narendra-modi-wants-to-rebrand-and-promote-yoga-in-india/2014/12/02/7c5291de-7006–11e4-a2c2–478179fd0489_story.html

38 Deepak Chopra, "Yoga Belongs to All of Us," The Chopra Foundation, April 28, 2010, https://www.choprafoundation.org/consciousness/yoga-belongs-to-all-of-us/

39 "The Great Yoga Debate: Aseem Shukla vs Deepak Chopra," Defense Forum India, May 19, 2010, https://defenceforumindia.com/threads/the-great-yoga-debate-aseem-shukla-vs-deepak-chopra.10442/

40 Jordan Susman, "Your Karma Ran Over My Dogma—Bikram Yoga and the (IM)Possibilities of Copyrighting Yoga," *Loyola of Los Angeles Entertainment Law Review*, 25, no. 2 (2005): 245–74.

41 Suzanne Newcombe, "Spaces of Yoga: Towards a Non-Essentialist Understanding of Yoga," in *Yoga in Transformation: Historical and Contemporary Perspectives on a Global Phenomenon*, ed. Karl Baier, Philip A. Maas, and Karin Preisendanz (Göttingen, The Netherlands: Vandenhoeck & Ruprecht Unipress, 2018), 557.

42 Newcombe, "Spaces of Yoga," 558. See also Candy Gunther Brown, *Debating Yoga and Mindfulness in Public Schools: Reforming Secular Education or Reestablishing Religion?* (Chapel Hill: University of North Carolina Press, 2019).

43 Newcombe, "Spaces of Yoga," 559.

44 Jain, *Selling Yoga*, 155.

45 Laurette Willis, "Why a Christian Alternative to Yoga?" PraiseMoves, accessed August 20, 2020, http://praisemoves.com/about-us/why-a-christian-alternative-to-yoga/

46 Andrea Jain, "Branding Yoga: The Cases of Iyengar Yoga, Siddha Yoga and Anusara Yoga," *Approaching Religion*, 2, no. 2 (2012): 6.

47 "Here to Be," Lululemon, accessed August 20, 2020, https://info.lululemon.com/heretobe/

48 Jain, *Selling Yoga*, 123–4.

49 "CorePower Yoga. Live Your Power (Home Page)," CorePower Yoga, accessed August 24, 2020, https://www.corepoweryoga.com/

50 Alice Hines, "Inside CorePower Yoga Teacher Training," *New York Times*, April 6, 2019, https://www.nytimes.com/2019/04/06/style/corepower-yoga-teacher-training.html

51 "Yoga," Ministry of Ayush, accessed August 20, 2020, https://main.ayush.gov.in/about-the-systems/yoga

52 Jain, *Selling Yoga,* 115.

53 Stuart Ray Sarbacker, "Swami Ramdev: Modern Yoga Revolutionary," in *Gurus of Modern Yoga*, ed. Mark Singleton and Ellen Goldberg (New York: Oxford University Press, 2014), 357.

54 Andrea Jain and Michael Schulson, "The World's Most Influential Yoga Teacher Is a Homophobic Right-Wing Activist," *Religion Dispatches*, October 1, 2016, http://religiondispatches.org/baba-ramdev/

55 "Will Give All Support to Ramdev, Says Shripad Naik," *The Indian Express*, November 12, 2014, https://indianexpress.com/article/india/india-others/will-give-all-support-to-ramdev-says-shripad-naik/

56 Robert F. Worth, "The Billionaire Yogi Behind Modi's Rise," *New York Times*, August 26, 2018, https://www.nytimes.com/2018/07/26/magazine/the-billionaire-yogi-behind-modis-rise.html

57 Jain and Schulson, "The World's Most Influential Yoga Teacher Is a Homophobic Right-Wing Activist."

58 Gigi Sukin, "Taking Corepower to the People," *ColoradoBiz Magazine*, March 7, 2016, https://www.cobizmag.com/taking-corepower-to-the-people/

59 "Report Intensive Reading | Yoga Blue Book: China Yoga Industry Development Report (2016–2017)," Social Sciences Academic Press, July 7, 3017, https://ssap.com.cn/c/2017-07-07/1057386.shtml

60 Zhang Yongjian, Huafeng Xu, and Zhu Tiayu, "Yoga Blue Book: China Yoga Industry Development Report (2016–2017)" (Chinese Academy of Social Sciences, June 2017).

61 "Report Intensive Reading | Yoga Blue Book: China Yoga Industry Development Report (2016–2017)."

10 Yoga therapies and the science of salvation

Without limiting ourselves to purely physical concerns, we might call yoga a self-development technique. If we wanted to use medical terms, we might call yoga (like other systems of exercise and stress reduction) a preventative measure. However, this would ignore the fact that many practitioners don't only do yoga to stay well. They do it to become "better than well," whether that's meant physically, mentally, or spiritually. Yoga therapy usually refers to a distinctly curative use of yoga. It is the application of yogic methods to solving some specific problem. The International Association of Yoga Therapists, for instance, positions yoga within a system of "comprehensive integrative pain management (CIPM)."[1] However, like many holistic systems of health management, it can also provide a framework for a healthy lifestyle, focusing on optimal wellness.

In this context, practitioners often hail yoga and Āyurveda (classical Indian medicine) as "sister sciences" in a regiment of care that holistically treats body, mind, and soul. The idea of yoga therapy (*cikitsā*) does have some premodern precedent, at least in the medieval texts of *haṭha* yoga, which present some techniques specifically for their curative purposes. However, today's intimate and symbiotic relationship between the two systems is rooted in the early 20th-century work of Indian innovators and popularizers of yoga, who went to great pains to establish the techniques of yoga as not only therapeutic but scientifically sound and evidence-based, in line with the standards of the then still-emergent field of professional medicine. Yogis like Swami Kuvalayananda (1883–1966) and Shri Yogendra (1897–1989) established institutes and authored publications to demonstrate the objective effectiveness of their methods. Another famous early modern yogi, Swami Sivananda (1887–1963), actually left a long and successful career as a medical doctor to start his Divine Life Society. Global gurus like B. K. S. Iyengar (1918–2014) and T. K. V. Desikachar (1938–2016), meanwhile, made a name for themselves as purveyors of precise, individually-attuned, and therapeutic styles of yoga.

Today, yoga therapists often work as part of an integrative health care model that crosses between modern evidence-based methods and premodern understandings of ways of being and knowing. While yoga therapists may have other (more formal) medical training and credentials, these are not required by their profession. Traditional medicine is not regulated in the same manner as mainstream modern medicine. However, it also relies on a radically different "paradigm," that is a scientific and philosophical model that structures concepts, theories, standards of evidence, and valid means of knowledge into an understanding of how the world (and, by extension, the human body) works. Even if a traditional therapy is deemed effective, modern medicine would differ in its explanations for how and why it works. For instance, we would say an herbal remedy is effective because of its particular biomolecular composition, and not because of the plant's astrological significance.

"Yoga therapy" is a holistic approach to therapeutics, bridging physiotherapy, psychotherapy, and, in many cases, some form of spiritual care. This model of treatment is often positively contrasted to the piece-meal model of modern Western medicine, which is said to treat the patient like a machine built from separate parts rather than an integrated being. However, here it's helpful to refer to Hugh Urban's argument that we are no longer dealing with a simple Westernization that turns everything (including yoga) into a commodity, but rather with a pervasive and truly global capitalist culture.[2] In a similar way, we might suggest that rather than thinking purely of the materialist tendencies of "Western" science, it would be more helpful to consider the way that global modernity produces an industrial, Balkanized, and profit-driven scientific and medical establishment. In such a context, traditional therapies (whether Asian or Western) become juxtaposed to the machine of mainstream global healthcare, especially as represented by highly commercial fields such as pharmaceuticals. At the same time, to bring things full circle, though turning to an alternative form of therapy can constitute an act of resistance to the status quo, it can also be seen as a symptom of the kind of neoliberal economy where the onus of "self-care" is placed on the individual.

Traditional therapies

The "sister sciences" of yoga and Āyurveda

Classical Indian medicine is known as Āyurveda (literally, "the knowledge of longevity"). Like classical Western (that is, Greek) medicine, Āyurveda's understanding of the body and therefore of health and disease is humoral, that is based on a model of internal vital fluids. The three Āyurvedic humors or *doṣas* are *vāta* (wind), *pitta* (choler), and *kapha* (phlegm). These must be kept in balance and confined to their proper spheres within the body. Note that translating these terms into English is problematic, not least because it forces a direct parallel with Greek humoral terminology. There are certainly some foundational similarities between the two, but the differences in their specifics are far greater. Beyond this basic framework, Āyurveda is a highly complex system that covers a variety of modern medical topics, from internal medicine, to surgery, to anatomy and embryology. The classical sources of Āyurveda are found in two Sanskrit texts, the *Caraka Saṃhitā* and the *Suśruta Saṃhitā*, compendia which were composed in multiple layers between approximately 300 BCE and 500 CE.[3]

It only stands to reason that the premodern authors of yogic philosophy (who were scholars, after all) would have had some basic familiarity with the medical system of their time. Even yogic practitioners whose knowledge was more practical rather than scholarly would have acquired that knowledge in a cultural context permeated by common understandings of the body that informed Āyurveda as much as it did yoga. So it shouldn't surprise us that yogic texts seem to have an awareness of Āyurvedic terminology and vice versa. Nor is it so unusual that yogis would view disease as an impediment to their practice and might therefore look to medicine to cure their bodily ailments.[4] The real question is: to what extent can we say that these two systems have not only complementary but perhaps overlapping goals?

Medieval texts on *haṭha* yoga, which lay out previously esoteric physical practices, tend to posit spiritual liberation as the final goal. However, in describing their methods of manipulating the body's subtle internal processes, they routinely catalog a range of mundane "therapeutic" benefits. For instance, by taming the breath, the yogi strengthens his internal (digestive) fire. This means that food is processed more quickly, and his vital substances (lymph; blood; muscle; fat; bone; marrow; and semen, or implicitly menstrual blood in females) all increase, which leads to health and great vigor.[5] The texts also describe diet, a number of purificatory personal hygiene techniques (collectively known at the *ṣaṭ karmāni* or the "six actions"), and advise on which herbs best enhance yogic practice and its worldly results.[6] The *Viveka Mārtaṇḍa*, a 13th-century *haṭha* yoga text, gives the following summary:

> The best of yogins cures diseases by Yogic posture (*āsana*), sin by breath retentions (*prāṇāyāma*) and mental problems by withdrawing [his mind from sense objects] (*pratyāhāra*). He obtains stability of mind by concentration (*dhāraṇā*), wondrous power by meditation (*dhyāna*) and liberation by *samādhi*, after having abandoned [all] action, good and bad.[7]

However, as philologist and historian of yoga Jason Birch has suggested, such claims are just as likely evidence that yogis and Āyurvedic *vaidyas* (doctors) were not allies but competitors. Not only did yogic traditions posit themselves as purveyors of the ultimate therapy in the form of spiritual liberation (*mokṣa*) but their increasing attention to curative methods can be seen as an attempt to take on a role that would otherwise be occupied by Āyurvedic methods. Thus, calling premodern yoga "alternative medicine" might be somewhat anachronistic, but there is certainly a potential parallel to be found.

However, if we truly want to consider a possible relationship between yoga and Āyurveda that translates into modern practice, we should also consider the Āyurvedic prescriptions regarding exercise (*vyāyāma*). The *Caraka Saṃhitā* (1.7.31–32), for instance, defines exercise as the kind of exertion that has a positive effect on the body, and results in steadiness and in physical strength. Exercise results in ease, capacity for action, ability to withstand suffering (*duḥkha*), the correction of humoral imbalance, and the strengthening of digestive fire.[8] Scholars like Joseph Alter have sketched out *vyāyāma*'s location the intersection between of ascetic yogic practices and martial arts traditions such as wrestling, while Jason

Birch, Mark Singleton, and Jerome Armstrong have pointed to the connections between *vyāyāma* manuals, early modern *haṭha* yoga texts, and the innovations of Colonial Era yogis.[9]

Western harmonial healing

The classical Western medical system contains a total of four humors, associated with the four natural elements: blood, related to the element of air; yellow bile related to fire; black bile, related to earth; and phlegm related to water. These were associated by the Greek physician Galen (129–210 CE) with four fundamental human temperaments: sanguine, choleric, melancholic, and phlegmatic. Health arose from a state of balance and harmony amongst the humors, while disease resulted from their imbalance. In addition to this humoral system of internal balance, the primary influence on the state of human body was astrological. In fact, "influence" derives from the Latin *influxus*, referring in this case to a literal "flowing in" of forces from the celestial bodies of the stars and planets (which would have originally been understood as divine beings). From this perspective, one would have wanted not only to maintain harmony with the movements of these cosmic forces, but also to maximize positive influences and minimize negative ones.

Variants of this system were standard in Europe through the Renaissance and into the early modern period. The spirit (*spiritus*) or subtle energy of the celestial bodies was believed to permeate everything in the natural world, including plants and minerals which could be used to treat disorders arising from bodily imbalance or disharmony with external forces. Methods of therapy that emphasized these metaphysical elements would have complemented their use of herbal and mineral compounds with other actions that were thought to enhance the influx of spirit both for the purposes of healing disease as well as promoting overall wellness. For instance, the Italian philosopher Marsilio Ficino (1433–1499) recommended a list of therapeutic methods including: well-composed images; medicines; pleasant odors; harmonious music (along with ritual movements, gestures, and dance); imagination; philosophy; and tranquil contemplation. When it came to bodily movement, Ficino stated: "exercise by keeping constantly in motion and make various circular movements like those of the heavenly bodies. Since by their movings and circlings you were engendered, by making similar motions you will be preserved."[10]

Therapeutic exercise was already present in the writings of Galen, who defined exercise as any movement that was vigorous, swift, or both, and that caused an acceleration of the breath. The Islamic philosopher Ibn Sīnā (aka Avicenna, 980–1037), who further systematized Galenic medicine, also included a range of passive motions, such as when a body is moved, carried, or rocked by another force, which he prescribed especially for the sick and otherwise frail.[11] Renaissance European texts expounding specifically on physical culture, such as *De Arte Gymnastica* (1569) by Geronimo Mercuriali (1530–1606), therefore articulated what had by then become standard wisdom. Namely the intentional nature of exercise, the assertion that such activities should be moderate rather than excessively vigorous or violent, and the notion that different forms of exercise were appropriate to various types of individuals (distinguished by age, gender, state of health, and class). One interesting feature of these systems, owing to the foundational role of harmony and therefore of musical theory in the Western tradition, is development of the voice, including attention to the chest, mouth, tongue, and breath, usually accomplished through declamations set to music.[12] Indeed, the most detailed and elaborate early modern treatment of breathing exercises can be found in the context of aesthetics and the art of oratory.

One of the chief early modern innovators of physical culture, both therapeutic and otherwise, was the Swedish Pehr Henrik Ling (1776–1839). Ling believed the human organism to be composed of three fundamental principles: the dynamic phenomena of the mental and moral faculties, the chemical phenomena of the body's internal processes, and the mechanical phenomena of the body's internal and external processes. The unified harmony of these vital orders signified a state of health and the necessary condition for an organism's development. Any effective system of medicine therefore had take all three orders into account when applying treatment. Movement, according to Ling, could be active, passive, or a combination of the two. Passive movements are characterized by external source of motion and can include an activity such as riding wherein the body is supported, or intentional manipulations such as aided flexion, pulling, shaking, and other actions many of which are generally akin to massage. By the middle of the 19th century, his system became well known in North America, where it was being touted by some as the "Movement Cure." Proponents of Ling's system, even in so-called secular contexts, hailed it as a complete regimen that addressed the "whole organism"—mind, body, and soul.[13]

The rise of "alternative" medicine

Calling something "alternative" only makes sense if there is a single established norm. Modern science-based medicine is typically referred to as "allopathy," deriving from Greek expression "other than the disease." As a continuation of Galenic humoral theory, the premodern versions of this school of thought maintained that disease could be cured by acting in opposition to a perceived humoral imbalance. Mainstream 19th-century medicine was still chiefly dominated by "heroic" allopathic methods, which were neither very effective nor particularly pleasant. Therapy was based on a logic of harsh purging as a means of rebalancing the body's vital substances. This could take the form of sweating, bloodletting, or gastrointestinal purging effected by administering emetics or laxatives. The most widely used of these was calomel, also known as mercurous chloride, which erodes the lining of the gastrointestinal tract, thereby acting as a powerful laxative, and also has the somewhat unfortunate effect of rotting away one's teeth and gums.[14] Eventually, gentler allopathic methods won out in the mainstream establishment, preserving the basic logic of counteracting disease but striving to do so without destroying the body along with it. This, of course, was greatly helped by scientific advancements in germ theory and understandings of the body's internal biological processes, which redefined what it meant to act in opposition to the disease by more accurately identifying the underlying causes of symptoms if not the ailment itself.

In this sense, the 19th century presented an interesting historical moment. Modern medicine was not yet truly modern—that is, many therapies were not based in sound science and were likely to do more harm than good. However, medicine was increasingly becoming professionalized in the modern sense of the term, as expansions in education and print culture created an international body of common medical knowledge. Throughout the 19th century, other schools of thought, such as homeopathy, naturopathy, osteopathy, and chiropractic, vied to reform the violent mechanisms of heroic medicine by advancing competing logics[15] (by emphasizing, for instance, astrological rather than humoral understandings of the body). The "alternative" methods of the time were thus not necessarily any less scientific, they just happened to fall outside the mainstream of the growing standard consensus. Thus, early modern sources that argue disease can be treated with sunlight, water, exercise and deep breathing, or positive thinking, should be placed in the context of their time as presenting more gentle and holistic solutions to the same basic problem of correcting imbalance. And, of course, a great number of these methods are not unsound, provided that they are not used to address issues that fall beyond their scope.

It's worth noting, however, that today the labels of "alternative" or "holistic" medicine are applied to a wide range of methods, including not only pre-modern (or early modern) Western methods, but also the traditional medical systems of non-European cultures. Such systems are also sometimes referred to as "ethnomedicine" and their legitimacy is often bound up in complex issues of cultural imperialism and colonialism. Modern medicine is often treated as being synonymous with Western medicine. Yet modern Western medicine itself exists on a continuum with (insofar as it evolved from) its own culturally specific premodern and traditional theories and methods.

In fact, for most of the 19th century (the heyday of British colonialism in India), Western medicine was no more modern or definitely effective than Indian medicine. As we mentioned, the major advancements that led to the rise of modern medicine, such as germ theory, the discovery of viruses, vaccines and antibiotics, advancements in biochemistry and genetics, and so on did not occur until the very late 19th century. In fact, many of these fields were still in their nascency over the first half of the 20th century. Thus, modern medicine as we know it today is by many measures barely a century old. In this sense, though its major discoveries are often treated as "Western," they must be considered in the context of unprecedented global connectivity that enabled them.

Yet it remains true that Western Europe (and increasingly North America) have exercised an outsize global influence during the historical period we refer to as modern, which can obscure the cultural evolution occurring in other parts of the world. In this context, non-Western methods are conflated with non-modern methods. Both can become sites of resistance to the mainstream medical establishment, though *what* precisely is being resisted varies from one cultural context to another. In India, for instance, indigenous methods are seen as pushing back against the legacy of colonial domination. In the United States, which lacks a universal and socialized healthcare system, alternative therapies can signal the rejection of a corporate and profit-driven medical industry. In both contexts, yoga (with or without reference to Āyurveda) is presented as one such means of resistance.

The shifting goals of early modern yoga

The Indian innovators who popularized yoga in the early 20th century went to great lengths to appeal to the modern authority of science, even as they emphasized the traditional Indian character of their methods. Even more importantly, they juxtaposed yoga with competing Western harmonial systems, claiming alternately that these were either not sufficiently scientific or not sufficiently spiritual. For instance, Swami Abhedananda (1866–1939), head of the New York Vedanta Society, wrote in 1902 that "faith-healers, mental-healers, and Christian Scientists cure disease without giving drugs; the Yogis of India do the same, but in a more scientific manner." He added that,

> if mental-healers and faith-healers knew the secret of controlling the Prāṇā [breath as life-force], they would have been undoubtedly more successful in their attempts. Some among them are now beginning to take up breathing exercises, and perhaps in time they will learn the truths contained in the wonderful science of breathing.[16]

At the same time, he maintained that

> by breathing exercises, however, is not meant here merely deep breathing, such as is taught by teachers of music, Delsarte, or physical culture. Deep breathing is very good for drawing a full supply or oxygen into the system, and undoubtedly has its value, especially for women who wear tight dresses. Many of the diseases from which they suffer are directly traceable to a lack of the adequate quantity of oxygen necessary for organic combustion and for the maintenance of the activity of organs. ... By breathing exercises we mean that process by which control over the motion of the lungs and of the nerve centers, as also, in the end, over the Prāṇā or vital energy can be acquired.[17]

Thus, by denying the fundamentally metaphysical assumptions behind harmonial breathing practices and reducing them to purely physiological techniques, yogic breathing is elevated as spiritually superior because more profoundly effective. Abhedananda's strategy can be seen as a kind of "divide and conquer" move. He isolates the two ends of the Western spectrum—exclusively spiritual practitioners of mental and faith healing from exclusively physical practitioners of breathing and physical culture—thereby erasing the substantial portion of those who would have practiced both. Yoga, then, is advanced as the only kind of practice that is capable of fulfilling both aims.

However, the line between the physical and spiritual was somewhat of a shifting marker in contemporary yoga as well. Early English-language practice manuals produced by Indian innovators of yoga tended to be eclectic affairs. They would typically include *āsana* (posture) and *prāṇāyāma* (breath control) along with a varying range of other *haṭha*-yogic practices such as *bandhas* (locks), *mudrās* (seals), and various purificatory techniques, which often blend into more generic hygienic advice rather than serving their more traditional functions. There would frequently be talk of diet and, somewhat less frequently though still regularly, a section devoted to sexual continence. When it came to goals, they gradually subsumed pre-modern *haṭha* techniques, which were built on a logic of manipulating the body's subtle energies, into modern scientific and hygienic paradigms. When dynamic standing *āsanas* were incorporated, they were often distinguished from the more static seated *āsanas* that are meant to be combined with *prāṇāyāma* practice. Kuvalayananda, for instance, went so far as to split the two into completely different sections under the headers of "Meditative Poses" versus "Cultural Poses."[18] Complex *prāṇāyāma* techniques were often treated separately, and relegated to a more specialized volume. References to the subtle body, the *kuṇḍalinī* (the coiled energy believed to rest at the base of the spine, which when awakened and raised into the head leads to enlightenment and immortality), and other more metaphysical aspects of *haṭha* yoga were either largely avoided or likewise relegated to a separate volume.

Another useful example here is the difference between Sivananda's *Kundalini Yoga* (1935) and his *Yogic Home Exercises* (1939). The former, despite containing some discussion and integration of modern anatomy, provides a fairly full account of classical *haṭha* yoga. The latter text, on the other hand, subtitled "Easy Course of Physical Culture for Modern Men and Women," contains only passing references to such concerns. This is despite incorporating the full range of *bandhas* and *mudrās* that might have traditionally been employed for *kuṇḍalinī*-related purposes. For instance, in his description of the "Yoga Mudrā," Sivananda stated obliquely that it "is very useful for rousing the Kuṇḍalinī Śakti" before immediately moving on to specify that "this pose removes all kinds of disorders of the abdominal viscera."[19]

Kuvalayananda took the emphasis on yoga's effects on the anatomy even further by packing his treatment of *āsana* and *prāṇāyāma* in tables and tables of experimental data in his *Yoga Mīmāṇsa* journal. However, for all his efforts, he never quite managed to consummate the synthesis with metaphysical aims. The scientifically demonstrated virtues of yogic practices inevitably stopped short of empirically illustrating more transcendent forms of self-realization. For instance, Kuvalayananda's *Popular Yoga: Prâṇâyâma* (1931) promises to expound not only the physical but the spiritual benefits of breathwork but, when the moment arrives, it includes only about a page and a half referring to the potential of nerve stimulation and the newly discovered hormonal fluctuations of the endocrine system to induce psychological changes. The short section closes, a bit anticlimactically, by asserting:

> Again we are hypothetically satisfied that the practice of Prāṇāyāma introduces high pressure both in the central canal of the spinal cord and the ventricles of the brain. These pressures centrally stimulate the whole nervous system. Owing to these central and peripheral stimuli, the human consciousness

> begins to be internalized and supersensuous perceptions begin to be possible. Worlds subtler and still subtler begin to be opened out in proportion to the consciousness itself getting more and more refined, till at last the individual consciousness merges into the cosmic and the individual becomes one with the Infinite.[20]

Kuvalayananda thus attempted to straddle the divide between lofty metaphysical goals and a different sort of self-realization—one that amounts to an optimization of the organism on its own terms, relying solely on biomechanical metrics.

However, even if they fell short of proving yoga's spiritual effects, such efforts were instrumental to representing the practice as an effective method of holistic therapeutic intervention. Many of the therapeutically-focused organizations founded by early 20th-century yogis, such as Yogendra's Yoga Institute in Mumbai (founded 1918), Kuvalayananda's Kaivalayadham in Lonavala (founded 1924), and Desikachar's Krishnamacharya Yoga Mandiram (founded 1976 in honor of his father's earlier teachings), still provide services today.

Legitimizing traditional medicine in India

In the 1990s, India established an official Central Council for Research on Yoga and Naturopathy (CCRYN), which was subsequently incorporated under the Ministry of Ayurveda, Yoga and Naturopathy, Unani, Siddha, and Homoeopathy (AYUSH) in 2014.[21] As indicated by its name, the ministry does not only seek to represent indigenous South Asian systems but also other therapies that ground themselves in claims to natural and ancient methods. Āyurveda is a Sanskritic tradition. Siddha, meanwhile, evolved in Tamil (South Indian) language and culture. Āyurveda and Siddha share many similarities, but also have some major differences in terms of how concepts are organized and understood, as well as in more practical matters such as the use of regionally specific plants.[22] Unani (*tibb yūnānī*, Urdu for "Greek medicine") is Indo-Muslim medicine, which, true to its name, derives heavily from Arabic elaborations on Greek (especially Galenic) sources, but also incorporates many other regional traditions that were drawn upon by the sprawling Islamic empire during its medieval golden age.[23] Naturopathy and Homeopathy are modern and more-or-less strictly Western systems, also deriving largely from Greek roots and subsequent European elaborations.

The Ministry or AYUSH is not identical to or directly connected to India's Ministry of Health. Its inception might be viewed as closely connected to the election of Prime Minister Narendra Modi in 2014 and the associated political prominence of the Hindu Nationalist party, the Bharatiya Janata Party (BJP), to which he belongs. Minister of AYUSH Shripad Yesso Naik has declared that yoga is "a way of medicine that belongs to India. After the British came to India, they suppressed Indian medicine and tried to foist Western medicine on us—that's why traditional medicine could not be promoted."[24]

The founding of the Ministry of AYUSH was accompanied by Modi's successful campaign with the United Nations to establish an International Day of Yoga

(June 21) and the introduction of the Common Yoga Protocol (CYP), a sequence of exercises to be performed annually on this day. AYUSH's published booklet outlining the protocol states that yoga is "a passport to health insurance, a key to fitness and wellness," positioning the practice as a solution for "non-communicable, lifestyle diseases" such as diabetes, hyper-tension, stress, and depression. [25]

Yoga therapy: a modern framework of holistic healing

Internationally, yoga therapy is not subject to formal medical licensing and accreditation, instead it is largely represented by a self-regulating body of practitioners represented by the International Association of Yoga Therapists (IAYT). The IAYT was founded in 1989 by Larry Paine and Richard Miller. Paine holds a doctoral degree in fitness education and has done graduate work in physical therapy. Miller holds a doctoral degree in clinical psychology. As of 2019, IAYT had over 5,000 individual members from over 50 countries. Since its founding, the organization has focused on research-based publications, conferences, standards-development, and relationships with integrative and complementary health care providers. In 2016, the IAYT launched an official accreditation program to outline training requirements and standardize standards and parameters around the ethics of yoga therapy.[26]

Though some yoga therapists may be licensed professionals practicing in related medical and therapeutic fields, IAYT does not provide, certify, or endorse medical credentialing. The IAYT model does not consider a yoga therapist to be diagnosing and treating a patient, the way a licensed medical doctor would, but rather empowering them to improve their own health and wellbeing. However, yoga therapists do receive more training than would be expected of a yoga instructor. The IAYT accreditation program requires a total of 800 hours of dedicated training in addition to the standard 200-hour minimum established by the Yoga Alliance, the (likewise self-regulating) organization that sets professional standards for yoga teachers.

The IAYT sees itself as engaging in a biopsychosocial-spiritual model of holistic therapy, grounded at least partially in the traditional methods of yoga. It defines this connection as follows:

> Yoga therapy can be understood as a salutogenic intervention that seeks to identify the contributors to health and assist individuals in progressing toward optimal well-being. Yoga teaches that in adverse life situations, including chronic pain, we can connect to states of calm, equanimity, and contentment; suffering arises from forgetting this connection to such states as one mis-identifies with the fluctuating stimuli of the body, mind, and environment. The teachings and practices of yoga can support equanimity and contentment within the specific circumstances of the individual. Improved well-being along the BPSS continuum is fostered as the person is supported in identifying the causes of suffering and experiences the potential for greater well-being along the BPSS continuum. A foundational philosophy that informs yoga therapy is the panchamaya kosha, or five sheaths, model. The kosha model is said to be

> more than 2,500 years old. Similar to the BPSS model, the kosha model recognizes that many layers of experience (physical, energetic, psychoemotional, social, spiritual) influence wellbeing. Yoga therapists evaluate and work with clients on each of these layers of well-being.[27]

Notably, the "yoga" portion of this definition is left very vague, which undoubtedly reflects the IAYT's efforts to bridge not only the many historical variants of yoga practice, but also the variability in interpretation among its members. The concept of *kośas* is indeed first mentioned in the *Taittirīya Upaniṣad* (2.1–5), a mystical text likely composed around the 6th century BCE. There, we learn that the *ātman*, or Self, is encased in a series of bodies, beginning with the gross physical body made of food (*anna*), followed by the vital breath (*prāṇa*), the mind (*manas*), discernment (*vijñāna*), and finally bliss (*ananda*). This model of the body becomes most prominent in Vedānta philosophical traditions and is not generally referenced as "yogic" (that is, it doesn't help us accomplish anything with regards to the goals of yoga) until the two traditions begin to blend in the late medieval and early modern periods. The *kośas* begin to be play a role in yogic texts around the 17th century,[28] which should not necessarily be taken to mean that this interpretation is somehow inauthentic but only that it is one of many historical models of the yogic body. Harmonial models, which form an implicit backdrop to Western understandings of psychology and spirituality, also tended to parse the human being into layers in this manner. And, in the end, neither model tended to explicitly include a "social" layer, as the BPSS model does. Again, this should not lead us to conclude that the model is not legitimate, but only serves to highlight the way that traditions and different understandings of the human body and its place in the larger world evolve across time and space.

Typically, a yoga therapist will have training in a specific style of yoga, whether affiliated with a distinct Indian lineage or a more eclectic modern synthesis, that provides additional ideological scaffolding to what is specifically "yogic" about their model of treatment. Thus, organizations like IAYT and Yoga Alliance, though they may set basic standards for competency and ethics, tend to avoid defining the scope of what counts as yoga. In the case of yoga therapy, especially, there is a focus on balancing the traditional with the modern when it comes to evidence-based therapeutic techniques.

In 2017, the Integrative Pain Care Policy Congress, hosted by the Academy of Integrative Pain Management in partnership with the Integrative Health Policy Consortium and PAINS (Pain Action Alliance to Implement a National Strategy) Project, brought together representatives from more than 75 different organizations and agencies to develop a consensus on comprehensive integrative pain management, which it defined as "biomedical, psychosocial, complementary health, and spiritual care. It is person-centered and focuses on maximizing function and wellness. Care plans are developed through a shared decision-making model that reflects the available evidence regarding optimal clinical practice and the person's goals and values."[29]

Research on the therapeutic effects of yoga

Below is a limited sample of some peer reviewed and evidence-based studies, documenting the therapeutic uses of yoga. It's worth noting that what is meant by "yoga" can vary from study to study. Generally speaking, the research is based on a common understanding of modern global yoga as a practice that combines bodily movement, intentional breathing, and mental concentration. Some of the techniques utilized are based in traditional Indian yogic practices, while others are more generic and can be found in other systems of physical culture and meditative practice. Some studies focused on one of these features, while others relied on a combination.

Managing and reducing stress

- Rinske Gotink et al., "Meditation and Yoga Practice Are Associated with Smaller Right Amygdala Volume: The Rotterdam Study," *Brain Imaging and Behavior*, 12, no. 6 (2018): 1631–9.
- Laura Schmalzl et al., "The Effect of Movement-Focused and Breath-Focused Yoga Practice on Stress Parameters and Sustained Attention: A Randomized Controlled Pilot Study," *Consciousness and Cognition*, 65 (2018): 109–25.
- Michaela C. Pascoe, David R. Thompson, and Chantal F. Ski, "Yoga, Mindfulness-Based Stress Reduction and Stress-Related Physiological Measures: A Meta-Analysis," *Psychoneuroendocrinology*, 86 (2017): 152–68.

Managing depression and anxiety disorders

- Zaimin Li et al., "Mind-Body Exercise for Anxiety and Depression in COPD Patients: A Systematic Review and Meta-Analysis," *International Journal of Environmental Research and Public Health*, 17, no. 1 (2020).
- Sy Atezaz Saeed, Karlene Cunningham, and Richard M. Bloch, "Depression and Anxiety Disorders: Benefits of Exercise, Yoga, and Meditation," *American Family Physician*, 99, no. 10 (2019): 620–34.
- Nadia K. Bukar, Luann M. Eberhardt, and Judy Davidson, "East Meets West in Psychiatry: Yoga as an Adjunct Therapy for Management of Anxiety," *Archives of Psychiatric Nursing*, 33, no. 4 (2019): 371–6.
- Klara Meister and Georg Juckel, "A Systematic Review of Mechanisms of Change in Body-Oriented Yoga in Major Depressive Disorders," *Pharmacopsychiatry*, 51, no. 3 (2018): 73–81.

Improving physical and neural function among aging populations

- Divya Sivaramakrishnan et al., "The Effects of Yoga Compared to Active and Inactive Controls on Physical Function and Health Related Quality of Life in Older Adults: Systematic Review and Meta-Analysis of Randomised Controlled Trials," *Journal of Behavioral Nutrition and Physical Activity*, 16, no. 1 (2019).

- Danilo Forghieri Santaella et al., "Greater Anteroposterior Default Mode Network Functional Connectivity in Long-Term Elderly Yoga Practitioners," *Frontiers in Aging Neuroscience*, 11 (2019).
- Bianca P. Acevedo, Sarah Pospos, and Helen Lavretsky, "The Neural Mechanisms of Meditative Practices: Novel Approaches for Healthy Aging," *Current Behavioral Neuroscience Reports*, 3, no. 4 (2016): 328–39.

Managing the symptoms of cancer, including treatment-related stress, sleep quality, inflammation, and immune function

(*Note*: Yoga is not being used to treat the disease itself.)

- Suzanne C. Danhauer et al., "Yoga for Symptom Management in Oncology: A Review of the Evidence Base and Future Directions for Research," *Cancer*, 125, no. 12 (2019): 1979–89.
- Cecile A. Lengacher et al., "Feasibility of the Mobile Mindfulness-Based Stress Reduction for Breast Cancer (mMBSR(BC)) Program for Symptom Improvement Among Breast Cancer Survivors," *Psycho-Oncology*, 27, no. 2 (2018): 524–31.
- Ram R. Amritanshu et al., "Effect of Long-term Yoga Practice on Psychological Outcomes in Breast Cancer Survivors," *Indian Journal of Palliative Care*, 23, no. 3 (2017): 231–6.

Yoga therapy in action

In 2007 Beryl Bender Birch, a prominent American teacher and one of the originators of Power Yoga, co-founded the Give Back Yoga Foundation, which aims to bring yoga to populations that might not normally have access to the practice. The organization's mission statement runs as follows: "We help yoga teachers, health workers, and charitable organizations offer yoga to those in need—including veterans, prisoners, and individuals facing mental and physical illness. We also work with community partners to increase access to yoga for populations that face systemic bias and prejudice."[30] One of its first grants was to James Fox, founder of the Prison Yoga Project, to help fund the publication and distribution of his book, *Yoga: A Path to Healing and Recovery*. Fox began teaching yoga to prisoners in 2002, when he was invited to teach at San Quentin by the Insight Prison Project. As of 2019, the Prison Yoga Project had trained over 2,000 teachers at over 350 jails and prisons in the United States, as well as Mexico, Canada, Sweden, the United Kingdom, The Netherlands and India, with more jails and prisons continually requesting information on how to start their own yoga programs. Fox's book, meanwhile, had been requested and sent free of charge to over 26,000 prisoners.[31]

The Prison Yoga Project centers a "Restorative Justice practice that focuses on recovery from trauma, development of resilience, and cultivation of empathy, compassion, and personal responsibility," stating that its "evidence-supported, trauma-informed approach to yoga and mindfulness supports people to face and release unresolved trauma safely and effectively."[32] According to the organization's materials, 99 percent of people in prison environments have experienced and are continuing to experience trauma. Fox refers to this phenomenon as "original pain," noting that "most prisoners suffer from Complex Trauma, chronic interpersonal trauma experienced early in life such as abandonment, hunger, homelessness, domestic violence, sexual abuse, bullying, discrimination, drug and alcohol abuse, and witnessing crime—including murder."[33] Advocates of trauma-sensitive yoga emphasize that trauma not only habituates the body to react to stimuli from a primal flight-or-flight nervous response but also makes the body itself feel like an unsafe space. Movement, breath, and concentration techniques such as those practiced in modern yoga can help rehabilitate the body to feel and respond differently, giving the practitioner a conscious sense of control.[34]

One Prison Yoga teacher based in Denver, Colorado emphasized the special nature of such work, as opposed to a typical modern yoga class. He highlighted the importance of remembering that this population of students is not practicing in a comforting and aesthetically pleasing yoga studio, but rather in a prison that is lit, loud, and threatening. He also explained that, from an institutional perspective, there is a "constant level of depersonalization and dehumanization of the prisoner." Because of this, part of his goal as a teacher is for his students to "know that he sees them as people, as equal and worthy of not only controlling themselves, but also making choices about how they react to their lives." Prison Yoga Project teachers are trained to use invitations rather than commanding or authoritative language, they place themselves within the experience as equals by practicing with the students, they remain on their own mat for the duration of the class, and they don't provide hands-on assists or otherwise touch the students. Their teaching style is direct and communicative, often incorporating real life or practical examples, and relying on clear English terminology for the poses. The practice focuses on "breath, movement, centering, connecting and calming" through simple postures and basic flow sequences, though the Denver-based teacher noted that he often incorporates "an arm balance like 'crow' as most male prisoners can do the pose, and it makes them feel empowered and successful."

However, the case of Prison Yoga also presents some crucial opportunities for criticism. Because the Prison Yoga Project's teachers are volunteers, the program requires no funding and little investment of resources, which makes it fiscally beneficial to the prison industrial complex. A Pew report found that Departments of Corrections collectively spent $8.1 billion on prisoner health care in 2015. The report cites 2011–2012 data from the Bureau of Justice Statistics, which reveals that 40 percent of all state and federal prisoners reported having at least one current chronic illness, with the highest rates occurring among older populations (73 percent) and women (63 percent).[35] In this context, yoga therapy presents a low-cost alternative to conventional medical treatments, making such altruistic projects a bandage applied to a fundamentally broken system. On this point, scholar Andrea Jain has argued that efforts like the Prison Yoga Project fail their students by doing nothing to "target the structural factors contributing to mass incarceration, suggesting that the task is primarily one of reforming the prisoners."[36] For Jain, this is part of a larger phenomenon where capitalist and neoliberal ideology focused on eternal optimization of everything from profits to human bodies, can lead to a focus on "self-care" that leaves the individual at the mercy of systemic iniquities that are by definition outside of individual control.

As Jain states, without a corresponding focus on structural (in addition to individual) change, yoga therapy joins the ranks of "therapeutically-focused applications of spirituality that concentrate on healing the broken person rather than undermining the system that broke that person in the first place."[37]

Conclusions

- Traditional Indian and Western medicines share a "humoral" model of the body where health is understood as a balance of internal fluids carrying vital forces. Indian Āyurveda and Galenic Western medicine both incorporated physical culture and exercise as a means of strengthening the body and preventing disease. Both cultures also integrated such medical understandings of the body, as in *haṭha* yoga and Western harmonial spirituality. As the mainstream medical establishment arose in the 19th century, such systems were increasingly relegated to "alternative" status.
- Early 20th-century innovators and modernizers of yoga were engaged in a complex project to simultaneously prove yoga's objective scientific effectiveness, while maintaining its holistic and especially spiritual character. On both grounds, they juxtaposed it to Western methods, with spiritual Western methods being portrayed as not sufficiently scientific and physical Western methods being seen as not sufficiently holistic and spiritual. However, even as early Indian manuals aimed at an English-speaking audience continued to gesture at yoga's spiritual dimensions, their goals and methods were increasingly framed in physical (rather than metaphysical) terms. Today, India's Ministry of AYUSH portrays yoga as standing among a range of traditional methods that provide holistic solutions to health and act as a form of resistance to colonialism.
- Internationally, yoga therapy is represented by the International Association of Yoga Therapists (IAYT), a self-regulating body that sponsors research and sets standards for training and credentialing. Yoga therapists are not required to have formal medical credentials, though many may have other training outside of yoga-specific methods. The IAYT adheres to a loose understanding of yoga as a tradition, allowing for flexibility among its members.
- In practice, yoga therapy aims to bridge the gap between evidence-based methods and traditional forms of knowledge. It also foregrounds patient-centered care and aims to be responsive to the specific needs and circumstances of the individual. Even in group settings, such as the classes taught

by the Prison Yoga Project, instruction is context-sensitive and adapted to helping the practitioners find an individual sense of agency and control over their wellness. However, especially in this sort of institutional context, rooted as it is in systems of social inequality, a focus on reforming the individual can cater to rather than dismantle the larger systems of oppression that lead to physical and psychological harm.

Notes

1 Neil Pearson, Shelly Prosko, Marlysa Sullivan, and Matthew J. Taylor, "Yoga Therapy and Pain—How Yoga Therapy Serves in Comprehensive Integrative Pain Management, and How It Can Do More" (Little Rock, AR: International Association of Yoga Therapists, 2020), 2, https://cdn.ymaws.com/www.iayt.org/resource/resmgr/docs_whitepapers/iayt_pain_white_paper.pdf
2 Hugh B. Urban, "Osho, from Sex Guru to Guru of the Rich: The Spiritual Logic of Late Capitalism," in *Gurus in America*, ed. Thomas A. Forsthoefel and Cynthia Ann Humes (Albany: State University of New York Press, 2005), 187.
3 Dominik Wujastyk, *The Roots of Ayurveda: Selections from Sanskrit Medical Writings* (London: Penguin Books, 2003), 40, 105.
4 Jason Birch, "Premodern Yoga Traditions and Ayurveda: Preliminary Remarks on Shared Terminology, Theory, and Praxis," *History of Science in South Asia*, 6 (2018): 5.
5 Birch, "Premodern Yoga Traditions and Ayurveda," 19.
6 Birch, "Premodern Yoga Traditions and Ayurveda," 35–44.
7 Birch, "Premodern Yoga Traditions and Ayurveda," 45.
8 For a translation see Avinash Chunder Kaviraj Kaviratna, *Charaka-Samhita: Translated into English*, vol. 1 (Calcutta: G. C. Chakravarti, 1896), 77.
9 Joseph S. Alter, *The Wrestler's Body: Identity and Ideology in North India* (Berkeley: University of California Press, 1992), 82–3; Jason Birch and Mark Singleton, "The Yoga of the Haṭhābhyāsapaddhati: Haṭhayoga on the Cusp of Modernity," *Journal of Yoga Studies*, 2 (2019): 47–8; Jerome Armstrong, "Uncovering Vyāyāma in Yoga: Haṭha Yoga, Sūrya Namaskār, Bikram Yoga, and Modern Yoga Asana Practice," in *Yoga and the Physical Practices of South Asia*, ed. Mark Singleton and Daniela Bevilacqua (Cambridge: Open Book Publishers, forthcoming).
10 Marsilio Ficino, *Three Books on Life*, trans. Carol V. Kaske and John R. Clark (Binghamton, NY: Center for Medieval and Early Renaissance Studies, 1989), 373.
11 Sandra Cavallo and Tessa Storey, *Healthy Living in Late Renaissance Italy* (New York and London: Oxford University Press, 2013), 146–7.
12 Cavallo and Storey 2013: 149.
13 Anya P. Foxen, *Inhaling Spirit: Harmonialism, Orientalism, and the Western Roots of Modern Yoga* (New York: Oxford University Press, 2020), 116.
14 James C. Whorton, *Nature Cures: The History of Alternative Medicine in America* (New York: Oxford University Press, 2004), 3–4.
15 Whorton, *Nature Cures*, 4–6. See also Norman Gevitz, ed., *Other Healers: Unorthodox Medicine in America* (Baltimore, MD: Johns Hopkins University Press, 1988).
16 Swami Abhedananda, *How to Be a Yogi* (New York: The Vedanta Society, 1902), 146–7.
17 Abhedananda, *How to Be a Yogi*, 157–8.
18 Srimat Kuvalayananda, *Popular Yoga: Âsanas* (Bombay: Kaivalyadhama, 1933).
19 Swami Sivananda, *Yogic Home Exercises: Easy Course of Physical Culture for Modern Men and Women* (Bombay: D. B. Taraporevala Son and Co., 1939), 51.
20 Srimat Kuvalayananda, *Popular Yoga: Prâṇâyâma* (Bombay: Kaivalyadhama, 1931), 128.

21 Joseph S. Alter, "Yoga, Nature Cure and 'Perfect' Health: The Purity of the Fluid Body in an Impure World," in *Yoga in Transformation: Historical and Contemporary Perspectives on a Global Phenomenon*, ed. Karl Baier, Philip A. Maas, and Karin Preisendanz (Göttingen, The Netherlands: Vandenhoeck & Ruprecht Unipress, 2018), 443.
22 Richard S. Weiss, *Recipes for Immortality: Medicine, Religion, and Community in South India* (New York: Oxford University Press, 2009).
23 Seema Alavi, *Islam and Healing: Loss and Recovery of an Indo-Muslim Medical Tradition, 1600–1900* (New York and London: Palgrave Macmillan, 2008), 22.
24 Harriet Alexander, "India's Yoga Minister Aims to Reclaim Practice from West," *The Telegraph*, December 3, 2014, https://www.telegraph.co.uk/news/worldnews/asia/india/11271782/Indias-yoga-minster-aims-to-reclaim-practice-from-West.html
25 "International Day of Yoga: Common Yoga Protocol" (Ministry of Ayurveda, Yoga and Naturopathy, Unani, Siddha and Homeopathy (AYUSH), May 2019), v–vi, https://yoga.ayush.gov.in/yoga/public/assets/front/pdf/CYPEnglishBooklet.pdf. See also Christopher Patrick Miller, "Soft Power and Biopower: Narendra Modi's 'Double Discourse' Concerning Yoga for Climate Change and Self-Care," *Journal of Dharma Studies*, 3, no. 1 (2020): 93–106.
26 "Learn about IAYT," The International Association of Yoga Therapists, accessed August 24, 2020, https://www.iayt.org/page/LearnAbout
27 Pearson et al., "Yoga Therapy and Pain," 7.
28 James Mallinson and Mark Singleton, *Roots of Yoga: A Sourcebook from the Indic Traditions* (London: Penguin Classics, 2017), 184.
29 Pearson et al., "Yoga Therapy and Pain," 4.
30 "About Us," Give Back Yoga Foundation, accessed August 24, 2020, https://givebackyoga.org/about-us/
31 "James Fox and the Prison Yoga Project," *Daily Good*, April 25, 2019, www.dailygood.org/story/2299/james-fox-and-the-prison-yoga-project-awakin-call-editors/
32 "Philosophy," Prison Yoga Project, accessed August 24, 2020, https://prisonyoga.org/our-mission/philosophy/
33 Prison Yoga Project, "Why We Teach Yoga and Mindfulness in Prison . . . Facebook Post," Facebook, September 3, 2018, https://www.facebook.com/prisonyoga/posts/why-we-teach-yoga-and-mindfulness-in-prison-by-james-fox-ma-founder-and-director/2054286137944482/
34 David Emerson and Elizabeth Hopper, *Overcoming Trauma Through Yoga: Reclaiming Your Body* (Berkeley, CA: North Atlantic Books, 2011).
35 "Prison Health Care: Costs and Quality," The Pew Charitable Trusts, October 2017, 3, 24, https://www.pewtrusts.org/-/media/assets/2017/10/sfh_prison_health_care_costs_and_quality_final.pdf
36 Andrea R. Jain, *Peace, Love, Yoga: The Politics of Global Spirituality* (New York: Oxford University Press, 2020), 166.
37 Jain, *Peace, Love, Yoga*, cover copy.

Glossary

agni "fire," most often the Vedic god of fire, the sacrificial, or the internal fire of the body.

ajīva non-sentient, a classification of matter in Jainism.

ākāśa the most subtle of the gross elements of Sāṅkhya and the physical medium of sound, usually translated as "ether" or "space."

amṛta the nectar of immortality believed to be stored in the cranial vault, associated with the moon and with *bindu* (semen).

Arjuna one of the protagonists of the *Mahābhārata* epic and of the *Bhagavad Gītā*.

āsana literally "seat," a pose, posture, or way of positioning the body.

asceticism severe self-discipline, austerity, including lifestyle observances and bodily practices.

ātman the true and absolute Self, usually understood to consist of pure consciousness.

Āyurveda literally "the knowledge of longevity," classical Indian medicine.

bandha a "lock" or a bodily technique applied in the practice of *haṭha* yoga.

bandhu a hidden connection or correspondence, especially between microcosm and macrocosm, that structures the cosmic order.

Bhagavad Gītā "The Song of the Blessed One," a scripture recounting the teachings of Kṛṣṇa to Arjuna, part of the *Mahābhārata* epic.

bhakta a practitioner of *bhakti* or devotion.

bhakti devotion to a deity.

bhūtaśuddhi the tantric practice of ritually purifying and ultimately meditatively dissolving the body's material elements.

bindu semen, a vital substance believed to be stored in the cranial vault and associated with *aṃṛta* or the nectar of immortality.

Bodhisattva "Awakened One," an enlightened being in Buddhism.

brahman "the expansion," the creative power of the Vedas and the idea of ultimate reality (the macrocosmic equivalent of *ātman* or the Self), especially in the Upaniṣads and Vedānta.

Brahmin (*brāhmaṇa*) pertaining to the priestly social class, the highest *varṇa* of Vedic society.

cakra "circle," specifically a circle of deities in tantra or a center of subtle energies in later yogic traditions.

cosmology a set of philosophical questions that tries to describe the universe in its totality: how it works, what it's made of, whether it has a meaning or purpose.

Delsarteism a 19th-century Euro-American school of physical culture based on the work of French composer François Delsarte.

dharma in Vedic society, one's rightful duty in both a social and a cosmic sense. Can also refer to the teachings of the Buddha or a basic constituent of reality in Buddhism.

dhātu one of the seven constituents (lymph, blood, muscle, fat, bone, marrow, and semen) of the gross material body. Can also refer to an element of reality in Buddhism.

dhyāna meditation.

doṣa one of the three bodily humors or essences of Āyurveda, *vāta* (wind); *pitta* (choler); and *kapha* (phlegm).

ether the fifth element of Greek philosophy, associated with the subtle matter of the heavens and of the heavenly bodies (planets and stars).

granthi "knot," an element of the tantric and *haṭha* yogic subtle body representing an obstacle or a blockage in the body's channels.

guṇa "quality," one of the three fundamental essences of *prakṛti* (nature) in Sāṅkhya, namely *sattva* ("existence"), *rajas* ("ardor"), and *tamas* ("darkness").

harmonialism a Western framework, grounded in ancient Greek philosophy, that understands the universe as arranged according to a framework of (often mathematically and musically) ordered proportions, which are interconnected on every level by a relationship of correspondence or sympathy. Harmonial traditions aim to use this web of connections between the levels of reality to bring all three (human, cosmos, and the divine) into alignment or harmony for the benefit of body on the one hand and soul on the other.

haṭha "force," describing a method of yoga defined by its use of physical techniques like *bandhas* (locks) and *mudrās* (seals) to manipulate the body's vital forces.

Haṭha Pradīpikā an influential 15th-century text on haṭha yoga compiled by Svātmārāma.

jhāna Pali equivalent of the Sanskrit *dhyāna*, meditation.

jīva a sentient Self, especially in Jainism.

jīvanmukti liberation while still embodied and living.

jñāna "gnosis," usually supreme knowledge of the true Self.

karma "action," specifically ritual action in the Vedic context, later any action and its consequent seeds of reaction, which keep the Self bound in the cycle of rebirth. When paired with yoga, as in the *Bhagavad Gītā*, a way of acting with a mental disposition of detachment so as not to bind the Self.

Kaula from *kula* (clan), one of the schools of tantra grounded in the worship of fierce goddesses often called Yoginīs.

keśin the long-haired ascetic wanderer of *Ṛg Veda* 10.136.

kośa one of the five bodily sheaths or frames of Vedānta, also grouped into the gross, subtle, and causal bodies.

Kṛṣṇa a god in Hinduism, often associated with Viṣṇu, the teacher and supreme deity in the *Bhagavad Gītā*.

kṣatriya the ruling "Warrior" social class (*varṇa*) of Vedic society.

kuṇḍalinī "coiled one," a goddess internalized as a feminine energy residing somewhere in the torso or at the base of the spine in tantric and later yogic traditions.

laṭīfa variously translated as "subtle substance," "subtle center," or "subtle body" in Sufi Islam.

laya dissolution of the mind, usually in Śiva, as in tantric Śaiva *layayoga*.

Mahābhārata "The Great Tale of the Bhāratas," one of the two principal Sanskrit epics.

Mahāvīra Vardhamāna Mahāvīra, the founder of Jainism, thought to have lived in the region of Greater Magadha sometime in the 6th to 5th century BCE.

maṇḍala "circle," a ritual diagram, mapping out both the human body and the cosmos, populated by deities or their *mantras*. Can also be called a *yantra* (instrument) depending on context.

mantra literally, "a mental instrument," an utterance, verse, or formula that represents something or produces some effect. In the Vedic tradition, it embodies the creative of the Vedic verses. In tantric traditions, a *mantra* is the literal sonic embodiment of a deity.

maqām in Arabic, a "place" or "station" such as a shrine that might be visited by a pilgrim, signifying stages of spiritual progress as understood within the subtle body in Sufi Islam.

mokṣa liberation from the cycle of *saṃsāra* or rebirth.

mudrā "seal," referring to a bodily technique in *haṭha* yoga or a ritual gesture in tantra. Can also refer to one of the impure substances of Kaula tantric ritual, or a gesture of the hands used to impose *mantras* onto the body in standard tantric ritual.

muni a silent wandering ascetic.

nāḍī one of the body's internal channels, through which vital substances are supposed to flow. Variously understood as physical nerves or veins, or something more subtle.

Nāths an order of Śaiva yogis that has historically leaned in both tantric and ascetic directions, and with whom many of the classical texts on *haṭha* yoga are associated.

nirvāṇa liberation from the cycle of *saṃsāra* or rebirth.

nyāsa "imposition," a step in tantric ritual where the practitioner assigns deities or divine energies, usually represented by their special *mantras*, to the various parts of his body.

ojas the body's basic vital material.

oṃ a sacred syllable or *mantra*, associated by the Upaniṣads with the highest reality of *brahman*.

padma "lotus," another way of talking about the *cakras* of the subtle body.

Pāśupatas an early ascetic Śaiva order.

Patañjali the author or compiler of the *Yoga Sūtras*.

pneuma in Greek philosophy, the subtle vital spirit within the human body, associated with breath and the bodily counterpart of ether, or the subtle matter of the heavenly bodies.

prakṛti material nature. In Sāṅkhya philosophy, it is one of the two basic principles of reality, the inert object to *puruṣa*'s conscious subject.

prāṇa the subtle vital force of breath.

prāṇāyāma the control and manipulation of *prāṇa*, breath-control.

puruṣa "person." In Sāṅkhya philosophy, it is one of the two basic principles of reality, the conscious subject to *prakṛti*'s inert object.

rāja "royal," when paired with yoga referring to the highest or best method or state, often synonymous with *samādhi*.

rajas one of the three fundamental essences (*guṇas*) of nature (*prakṛti*) in Sāṅkhya, translated as "ardor" and signifying movement and energy. Can also refer to female sexual fluid or menstrual blood, analogue of the male *bindu*.

Ṛṣi in the Vedic tradition, the semi-divine poet mystics who originally intuited the verses of the Vedic hymns.

Śaiva associated with the god Śiva.

Śākta associated with the Goddess, derived from *śakti* (feminine energy).

śakti feminine energy, associated with the Goddess.

saṃketa one of the "methods" prescribed by Śaiva tantric texts to achieve dissolution of the mind in Śiva.

saṃsāra the cycle of transmigration and rebirth.

Śaṇkara an 8th-century philosopher and theologian who founded the non-dual Advaita Vedānta school, maintaining that the material world is simply an illusion that conceals the oneness of all reality, specifically the *ātman* and *brahman*.

Sāṅkhya a dualistic school of ancient Indian philosophy that understands reality as a series of 25 emanated principles (*tattvas*).

sattva one of the three fundamental essences (*guṇas*) of nature (*prakṛti*) in Sāṅkhya, translated as "existence" and signifying lucidity and pure being.

Siddha "accomplished one," an enlightened being and tantric master.

siddhi "accomplishment" or "superpower" gained through yogic or tantric practice.

Śiva a god in Hinduism, often associated with asceticism and yoga.

soma a psychoactive substance (usually a milky juice, pressed from an unknown plant) spoken of in the Vedic hymns and offered as part of the Vedic fire sacrifice. Associated with the moon and the elixir of immortality.

śramaṇa a non-Vedic movement of asceticism.

śūdra the lowest "Servant" social class (*varṇa*) of Vedic society.

suṣumnā the central channel (*nāḍī*) of the body believed to run either from the heart or from the bottom of the torso up to the crown of the head.

tamas one of the three fundamental essences (*guṇas*) of nature (*prakṛti*) in Sāṅkhya, translated as "darkness" and signifying inertia and ignorance.

tantra theistic systems of religious ritual that emerged in South Asia during the second half of the first millennium CE, usually viewing the world as permeated with divine energy.

tapas "heat," often referring to the performance of ascetic practices and the energy generated through them.

tattva one of Sāṅkhya's 25 emanated principles of reality, also used in later schools of tantra and Vedānta.

tejas the body's vital energy.

Tīrthaṅkara "Ford-Maker," an enlightened being in Jainism.

Upaniṣads a set of mystical texts in the Vedic tradition, the first of which were composed between the 5th century BCE and the 1st century CE.

Vaiṣṇava associated with the god Viṣṇu.

vaiśya the common "People," the productive social class (*varṇa*) of Vedic society.

varṇa one of the four social classes of Vedic society.

vāyu one of the winds that govern the internal movement of the body's vital substances.

Vājrayana the tantric school of Buddhism.

Veda/Vedic refers to the traditions stemming from the four *saṃhitās* or "compilations" of verses (*Ṛg*, *Yajur*, *Sāma*, and *Atharva*) belonging to an ancient nomadic culture that settled in the northern region of the South Asian continent beginning around 1500 BCE.

Vedānta literally the "end" or "culmination" (*anta*) of the Vedas, a set of philosophical schools that evolved to interpret and reconcile the seemingly diverse perspectives on reality that can be found in the Upaniṣads. The most famous of these is Advaita (or Non-Dual) Vedānta.

Viṣṇu a god in Hinduism, often associated with Kṛṣṇa.

Vivekananda born Narendranath Datta (1863–1902), a monk who is credited, among other things, with becoming one of the first global popularizers of yoga when he toured North America and Europe between 1893 and 1900. Founder of the first global Vedanta Society and author of *Rāja Yoga* (1896).

yajña the sacrificial order of fire rites of early Vedic society.

Yoga Sūtras a compilation of verses on yoga compiled by Patañjali sometime between 325 and 425 CE as part of the *Pātañjala-Yoga-Śāstra-Sāṅkhya-Pravacana* ("the authoritative exposition of yoga that originates with Patañjali, the mandatory Sāṅkhya teaching").

Yogananda born Mukunda Lal Ghosh (1893–1952), a monk and practitioner of a tantric method called Kriya Yoga, who came to the United States in 1920 and became one of the first global gurus. Founder of the Self-Realization Fellowship and author of *Autobiography of a Yogi* (1946).

yogi a practitioner of yoga.

Yoginī one of the fierce goddesses worshipped in some tantric traditions, equivalent to the Buddhist Ḍākinī. Can also refer to a female practitioner of yoga.

Index